Professional Post-Graduate Diploma in Marketing

PAPER 11:
MANAGING MARKETING PERFORMANCE

For exams in December 2006 and June 2007

Study Text

In this July 2006 edition

- A new user-friendly format for easy navigation

- Regular *fast forward* summaries emphasising the key points in each chapter

- Recent examples of marketing practice

- Fully revised

- A full index

BPP)))
PROFESSIONAL EDUCATION

Third edition July 2006

ISBN 0 7517 2706 7 (Previous edition 07517 2254 5)

British Library Cataloguing-in-Publication Data
A catalogue record for this book
is available from the British Library

Published by

BPP Professional Education
Aldine House, Aldine Place
London W12 8AW

www.bpp.com

Printed in Great Britain by
WM Print
45-47 Frederick Street
Walsall
WS2 9NE

We are grateful to the Chartered Institute of Marketing
for permission to reproduce in this text the syllabus,
tutor's guidance notes and past examination
questions.

Contents

The BPP Study Text

Aims of this Study Text

> To provide you with the knowledge and understanding, skills and application techniques that you need if you are to be successful in your exams

This Study Text has been written around the **Managing Marketing Performance** syllabus.

- It is **comprehensive**. It covers the syllabus content. No more, no less.

- It is targeted to the **exam**. We have taken account of the pilot paper, guidance the examiner has given and the assessment methodology.

> To allow you to study in the way that best suits your learning style and the time you have available, by following your personal Study Plan (see below)

You may be studying at home on your own until the date of the exam, or you may be attending a full-time course. You may like to (and have time to) read every word, or you may prefer to (or only have time to) skim-read and devote the remainder of your time to question practice. Wherever you fall in the spectrum, you will find the BPP Study Text meets your needs in designing and following your personal Study Plan.

> To tie in with the other components of the BPP Effective Study Package to ensure you have the best possible chance of passing the exam

Recommended period of use	Elements of the BPP Effective Study Package
3-12 months before exam	**Study Text** Acquisition of knowledge, understanding, skills and applied techniques
1-6 months before exam	**Practice & Revision Kit (9/2006)** Tutorial questions and helpful checklists of the key points lead you into each area. There are then numerous Examination questions to try, graded by topic area, along with realistic suggested solutions prepared by marketing professionals in the light of the Examiner's Reports. The September 2006 edition will include the Specimen Paper and December 2005 paper.
From three month before the exam until the last minute	**Passcards** Work through these short memorable notes which are focused on what is most likely to come up in the exam you will be sitting..

Settling down to study

By this stage in your career you may be a very experienced learner and taker of exams. But have you ever thought about *how* you learn? Let's have a quick look at the key elements required for effective learning. You can then identify your learning style and go on to design your own approach to how you are going to study this text – your personal Study Plan.

Key element of learning	Using the BPP Study Text
Motivation	You can rely on the comprehensiveness and technical quality of BPP. You've chosen the right Study Text – so you're in pole position to pass your exam!
Clear objectives and standards	Do you want to be a prizewinner or simply achieve a moderate pass? Decide.
Feedback	Follow through the examples in this text and do the Action Programme and the Quick Quizzes. Evaluate your efforts critically – how are you doing?
Study Plan	You need to be honest about your progress to yourself – don't be over-confident, but don't be negative either. Make your Study Plan (see below) and try to stick to it. Focus on the short-term objectives – completing two chapters a night, say – but beware of losing sight of your study objectives.
Practice	Use the Quick Quizzes and Chapter Roundups to refresh your memory regularly after you have completed your initial study of each chapter.

These introductory pages let you see exactly what you are up against. However you study, you should:

- **Read through the syllabus** – this will help you to identify areas you have already covered, perhaps at a lower level of detail, and areas that are totally new to you

- **Study the examination paper section**, where we show you the format of the exam (how many and what kind of questions and so on)

Key study steps

The following steps are, in our experience, the ideal way to study for professional exams. You can of course adapt it for your particular learning style (see below).

Tackle the chapters in the order you find them in the Study Text. Taking into account your individual learning style, follow these key study steps for each chapter.

Key study steps	Activity
Step 1 **Chapter Topic list**	Study the list. Each numbered topic denotes a **numbered section** in the chapter.
Step 2 **Introduction**	Read it through. It is designed to show you **why the topics in the chapter need to be studied** – how they lead on from previous topics, and how they lead into subsequent ones.
Step 3 **Explanations**	Proceed **methodically** through the chapter, reading each section thoroughly and making sure you understand.
Step 4 **Key Concepts**	**Key concepts** can often earn you **easy marks** if you state them clearly and correctly in an appropriate exam.
Step 5 **Exam Tips**	These give you a good idea of how the examiner tends to examine certain topics – pinpointing **easy marks** and highlighting **pitfalls**.
Step 6 **Note taking**	Take **brief notes** if you wish, avoiding the temptation to copy out too much.
Step 7 **Marketing at Work**	Study each one, and try if you can to add flesh to them from your **own experience** – they are designed to show how the topics you are studying come alive (and often come unstuck) in the **real world**. You can also update yourself on these companies by going on to the World Wide Web.
Step 8 **Action Programme**	Make a very good attempt at each one in each chapter. These are designed to put your **knowledge into practice** in much the same way as you will be required to do in the exam. Check the answer at the end of the chapter in the **Action Programme review**, and make sure you understand the reasons why yours may be different.
Step 9 **Chapter Roundup**	Check through it very carefully, to make sure you have grasped the **major points** it is highlighting.
Step 10 **Quick Quiz**	When you are happy that you have covered the chapter, use the **Quick Quiz** to check your recall of the topics covered. The answers are in the paragraphs in the chapter that we refer you to.
Step 11 **Illustrative question(s)**	Either at this point, or later when you are thinking about revising, make a full attempt at the **illustrative questions**. You can find these at the end of the Study Text, along with the **Answers** so you can see how you did.

Developing your personal Study Plan

Preparing a Study Plan (and sticking closely to it) is one of the key elements in learning success.

First you need to be aware of your style of learning. There are four typical learning styles. Consider yourself in the light of the following descriptions. and work out which you fit most closely. You can then plan to follow the key study steps in the sequence suggested.

Learning styles	Characteristics	Sequence of key study steps in the BPP Study Text
Theorist	Seeks to understand principles before applying them in practice	1, 2, 3, 7, 4, 5, 8, 9, 10, 11 (6 continuous)
Reflector	Seeks to observe phenomena, thinks about them and then chooses to act	
Activist	Prefers to deal with practical, active problems; does not have much patience with theory	1, 2, 8 (read through), 7, 4, 5, 9, 3, 8 (full attempt), 10, 11 (6 continuous)
Pragmatist	Prefers to study only if a direct link to practical problems can be seen; not interested in theory for its own sake	8 (read through), 2, 4, 5, 7, 9, 1, 3, 8 (full attempt), 10, 11 (6 continuous)

Next you should complete the following checklist.

Am I motivated? (a) [ ]

Do I have an objective and a standard that I want to achieve? (b) [ ]

Am I a theorist, a reflector, an activist or a pragmatist? (c) [ ]

How much time do I have available per week, given: (d) [ ]

- The standard I have set myself

- The time I need to set aside later for work on the Practice and Revision Kit

- The other exam(s) I am sitting, and (of course)

- Practical matters such as work, travel, exercise, sleep and social life?

Now:

- Take the time you have available per week for this Study Text (d), and multiply it by the number of weeks available to give (e)   (e) [ ]

- Divide (e) by the number of chapters to give (f)   (f) [ ]

- Set about studying each chapter in the time represented by (f), following the key study steps in the order suggested by your particular learning style

This is your personal **Study Plan**.

Short of time?

Whatever your objectives, standards or style, you may find you simply do not have the time available to follow all the key study steps for each chapter, however you adapt them for your particular learning style. If this is the case, follow the Skim Study technique below (the icons in the Study Text will help you to do this).

Skim Study technique

Study the chapters in the order you find them in the Study Text. For each chapter, follow the key study steps 1–2, and then skim-read through step 3. Jump to step 9, and then go back to steps 4–5. Follow through step 7, and prepare outline Answers to the Action Programme (step 8). Try the Quick Quiz (step 10), following up any items you can't answer, then do a plan for the illustrative question (step 11), comparing it against our answers. You should probably still follow step 6 (note-taking).

Moving on...

However you study, when you are ready to embark on the practice and revision phase of the BPP Effective Study Package, you should still refer back to this Study Text:

- As a source of **reference** (you should find the list of key concepts and the index particularly helpful for this)

- As a **refresher** (the Chapter Roundups and Quick Quizzes help you here)

A note on pronouns

On occasions in this Study Text, 'he' is used for 'he or she', 'him' for 'him or her' and so forth. Whilst we try to avoid this practice it is sometimes necessary for reasons of style. No prejudice or stereotyping accounting to sex is intended or assumed.

Syllabus

Aims and objectives

The **Managing Marketing Performance** module covers the implementation of a customer-focused business strategy in a strategic and global context. It aims to provide participants with the knowledge and skills required to contribute to the successful implementation of a customer-oriented and competitive strategy for the organisation. Its emphasis is on facilitating change in the organisation, ideally towards a stronger market orientation, managing and integrating the marketing function as part of the organisation's response, and measurement.

Learning outcomes

Participants will be able to:

- Critically evaluate the techniques available for integrating teams and activities across the organisation, specifically relating to brands and customer-facing processes, and instilling learning within the organisation.

- Identify the barriers to effective implementation of strategies and plans involving change (including communications) in the organisation, and develop measures to prevent or overcome them.

- Demonstrate an ability to manage marketing activities as part of strategy implementation.

- Assess an organisation's needs for marketing skills and resources and develop strategies for acquiring, developing and retaining them.

- Initiate and critically evaluate systems for control of marketing activities undertaken as part of business and marketing plans.

Knowledge and skill requirements

Element 1: Creating the organisational context for effective implementation of strategy. (15%)	
1.1	Appraise the requirements of a given set of tasks and their context, and assess the impact of relevant factors on the creation or development of a team to perform those tasks.
1.2	Determine the skills, characteristics and roles required within a team to carry out specific tasks effectively.
1.3	Prepare a plan showing how the team should be structured, selected, formed and developed to ensure effective performance.
1.4	Demonstrate an ability to manage the work of teams and individuals to achieve objectives, and create effective working relationships within the team and with other teams.
1.5	Critically evaluate the productivity, satisfaction and effectiveness of teams against their objectives using appropriate techniques.
1.6	Analyse the causes of any sub-optimal performance and recommend how to improve the team's performance, including plans to improve motivation, commitment and loyalty.

Element 2: Managing change and internal marketing. (20%)	
2.1	Recommend how an organisation should become more strongly market oriented, taking into account the nature of its environment and culture.
2.2	Assess the main pressures on an organisation to change and the initiatives available or being used to respond.
2.3	Identify and evaluate the sources and the techniques for overcoming any resistance to change.
2.4	Assess the impact of, and prepare a plan for, change in a marketing department, including the development of appropriate skills and capabilities to meet the new objectives.
2.5	Critically evaluate the role and content of an internal marketing communications plan and its contribution to managing change in an organisation.

Element 3: Implementing the business strategy through marketing activities. (30%)	
3.1	Explain the link between marketing activities and shareholder value, and measurement using economic value added.
3.2	Determine the contribution to shareholder value of marketing activities undertaken.
3.3	Build sustainability and ethics into business and marketing activities (including the mix) through planning, the instillation of values and day-to-day management.
3.4	Critically appraise methods available for valuing brands and building brand equity, and recommend an appropriate approach for the organisation.
3.5	Propose a contingency plan and procedures to be taken in the event of a 'crisis' or threat to the reputation of the brand or the organisation (including communications with the press and stakeholders).
3.6	Identify 'moments of truth' in delivering a service and activities that may add further value, and assess their likely impact on customers and intermediaries.
3.7	Propose and implement appropriate improvements to customer service by developing or enhancing customer care programmes.
3.8	Establish and apply techniques for managing and monitoring service quality, including the use of specific measures.
3.9	Develop and manage integrated marketing and communications programmes to establish and build relationships appropriate to the needs of customers, clients or intermediaries.
3.10	Develop support for relationships with customers, clients and intermediaries using appropriate information systems and databases and adhering to relevant privacy and data protection legislation.

Element 4: Management techniques for managing the marketing function. (20%)	
4.1	Assess the relevance to an organisation of the key concepts of quality management, including structured approaches to continuous improvement and problem solving, and their use in conducting marketing activities.
4.2	Develop a plan for compliance of a marketing function's activities with an organisation's quality management system.
4.3	Assess the relevance to a marketing function of the concept of process and techniques for process management, and develop a plan for their use in conducting marketing activities.
4.4	Assess the relevance to an organisation of the key concepts and techniques of project (or programme) management, and develop plans for their use in conducting marketing and other business activities.
4.5	Assess the capabilities of an organisation to exploit innovation and creativity in its products/services and processes.
4.6	Develop and nurture processes and techniques within marketing teams to exploit innovations in marketing.
4.7	Establish a mechanism, which is consistent with organisational policy, for deciding the activities to be undertaken by external suppliers, including agencies and outsourcing, and gain approval for the relevant expenditure.

Element 5: Measurement, evaluation and control. (15%)	
5.1	Develop and use 'accounting' measures of the performance of marketing activities against objectives.
5.2	Define and use customer-related and innovation measures as part of the organisation's balanced scorecard.
5.3	Measure the financial returns achieved on specific investments in marketing activities and programmes and compare them with the original business case or investment appraisal.
5.4	Propose measures of the value generated by developing a position based on sustainability or ethics and of the progress of the organisation in achieving the desired position.
5.5	Assess the value that marketing activities generate and contribute to shareholder value, as appropriate working with colleagues from other disciplines, using appropriate models and techniques.

Assessment

CIM will offer a single form of assessment based on the learning outcomes for this module. It will take the form of an invigilated, time-constrained assessment throughout the delivery network. Candidates' assessments will be marked centrally by CIM.

Overview and rationale

This module is an entirely new departure for CIM, but one which reflects the very real challenges that organisations face in implementing strategy and delivering against plans. As a new syllabus, it is not yet as well served with support materials as other modules, so participants and tutors should be prepared to draw materials from a range of sources.

This module introduces the knowledge and skills required to implement the organisation's strategy by managing its marketing activities. It is important to emphasise that, at this level, we are dealing with business, not purely marketing, decisions. As such, marketing has to integrate with the other functions. This module builds on the Strategic Marketing Decisions module and provides a valuable foundation for the application of implementation knowledge and skills in the final module, Strategic Marketing in Practice. It places a strong emphasis on cross-functional working to integrate teams across the organisation to brand and customer processes.

This module builds on some of the concepts and skills introduced in the Marketing Management in Practice module at Stage 2.

Approach

The challenge in delivering this syllabus is to avoid the pitfall of treating it as a loosely linked set of aspects, each drawn from a different academic discipline. The Statements of Marketing Practice should be used to provide focus on the marketing activities that participants at this level will have to perform in the workplace. The syllabus envisages marketing as either a discrete function or a set of activities spread throughout the organisation. Both of these contexts need to be brought out during delivery.

It is important to emphasise the links between everything the organisation does (its activities), how it does it (people and processes) and why it is doing it (strategic goals, competitive position and customer satisfaction). Success may just be out of reach because of the lack of co-ordination and integration of these important issues. The role of strategic marketing managers, for which this module prepares participants, demands a high level of coordination with colleagues in other disciplines or functions.

Similarly, it is important throughout the delivery of this module to emphasise the marketing and wider organisational context. International marketing strategy is no longer treated as a discrete module but is integrated into all the modules at Stage 3. No organisation is detached from international influences even if the organisation does not have or deal with international customers. Tutors should ensure that they reflect in their delivery approach and materials used the international dimension of implementation.

They should also reflect the different contexts (B2B, B2C, services, capital projects, not-for-profit, voluntary and public sector) in which marketing activities are carried out. A key role of the tutor is to ensure that participants cover a range of contexts and are able to see how marketing may be applied differently. Again this can be achieved through their delivery approach and materials.

Syllabus content

Element 1: Creating the organisational context for effective implementation of strategy. (15%)

This element develops an understanding of the formation, development and performance of marketing teams. It draws on the academic theories contained in the academic disciplines of organisational behaviour (OB) and, to a lesser extent, organisational development (OD).

Element 2: Managing change and internal marketing. (20%)

This element provides an understanding of how the strategic marketing manager can influence the organisational culture, in particular into adopting a stronger market orientation. It goes on to address the planning and implementation of change, using the concept of internal marketing, to facilitate and manage the consequent change in the organisation and marketing team. This part of the syllabus draws on the theories of culture and change management.

Element 3: Implementing the business strategy through marketing activities. (30%)

This element covers the strategic marketing manager's role in managing marketing activities within an organisation. It emphasises the link with shareholder value and corporate reputation, reflecting on the increasing importance of sustainability, social responsibility and ethics. It goes on to explore the marketing activities needed to enhance reputation: brand management, service quality and relationships. This part of the syllabus is based on marketing theory but reflects up-to-practice that may not be covered in some marketing texts.

Element 4: Management techniques for managing the marketing function. (20%)

This element aims to equip strategic marketers with some of the key management techniques needed to manage the organisation's marketing activities. It covers concepts and their application drawn from quality, process and project management. It also places importance on instilling creativity and innovation as a means of overcoming obstacles to implementation within organisations. Finally, it touches on the management of external resources and ensuring they contribute to the overall value generated by marketing. The syllabus for this element draws on operations management, including quality management.

Element 5: Measurement, evaluation and control. (15%)

This final element closes the loop in the strategic management process started in the *Analysis & Evaluation* module at Stage 3 by focussing on the measurement of performance and control. It develops an understanding of the various measures and associated techniques available and processes for appraising and evaluating activity, team and business performances. This part of the syllabus draws on financial management and control theory.

Delivery approach

Although it is expected that the learning outcomes should be achieved as discrete goals of attainment, it is assumed that tutors will also recognise and impart an understanding of the integrated nature of the syllabus content. Practical exercises, such as data gathering and the application of models and frameworks are critical to the development of skills required in this module. Particular emphasis should be placed on the critical and objective evaluation of data, being aware of potential bias. It is important that the projects or case studies illustrate the integration of analysis and evaluation within the process of strategy formulation.

Websites

The Chartered Institute of Marketing	
www.cim.co.uk	CIM website with information and access to learning support for participants.
www.cim.co.uk/learningzone	Direct access to information and support materials for all levels of CIM qualification
www.cim.co.uk/tutors	Access for Tutors
www.shapethagenda.com	Quarterly agenda paper from CIM

Publications on line	
www.ft.com	Extensive research resources across all industry sectors, with links to more specialist reports. (Charges may apply)
www.thetimes.co.uk	One of the best online versions of a quality newspaper.
www.economist.com	Useful links, and easily-searched archives of articles from back issues of the magazine.
www.mad.co.uk	Marketing Week magazine online.
www.brandrepublic.com	Marketing magazine online.
www.westburn.co.uk	Journal of Marketing Management online, the official Journal of the Academy of Marketing and Marketing Review.
http://smr.mit.edu/smr/	Free abstracts from Sloan Management Review articles
www.hbsp.harvard.edu	Free abstracts from Harvard Business Review articles
www.ecommercetimes.com	Daily enews on the latest ebusiness developments
www.cim.co.uk/knowledgehub	3000 full text journals titles are available to members via the Knowledge Hub – includes the range of titles above - embargoes may apply.
www.cim.co.uk/cuttingedge	Weekly round up of marketing news (available to CIM members) plus list of awards and forthcoming marketing events.

Sources of useful information	
www.1to1.com	The Peppers and Rogers One-to-One Marketing site which contains useful information about the tools and techniques of relationship marketing
www.balancetime.com	The Productivity Institute provides free articles, a time management email newsletter, and other resources to improve personal productivity
www.bbc.co.uk	The Learning Zone at BBC Education contains extensive educational resources, including the video, CD Rom, ability to watch TV programmes such as the News online, at your convenience, after they have been screened
www.busreslab.com	Useful specimen online questionnaires to measure customer satisfaction levels and tips on effective Internet marketing research
www.lifelonglearning.co.uk	Encourages and promotes Lifelong Learning through press releases, free articles, useful links and progress reports on the development of the University for Industry (UFI)
www.marketresearch.org.uk	The Market Research Society. Contains useful material on the nature of research, choosing an agency, ethical standards and codes of conduct for research practice
www.nielsen-netratings.com	Details the current levels of banner advertising activity, including the creative content of the ten most popular banners each week (within Top Rankings area)
www.open.ac.uk	Some good Open University videos available for a broad range of subjects
www.direct.gov.uk	Gateway to a wide range of UK government information

www.srg.co.uk	The Self Renewal Group – provides useful tips on managing your time, leading others, managing human resources, motivating others etc
www.statistics.gov.uk	Detailed information on a variety of consumer demographics from the Government Statistics Office
www.durlacher.com	The latest research on business use of the Internet, often with extensive free reports
www.cyberatlas.com	Regular updates on the latest Internet developments from a business perspective
http://ecommerce.vanderbilt.edu	eLab is a corporate sponsored research centre at the Owen Graduate School of Management, Vanderbilt University
www.kpmg.co.uk www.ey.com/uk www.pwcglobal.com	The major consultancy company websites contain useful research reports, often free of charge
http://web.mit.edu	Massachusetts Institute of Technology site has extensive research resources
www.adassoc.org.uk	Advertising Association
www.dma.org.uk	The Direct Marketing Association
www.theidm.co.uk	Institute of Direct Marketing
www.export.org.uk	Institute of Export
www.bl.uk	The British Library, with one of the most extensive book collections in the world
www.managers.org.uk	Chartered Management Institute
www.cipd.co.uk	Chartered Institute of Personnel and Development
www.emerald-library.com	Article abstracts on a range of business topics (fees apply)
www.w3.org	An organisation responsible for defining worldwide standards for the Internet

Case studies

Case studies

www.1800flowers.com	Flower and gift delivery service that allows customers to specify key dates when they request the firm to send them a reminder, together with an invitation to send a gift
www.amazon.co.uk	Classic example of how Internet technology can be harnessed to provide innovative customer service
www.broadvision.com	Broadvision specialises in customer 'personalisation' software. The site contains many useful case studies showing how communicating through the Internet allow you to find out more about your customers
www.doubleclick.net	DoubleClick offers advertisers the ability to target their advertisements on the web through sourcing of specific interest groups, ad display only at certain times of the day, or at particular geographic locations, or on certain types of hardware
www.facetime.com	Good example of a site that overcomes the impersonal nature of the Internet by allowing the establishment of real time links with a customer service representative
www.hotcoupons.com	Site visitors can key in their postcode to receive local promotions, and advertisers can post their offers on the site using a specially designed software package
www.superbrands.org	Access to case studies on international brands

The Exam Paper

Assessment methods and format of the paper

		Number of marks
Part A:	one compulsory question based on an industry scenario or a company mini-case study: this question will be broken down into parts, typically three	50
Part B:	choice of two questions from four	50
		100

The examination will be based on the stated learning outcomes and every examination will cover at least 80% of the syllabus content.

Time allowed: 3 hours

Note. Earlier drafts of the assessment methodology for this paper spoke in terms of Parts A, B and C, with one question from a choice of two being answered in each of Parts B and C. This proposal has been superseded by the format described above.

Analysis of past papers

December 2004

Part A (compulsory case study: 50 marks)

1   A major government department is relocating to a rural area but objections have been raised both within the department and in the relocation area.

   (a)   Discuss the marketing techniques that could build support.
   (b)   Using a graphic method, show how the move can be organised and co-ordinated.

Part B (two from four: 25 marks each)

2   Performance measures for the relocation in question 1.

3   Developing a marketing orientation in commercial and not-for-profit organisations

4   Using account data for marketing purposes

5   Methods of managing team performance

Specimen paper

Part A (compulsory case study: 50 marks)

1   A food manufacturing company is facing pressure on margins and consumer suspicions about wholesomeness and animal welfare.

   (a)   Action priorities for the response to the meat contamination issue
   (b)   Selection and implementation of product-market vector

Part B (two from four: 25 marks each)

2   Internal marketing: functional co-operation

3   Business case for recruitment of Product Manager

4   Balanced scorecards: difference between service and manufacturing companies

5   Setting and maintaining after sales service quality standards

About this BPP Study Text

The CIM qualification scheme

The CIM Professional Post-Graduate Diploma (PPGD) is very different from its predecessor. Like the Professional Certificate and the Professional Diploma, it is the result of an extensive research, consultation and course design project. As a result of this work, the three levels of qualification are embedded in a supporting **conceptual framework**.

Statements of Marketing Practice

Statements of Marketing Practice (SOMPs) define what marketers actually do at various levels in organisations. They are based on research and provide the foundation for the examination syllabuses. You will find a section headed 'Related Statements of Practice' preceding the syllabus in each BPP Study Text. These are the SOMPs that that unit of study is intended to support. The knowledge and skill requirements given in the syllabus for each unit underpin the SOMPs.

Strategic marketing and the PPGD

The PPGD is intended for the **aspiring strategic marketer**, that is, for the person who is moving or will shortly move into a role with influence at the strategic level. The primary role of strategic marketing is to identify and create value for the business through strongly differentiated positioning. It does this by influencing the strategy and culture of the organisation towards a strong customer focus.

The PPGD

The PPGD is organised into four units: Analysis and Evaluation, Strategic Marketing Decisions, Managing Marketing Performance and Strategic Marketing in Practice. Just as at the lower levels of the CIM qualification, the fourth unit, Strategic Marketing in Practice, is an integrative unit that draws together the threads of the other three units. However, perhaps more than is the case at the lower levels, the first three units **are themselves highly integrated**. They proceed in a logical sequence, which is based on the well-known rational model of strategy. This is split into three consecutive parts that are accurately reflected in their titles. Between them, they cover the whole field of strategic marketing, but they are not separate from each other, because business strategy itself is not compartmentalised. The split is merely one of convenience. It is important that you understand this, because you must make appropriate connections in your understanding and not regard the units as hermetically sealed off, one from another.

There is, in fact a great deal of commonality of subject matter in the first three units; the distinction between them lies in the way the ideas and techniques are used and the purposes they serve. This is reflected in the syllabuses for the three units. Let us take an important example that appears in all three: the idea of **shareholder value**.

Creating, safeguarding and enhancing the wealth of shareholders are what business is about. For marketing to play its proper role it must be able to demonstrate that it generates a return on the assets it uses and that in specifically financial terms it is worthwhile. The only satisfactory way to do this is by using the techniques of financial appraisal, such as ratio analysis and discounted cash flow. Now the idea of shareholder value is important at all stages of strategic management. At the analysis stage it is used to measure the current and past success of the company and its competitors. At the stage of strategic choice, it is the yardstick by which competing future strategies are measured. And at the implementation stage it is the basis of the strategic control system, setting the desired standard for performance.

Study Text coverage

As always, we have aimed to provide you with comprehensive coverage of your exam syllabus and the three Study Texts covering the first three units have been prepared with this aim in mind. This means that there is considerable repetition of material in these three Study Texts, reflecting as they do, the repetition in the syllabuses. This has the advantage that each Study Text is complete in its coverage. On the other hand, it also means that each one is perhaps rather larger than it otherwise might be. Nevertheless, we feel that completeness of coverage is more important than mere handiness.

Part A

Managing marketing performance

Managing the team

Syllabus content

- Managing the requirements of tasks and their context and the creation and development of a team to perform them
- Determining the skills, characteristics and roles required within a team to carry out specific tasks effectively
- Planning for the structure, selection, formation and development of the team to ensure effective performance

Introduction

In this chapter, we discuss some of the issues in managing a team. In Section 1 we discuss teams and groups in general, why they are needed, what they do, some examples in a marketing context, and some key management issues.

In Section 2, we discuss the problems of forming new teams, and the type of developmental stages a team goes through before it can get down to work. Team formation in difficult or unusual circumstances has been stressed as important for this paper. In Section 3, we offer some rules of thumb for you to assess whether a team is effective or not, with the proviso that a team which is too cohesive can be blind to new or different ideas – group think.

Sections 4 and 5 deal with some more enterprising ideas about how teams might be set up and run. In Section 6 we focus on your role as a possible team leader. Teams often need some sort of direction, but the approach to leadership you adopt (leadership style) can vary, depending on the task and the followers.

1 Teams and groups: dynamics and needs

FAST FORWARD

A group is 'any collection of people who perceive themselves to be a group'. An 'effective' group is one which achieves its allotted task and satisfies its members. Teams are becoming more important as a means of organising work.

Groups function through interaction between individual members and the blend of their skills and abilities.

In *Understanding Organisations, Handy* defines a group as **'any collection of people who perceive themselves to be a group'**. The point of this definition is the distinction it implies between a random collection of individuals and a group of individuals who share a **common sense of identity and belonging**.

Key concept

Group dynamics is the name given to the system of relationships and behaviour which exists in any group of people. Membership of a group tends to modify or develop personal characteristics to the extent that the group appears to have a personality of its own.

A group has certain attributes that a random crowd does not possess.

(a) **The members have a sense of identity**: there are acknowledged boundaries to the group which define it.

(b) **Members are loyal to the group**, and conform to the norms of behaviour and attitude that bind the group together.

(c) **Purpose and leadership**. Most groups have a **purpose or set of objectives** and will, spontaneously or formally, choose individuals or sub-groups to lead them towards those goals.

1.1 Why people form groups

People are drawn together into groups for many reasons.

- The **need to belong and to make a contribution** that will be noticed and appreciated
- **Familiarity**: a shared office or canteen
- Common rank, specialisms, objectives and interests
- The attractiveness of a particular **group activity** (for example joining a club)
- **Power** greater than the individuals alone could muster (for example a trade union)

1.2 Formal and informal groups in organisations

Some groupings will be part of the **formal organisation**: for example, specialists may be in a committee investigating a particular problem; a department split into small work teams to facilitate supervision. Other groups are **informal**.

(a) **Formal groups** will have a formal structure; they will be consciously organised for a function allotted to them by the organisation, and for which they are held responsible – they are task oriented, and become **teams**. Leaders may be chosen within the group, but are typically given authority by the organisation. Permanent formal groups include work sections and management teams such as the board of directors. **Temporary** formal groups include ad hoc committees and project teams.

(b) **Informal groups** will invariably be present in any organisation. Informal groups include workplace cliques and networks who socialise outside work. They have a constantly fluctuating membership and structure, and leaders usually emerge because of their personal qualities. The purposes of informal groups are usually related to group and individual member satisfaction, rather than to a task.

1.3 The functions of groups

From the organisation's standpoint groups and teams have several purposes.

- Performing tasks which require the collective skills of more than one person

- Testing and ratifying decisions made outside the group

- Consulting or negotiating, especially to resolve disputes within the organisation

- Creating ideas

- Collecting and transmitting information and ideas

- Co-ordinating the work of different individuals or other groups

- Motivating individuals to devote more energy and effort into achieving the organisation's goals

There may be no strict division between these different functions. They will inevitably overlap in practice. A group will be most effective if its members are not attempting to cope with different functions simultaneously.

From the individual's standpoint, groups also perform some important functions.

(a) They satisfy social needs for friendship and belonging.

(b) They help individuals in developing images of themselves.

(c) They enable individuals to help each other on matters which are not necessarily connected with the organisation's purpose, for example, people at work may organise a baby-sitting circle.

(d) They enable individuals to share the burdens of any responsibility they may have.

1.4 Examples of groups

Examples of groups or teams in marketing

(a) **Quality circles** discussing and improving quality of service

(b)   **Project groups**

- **A new product development team**

- A **key account team** responsible for all aspects of a marketing for a key client or customer segment

- A **specialist marketing function team** responsible for research or the creative dimensions of marketing

(c)   **Brainstorming groups**, brought together to generate new ideas and suggestions, for problem-solving or planning

(d)   **Training or study groups**

Action Programme 1

What (a) formal and (b) informal groups are you involved with? What are their functions? Why can these functions be performed better by a group than by an individual?

Pick a group of which you are a member. How do you define who is 'in' the group and who isn't? Does the leader of the group make a positive effort to keep the group close-knit and to make it **feel** like a team? Would you say your department or section was a team?

Do you personally **like** working in a group, or do you prefer to be and function better alone? Do you think you could succeed by being either a team player or a loner? Or does your work and the marketing culture require you to be both, at appropriate times?

1.5 Issues in managing groups

FAST FORWARD

John Adair's work on leadership identified three overlapping sets of **needs** which need to be satisfied when teams are managed, and the **roles the team leader needs to play** to satisfy these needs.

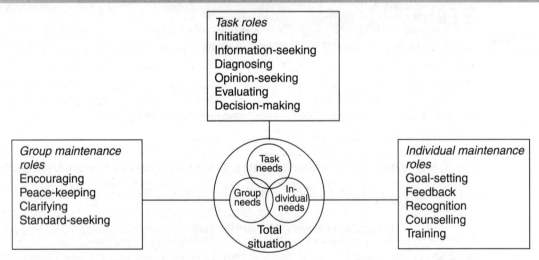

For effective performance all three sets of needs must be identified and satisfied. Without an overlap of these three circles, the group will be unsuccessful.

The total situation dictates the relative priority that must be given to each of the three sets of needs. Effective leadership involves identifying and acting on those priorities to create a balance between the needs. Meeting the various needs implies specific management roles.

Around this framework, *Adair* developed a scheme of leadership training based on precept and practice in each of **eight leadership activities** as applied to task, team and individual.

- Defining the task
- Planning
- Briefing
- Controlling

- Evaluating
- Motivating
- Organising
- Setting an example

Adair argued that the common perception of leadership as 'decision-making' was inadequate to describe the range of action required by the complex situations in which managers find themselves. This model is therefore more practical. It clearly identifies the responsibilities of the manager or leader in ensuring that the required task is achieved, but also that team and individual needs are satisfied as part of the process.

1.6 New trends

Teams and groups will become increasingly popular in a marketing context, and will replace the type of hierarchical organisation structure that stifles innovation and hampers communication in many organisations. *Freeling* suggests that teams from a number of business functions will carry out most marketing functions.

- '**Integrators** are responsible for serving each distinct consumer, channel or product.' They will co-ordinate the organisation's resources for the customer's benefit. They will lead teams with a variety of skills.

- '**Specialists** will create competitive advantage by helping the company build world class skills in the two or three most important areas of marketing.' A team might contain a pricing specialist and a specialist in database marketing, for instance.

'The teams will be organised around key **cross functional** business processes like building **brand unity** and ensuring superior **customer service**.'

A problem is the need to adjust people's behaviour. The 'integrators' are co-ordinators, not bosses: they rely on the **specialist** expertise of the people in the team.

2 Forming teams

FAST FORWARD

A team differs from a simple group in that it has some kind of formal purpose and this in turn implies some degree of both organisation and management. The team members are likely to have to play a range of roles (as observed by Belbin) and the team is likely to pass through the four stages of development described by Tuckman. Handy's model of effectiveness describes the outcomes of the team's work as contingent on the nature of the given and intervening factors in its work setting.

Simply bringing a group of individuals together does not make a team. The word 'team' implies **synergy**. Its output collectively would be greater than the sum of the outputs of individuals working in isolation.

But what constitutes a team? The eleven players on the football field may seem to be a team, but their manager is seldom a player and there are dozens of others supporting their activities behind the scenes.

If you are faced with starting a team from scratch, you can begin by identifying what the **task** is and what **skills** and **characteristics** are needed to achieve it. Then group members can be identified from within or outside the organisation.

In the supposedly flatter, more matrix structured organisation of today the formation of teams for relatively short periods is becoming more common. These may be **project teams** which bring together individuals from different disciplines, backgrounds and even different companies. In these situations the manager has two key roles.

- Selecting the right mix of individuals
- Actively working to turn individuals into effective teams in as short a time as possible

Imagine for a moment you are free to choose individuals to make up a new business team: perhaps a creative marketing team. Who would you choose? All the best known experts in their fields? Common sense would suggest that a team of the best must generate the best results.

In practice, however, this is not always the case. A team drawn from a combination of stars and workhorses is more likely to be effective. The individual needs of stars can sometimes take precedence over the needs of group or task.

2.1 Team roles

Belbin drew up a list of the characteristics of an ideal team. More than one role can be played by each team member.

Member	Role
Co-ordinator	Presides and co-ordinates; balanced, disciplined, good at working through others.
Shaper	Highly strung, dominant, extrovert, passionate about the task itself, a spur to action.
Plant	Introverted, but intellectually dominant and imaginative; source of ideas and proposals but with disadvantages of introversion.
Monitor-evaluator	Analytically (rather than creatively) intelligent; dissects ideas, spots flaws; possibly aloof, tactless – but necessary.
Resource-investigator	Popular, sociable, extrovert, relaxed; source of new contacts, but not an originator; needs to be made use of.
Implementor	Practical organiser, turning ideas into tasks; scheduling, planning and so on; trustworthy and efficient, but not excited; not a leader, but an administrator.
Team worker	Most concerned with team maintenance – supportive, understanding, diplomatic; popular but uncompetitive – contribution noticed only in absence.
Finisher	Chivvies the team to meet deadlines, attend to details; urgency and follow-through important, though not always popular.

Once you have a group of individuals selected (or inherited) as your basis, you now have the task of turning them into a team.

2.1.1 Principles of team design

Belbin suggests there are five closely related constraints on the design of effective teams.

(a) Team members should **perform effectively** in their team roles and in their functional specialisation.

(b) There should be a **proper balance** of both team and functional roles among the members of the team.

(c) The technical effectiveness of the team depends on the presence of members able to perform the necessary team roles.

(d) Team effectiveness also depends on members' ability to assess relative strengths and weaknesses in team and functional roles and adjust their contributions accordingly.

(e) Team members' personalities will predispose them to some team roles and limit their ability to play others.

Marketing at Work

Nicky Wnek described the 'innovation squad' in *Marketing Business*.

'**Mr Blue Skies** is the broad thinker who keeps the long-term vision but needs to be kept-in-touch with reality. His colleague, **Mr Margin** gets margins up and thus delivers the all-important profit. However, he cannot see that innovation relies on intangibles such as faith and judgement.

Ms Misery takes her name from her tendency to focus on the negative. But innovation needs her rigorous approach.

Ms Me-Too could bring about a first-to-market situation by keeping a valuable eye on the competition – for instance an innovation abroad. Every innovation needs someone to champion the cause but **Mr Hobby-Horse** can be in danger of backing the wrong horse. **Mr Cavalier** is the classic self-confident entrepreneur with high energy levels and a healthy disregard for the established way of doing things; he genuinely cares about a result and is faster at effecting change.

Ms Brands is the player who contributes the strong understanding of the consumer, but unfortunately not everyone shares her passion for her particular brand. **Mr Out-of-Depth** is unlikely to have that big idea, but he is keen, hard-working and sufficiently junior to do the essential donkey work.'

2.2 Team development

Groups are not static. They mature and develop. Four stages in this group development were identified by *Tuckman*.

- **Forming**
- **Storming**
- **Norming**
- **Performing**

Each of these stages has different implications for the **task** and the **interpersonal relationships** between team members.

Forming

The group is beginning to establish personal relationships. Members will be cautiously testing boundaries, trying to find out about each other, and about the aims and norms of the group, which will at this stage be primarily organisational traditions and standards.

Interpersonal focus		Task focus	
Main concerns:	*Resulting in:*	*Main concerns:*	*Resulting in:*
Inclusion	Cautious behaviour	Task orientation	'What are we supposed to do?'
Rejection	Avoiding conflict		
Acceptance			'What are the goals?'

Storming

Interpersonal behaviours and greater confidence in self expression begin to cause conflict. There is resistance to group influence and task requirements, as a struggle for control and leadership emerges.

Interpersonal focus		Task focus	
Main concerns:	*Resulting in:*	*Main concerns:*	*Resulting in:*
Control	Conflict	Organisation of the task	'Are these the rules we want to follow?'
Status/authority	Power struggles	Rules and agenda decisions	Questioning decisions already reached
Stress	Criticism		
Values & ideas	Challenging ideas and practices		'Is the task possible?'

Norming

A settling down period. Group cohesion increases as roles (including leadership) are established. Norms and processes are evolved for group functioning: work sharing, output levels, interactions, decision making and so on.

Interpersonal focus		Task focus	
Main concerns:	*Resulting in:*	*Main concerns:*	*Resulting in:*
Being liked	Cohesion	Getting on with the job	Willingness to change
Being accepted	Group focus		Compromise and
Open-mindedness	Building team spirit	Data flow	collaboration
Listening			Information sharing

Performing

Members perform tasks through genuine collaboration (working together). Roles have been clarified.

Interpersonal focus		Task focus	
Main concerns:	*Resulting in:*	*Main concerns:*	*Resulting in:*
Interdependence and	Acceptance of others' point of view	Creative problem-solving and decision-making	Adapting to change
independence	Agreeing to		All-member contribution and support
Commitment	disagree		No complacency
Affection			
Autonomy			

Mourning or adjourning

The group sees itself as having fulfilled its purpose. If it is a temporary group, it may physically disband. Otherwise, on-going changes in function and/or personnel must be absorbed.

Interpersonal focus		Task focus	
Main concerns:	*Resulting in:*	*Main concerns:*	*Resulting in:*
Withdrawal of key personnel	Disillusionment, frustration	Restating direction	Some confusion
Break-up of group support and security	Confusion, sadness and anxiety	Questioning support structures	Re-norming, re-negotiating roles
Perception that the task is finished	Evaluation, withdrawal	Opting out/disbanding	Returning to forming stage

These stages reflect increasing group effectiveness over time. While the stages are clearly defined, however, they do not form a swift or inevitable progression. Not all groups develop through all the stages: some may get stuck on particular interpersonal or task issues and remain immature, conflicted or cohesion-focused without reaching the effective team-working stage. Some stages may have to be re-negotiated as interpersonal and task issues change or emerge.

Adair identifies a fifth stage, **dorming**, in which the team becomes sleepy and complacent. The danger of this development is obvious.

Marketing at Work

It may be possible to apply Tuckman's ideas to the **management of work groups**.

The Nationwide Building Society has introduced self-managed teams into its administrative centre. The progress of the change can be described in Tuckman's terms. The project also illustrates how *management input* can contribute to the process.

At the **forming** stage, management provided extra training in team building, conflict management and job-specific skills. Leaders were appointed, but in coaching rather than directive roles. The need to learn new skills produced a temporary dip in performance.

The **storming** stage started at the same time, with some leaders fearing a loss of control and some team members objecting to what they saw as more work for the same rewards.

Norming was an important part of the project and crucial to the management's intentions. One management input was the publication of a series of **performance measures** for each team. A **sense of ownership and responsibility** caused the teams to work to improve their results. For instance, peer pressure led to a 75% reduction in sickness absence. Similarly, a low-achieving group took advice from other groups and made a significant improvement in its performance. Consistent comment from team members during annual appraisals indicates that they are now committed to the new norms.

The **performing** stage has now been reached. Productivity is up by 50% and the centre's staff are now at the top of the organisation's annual staff survey in terms of job satisfaction.

Action Programme 2

What norms and customs are there in the group you are part of or familiar with? What do you have to do to become part of its culture? Is there a non-conformist in the group – someone who doesn't fit in: how i that person treated?

2.3 Creating an effective team

The criteria of group effectiveness are first, the fulfilment of task and organisation goals and, second, the satisfaction of group members.

A useful way of looking at the problem of how a supervisor or manager can create an effective team is to take a **contingency approach**. *Handy* suggested that group effectiveness (**outcomes**) depends on the **givens** and **intervening factors** in the diagram below.

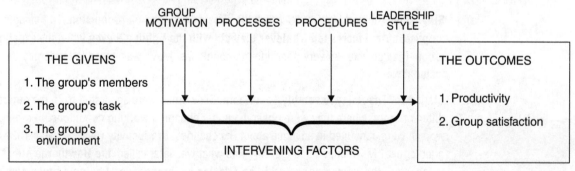

2.3.1 The givens

The personalities of the members of the team, and their personal goals, will help to determine the group's personality and goals. Individuals are likely to be influenced more strongly by a small group than by a large group in which they may be unable to participate effectively in team decisions.

The nature of the task must have some bearing on how a group should be managed.

(a) If a job must be done urgently, it is often necessary to dictate how things should be done, rather than to encourage a participatory style of working.

(b) Jobs that are routine, unimportant and undemanding will be insufficient to motivate either individuals or the group as a whole.

The group's **environment** is both the physical surroundings at work and its inter-group relations. An open-plan office, in which the members of the group are closely situated, is conducive to **group cohesion**. A group's attitudes will also be affected by its relationship with other groups, which may be friendly, neutral or hostile. Where groups are in competition with other groups, they become more closely knit among themselves, are better motivated and more task-focused. Teams playing games show this kind of motivation.

2.3.2 Intervening factors

Of the intervening factors, we will be discussing motivation in more detail later and we will go on to talk about leadership and leadership style in the following section. With regard to processes and procedures, groups are much the same as individuals: research indicates that a team which tackles its work systematically will be more effective than one which muddles through. Note that it is the intervening factors that a manager is likely to be able to manipulate.

2.4 The outcomes

FAST FORWARD

Groups prize loyalty, which usually expresses itself in conformity to **norms of behaviour** which bind the group together. Groups are capable of exerting considerable social pressure on individuals to conform.

Ideally, the group and its work will be managed so that efforts towards high productivity will also lead to the satisfaction of personal and group needs such as job satisfaction, respect and cohesion. A **participative style of management** (see below) may contribute to this. However, as in the Bank Wiring observation room discussed below, individuals and the groups may have goals which prevent high output.

 Marketing at Work

Elton Mayo's work sheds light on the importance of groups within an organisation. The **Hawthorne Studies** were conducted at the Hawthorne plant of the Western Electric Company.

(a) **Stage one**. The company investigated the effects of lighting on production. To management's surprise, **output increased whatever they did with the lighting** – even when the experimental group was subjected to very poor lighting conditions. Mayo was called in to identify the 'mystery' factor at work.

(b) **Stage two**. The **Relay Assembly Test Room**. Six women were separated from the others in a different room, where they were observed under changing working conditions. In most cases, the women were consulted in advance about the changes. Productivity rose – whatever the changes, good or bad! Mayo concluded that this was what was later called **'the Hawthorne effect'**: the **response of the women appeared to be affected by their sense of being a group singled out for attention.**

(c) **Stage three**. Stage two had suggested that employee attitudes and values were important. The company set up an interview programme designed to survey attitudes towards supervision, jobs and working conditions. The major conclusion was that relationships with people at work were important to employees.

(d) **Stage four**. The **Bank Wiring Observation Room**. Fourteen men were put in an observation room to work under more or less normal conditions. **The group was seen to set its own rules, attitudes and standards of output**. Its behaviour became oriented towards its own interests in a way that seemed beyond the supervisor's control. In other words, the group had developed into a powerful, self-protecting informal organisation.

The conclusions of the studies were that individual members must be seen as part of a group, and that **informal groups exercise a powerful influence in the workplace**: supervisors and managers need to take account of **social needs** if they wish to secure commitment to organisational goals.

3 Effective and ineffective teams

FAST FORWARD

Teams do not always work as well as hoped. Motivation, communication and mutual support may not develop and the team may be hampered by conflict, alienation, groupthink and divisive management.

3.1 Characteristics of an ideal team

(a) Each individual gets the **support of the team and a sense of identity and belonging** which encourages loyalty and hard work on the group's behalf.

(b) **Skills, information and ideas are shared**, so that the team's capabilities are greater than those of the individuals.

(c) New ideas can be tested, reactions taken into account and persuasive skills brought into play in **group discussion for decision making and problem solving**.

(d) Each individual is encouraged to participate and contribute and thus becomes personally **involved in and committed to the team's activities**.

(e) Goodwill, trust and respect can be built up between individuals, so that **communication is encouraged** and potential problems more easily overcome.

Unfortunately, team working is rarely such an undiluted success.

(a) Awareness of **group norms** and the desire to be acceptable to the group may **restrict individual personality** and flair.

(b) **Too much discord**. Conflicting **roles and relationships** can cause difficulties in communicating effectively.

(c) **Personality problems** will harm performance if one member dislikes or distrusts another; is too dominant or so timid that the value of his ideas is lost; or is so negative that constructive communication is rendered impossible.

(d) **Rigid leadership** and procedures may **strangle initiative and creativity** in individuals.

(e) **Differences of opinion** and political conflicts of interest are always likely.

(f)   **Too much harmony**. Teams work best when there is room for disagreement. The cosy consensus of the group may prevent consideration of alternatives, constructive criticism or conflict. *I L Janis* called this **group think**. Similarly, efforts to paper over differences lead to bland recommendations.

(g)   **Corporate culture and reward systems**. Teams may fail if the company promotes and rewards the individual at the expense of the group.

(h)   **Too many meetings**. Teams should not try to do everything together. Not only does this waste time in meetings, but team members are exposed to less diversity of thought.

(i)   **Powerlessness**. People will not bother to work in a team or on a task force if its recommendations are ignored.

3.1.1 Team problems

Problems of team effectiveness may be analysed under four headings.

(a)   **Goals**. Team members may not have a clear or complete understanding of team goals and their detailed implications. This problem may be particularly apparent when functional specialists place too much emphasis on their own areas of expertise.

(b)   **Roles**. Clarity about roles depends on clarity about goals. Authority, responsibility accountability and boundaries define roles; in the absence of clear understanding on roles there will be disputes.

(c)   **Processes**. Process is about the way things are done. There are issues of communication, record-keeping and audit trail that are simple to arrange. Wider issues depend on the aspects of role definitions listed above. Decision-making is crucial and hand in hand with those matters.

(d)   **Relationships**. Problems that appear to derive from personal relationships may, in fact, reflect confusion on goals, roles and processes. Genuine relationship problems are the most difficult to resolve.

3.1.2 Team building

Where people are unused to team working, or if there are general problem areas, it may be necessary to place great emphasis on team-building activity. Adair's model of leadership explicitly recognises this under the heading of dealing with team needs.

Generally, in today's service businesses, careful attention to communication, especially through effective meetings, will go a long way towards promoting team effectiveness. Communication must be two-way and team leaders must be committed to balancing team and individual needs in order to promote task success.

3.2 The dangers of group think

Handy notes that 'ultra-cohesive groups can be dangerous because in the organisational context the group must serve the organisation, not itself'. If a group is completely absorbed with its own maintenance, members and priorities, it can become dangerously blinkered to what is going on around it, and may confidently forge ahead in a completely wrong direction.

The cosy consensus of the group may prevent consideration of alternatives, constructive criticism or conflicts. There are several symptoms of **group think**.

- A sense of invulnerability and blindness to the risk involved in pet strategies
- Rationalisation of inconsistent facts
- Moral blindness and a feeling that might is right
- A tendency to stereotype outsiders and enemies

- Strong group pressure to quell dissent
- Self-censorship by members
- Mutual support and solidarity to guard decisions

Group think is rife at the top and centre of organisations. Victims take great risks in their decisions, fail to recognise failure, and are highly resistant to unpalatable information. Such groups must actively encourage **self-criticism**; welcome **outside ideas** and evaluation; and respond positively to **conflicting evidence**.

3.3 Appraising group effectiveness

Supervisors who wish to improve the effectiveness of their work groups must be able to identify the different characteristics of an effective and an ineffective group. No one factor on its own will be significant, but taken collectively the factors may indicate how well or badly the group is doing.

Action Programme 3

How would you determine whether a team was effective or ineffective? Think about both quantitative and qualitative factors which may characterise the two extremes. Remember that individual attitudes will affect many things, as well as the dynamics of the group.

Action Programme 4

Consider your group at work. How effective is it in terms of (a) doing what the organisation wants it to do in the way of tasks and (b) offering satisfaction to its members?

What can you (or your manager) do to improve the effectiveness of the group? Think about your contribution, if you are a member, and your ability to adjust the 'intervening factors' in the group situation, if you are its leader. What is there in the group membership, the task and the environment (ie the 'givens') that hold the group back from being as effective as it might be?

3.3.1 Example case study

You have recently been appointed to manage a group of 10 people and you have found evidence that all is not well. The output of the section is not high. Although overtime is regularly worked, there are substantial backlogs and targets are missed. Absenteeism is high with the same people absent regularly. They produce poor excuses or none at all. People fall out over trivial issues and the lack of co-operation impairs efficiency. You feel a general air of lethargy, if not hostility. What do you propose to do about it? How will you know when you are succeeding?

Solution

There are various possible causes of this serious situation. The failure to achieve targets might be due to inadequate planning, failure of the manager to tell individuals what their targets are, and lack of a feedback and control system to ensure that action is taken when needed. Some individual group members might be unsuited to their jobs and this might help to explain poor efficiency. Inadequate working conditions and poor organisation of the group's work routines might also be at fault. The workload of the group might be excessive so that group members no longer try to achieve targets. However, an improvement in efficiency would increase output and the group is clearly not performing well enough.

The problem of absenteeism might be caused by low morale, but the absence of disciplinary action against persistent offenders can only create a sense of unfairness amongst the others. This could help to explain the hostility and conflicts over trivial matters between group members.

The lack of co-operation might be caused by poor planning and supervision, or by poor motivation of staff and inter-personal dislikes. Staff have clearly been reluctant to refer matters to their manager, since conflicts have arisen over trivial matters. Good supervision should prevent minor disagreements from escalating into conflict in the first place.

3.3.2 What should be done?

The effectiveness of the group should be assessed initially in terms of the group itself, the group's task and the group's working environment.

(a)   The **personalities, characteristics, skills and experience** of each individual group member should be assessed. Inter-personal hostility between particular individuals should be identified. Habitual absentees should be identified.

(b)   The **tasks** of the group should be assessed. Are the tasks of the group too difficult for the group members? Is the workload too heavy for a group of ten?

(c)   The **environment** of the group should be examined. Do the individuals who have to co-operate closely with each other actually sit close together? Is the equipment used by the group adequate for their job?

After an initial assessment of these matters, you should call a group meeting. At the meeting, you should express disquiet at the state of affairs, and explain why. The group members should be encouraged to state their own views, after which you should state your intention to do something about the problem. An outline of the proposed steps should be given.

(a)   The group as a whole must know what its **planning targets** are, and each individual member of the group should be given standards or targets to work towards.

(b)   If there is a need for **overtime**, the quantity of overtime that ought to be required should be built into the plan. You should ask individuals whether they are unable or unwilling to work these amounts of overtime. If there is a need for more staff, you could pursue the matter through your superior, and let the staff know what is happening about it.

(c)   There should be regular **feedback** to individual group members on their performance, against target. If performance is below standard, you should discuss what control action or remedies might be necessary.

(d)   **Persistent absenteeism** must be **stopped**. It should be made clear to all group members that disciplinary measures will be taken against offenders. You should than apply discipline consistently and keep to your word.

(e)   The need for **co-operation** between group members should be made clear and can be improved by good planning. You should set a timescale for improvements and use regular group meetings to review progress, identify problems and work out difficulties.

(f)   You should give **time and attention to individual members** of the group. **Training needs** should be identified, and group members given appropriate training where required. You should get to know each individual, identifying their needs and interests, and trying to encourage them. If some individuals continue to show personal animosity, or to perform badly, you should express concern, and indicate that their next formal appraisal will not be favourable.

(g)   The **techniques and equipment** used by the group should be improved where necessary (and if resources are available). You should make whatever alterations to the office layout and environment seem beneficial and practicable.

3.3.3 How to gauge success

Two things should happen when matters are improving.

- The productivity of the group should improve and targets will be achieved.
- There should be an apparent improvement in the **attitudes** of group members.

More specific improvements will occur. Several of these can be quantified and monitored.

- **Absenteeism** should be much lower.

- There should be **higher output**.

- Individual targets as well as group targets should be achieved.

- Individuals should display a **greater commitment** to their work and the achievement of targets.

- **Communication** between group members should be more free and open.

- **Conflicts** over minor matters should no longer occur.

- Group members should show signs of trying to help each other by offering **constructive suggestions and ideas**.

- Group members will show signs of wanting to develop their abilities further.

It is the manager's responsibility to monitor the effectiveness of the group and be constantly seeking ways of improving it. The manager should bring in new ideas and people and set new challenges and targets Although there is a tendency not to change a winning team, **even a successful group can become complacent and stale**.

Action Programme 5

Draft a short report to the manager of a team you are involved with. In it you should make three specific recommendations for improving team performance and the ways in which you suggest the effect of these changes is monitored.

3.4 Groups and decision making

<img src="data:image/png;base64..."/>
FAST FORWARD

Group decision-making can benefit from the range of inputs provided by the members and it can promote acceptance of decisions. However, it can blur responsibility, promote harmful agendas and waste time.

Group decision making can be useful.

(a)   Pooling skills, information and ideas from different functions, specialisms and levels in the organisation could increase the quality of the decision. Groups have been shown to produce better evaluated decisions than individuals working separately.

(b)   Participation in the decision-making process makes the decision acceptable to the group either because it represents a compromise or consensus of all their views, or because the group has simply been consulted and given a sense of influencing the decision.

With critical decisions, where quality is the prime objective, it may be more helpful for a manager to involve work groups in areas such as problem definition and formulation of alternative solutions to take advantage of collective skills and experience and the creativity of group idea-generation. The decision might be best left to the manager responsible. Acceptance might have been enhanced by the consultative process.

The same criteria apply as deciding whether to delegate.

- Do you need employee acceptance?
- Do you have the power to do without employee acceptance?
- Do you trust employees' judgement and ability to reach consensus?
- Do you need employee input, or is the solution clear-cut?
- Do you need a fast decision or a well sold decision?

3.4.1 Risks in group decision-making

(a)   Shared responsibility can be blurred responsibility, and groups tend to make riskier decisions than individuals.

(b)   The desire for consensus in a group can make it ignore dissent and any information that contradicts its pet theory.

(c)   Groups may have their own agenda and make decisions to further their own objectives rather than the organisation's.

(d)   Group decisions take longer to reach (although they are easier to implement later) especially if there is conflict and disagreement in the group. This is not regarded as a drawback by the Japanese, however. Argument leading to eventual consensus is common managerial practice in Japanese business.

4 Teams from different parts of the organisation

FAST FORWARD

There are two basic approaches to the organisation of cross-functional team working: **multi-disciplinary** teams and **multi-skilled** teams.

4.1 Multi-disciplinary teams

Multi-disciplinary teams bring together individuals from different functional specialisms, so that their competencies can be **pooled or exchanged**. They are appropriate when a significant degree of technical expertise in divergent disciplines is required, as in most large technical projects.

Multi-disciplinary teams:

(a)   Increase team members' **awareness of the big picture** of their tasks and decisions, by highlighting the dovetailing of functional objectives

(b)   Help to generate **solutions to problems**, and suggestions for performance or process improvements, by integrating more pieces of the puzzle

(c)   Aid **co-ordination across functional boundaries**, by increasing the flow of communication, informal relationships and co-operation.

On the other hand, the members of multi-functional teams have different reporting lines and responsibilities within their line departments, creating the **ambiguity of dual responsibility**. They may have a range of different backgrounds, work cultures, specialist skills and terminology. This creates a particular challenge for the team leader: to build a sense of team identity, role clarity and co-operative working.

4.2 Multi-skilled teams

Multi-skilled teams bring together a number of functionally versatile individuals, each of whom can perform *any* of the group's tasks: work can thus be **allocated flexibly**, according to who is best placed to do a given job when required. The advantages of multi-skilling may be as follows.

(a) Performing a **whole, meaningful job** is more satisfying to people than performing only one or two of its component operations (as in scientific job design).

(b) Allowing team members to see the big picture enables and encourages them to **contribute information and ideas** for improvements.

(c) Empowering team members to take initiative **enhances organisational responsiveness** to customer demands and environmental changes (particularly in 'front-line' customer service units).

(d) A focus on overall task objectives **reduces the need for tight managerial control** and supervision.

(e) Labour resources can be allocated more **flexibly and efficiently**, without potentially disruptive demarcation disputes.

Multi-skilled teams are particularly appropriate when a high degree of flexibility is required. However, because of human limitations, there are likely to be large areas of competence outside their capabilities. They are thus suited to broad but still limited areas of activity, whereas a multi-disciplinary team can be assembled to cover any desired range of functions.

4.3 Project teams

Project teams may be set up to handle specific **strategic developments** (such as the introduction of a Just in Time approach), tasks relating to **particular processes** (such as the computerisation of the payroll system), tasks relating to particular **cases or accounts** (such as co-ordination of work for a client or client group) or special **audits or investigations** of procedures or **improvement opportunities** (such as a review of recruitment and selection methods).

Short-term projects pose particular time constraints on building and managing a successful team. The challenge for project managers and co-ordinators is to accelerate the process of team development, whilst at the same time keeping pace with the immediate targets set out in the project plan.

5 Virtual and self-managed teams

FAST FORWARD

It is no longer essential that teams have all their members in a single location, or even have a single formal leader. Virtual teams function via electronic links; self-managed teams collaborate to discharge most routine management functions themselves.

5.1 Virtual teams

The development of information and communications technology has enabled communication and collaboration among people at a diverse and far-flung range of locations, via teleconferencing and video-conferencing, locally networked PCs and the Internet. This has created the concept of the **virtual team**: an interconnected group of people who may never be present in the same office – and may even be on different sides of the world – but who share information and tasks, make joint decisions and fulfil the collaborative functions of a physical team.

'Virtual teams may be composed of full-time or part-time employees. They might have a global reach, or involve combinations of local telecommuting members and more traditional In-house workers. A senior executive might be on one planning committee for a product release, for example, another for identifying minority vendors, another to study relocating a plant, and another to evaluate software tracking. He may deal with key players who not only are out of the country but also are working for another company, or perhaps as suppliers who are on the virtual team to add information and technical support.'

(Solomon, 2001)

Localised virtual teams have been used for some time in the form of **teleworking**: the process of working from home, or from a satellite office close to home, with the aid of computers, facsimile machines, modems or other forms of telecommunication equipment. The main benefits cited for such work include savings on office overheads and the elimination of the costs and stresses of commuting for employees.

More recently, however, the globalisation of business, the need for fast responses to marketplace demands and the increasing sophistication of available technologies has brought about an explosion in global virtual teamworking. More and more organisations are attempting to conduct business 24 hours a day, seven days a week, with people on different continents and in different time zones. Electronic collaboration allows organisations to do the following things.

(a) Recruit and collaborate with the best available people without the constraints of **location** or **relocation**. A team can co-opt a specialist when required, from a global pool of skills.

(b) Offer more **scheduling flexibility** for people who prefer non-traditional working hours (including the handicapped and working parents, for example).

(c) Maintain close contact with customers **throughout the world**.

(d) Operate **24-hour working days** (for example, for global customer support) – without having to have staff on night shifts.

5.2 Self-managed teams

Self-managed teams are the most highly-developed form of team working. They are permanent structures in which team members collaboratively decide all the major issues affecting their work: work processes and schedules, task allocation, the selection and development of team members, the distribution of rewards and the management of group processes (problem-solving, conflict management, internal discipline and so on). The team leader is a member of the team, acting in the role of coach and facilitator: leadership roles may be shared or rotated as appropriate.

Self managed teams generally have the following features.

(a) They contract with management to assume various degrees of **managerial responsibility** for planning, organising, directing and monitoring (which may increase as the team develops). Team members learn and share the jobs usually performed by a manager: no 'visible' immediate manager is present. They often report to 'absentee' managers with broad responsibilities for several functions, whose role is to act as integrators/facilitators.

(b) They perform **day-to-day planning and control functions**: scheduling and co-ordinating the daily and occasional tasks of the team and individuals; setting performance goals and standards; formulating and adopting budgets; collecting performance data and reviewing results.

(c) They perform **internal people management functions**: screening and interviewing candidates to join the team, and contributing to selection/hiring decisions; providing orientation for new members; coaching and providing feedback on member performance; designing and conducting cross-training on all tasks.

(d)   Team members cross-train in all the tasks necessary for a particular process, and members rotate flexibly from job to job.

(e)   Weekly team meetings are used to identify, analyse and solve task and relationship problems within the team: reviewing team working and progress; getting team members to research and present team issues and so on.

Self-managed teamworking is said to have advantages in:

(a)   Saving in managerial costs

(b)   Gains in quality and productivity, by harnessing the commitment of those who perform work

6 The manager's role within the team

FAST FORWARD

> Managers are responsible for **planning** and **controlling** the work of the teams they lead. This is often done using a **budget**, which can be used as a forecast, a yardstick, a target and a means of allocating resources.

The manager has many functions and must take responsibility for a range of business activities. In this section, we provide you with an overview of these activities as they relate to the management of the team.

6.1 Prioritisation

Each of us has to identify a system for prioritising our work and this involves planning. If you treat work in a reactive and ad hoc way, then you will respond to tasks as they land on your desk with no consideration of their importance. Effective managers take the time to review what has to be done and consider each activity in terms of its importance, priority and urgency, as well as the potential for delegation.

Key concept

> **Prioritisation** involves identifying **key results** (objectives which *must* be achieved if the section is to fulfil its aims) and **key tasks** (those things that *must* be done on time and to the required standard if the key results are to be achieved).

A job will be **important** compared to other tasks, if it satisfies at least one of three conditions.

- It adds value to the organisation's mission.

- It comes from a source deserving high priority, such as a customer or senior manager.

- The potential consequences of failure are long-term, difficult to reverse, far reaching and costly.

One of the problems managers have in allocating their time, comes from determining what tasks are **important** as defined above and distinguishing these from **urgent** tasks, which may have a deadline but less importance.

- Tasks both urgent and important should be dealt with now, and given a fair amount of time.

- Tasks **not** urgent but still important will become urgent as the deadline looms closer. Some of these tasks can be delegated.

- Tasks urgent but not important should be delegated, or designed out of your job. The task might be urgent to someone else, but not to you.

- Tasks neither urgent nor important should be delegated or binned.

6.2 Planning

Planning enables the organisation to cope with the uncertainty of the future in a way that will allow its objectives to be achieved. There are three important steps to planning.

(a) **Objective-setting**. Deciding what the organisation, and units within it, should achieve

(b) **Forecasting**. Anticipating, as far as possible, what opportunities and threats are likely to be offered by the future

(c) **Detailed planning**. Making decisions about what to do, how and when to do it and who should be responsible for it

Even the best plans may go wrong, but plans give direction and predictability to the work of the organisation, and enable it to adapt to environmental changes without crisis.

Planning affects all levels of management from the determination of overall direction, down to the detail of day-to-day operational tasks. There is a **hierarchical structure** of plans in which broad, long-term strategies lead to medium-term policies which are supported by short-term operational decisions.

6.2.1 An approach to planning

A systematic approach to planning, based on results and objectives involves:

Step 1   **aims**; which dictate

Step 2   **priorities**, or '**key result areas**'; for which there should be

Step 3   **standards**; and

Step 4   **detailed targets**; so that

Step 5   **action plans**; can be formulated and implemented, subject to

Step 6   **monitoring**; and

Step 7   **control** action where required.

Through your studies at Advanced Certificate and Diploma Level and your work as a practising marketer you will be called upon to produce specific and often detailed plans. The above framework can be used as a basis for section headings within a report or plan.

Key concept

> **Control** is the process of monitoring the activities of individuals and units, and taking whatever actions may be necessary to bring performance into line with plans, by adjusting performance or, possibly, the plans themselves.

6.3 Control

Control is required because unpredictable events occur and actual performance deviates from what was expected and planned. For example, a powerful new competitor may enter the market, or there may be an unexpected rise in labour costs. Control systems allow managers to identify deviations from plan and to do something about them before they have adverse consequences.

Planning and control are intimately linked.

(a) It is necessary to verify whether or not the plan has worked or is working, and whether the objectives of the plan have been/are being achieved. This is where control becomes part of the planning process.

(b)   Actual results and performance are therefore compared to the plan. If there are deviations, weaknesses or errors, control measures will be taken – which involves adjusting or setting further plans for ongoing action. Thus planning becomes part of the control process.

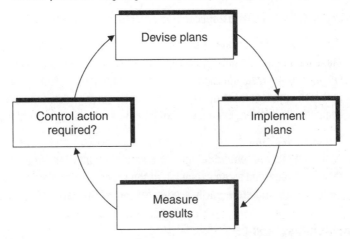

6.4 Budgets

An important aspect of both planning and control activity is the **budget** and you may be asked to make budget recommendations in the examination. Do not worry about the actual costs of various activities; the examiners are more interested in the fact you have been through the process of **identifying the key cost areas**.

A budget, since it has different purposes, might mean different things to different people.

(a)   As a **forecast** of the expected performance of the organisation, it helps managers to look into the future. Given conditions of rapid change and uncertainty, however, this function will only be helpful over short periods of time. Budgets will often be updated or superseded.

(b)   As a **means of allocating resources**, it can be used to decide what resources are needed and how much should be given to each area of the organisation's activities. Resource allocation is particularly important when some resources (usually finance and qualified staff) are in short supply. Budgets often set ceilings on spending by administrative and service departments – or project teams.

(c)   As a **yardstick** against which to compare **actual performance**, the budget provides a means of indicating where and when **control action** may be necessary (and possibly where some managers or employees are open to censure for achieving poor results).

(d)   As a **target** for achievement, a budget might be a means of **motivating the workforce** to greater personal accomplishment.

6.5 Decision making and problem solving

FAST FORWARD

Decision-making may be approached in a rational manner, though it is possible to spend far too much time thinking about decisions.

Once a decision has been made, an **action plan** to implement it may be needed.

In a business, a **decision** is usually the result of choosing between available or anticipated options and is often taken on the grounds of future projections. **The decision-making process thus involves value judgements and risk taking**. The earlier management authors highlighted decision-making as one of the key differences between management and workers.

How systematic should decision-making be? It has been suggested that too much time is spent thinking about decisions; and that the essence of good decisions is to make them firmly and quickly, and then get on with the work. However, risky or important decisions do need to be taken with care.

There are two approaches, which are applicable to different types of decision.

(a) **Scientific decision making** depends on the quantitative techniques of management, which measure and express all viable alternatives. It assumes that full and complete information will lead to the ideal solution. This approach ignores individual flair and fails to recognise that many management decisions have to be taken without the luxury of time in which to evaluate alternatives. Events will continue to evolve and may enforce a decision.

(b) **Reaction decision** theory assumes that once policies and corporate plans are established, decisions that are required follow as a natural result of those plans. In this way, decision making is regarded as an extension of the process of implementing corporate plans. Decisions are therefore partly predetermined by the detail of the plans.

6.5.1 The decision sequence

There is a generally accepted rational model of decision making and problem solving.

We have a problem	Identify and define the problem
	Analyse the problem
What solution can we find?	Appraise available resources
	List and compare alternative solutions
	Select the optimum solution
Now implement the solution	Draw up action plan to implement solution
	Carry out plan
	Monitor progress/effectiveness of plan

You cannot find an answer unless you are asking the right question. Careful **definition of the problem** and examination of its causes frequently produce a definition of the solution. For example, a manager concerned with declining sales volume might concentrate on improving sales staff performance because there appears to be a direct link, while ignoring more subtle effects like product obsolescence and changes in fashion.

Decisions should be based on as many **facts about the situation** as it is possible to obtain with reasonable effort and at reasonable cost. However, most decisions are based on **incomplete information**, because all the information is not available or because, beyond a certain point, the gathering of **more** information would not be worth the extra time and cost involved. A good decision can be made without all the facts, but a manager must know what information is missing in order to evaluate the degree of risk involved in the decision.

There is rarely only one solution to a problem and much of a manager's skill will be exercised in framing, comparing and finally choosing between alternative solutions. Especially where creativity or innovation is required, it is advisable to generate as many options as possible. **Brainstorming** is a technique usually involving a group, where ideas are generated without immediate evaluation or comment so that creativity is not stifled.

An **action plan** to implement the chosen decision should be drawn up by the supervisor responsible in consultation with the subordinates who must put it into action. If a manager has to sell a decision to subordinates, it probably means that they have not been consulted properly in the evaluation of alternatives. We will discuss consensus decision making, and gaining acceptance of decisions later.

6.6 Leadership

FAST FORWARD

Leadership is the process of influencing others to work willingly towards the achievement of organisational goals. Theories of leadership have taken several different approaches.

Traits: common characteristics of leaders, which are innate.
Styles lying on one of several similar continua
Wholly **task centred** to wholly human centred
Functions, in the context of task, group and individual needs.

Leadership is fundamental to the effective working of a group and **skills of leadership can be learnt and improved**.

Leadership is the process of influencing others to work **willingly** towards a goal, and to the best of their capabilities. 'The essence of leadership is **followership**. In other words it is the willingness of people to follow that makes a person a leader' (*Koontz, O'Donnell, Weihrich*).

Leadership comes about in a number of different ways.

(a)   A manager is **appointed** to a position of authority within the organisation. Leadership of subordinates is a function of the position.

(b)   Some leaders are **elected**.

(c)   Other leaders **emerge** by popular choice or through their personal drive.

The personal, physical or expert power of leaders is more important than position power alone. Within teams and groups of equal colleagues leadership can and does change.

If a manager has indifferent or poor leadership qualities then the team would still do the job, but not efficiently. A good leader can ensure more than simply a compliance with orders. **Leadership and management are different but linked activities; two sides of the same coin. Managing** is concerned with logic, structure, analysis and control. If done well, it produces predictable results on time. **Leadership** requires a different mind set and the leader has different tasks.

- Creating a sense of direction
- Communicating the vision
- Energising, inspiring and motivating

All of these activities involve dealing with people rather than things. A manager needs leadership skills to be effective.

6.7 Leadership traits

Early writers believed that leadership was an **inherent characteristic**: you either had it, or you didn't: leaders were born, not made. Studies on leadership concentrated on the personal traits of existing and past leadership figures.

It is now felt that leadership appropriate to a given work situation can be **learned**.

Action Programme 6

Think about your own supervisor or manager. Would you consider him or her a leader? Are you a leader to your subordinates (if you are in an appropriate position)? Why, or why not?

Identify someone who you would consider a real leader. What qualities can you identify in that person that makes them a leader in your eyes? Could those qualities be taught somehow?

Does your organisation create or encourage leaders? What training courses offered by your employer are aimed at developing leadership qualities and skills?

6.8 Leadership styles

The terms **leadership style** and **management style** are almost interchangeable, but as the matters under discussion here concern the way managers deal with their subordinates, we will use leadership style.

Four different types or styles of leadership were identified by *Huneryager and Heckman*.

(a) **Dictatorial**. The manager **forces** subordinates to work by threatening punishment and penalties.

(b) **Autocratic**. Decision making is centralised in the hands of the leader, who does not encourage participation by subordinates; indeed, subordinates' ideas might be actively discouraged and obedience to orders would be expected from them.

(c) **Democratic**. Decision-making is decentralised, and shared by subordinates in **participative group action**. To be truly democratic, the subordinate must be willing to participate.

(d) **Laissez-faire**. Subordinates are given **little or no direction at all**, and are allowed to establish their own objectives and make all their own decisions.

These four divisions of management style are really a simplification of a continuum or range of styles, from the most dictatorial to the most laissez-faire.

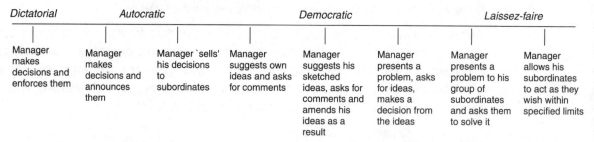

This **continuum of leadership styles** was first suggested by *Tannenbaum and Schmidt* in the *Harvard Business Review* in 1973.

A similar spectrum from autocratic to democratic, but without the extremes at either end, was suggested by the research unit at Ashridge Management College (**the Ashridge studies**).

(a) The **autocratic or *tells* style**. This is characterised by one-way communication between the manager and the subordinate, with the manager telling the subordinate what to do. The leader makes all the decisions and issues instructions, expecting them to be obeyed without question.

(b) The **persuasive or *sells* style**. Managers make all the decisions, but believe that subordinates need to be **motivated** to do what is required.

(c) The **consultative style**. This involves discussion between the manager and the subordinates involved in carrying out a decision, but the manager retains the right to make the decision.

(d) The **democratic or *joins* style**. The leader joins the group of subordinates to make a decision on the basis of consensus. It is the most democratic style of leadership. The joins style is most effective where all subordinates have equal knowledge and can therefore contribute in equal measure to decisions.

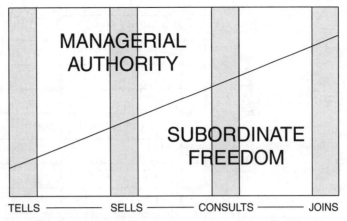

TELLS ———— SELLS ———— CONSULTS ———— JOINS

There are differing views as to which of these leadership styles is most effective. The probable truth is that the degree of effectiveness of a particular leadership style will depend on the work environment, and the character of the leader and subordinates.

The Ashridge studies made the following findings with regard to leadership style and employee motivation.

(a)   Subordinates preferred the **consults** style of leadership, but mainly thought their managers exercised the **tells** or **sells** style.

(b)   The attitude of subordinates towards their work was most favourable amongst those who thought that their boss exercised the 'consults' style.

(c)   The least favourable attitudes were found amongst subordinates who were unable to perceive a consistent style of leadership in their boss. In other words, subordinates are unsettled by a boss who chops and changes between autocracy, persuasion, consultation and democracy.

Action Programme 7

Take some time to consider these four styles and produce a list of the strengths and weaknesses of the following leadership styles.

Tells
Sells
Consults
Joins

6.9 Blake and Mouton

By emphasising style of leadership and the importance of human relations, it is all too easy to forget that a manager is **primarily responsible for ensuring that tasks are done** efficiently. *Blake and Mouton* tried to address the balance of management thinking, with their **management grid** based on two aspects of managerial behaviour.

- Concern for production, ie the **task**
- Concern for people and human relations

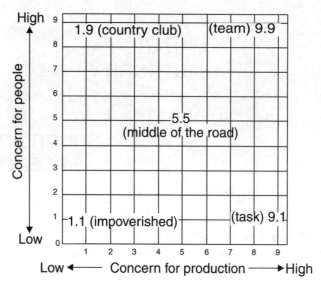

R Blake and J Mouton The Managerial Grid III, 1985

The extreme cases shown on the grid are:

(a) 1.1 **impoverished**: manager is lazy, showing little effort or concern for staff or work targets.

(b) 1.9 **country club**: manager is attentive to staff needs and has developed satisfying relationships. However, little attention is paid to achieving results.

(c) 9.1 **task management**: almost total concentration on achieving results. **People's needs are virtually ignored** and conditions of work are so arranged that people cannot interfere to any significant extent.

(d) 5.5 **middle of the road or the dampened pendulum**: adequate performance through balancing the necessity to get out work while maintaining morale of people at a satisfactory level.

(e) 9.9 **team**: high performance manager who achieves high work accomplishment through leading committed people who identify with the organisational aims.

 Action Programme 8

Think about yourself and other managers you know. Where would you place them on the grid?

6.10 McGregor Theory X and Theory Y

Key concept

> **Theory X and Theory Y**
>
> In *The Human Side of Enterprise, Douglas McGregor* discussed the way in which managers handle people according to the assumptions they have about them, and about what kind of management style will obtain their efforts. He identified two extreme sets of assumptions (Theory X and Theory Y) and explored how management style differs according to which set of assumptions is adopted.

Theory X is the theory that the average human being has an **inherent dislike of work** and will avoid it if possible. Human beings **prefer to be directed**, wishing to avoid responsibility. They have relatively little ambition and want security above all. They are self-centred, with little interest in the organisation's needs. They are **resistant to change**, gullible and easily led. They **must be coerced, controlled, directed, offered reward or threatened with punishment to get them to put forth adequate effort** towards the achievement of the organisation's objectives.

According to **Theory Y**, however, the expenditure of physical and mental effort in **work is as natural as play or rest**. The ordinary person does **not** inherently dislike work: according to the conditions it may be a source of satisfaction or punishment. Extensive control is not the only means of obtaining effort. **People exercise self-direction** and self-control in the service of **objectives to which they are committed**: they are not naturally passive, or resistant, to organisational objectives, **but have been made so by experience**.

The most significant reward that can be offered is the satisfaction of the individual's need for personal growth and development. The average human being can learn not only to accept but also to seek responsibility. Managements should create conditions and methods that will enable individuals to integrate their own and the organisation's goals, by personal development.

McGregor intentionally polarised his theories, and recognised that managers' assumptions may be somewhere along the line between the two extremes. He also recognised that the **assumptions were self-perpetuating**. If people are treated as though they are Theory X people, because of management assumptions, Theory X behaviour will in fact be induced – thus confirming management in its beliefs and practices.

Action Programme 9

What is the most common leadership style used in your office? What is it about the culture and work of the firm, or the personalities involved, that make this the most-used style?

What style would you like your boss to adopt? What drawbacks, if any, can you see in that style from the leader's point of view?

6.11 Example case study

Derek is a young retail manager who, after completing his Stage 2 examinations recently, was transferred to a small old-established company outlet.

At his first progress review with his superior, he was very confident and enthusiastic about numerous initiatives which he had already taken or was about to take. Derek expressed disappointment that his staff were so reactionary and unco-operative.

Enquiries by Derek's superior among the staff uncovered general dissatisfaction about Derek's leadership. The younger ones are frightened of him, and feel he has no interest in them. They say he is always in a hurry, and they have no idea of whether their work is up to his requirements or not.

The older ones, who have worked in the company for years, are very worried about his apparently arbitrary and risky decisions. Others are resentful and frustrated that Derek never bothers to listen to their ideas. Derek has been informed of these comments.

Recommend the behaviour which Derek should adopt to improve the situation.

Solution

Derek's problem is one of leadership style.

We are told that Derek is very confident and takes many initiatives, but does not understand why others resist his decisions. He appears to take decisions without consulting his subordinates and then tells them what his decision is. Having taken decisions, he appears to leave his staff to get on and shows no obvious interest in what they are doing. This is a self-contradictory combination of the **autocratic** and **laissez-faire** styles.

The problems with his leadership style are evident in the dissatisfaction of the subordinates.

(a)   The younger ones want to do their job well but get no personal interest or attention from Derek. They do not know whether they are doing well or badly nor by what standards they may be judged.

(b)   Some people are frustrated because they are not allowed to participate in the decision-making process. Their opinions are not asked for, and their ideas are ignored.

(c)   The older ones are upset by Derek's radical approach to the decisions he takes. Derek is failing to explain his reasons and persuade the older ones of the need for change.

Advice to Derek

The advice to Derek should be to urge him to **recognise his supervisory responsibilities**.

(a)   He seems unaware of the problems his leadership style is causing. His performance will be judged on the achievements of his store **as a whole**, not just on his own personal efforts. If his subordinates are performing badly, he will be held responsible.

(b)   His attitude to his staff should change. In general terms, a more participative style of leadership is needed.

(c)   Derek should give each of his staff individual attention, counselling and encouragement. He must find time to devote to this task, and he must not be too busy with other work to bother about his subordinates.

(d)   In addition to giving subordinates individual attention, he should also try to encourage a group identity and cohesiveness. Regular meetings in a group with his subordinates should be recommended to him.

Derek should tackle each of the specific worries of his staff.

The younger ones require **closer supervision**, and Derek should spend more time with them. He should set clear standards for their work and, at regular appraisal sessions, let them know whether they are meeting these standards.

In the case of those who are **resentful** that Derek never listens to their ideas, Derek should be much more prepared to **listen**. Their ideas might not always be good ones, but a task of supervision is to develop staff. This can be done by encouraging ideas and initiatives, discussing them, and then explaining why they might or might not be good ones. A more consultative or participative style of leadership will almost certainly reduce their frustrations, and also help to develop his own skills and experience.

The older staff have a lot of **experience** in the department and Derek should try to see the benefit of making use of that. Derek should explain his reasons for changes. Knowing why change is needed helps to **reduce resistance** to it. He should also explain how the staff will be affected personally by any changes, and how they can adapt to them. Their specific responsibilities and targets as a result of any change should be spelled out clearly, and Derek should try to convince them that they are capable of carrying out new tasks well. Their experience should be used constructively, whereas currently it is being expressed negatively in frustration and resistance to change.

It is not easy for a manager to change his leadership style overnight, and Derek should seek **advice** as to how to introduce the necessary changes. Regular staff meetings would be one suggestion.

Derek should be **counselled** regularly by his boss as he tries to change. A formal review of his success in changing his style, and the effects of his new approach on the branch's performance and attitudes, should be made after some months.

6.12 Leadership and employee development

An aspect of the leader's role is sometimes held to be that of developing employees, rather than simply managing or leading them. To help employees develop and grow in the role may require coaching skills, traditionally associated with training activities.

The advantages of coaching people into new roles in that it broadens the management skills base, and thereby makes succession easier to plan.

Marketing at Work

The most important thing for those at the top is to tap into the roots of our organisations and understand what makes people tick and what frustrates them. The late John Garnett of the then Industrial Society gave me the compelling image of the 'gardener boss'. This means giving people the support and headroom to develop their own style, not racing out in front of them shouting: 'I'm off to the wild blue yonder with a vision and I expect you to follow'. You're sunk if they don't – or perhaps you move into the more bullying mode known as 'robust management'. Fear can drive performance for a while, but sustained high performance and morale can be achieved only by nourishing the roots.

Sue Street, permanent secretary at the DCMS, *Management Today, 1 August 2004*

6.13 The manager as a team member

Besides taking the role as leader the manager may also be a team member. The marketing director may lead the marketing team, but be a member of the senior management team. Recognising which 'hat' you are wearing is important in these situations. There is only room for one leader at a time and it is important not to usurp the authority of the established leader. A team player should support by playing a full part, contributing to discussions but not overriding the leader's approach.

Chapter Roundup

- A group is 'any collection of people who perceive themselves to be a group'. An 'effective' group is one which achieves its allotted task and satisfies its members. Teams are becoming more important as a means of organising work.

- Groups function through interaction between individual members and the blend of their skills and abilities.

- *John Adair's* work on leadership identified three overlapping sets of **needs** which need to be satisfied when teams are managed, and the **roles the team leader needs to play** to satisfy these needs.

- A team differs from a simple group in that it has some kind of formal purpose and this in turn implies some degree of both organisation and management. The team members are likely to have to play a range of roles (as observed by Belbin) and the team is likely to pass through the four stages of development described by Tuckman. Handy's model of effectiveness describes the outcomes of the team's work as contingent on the nature of the given and intervening factors in its work setting.

- Groups prize loyalty, which usually expresses itself in conformity to **norms of behaviour** which bind the group together. Groups are capable of exerting considerable social pressure on individuals to conform.

- Teams do not always work as well as hoped. Motivation, communication and mutual support may not develop and the team may be hampered by conflict, alienation, groupthink and divisive management.

- Group decision-making can benefit from the range of inputs provided by the members and it can promote acceptance of decisions. However, it can blur responsibility, promote harmful agendas and waste time.

- There are two basic approaches to the organisation of cross-functional team working: **multi-disciplinary** teams and **multi-skilled** teams.

- It is no longer essential that teams have all their members in a single location, or even have a single formal leader. Virtual teams function via electronic links; self-managed teams collaborate to discharge most routine management functions themselves.

- Managers are responsible for **planning** and **controlling** the work of the teams they lead. This is often done using a **budget**, which can be used as a forecast, a yardstick, a target and a means of allocating resources.

- **Decision-making** may be approached in a rational manner, though it is possible to spend far too much time thinking about decisions.

- Once a decision has been made, an **action plan** to implement it may be needed.

- **Leadership** is the process of influencing others to work willingly towards the achievement of organisational goals. Theories of leadership have taken several different approaches.

    Traits: common characteristics of leaders, which are innate
    Styles lying on one of several similar continua
    Wholly **task centred** to wholly human centred
    Functions, in the context of task, group and individual needs.

- Leadership is fundamental to the effective working of a group and **skills of leadership can be learnt and improved**.

Quick Quiz

1 What attributes distinguish a group or team from a random collection of individuals?

2 What are the functions of groups from the point of view of the organisation?

3 What are the main issues to be taken into account when managing a group?

4 What stages does a team go through as it matures?

5 What happens during the norming stage?

6 What does Handy mean by the term 'outcomes' in his contingency approach?

7 List four of the characteristics you would expect in an ideally functioning group.

8 What is meant by the term *group think* and why is it a problem?

9 Give four different uses of a budget.

10 Are all managers leaders?

11 What were the four leadership styles identified by Huneryager and Heckman?

12 What leadership style, if any, do employees prefer?

13 What are the axes of the management grid?

14 What is Theory X?

Answers to Quick Quiz

1 Sense of identity, loyalty to the group, purpose and leadership

2 Using collective skills; testing and ratifying decisions made

3 Group maintenance needs, individual needs, task needs

4 Forming, storming, norming, performing

5 Group cohesion increases; norms and processes emerge; the group begins to function

6 Productivity and group satisfaction

7 Support and identification for individuals; sharing of skills, ideas and information; group input into problem solving and decisions; individual involvement and commitment; improved communication

8 Cohesiveness and consensus may effectively blind the group to changes in its environment

9 Forecast, yardstick, target and means of allocating resources

10 No

11 Dictatorial, autocratic, democratic, laissez-faire

12 The consults style

13 Concern for people and concern for production

14 A set of assumptions about human behaviour: the average person dislikes work and will avoid it if possible

Action Programme Review

3

Effective teams	Ineffective teams
Quantifiable factors	
Low rate of labour turnover	High rate of labour turnover
Low absenteeism	High absenteeism
High output and productivity	Low output and productivity
Good quality of output	Poor quality of output
There are few stoppages and interruptions to work	Much time is wasted owing to disruption of work flow
Qualitative factors	
There is a high commitment to the achievement of targets and organisational goals	There is a low commitment to targets
There is a clear understanding of the group's work	There is no understanding of organisational goals or the role of the group (or there are no clear organisational goals)
There is a clear understanding of the role of each person within the group	There is confusion about the role of each person and uncertainty
There is free and open communication between members of the group and trust between members	There is mistrust between group members and suspicion of group's leader
There is idea sharing	There is little idea sharing
The group is good at generating new ideas	The group does not generate any good new ideas
Group members try to help each other out	Group members make negative and hostile criticisms about each other's work
There is group problem solving which gets to the root causes of the work problem	Work problems are dealt with superficially, with attention paid to the symptoms but not the cause.
Group members seek a united consensus of opinion	Group members hold strongly opposed views
The group is sufficiently motivated to be able to carry on working in the absence of its leader	The group needs its leader there to get work done

7

Style	Characteristics	Strengths	Weaknesses
Tells (autocratic)	The manager makes all the decisions, and issues instructions which must be obeyed without question	1 Quick decisions can be made when speed is required 2 It is the most efficient type of leadership for highly-programmed routine work	1 It does not encourage the subordinates to give their opinions when these might be useful 2 Communications between the manager and subordinate will be one-way and the manager will not know until afterwards whether the orders have been properly understood

Style	Characteristics	Strengths		Weaknesses	
				3	It does not encourage initiative and commitment from subordinates
Sells (persuasive)	The manager still makes all the decisions, but believes that subordinates have to be motivated to accept them in order to carry them out properly	1	Employees are made aware of the reasons for decisions	1	Communications are still largely one-way. Subordinates might not accept the decisions
		2	Selling decisions to staff might make them more committed	2	It does not encourage initiative and commitment from subordinates
		3	Staff will have a better idea of what to do when unforeseen events arise in their work because the manager will have explained his intentions		
Consults	The manager confers with subordinates and takes their views into account, but has the final say	1	Employees are involved in decisions before they are made. This encourages motivation through greater interest and involvement	1	It might take much longer to reach decisions
		2	An agreed consensus of opinion can be reached and for some decisions consensus can be an advantage rather than a weak compromise	2	Subordinates might be too inexperienced to formulate mature opinions and give practical advice
		3	Employees can contribute their knowledge and experience to help in solving more complex problems	3	Consultation can too easily turn into a façade concerning, basically, a sells style
Joins (democratic)	Leader and followers make the decision on the basis of consensus	1	It can provide high motivation and commitment from employees	1	The authority of the manager might be undermined
		2	It shares the other advantages of the consultative style (especially where subordinates have expert power)	2	Decision-making might become a very long process, and clear decisions might be difficult to reach
				3	Subordinates might lack enough experience

Now try Question 1 at the end of the Study Text

Improving team performance

2

Syllabus content

- Managing the work of teams and individuals to achieve objectives and create effective working relationships within the team and with other teams
- Evaluating the productivity, satisfaction and effectiveness of teams against their objectives using appropriate techniques
- Analysing and improving team performance, including plans to improve motivation, commitment and loyalty

Introduction

It is very easy to fall into simplistic, common sense attitudes of the Theory X/Y variety when wondering how to get employees to work well. The motivation theories described in this chapter will help you avoid falling into this trap.

In Section 1 we discuss **different approaches to motivation** and what factors encourage people to work hard and well, and how the manager can understand and use these factors: do people have needs which managers can satisfy? Do people weigh up the options?

In Section 2, we go on from identifying the needs which people have to how they can be satisfied, using pay, the job itself, participation and empowerment to enhance motivation. **People are often motivated by things other than money**, and in times when funds are scarce, attention to the non-financial aspects can help motivate a team.

Motivation has to be translated into performance: a person can be well motivated but incompetent. Consequently we have to review the **performance of the individual or team**, the subject of Section 3. The purpose of **appraisal** is to develop a review of a person's performance, with a view to improving it. Sometimes this might be achieved by training, which we discuss in Section 4.

On occasions, performance may be such that people require **counselling or advice** outside of the normal appraisal system. In extreme cases, **disciplinary action** might be necessary. We discuss these aspects in Sections 5 and 6. You must appreciate the differences between appraisals, counselling and disciplinary interviews.

Information technology and the new flexible job market can affect the management of the team, so in Section 7 we highlight some of the issues relating to people who work from home and/or who are not part of the organisation's full-time, permanent workforce.

1 Motivational theory and its value to the manager

FAST FORWARD

Motivation is an essential ingredient in ensuring that the individual and the team perform efficiently and effectively.

Management writers have devoted considerable time to understanding motivation because it is believed improvements here can generate competitive advantage.

Key concept

Motivation is simply reasons for behaviour. People at work display varying degrees of motivation to achieve the goals set by management. It is an important task of managers at all levels to enhance the individual's motivation to work effectively.

Managers can provide the team with the opportunity and resources to work, but without motivation, little effective work will result. Motivation is the magic ingredient or catalyst which the manager has to add to the work situation to generate results.

Earlier we considered the role and responsibilities of the leader. Responsibility for motivation is an integral part of that job. You must be aware of the theory and importance of motivation and be able to suggest solutions to motivational problems for the examiner.

Marketers may have a head start in this area of management, as they have studied motivation frequently in the context of understanding customer behaviour.

1.1 Why is motivation important?

You may be wondering why motivation is important. It could be argued that a person is employed to do a job, and so will do that job and no question of motivation arises. A person who does not want to do the work can resign. The point at issue, however, is the **efficiency** with which the job is done. It is suggested that if individuals can be motivated, by one means or another, they will produce a **better quality of work**.

1.2 Motivators and motivation

In the most basic terms, an individual has **needs** which he or she wishes to satisfy. The means of satisfying the needs are **wants**. For example, an individual might feel the need for power, and to fulfil this need, might want money and a position of authority. Depending on the strength of these needs and wants, he or she may take action to achieve them. Success will bring satisfaction. This can be shown in a simple diagram.

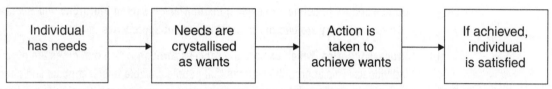

Motivators can be established to act as the wants of the individual. For example, the position of sales director might serve as a want to satisfy an individual's need for power, or access to the senior executive's dining room might serve as a want to satisfy a need for status. Motivators may exist that are **not directly controllable** by management; for example, an individual might want to be accepted by work mates, to satisfy a need for friendship and affiliation with others, and might therefore choose to conform to the norms and adopt the attitudes of the work group, which are not necessarily shared by the organisation as a whole.

Management has the problem of creating or manipulating motivators which will actually motivate employees to perform in a desired way.

Action Programme 1

Before you start reading about motivation theories, answer the following questions. What factors in yourself or in your organisation motivate you:

- To turn up at work at all?
- To do an average day's work?
- To work particularly hard?

Talk to friends and colleagues – find out what makes them tick.

1.3 Motivation theories

FAST FORWARD

There are basically two types of motivational theory.

- **Content theories**: motivation is driven by needs. Maslow's hierarchy of needs is the basic form of this approach.

- **Process theories**: motivation is a process of making choices about how best to satisfy needs.

What we believe motivation is and what can be done with it will influence all our attitudes to individuals in organisations and to our management style.

(a)   Some suggest that a **satisfied** worker will work harder, although there is little evidence to support the assumption. Satisfaction may reduce labour turnover and absenteeism, but will not necessarily increase individual productivity. Some hold that people work best within a compatible work group, or under a well-liked leader.

(b)   There is a common assumption that individuals will work harder in order to obtain a desired reward. **Incentives** can work if certain conditions are satisfied.

- The individual perceives the increased reward to be worth the extra effort
- The performance can be measured and clearly attributed to that individual
- The individual wants that particular kind of reward
- The increased performance will not become the new minimum standard

One way of grouping the major theories of motivation is by making the following distinction.

(a)   **Content theories**, which assume that human beings have a package of needs that they pursue and try to define and explain them. *Maslow's* **need hierarchy** and *Herzberg's* **two-factor theory** are two of the most important approaches of this type.

(b)   **Process theories**, which explore the process through which outcomes are pursued by individuals. This approach assumes that people are able to select goals and choose the paths towards them, by a conscious or unconscious process of calculation. *Vroom's* **expectancy theory** and *Handy's* **motivation calculus** are theories of this type.

Exam tip

> You are unlikely to be asked detailed questions on the theories of motivation in this examination but you will be required to understand the alternative approaches to motivation. It will be useful to have a feel for the ideas of the leading writers on motivation that you can call upon to illustrate your work.

1.4 Content theories

FAST FORWARD

> Maslow described a **hierarchy of needs** of relative strength. Herzberg's work was important because it encourages managers to recognise the **hygiene** factors, which can cause dissatisfaction if they are absent, but are unlikely to generate positive motivation.
>
> Herzberg also highlighted the motivational opportunities from job enlargement, enrichment and rotation, all of which are quite commonly used for both motivation and for training and development.

1.4.1 Maslow's hierarchy of needs

In his motivation theory, *Maslow* put forward certain propositions about the motivating power of people's **needs**.

(a)   Every person's needs can be arranged in a **hierarchy of relative strength**.

(b)   Each **level of need is dominant until satisfied**; only then does the next higher level of need become a motivating factor.

(c)   A **need which has been satisfied no longer motivates** an individual's behaviour. The need for self-actualisation can never be satisfied.

A Maslow, A Theory of Human Motivation, *Psychological Review*, July 1943

There is a certain intuitive appeal to Maslow's theory. After all, you are unlikely to be concerned with status or recognition while you are hungry or thirsty: primary survival needs will take precedence. Likewise, once your hunger is assuaged, the need for food is unlikely to be a motivating factor.

Maslow's theories may be of general interest, but they have no clear practical application.

(a) The same need may cause different behaviour in different individuals. One person might seek to satisfy his need for esteem by winning promotion whereas another individual might seek esteem by leading a challenge against authority.

(b) It is occasionally difficult to reconcile the willingness of individuals to forgo the immediate satisfaction of needs and to accept current suffering to fulfil a long-term goal (eg the long studentship of the medical or accounting professions), in terms of Maslow's hierarchy.

1.4.2 Herzberg's two-factor theory of job satisfaction

Herzberg contrasted the factors which cause job **dissatisfaction** and those which can cause job **satisfaction**. He called the former **hygiene** or **maintenance** factors, because they are essentially preventative. They prevent or minimise dissatisfaction **but do not give satisfaction**, in the same way that sanitation minimises some threats to health, but does not ensure good health.

Action Programme 2

What factors can you identify that cause dissatisfaction at work?

The important point is that **motivation** cannot be achieved by addressing the above-mentioned factors. All that will be attained is a neutral state in which there is neither motivation or dissatisfaction.

Motivator factors actively **create job satisfaction** and *are* effective in motivating an individual to superior performance and effort.

- Status (although this may be a hygiene factor as well as a motivator factor)
- Advancement
- Recognition
- Responsibility
- Challenging work
- Achievement
- Growth in the job

Herzberg saw two separate need systems in individuals.

(a) **A need to avoid unpleasantness**. This need is satisfied at work by **hygiene factors**. **Hygiene satisfactions** are short-lived; individuals come back for more as their expectations rise.

(b) **A need for personal growth**. This is satisfied by **motivator factors**.

Some individuals are not **mature** enough to want personal growth; they are **'hygiene seekers'** because they are only bothered about hygiene factors. A lack of motivators at work will encourage employees to concentrate on shortcomings in hygiene factors. These may be real or imagined. The result will be an endless series of demands relating to pay and conditions of work.

Herzberg suggested means by which motivator satisfactions could be supplied. Stemming from his fundamental division of motivator and hygiene factors, he encouraged managers to **study the job itself** (the type of work done, the nature of tasks, levels of responsibility) rather than **conditions of work**. Only this way will motivation improve. (Concentrating on hygiene factors will merely stave off job dissatisfaction.)

If there is sufficient challenge, scope and interest in the job, there will be a lasting increase in satisfaction and the employee will work well; productivity will be above 'normal' levels. The extent to which a job must be challenging or creative to a motivator seeker will, in relation to each individual, depend on his ability and his tolerance for delayed success.

Herzberg specified three typical means whereby work can be revised to improve motivation.

(a) **Job enrichment**: this is the main method of improving job satisfaction and can be defined as 'the planned process of up-grading the responsibility, challenge and content of the work'. Typically, this would involve increasing **delegation** to provide more interesting work and problem solving at lower levels within an organisation.

(b) **Job enlargement**: although often linked with job enrichment, it is a separate technique and is **rather limited** in its ability to improve staff motivation. Job enlargement is the process of increasing the number of operations in which a worker is engaged This is more limited in value, since a person who is required to complete several tedious tasks is unlikely to be much more highly motivated than a man performing one continuous tedious task.

(c) **Job rotation**: this is the planned operation of a system whereby staff members exchange positions with the intention of breaking monotony in the work and providing fresh job challenge.

1.5 Process theories

1.5.1 Vroom's expectancy theory

FAST FORWARD

Victor Vroom suggested that the strength of an individual's motivation to do something will depend on the extent to which he **expects** the results of his efforts to contribute towards his personal needs or goals, to reward him or to punish him.

Expectancy theory states that people will effectively decide how much they are going to put into their work as a result of two considerations.

(a) The **value** that they place on the expected outcome, whether the positive value of a reward, or the negative value of a punishment. *Vroom* called this **'valence'**.

(b)   The strength of their **expectation** that behaving in a certain way will in fact bring out the desired outcome. Vroom called this **expectancy**.

Expectancy x Valence = Force of motivation

1.6 Models of man

Schein summarises the historical development of thinking about motivation by describing **three sets of assumptions about people**. These correspond to the scientific management, human relations and Maslow/Herzberg schools of thought. Schein then describes his own model, which may be thought of as a **contingency approach**.

Schein suggested that none of the models proposed in the first half of the twentieth century was adequate to describe the behaviour of people at work. He suggested that people's motivations and concerns were **highly complex** and that many influences had a part to play in determining motivation. He described three models to summarise earlier models and then his own model of **complex man**.

Rational-economic man is primarily motivated by economic incentives. He is mainly passive and can (and must) be manipulated by the organisation into doing what it wants. In the context of an employing organisation, such a person would be influenced mainly by salary and fringe benefits. Fortunately, not all people are like this, and the self-motivated, self-controlling individuals must assume responsibility for those that are.

Social man looks for self-fulfilment in social relationships. In the context of an employing organisation, this would imply that an individual's major motivation would be not so much the job itself as the opportunity to mix with other people. Considerable implications exist here for the development of home working.

Self-actualising man is influenced by a wider range of motivations. Ultimately, the self-actualising man wishes to realise his own full personal potential. He is capable of maturity and autonomy and will (given the chance) voluntarily integrate his goals with the organisation.

Complex man represents Schein's own view of people. According to his model, individuals are variable and driven by many different motives. The motives influencing a particular individual may change from time to time, and their relative importance may also vary, depending on the situation. The complex man will respond to no single managerial strategy, but will consider its appropriateness to circumstances and his own needs.

1.6.1 Psychological contracts

According to Schein a **psychological contract** exists between individuals in an organisation and the organisation itself. An individual belongs to many organisations, and he or she has a different psychological contract with each. A psychological contract might be thought of as a **set of expectations**.

(a)   The individual expects to derive certain benefits from membership of the organisation and is prepared to expend a certain amount of effort in return.

(b)   The organisation expects the individual to fulfil certain requirements and is prepared to offer certain rewards in return.

Three types of psychological contract can be identified.

(a)   **Coercive contract**. The individual **feels** that he is being forced to contribute his efforts and energies involuntarily, and that the rewards he receives in return are inadequate compensation. For example, if an individual believes that he does not receive enough pay for the work he does, or if he is forcibly transferred to another job he does not like, there would be a coercive psychological contract between the individual and the organisation.

(b)   **Calculative contract**. This is a contract, **accepted voluntarily by the individual**, in which he expects to do his job in exchange for a readily identifiable set of rewards (for example pay, promotion, job content, status, or simply having a job of work to keep him occupied). This form of contract is the most frequent in industrial and commercial organisations. With such psychological contracts, motivation can only be increased if the rewards to the individual are improved. If the organisation demands greater efforts without increasing the rewards, the psychological contract will revert to a coercive one, and **motivation may become negative**.

(c)   **Co-operative contract**. This is a contract in which the individual **identifies himself with the organisation and its goals**, so that he actively seeks to contribute further to the achievement of those goals. **Motivation comes out of success at work, a sense of achievement, and self-fulfilment**. The individual will probably want to share in the planning and control decisions which affect his work, and co-operative contracts are therefore likely to occur where employees **participate in decision making**. Since these contracts are likely to result in high motivation and high achievement, the lesson for management would be that employee participation in decision making is the most desirable way to structure manager-subordinate relations at work, but **only if subordinates want participation**.

Motivation happens when the psychological contract, within which the individual's motivation calculus operates for new decisions, is viewed in the same way by the organisation and by the individual.

Action Programme 3

In *Brits at Work*, John Mole (a former manager) describes various work environments which he explored in order to gain a worm's eye view of life in British companies. In this quotation he is talking to a manager about scientists and researchers.

'"...but once you've provided them with the money (ie resources to finish research projects) and support (laboratory assistants), what motivates them?" "They motivate themselves, don't they?" There were certainly no material incentives for working in medical research. After a degree and a doctorate...you might be taken on at the salary I used to pay my secretary!'

Why is the narrator slightly confused?

2 Motivating teams and individuals

FAST FORWARD   Drucker suggested that job satisfaction comes from acceptance of responsibility.

We have already talked about job satisfaction in connection with the work of Herzberg. He conducted a survey of employees in Pittsburgh and analysed their accounts of times when they 'felt good' about their jobs; this was taken to be a sign of **job satisfaction** (as opposed to **job dissatisfaction**, arising from events which made them 'feel bad' about their jobs).

Drucker suggested that motivation through employee satisfaction or morale is not a useful concept because it is such a wishy-washy idea. It has no particular meaning, and if it is to have meaning, it must be defined more constructively. His suggestion was that employee satisfaction comes about through encouraging employees to accept **responsibility**. There are four ingredients to this.

(a) **Careful placement of people in jobs**. The person selected should see the job as one which provides a challenge to their abilities. There will be no motivation for a university graduate in the job of shop assistant, whereas the same job can provide a worthwhile challenge to someone of lesser academic training and intelligence.

(b) **High standards of performance in the job**. Targets for achievement should be challenging. However, they should not be imposed in an authoritarian way by the employee's bosses. The employee should be encouraged to set high standards of performance.

(c) **Providing the worker with the information needed to control personal performance**. The employee should receive routine information about how well or badly they are doing without having to be told by the boss. Being told by a boss comes as a praise or reprimand, and the fear of reprimand will inhibit performance. Access to information as a routine matter overcomes this problem of inhibition.

(d) **Opportunities for participation in decisions that will give the employee managerial vision**. Participation means having some say and influence in the way the employee's work is organised and the targets for work are set.

2.1 Methods of improving motivation and job satisfaction

FAST FORWARD

A wide variety of options are available to motivate the individual and the team. The important thing is to develop motivational strategies which suit both the situation and the individual. Schemes should be simple to administer, easy to understand and perceived to be fair, and any incentives should be clear.

There are various ways in which managers can attempt to increase the motivation of their subordinates.

(a) Herzberg and others recommended better **job design**.

(b) Various writers have suggested that subordinates' **participation in decision making** will improve motivation through self-realisation and **empowerment**.

(c) **Pay and incentive schemes** are frequently regarded as powerful motivators.

We shall discuss each of these ways in turn.

2.1.1 Job design

Job design is the process of deciding three issues.

- The **content** of a job in terms of its duties and responsibilities

- The **methods** to be used in carrying out the job, in terms of techniques, system and procedures

- The **relationship** that should exist between the job holder and his/her superiors, colleagues and subordinates

Action Programme 4

Write out a job design for the work you do. Assess the design in terms of motivation.

The objectives of the job design process are to improve productivity, efficiency and quality and to satisfy the individual's needs for interest, challenge and accomplishment.

2.1.2 Job enrichment

Job enrichment is planned, deliberate action to build greater responsibility, breadth and challenge of work into a job. A job may be enriched in a variety of ways, such as allowing the employee in the job greater freedom to decide how the job should be done.

Job enrichment attempts to add further responsibilities to a job by giving the job holder decision-making opportunities of a higher order.

Marketing at Work

At first, a **market researcher's** responsibilities for producing quarterly management reports ended at the stage of producing the figures. These duties were then extended so that she prepared the actual reports and submitted them, under her own name, to the senior management. This alteration in responsibilities not only enriched the job but also increased the work-load. This in turn led to delegation of certain responsibilities to clerks within the department. These duties were in themselves job enrichment to the clerks and so a cascading effect was obtained. This highlights one of the basic elements of job enrichment – that what is tedious, mundane detail at a high level can represent significant job interest and challenge at a lower level in the organisation where a person's experience and scope is much less.

Some experiments have been made whereby **work groups** were given collective job enrichment. *Child* gives the example in the UK of the Dutch company, *Phillips*. A work group responsible for manufacturing television sets carried out the entire assembly operation and also had authority to deal directly with purchasing, stores and quality control, without a supervisor acting as intermediary. The change in work organisation meant, however, that the **company had to incur additional costs in re-equipment and training**.

The opportunity for job enrichment may be constrained.

- Technology and working conditions may dictate how work must be done.
- Jobs utilising a low level of skill may be difficult to enrich.
- Job enrichment should be wanted by subordinates.

Job enrichment alone will not automatically make employees more productive. If jobs are enriched, employees will expect to be paid fairly for what they are doing. It might be more correct therefore to say that **job enrichment might improve productivity through greater motivation, but only if it is rewarded fairly**.

Action Programme 5

In what ways could your work or the work of your team be enriched?

2.1.3 Job enlargement

Job enlargement is frequently confused with job enrichment. Job enlargement is the attempt to widen jobs by increasing the number of operations in which a job holder is involved.

This has the effect of lengthening the cycle time of repeated operations; by reducing the number of repetitions of the same work, the dullness of the job should also be reduced. Job enlargement is therefore a horizontal extension of an individual's work, whereas job enrichment is a vertical extension. For most **knowledge workers**, like marketing staff, this may be less useful than job enrichment.

Job enlargement is the opposite of the **micro-division of labour** approach to the organisation of work, in which a job is divided up into the smallest number of sequential tasks possible. Each task is so simple and straightforward that it can be learned with very little training.

There are several arguments against the micro-division of labour:

(a) The work is monotonous and makes employees bored and dissatisfied. The consequences will be high labour turnover, absenteeism and spoilage.

(b) People, unlike machines, work more efficiently when their work is varied.

(c) Excessive specialisation isolates the individual in his work and inhibits social contacts with work-mates.

Aspects of well-designed jobs

- Scope for the individual to set work standards and targets
- Individual control over the pace and methods of working
- Provision of variety by allowing for inter-locking tasks to be done by the same person
- Opportunity to comment about the design of the product, or job
- Feedback to the individual about performance

Arguably, **job enlargement is limited in its ability to improve motivation** since, as Herzberg points out, to ask a worker to complete three separate tedious, unchallenging tasks is unlikely to motivate him more than asking him to fulfil one single tedious, unchallenging task.

2.1.4 Job enrichment and job enlargement combined

Nevertheless, job enlargement might succeed in providing job enrichment as well, provided that the nature of the extra tasks to be done in the bigger job are possible and give the employee a greater challenge and incentive.

Enlarged jobs might also be regarded as high status jobs within the department, and as stepping stones towards promotion.

2.1.5 Job rotation

Job rotation may take two forms.

(a) An employee might be transferred to another job in order to give him or her a new **interest** and **challenge**, and to bring a fresh person to the job being vacated.

(b) Job rotation might be regarded as a form of training. Trainees might be expected to learn a bit about a number of different jobs, by spending six months or one year in each job before being moved on.

Job rotation is often practised unofficially among the members of small work groups.

No doubt you will have your own views about the value of job rotation as a method of training or career development. It is interesting to note *Drucker's* view: 'The whole idea of training jobs is contrary to all rules and experience. A person should never be given a job that is not a real job, that does not require performance from him'.

2.2 Participation in decision making and empowerment

FAST FORWARD

Participation in the decision-making process can be a powerful source of motivation and improved decisions. However, it must be genuine or it may be negative in its effects. Empowerment can improve efficiency and motivation and reduce management costs.

2.2.1 Participation

Much research suggests that if a superior invites subordinates to participate in planning decisions which affect their work, if the subordinates voluntarily accept the invitation, and if results about actual performance are fed back regularly so that they can make their own control decisions, then the subordinates' motivation will rise.

- **Efficiency** may rise
- They may become more conscious of the organisation's **goals**
- It may be possible to **raise planning targets** to reasonably challenging levels
- They may be ready to take appropriate **control actions** when necessary

It is obvious that participation will only be feasible if the superior is willing to apply it, and if it is acceptable within the culture of the organisation.

2.2.2 What does participation mean and why is it desirable?

Handy commented that: 'Participation is sometimes regarded as a form of job enlargement. At other times it is a way of gaining commitment by workers to some proposal on the grounds that if you have been involved in discussing it, you will be more interested in its success.

2.2.3 Merits of participation schemes

(a) **They bring into play the employees' own experiences to decide the best methods**. Someone who is actually doing the job may be able to see where improvements can be made, and where the impact of decisions will be.

(b) **Employees may actually set targets higher than managers expect**. In the Hawthorne experiment, a group who participated in decisions affecting them became much more productive.

(c) **If employees can control their performance, many supervisory jobs will be removed** making supervision more effective and helping in the **delayering of organisations**.

(d) **Improved quality of work may result where employees are interested**. A group that feels involved will perform better.

(e) **Unexpected events will not be so traumatic**. Employees will have learned to think for themselves and will be willing to take decisions. This may have the additional effect of greater job satisfaction and reduced labour turnover and absenteeism.

The advantages of participation should also be considered from the opposite end: what would be the disadvantages of not having participation? The answer to this is that employees would be told what to do, and would presumably comply with orders. However, their compliance would not be enthusiastic, and they would not be psychologically committed to their work.

Participation can involve employees and make them committed to their task, if the following conditions are met.

(a) Participation should be **genuine**. It is very easy for a manager to invite participation from his subordinates and then ignore their views. A **culture change** may be needed within management.

(b) The efforts to establish participation by employees should be pushed over a **long period of time** and with a lot of energy. However, 'if the issue or the task is trivial...and everyone realises it, participative methods will boomerang. Issues that do not affect the individuals concerned will not, on the whole, engage their interest'. (Handy).

(c)   The **purpose** of the participation of employees in a decision is made quite clear from the outset. 'If employees are consulted to make a **decision**, their views should carry the decision. If, however, they are consulted for **advice**, their views need not necessarily be accepted.'

(d)   The individuals must have the **abilities** and the **information** to join in decision making effectively.

(e)   The supervisor or manager **wishes** for participation from the subordinates, and does not suggest it merely because he/she thinks it is the done thing.

Worldwide social and educational trends show that **people's expectations** have risen above the basic requirement for money. The current demand is for more interesting work and for a say in decision making. These expectations are a basic part of the movement towards greater participation at work.

2.2.4 Empowerment

Improvements in ICT have made obsolete many management functions relating to reporting and communicating. At the same time, competitive pressures to cut costs have encouraged processes such as **delayering** (cutting out levels of (mainly middle) management) and **downsizing**, leading to **flatter hierarchies**, with more delegation and more decentralisation of authority. All this involves **shifting responsibility** to employees further down the management hierarchy, a process recently given the broad name of **empowerment**.

The argument is that by empowering workers the job will be done more effectively.

This thinking is very much in line with that of the neo-human relations theorists such as Maslow, Herzberg and McGregor, who believed that organisational effectiveness is determined by the extent to which people's higher psychological needs for growth, challenge, responsibility and self-fulfilment are met by the work that they do.

 Marketing at Work

The validity of this view and its relevance to modern trends appears to be borne out by the approach to empowerment adopted by *Harvester Restaurants*, as described in *Personnel Management*. The management structure comprises a branch manager and a 'coach', while everyone else is a team member. Everyone within a team has one or more 'accountabilities' (these include recruitment, drawing up rotas, keeping track of sales targets and so on) which are shared out by the team members at their weekly team meetings. All the team members at different times act as 'co-ordinator' – the person responsible for taking the snap decisions that are frequently necessary in a busy restaurant. Apparently all of the staff involved agree that empowerment has made their jobs more interesting and has hugely increased their motivation and sense of involvement.

2.2.5 Problems with participation schemes

It must be remembered that participation and other schemes that enhance job satisfaction **do not necessarily lead to improvements in output and efficiency**. This has been shown empirically. Also, in the particular case of empowerment, a common reaction among people who are offered greater responsibility is that they should be paid more for accepting it.

2.3 Pay and incentive schemes

Incentive schemes are an attempt to use pay as a motivator. This is very difficult to do, since pay is widely seen as a hygiene factor rather than a motivator.

2.3.1 Pay as a motivator

Employees need income to live. The size of that income will affect the standard of living, and although they would obviously like to earn more, they are probably more concerned about two other aspects of pay.

- That they should earn **enough**
- That pay should be **fair in comparison** with the pay of others

There is no doubt that pay does have some motivating effect, but it is fundamentally a **hygiene** factor.

2.4 Incentive schemes

Pay as a motivator is commonly associated with payment by results or incentive schemes, where a worker's pay is dependent upon output. These are common in production settings but less appropriate for knowledge workers.

All such incentive schemes are based on the principle that people are willing to work harder to obtain more money. However, the work of *Mayo* has shown that there are several constraints that can nullify this basic principle.

(a)   The average employee is not generally capable of influencing the timings and control systems used by management.

(b)   Employees remain suspicious that if they achieved high levels of output and earnings then management would **alter the basis of the incentive rates** to reduce future earnings. As a result they **conform to a group output norm**. The need to have the approval of their fellow workers by conforming is more important than the money urge.

(c)   High taxation rates would mean that workers do not believe that extra effort produces an adequate increase in pay.

A short-term incentive scheme involves a direct observable link between personal or team efforts and the reward gained. However a long-term scheme such as a profit sharing scheme, has a less personal relevance and a slower pay-back.

2.4.1 Common types of short-term incentive schemes

Individual payment by results, such as a sales bonus over and above a basic wage for achieving set standards of sales over a prescribed period. There is thus a direct link between performance and earnings for each individual so the motivating effect is strong. However, it has its disadvantages.

(a)   The system is complex and expensive to administer.

(b)   If **quantity** of sales is the relevant index, margins may suffer as sales staff negotiate lower prices to make sales.

(c)   Employees may **manipulate** sales, because of fears that high sales will become a new norm, with a reduction in the pay incentive.

(d)   **Employees outside the scheme may resent the wages levels of those inside**: pay differentials may be eroded. It has been known for top sales people to earn more than the Managing Director.

Group payment by results such as team bonus schemes mean that bonus pay for group performance is distributed equally among members. The cohesion of the team may then be built up in an effort to improve collective performance. This type of scheme works well where individual contributions are hard to isolate: the calculation is fairer. However, there are still disadvantages to schemes of this type.

(a) In addition to the disadvantages of the individual system, the **larger the group, the less direct the link** between individual effort and reward – so the motivating effect may be reduced.

(b) The system may be **unfair to harder-working individuals** within the group.

(c) Political conflicts and rivalries **between groups** may work to the detriment of the organisation as a whole.

It has become clear from the experiences of many companies that profit sharing schemes, incentive schemes (productivity bonuses) and joint consultation machinery do not in themselves improve productivity or ease the way for work to get done. Company-wide profit sharing schemes cannot be related directly to extra effort by individuals and are probably a hygiene factor rather than a motivator.

2.5 Non-financial incentives

Marketing managers may already have considerable experience at developing non financial incentives to influence sales teams and the purchase behaviour of customers. Competitions, gifts and prizes can all be utilised as the basis of specific motivation schemes. They create interest, add status for the winner and often have a higher **perceived value** than financial incentives do. Non financial incentives can be cheaper than their cash equivalent; for example, retail vouchers can be purchased at a discount on face value.

Such incentives must satisfy two conditions.

- They must give recipients a choice.
- They must be valued by recipients.

Offering extra time off or holiday are typically very acceptable and an early finish on a Friday is the sort of incentive which can often be organised fairly informally at team level.

 Marketing at Work

Motivation

UK organisations spent more than £900 million last year on non-cash incentives. At least a quarter of that sum was spent on trying to improve people's performance at work.

Understandably, it is the more off-the-wall ideas that attract attention. A computer company in Oxfordshire, for example, appointed an 'apology man', who was employed to say sorry to individuals on behalf of others for day-to-day misunderstandings. The directors claim this saves a lot of management time and makes for a happier and more productive workforce.

Business systems specialist SAS also achieved some notoriety recently when it gave up providing free jelly beans to all employees and switched to providing share options instead. Such examples can cause people to take employee incentives less seriously, but millions of pounds of investment cannot be wrong. There are sound principles behind the work of Freud and Jung, and the idea that most people's actions are driven by the pursuit of pleasure and the fear of pain.

Clark Hull was the first academic to establish that behaviour is rooted in the individual's inner drive, habits and the incentive to change. Within a business context, we all recognise that some people appear well motivated all the time, while others need to establish a behaviour pattern or habit before they begin to perform well. A third group of people perform at their best only when there is something in it for them.

But all individuals make choices based on maximising personal pleasure. We see this when organisations set incentive or behaviour targets. Employees are usually very canny at working out whether the effort to change is worth the reward. Several studies have shown that few individuals will change their behaviour for less than 10 per cent of their take-home benefits. I'm afraid that the idea of jelly beans all round simply doesn't cut it.

In 1938 personality theorist Henry Murray established 20 basic human needs that could be exploited in order to improve people's performance. They included the need to accomplish something difficult; to master, manipulate or organise objects, human beings or ideas; and to rival and surpass other people.

All of these needs feed straight into recognition systems and methods of devising challenging work that have their origins in the studies of Maslow, Herzberg and other job enrichment specialists.

Incentive strategy

To devise effective incentive programmes, employers need to:

- take account of the corporate environment and trading background of the organisation
- combine goals with emotions
- keep organisational goals congruent with each other
- use success stories to spur people on
- provide adequate skills training
- establish a gradual change process, rather than a sudden switch
- respond to feedback from employees quickly and directly

John Fisher, *People Management*, 11 January 2001

3 The role of appraisal

FAST FORWARD

Appraisal can improve performance by providing a formal system of feedback which is also a useful benchmark for monitoring performance changes. Most appraisal systems require a manager to appraise a subordinate, but alternatives can be suggested.

Motivation is concerned with attempts to improve the performance of groups and individuals. We saw in the last section how important regular **feedback** was to the basic concepts of motivation. Appraisal is a systematic approach to providing that feedback and for putting praise and criticism in context. It also provides an assessment of current performance against which future improvements can be measured and **training needs** established.

The general purpose of any staff assessment system is to improve the efficiency of the organisation by ensuring that the individuals within it are performing to the best of their ability and developing their potential for improvement. Within this overall objective, staff assessments have several specific purposes.

- To review **performance**, to plan and follow up training and development programmes; and to set targets for future performance
- To review **potential**, as an aid to planning career development by predicting the level and type of work the individual will be capable of in the future
- To increase **motivation by providing feedback**
- To review **salaries**: measuring the extent to which an employee is deserving of a salary increase as compared with peers

Features of a typical system

- **Identification of criteria for assessment**, perhaps based on job analysis, performance standards and person specifications
- The preparation by the subordinate's manager of an **assessment report**
- An **appraisal interview**, for an exchange of views about the results of the assessment and targets for improvement
- **Review of the assessment by the assessor's own superior**, so that the appraisee does not feel subject to one person's prejudices. Formal appeals may be allowed, if necessary to establish the fairness of the procedure
- The preparation and implementation of **action plans** to achieve improvements and changes agreed
- **Follow-up**: monitoring the progress of the action plan

There may not need to be standard forms for appraisal (and elaborate form-filling procedures should be avoided) as long as managers understand the nature and extent of what is required, and are motivated to take it seriously. Most systems, however, provide for assessments to be recorded, and report forms of various lengths and complexity may be designed for standard use, A written record of some form is essential to prevent doubts and uncertainties at a later date.

3.1 The assessment report

The basis of assessment must first be determined. Assessments must be related to a **common standard**, in order for comparisons to be made between individuals, and of a particular individual's progress over time. They should also be related to meaningful performance criteria, which take account of the critical variables in each different job.

Various appraisal techniques may be used.

(a) **Overall assessment** is the simplest method, simply requiring the manager to write in narrative form judgements about the appraisee, possibly with a checklist of personality characteristics and performance targets to work from. There will be no guaranteed consistency of the criteria and areas of assessment, however, and managers may not be able to convey clear, effective judgements in writing.

(b) **Guided assessment** requires assessors to comment on a number of specified characteristics and performance elements, with guidelines as to how the terms (eg 'application', 'integrity', 'adaptability') are to be interpreted in the work context. This is a more precise, but still rather vague method.

(c) **Grading** adds a comparative frame of reference to the general guidelines, whereby managers are asked to select one of a number of levels or degrees to which the individual in question displays the given characteristic. These are also known as **rating scales**, and are much used in standard appraisal forms. Their effectiveness depends to a large extent on the **relevance** of the factors chosen for assessment and the definition of the agreed standards of assessment.

(i) Numerical values may be added to ratings to give rating 'scores'. Alternatively a less precise **graphic scale** may be used to indicate general position on a plus/minus scale, for example:

Factor: job knowledge

High _____ Average ✓_____ Low

(ii)   The principal drawback of such schemes is that the subordinate may not agree with the precise ratings given. This may lead to the subordinate questioning the judgement of the appraiser. The appraisal may degenerate into an argument about the appraiser's use of the grading system rather than what the assessment tells the subordinate about his or her performance.

(d)   **Results-orientated schemes**. The above techniques will be concerned with results but are commonly based on behavioural appraisal. A wholly results-orientated approach, such as Management by Objectives, reviews performance against specific targets and standards of performance agreed in advance by manager and subordinate together. Such an approach has a number of advantages.

(i)   The subordinate is more involved in appraisal because success or progress is measured against specific, jointly agreed targets.

(ii)   The manager is relieved, to some extent, of the role of **critic**, and becomes a **counsellor**.

(iii)   Learning and motivation theories suggest that clear and known targets are important in modifying and determining behaviour.

(e)   **Self-appraisals**, where the individuals carry out their own self-evaluation, can be an alternative to management/subordinate appraisals. They have the advantage that the system is evidently aimed at the needs of the individual. Self-appraisal schemes can also be combined with training schemes where the individuals decide on the training they require.

The effectiveness of any scheme will depend on the realistic and clear statement of targets; and the commitment of both parties to make it work. The **measurement of success or failure is only part of the picture: reasons** for failure and opportunities arising from success must be evaluated.

Managers will need guidance, or perhaps training to help them make a relevant, objective and helpful report. Most large organisations with standard review forms also issue detailed guidance notes to aid assessors with the written and discussion elements.

3.2 Appraisal interview

FAST FORWARD

As with all interviews, an appraisal interview must be well planned and taken seriously. It should be part of an appraisal system or scheme which is seen to be of value to both appraiser and appraisee. It should encourage two-way communication.

The report may be shown to the appraisee and thus form a basis for discussion. Some organisations, however, do not show the report to the employee; this is likely to lead to resentment and anxiety about the correctness or otherwise of its contents.

3.2.1 Approaches to appraisal interviews

(a)   The **tell and sell** method. The manager gives details of the assessment to the subordinate and then tries to **gain acceptance** of the evaluation and the improvement plan. This requires unusual human relations skills in order to convey constructive criticism in an acceptable manner, and to motivate appraisees to alter their behaviour.

(b)   The **tell and listen** method. The manager gives the assessment and then **invites response**. The manager no longer dominates the interview, and there is greater opportunity for **counselling**. The employee is encouraged to participate in the assessment and the working out of improvement targets and methods. Managers using this method will need to have good listening skills.

(c)	The **problem solving** approach. The manager abandons the role of critic altogether, and becomes a counsellor and helper. The discussion is centred not on the assessment, but on the employee's work problems. The employee is encouraged to think solutions through, and to commit to the recognised need for personal improvement.

Many organisations waste the opportunities for **upward communication** embedded in the appraisal process. In order to get a positive contribution from employees, the appraisal interviewer should ask positive and thought-provoking questions. Here are some examples.

- What parts of your job do you do best?
- Could any changes be made in your job which might result in improved performance?
- Have you any skills, knowledge, or aptitudes which could be made better use of in the organisation?

3.2.2 Follow-up procedures

- Having the report agreed and counter-signed by a more senior manager
- Informing appraisees of the final results of the appraisal, if this has been contentious in the review interview
- Carrying out agreed actions on training, promotions and so on
- Monitoring the appraisee's progress with agreed actions
- Taking necessary steps to help the appraisee for example by guidance, providing feedback or upgrading equipment

3.3 The effectiveness of appraisal

In practice, the system often goes wrong.

(a)	There may be a divergence between the subordinate's and interviewer's perceived and actual needs. A subordinate may **want** praise but **need** constructive criticism. The interviewer may wish to concentrate on criticising, whereas the appraisal could be used to give feedback on management practice.

(b)	Appraisal interviews are often **defensive on the part of the subordinate**, who believes that any criticism will bring sanctions. There may also be some mistrust of the validity of the scheme itself.

(c)	Interviews are also often **defensive on the part of the superior**, who cannot reconcile the role of judge and critic with the constructive intent of the interview. As a result there may be many unresolved issues left at the end.

(d)	The superior might show **conscious or unconscious bias** in the report. Systems without clearly defined standard criteria will be particularly prone to the subjectivity of the assessor's judgements.

(e)	The general level of ratings may vary widely from manager to manager.

(f)	Appraisals may deal with specific problems which should have been dealt with at the time they arose by counselling. Appraisals ought to concentrate on ongoing matters that are important to career development.

(g)	Appraisals may be seen merely as a bureaucratic form-filling exercise or as no more than an annual formality.

4 Training and development for staff

FAST FORWARD

One of the common follow-up outcomes will relate to **training and development**, and identified training needs.

- To tackle an identified weakness
- To develop skills in anticipation of a change in the job, environment or technology
- In preparation for promotion

Procuring the most appropriate human resources for the task and environment is an on-going process. It involves not only recruitment and selection, but the training and development of employees prior to employment, or at any time during their employment, in order to help them meet the requirements of their current, and potential future job.

Purposes of selection and training

- Fitting people to the requirements of the job
- Securing better occupational adjustment
- Defining performance criteria against which the success of the process can be monitored

Training may be defined as: 'the systematic development of the attitudes, knowledge and skill patterns required by an individual in order to perform adequately a given task or job'.

4.1 The contribution of training

Modern business is increasingly **dynamic**, with changes in technology, products, processes and control techniques. The need for planned growth combined with this dynamism mean that a working organisation's competitiveness depends increasingly on the **continuous reassessment** of **training needs** and the **provision of planned training** to meet those needs.

Training can contribute to success, but has its **limitations**.

(a) It must be the correct tool for the need: it cannot solve problems caused by faulty organisation, equipment or employee selection.

(b) Reasons for neglecting training must be overcome: these include cost, inconvenience, apathy and an unrealistic expectation of training in the past.

(c) Limitations imposed by intelligence, motivation and the psychological restrictions of the learning process must be understood.

Internal formal training courses are run by the organisation's training department. External training courses are available in many forms.

- Day-release courses

- Evening classes, which make demands on the individual's time outside work

- Revision courses for professional examinations

- Block-release courses which may involve some weeks at a college followed by a period back at work

- Sandwich courses, usually involving six months at college then six months at work, in rotation, for two or three years

- A sponsored full-time course at a university or polytechnic for one or two years

4.1.1 Disadvantages of formal training

(a) Individuals will not benefit from formal training unless they want to learn. The individual's superior may need to provide encouragement in this respect.

(b) If the subject matter of the training course does not relate to an individual's job, the learning will be quickly forgotten.

(c) Individuals may not be able to accept that what they learn on a course applies in the context of their own particular job. For example, managers may attend an internal course on management that suggests a participatory style of leadership, but may consider it irrelevant, because their subordinates are 'too young' or 'too inexperienced'.

4.2 Management training

FAST FORWARD

Training methods are many and varied. They must be selected with care to be best suited to the needs of the organisation in terms of cost, time, approach and the individual in terms of level, style, relevance and commitment needed.

4.2.1 A systematic approach to training

- **Identify areas** where training will be beneficial.

- **Establish learning targets**. The areas where learning is needed should be identified and specific, realistic goals stated, including standards of performance.

- Decide on the **training methods to be used**.

- **Plan a systematic learning and development programme**. This should allow for practice and consolidation.

- **Identify opportunities for broadening the trainee's knowledge and experience** such as involvement in new projects, extending the job or greater responsibility.

- **Take into account the strengths and limitations of the trainee**. A trainee from an academic background may learn best through research-based learning like fact-finding for a committee; whilst those who learn best by doing may profit from project work.

- **Implement** the scheme in full.

- **Exchange feedback**. The manager will want performance information in order to monitor the progress, adjust the learning programme, identify further needs and plan future development.

- **Validate the results** to check that the training works and benefits exceed costs.

4.2.2 Analysis of training needs

Training needs can be identified by considering the **gap** between **job requirements**, as determined by job analysis, job description and so on, and the **ability of the job holder**, as determined by testing or observation and appraisal.

The training department's management should make an initial investigation of the problem. Even if work is not done as well as it could be, training is not necessarily the right answer. We have seen that poor working standards might also be caused by other factors.

Marketing at Work

People Management reported that a number of *Whitbread* pubs had improved performance as a result of a change in the company's training scheme. Previously the company's training scheme had aimed to improve the service standards of individuals, and there were also discussions with staff on business developments. It was felt however that other companies in the same sector had overtaken Whitbread in these respects.

Whitbread therefore introduced an integrated approach to assessment of the performance of pubs. Assessment is by four criteria; training (a certain percentage of staff have to have achieved a training award), standards (suggested by working parties of staff), team meetings and customer satisfaction. Managers are trained in training skills and they in turn train staff, using a set of structured notes to ensure a consistent training process.

Pubs that fulfil all the criteria win a team hospitality award, consisting of a plaque, a visit from a senior executive, and a party or points for goods scheme. To retain the award and achieve further points, pubs have then to pass further assessments which take place every six months.

The scheme seemed to improve standards. Significantly staff turnover was down and a survey suggested morale had improved, with a greater sense of belonging particularly by part-time staff. A major cause of these improvements may well be the involvement of staff and management in the design process.

4.2.3 Training objectives

If the training department concludes that the provision of training could improve work performance, it must **analyse the work in detail** in order to decide what the **requirements** of a training programme should be. In particular, there should be a **training objective** or **objectives**. These are tangible, observable targets which trainees should be capable of reaching at the end of the course.

The training objectives should be **clear, specific and measurable**, for example: 'at the end of a course a trainee must be able to describe ..., or identify ..., or list ..., or state ..., or distinguish x from y ...'. It is insufficient to state as an objective of a course 'to give trainees a grounding in ...' or 'to give trainees a better appreciation of ...'. These objectives are too woolly, and actual achievements cannot be measured against them.

4.2.4 Training methods

Having decided what must be learned and to what standard of achievement, the next stage is to decide what method of training should be used.

4.2.5 On-the-job training (OJT)

OJT is very common, especially when the work involved is not complex. Trainee managers require more coaching, and may be given assignments or projects as part of a planned programme to develop their experience. Unfortunately, this type of training will be unsuccessful if the assignments do not have a specific purpose or the organisation is intolerant of any mistakes which the trainee makes.

Action Programme 6

What different methods of on-the-job training can you identify?

4.2.6 Coaching

Coaching is a common method of on the job training; the trainee is put under the guidance of an experienced employee who demonstrates how to do the job and helps refine the trainee's technique.

All forms of training require the commitment of the organisation to the learning programme. It must believe in training and developing employees, and be prepared to devote both the money and the time. The manager will largely dictate the department's attitude to these things.

4.2.7 Course training methods

(a) **Lectures**. Lectures are suitable for large audiences and can be an efficient way of putting across information. However lack of participation may lead to lack of interest and/or failure to understand by most of the audience.

(b) **Discussions**. Discussions aim to impart information but allow much greater opportunities for audience participation. They are often suitable for groups up to 20 and can be a good means of maintaining interest.

(c) **Exercises**. An exercise involves a particular task being undertaken with pre-set results following guidance laid down. They are a very active form of learning and are a good means of checking whether trainees have assimilated information.

(d) **Role plays**. Trainees act out roles in a typical work situation. They are useful practice for face-to-face situations. However, they may embarrass some participants and may not be taken seriously.

(e) **Case studies**. Case studies identify causes and/or suggest solutions. They are a good means of exchanging ideas and thinking out solutions. However trainees may see the case study as divorced from their real work experience.

Programmed learning can be provided on a computer terminal, but it is still associated with printed booklets which provide information in easy-to-learn steps. The booklet asks simple questions which the trainee must answer. If they are answered correctly, the trainee is instructed to carry on with more learning. If the questions are answered wrongly, the booklet gives an alternative set of instructions to go back and learn again. Programmed learning has a number of advantages.

(a) Trainees can work through the course in simple stages and continually checks their progress. Misunderstandings are quickly put right.

(b) Trainees are kept actively involved in the learning process because they must keep answering questions put to them in the booklet.

(c) Giving correct answers immediately reinforces the learning process.

(d) Trainees can work at their own pace.

4.2.8 Cost/benefit analysis of training

The training course should only go ahead if the **likely benefits are expected to exceed the costs** of designing and then running the course. Costs include training materials, the salaries of the staff attending training courses, their travelling expenses, the salaries of training staff and training overheads. **Benefits** might be measured in a variety of ways.

- Quicker working and therefore reductions in overtime or staff numbers
- Greater accuracy of work
- More extensive skills
- Improved motivation

As you will appreciate, the **benefits are more easily stated in general terms than quantified in money terms**. Indeed, it is often difficult to measure benefits such as increased Identification with business objectives and increased cohesion as a team, but these benefits may nevertheless be significant.

4.2.9 Implementation and evaluation of training

When the training course has been designed, **a pilot course may be run**. The purpose of the test would be to find out whether the training scheme appears to achieve what it has set out to do, or whether some revisions are necessary. After the pilot test, the scheme can be implemented in full.

Implementation of the training scheme is not the end of the story. The scheme should be **validated** and **evaluated**.

(a)   **Validation** means observing the results of the course, and measuring whether the training objective has been achieved.

(b)   **Evaluation** means comparing the actual costs of the scheme against the assessed benefits which are being obtained. If the costs exceed the benefits, the scheme will need to be re-designed or withdrawn.

4.2.10 Validation methods

(a)   **Asking the trainees** whether they thought the training programme was relevant to their work, and whether they found it useful. This is rather inexact and does not measure results for comparison against the training objective.

(b)   **Measuring what the trainees have learned** on the course, perhaps by means of a test at the end of the course.

(c)   Studying the **subsequent behaviour of the trainees** in their jobs to measure how the training scheme has altered the way they do their work. This is possible where the purpose of the course was to learn a particular skill.

(d)   Finding out whether the training has affected **the work or behaviour of other employees not on the course**. This form of monitoring would probably be reserved for senior managers in the training department.

(e)   Seeing whether training in general has contributed to the **overall objectives of the organisation**. This too is a form of monitoring reserved for senior managers and would perhaps be discussed at board level in the organisation.

 Marketing at Work

An article in *Marketing Business* in March 1998 highlighted recent trends in marketing training, particularly its interaction with the rest of the organisation. This reflects a change in emphasis in the role of marketing in many companies, away from product management and towards anticipating and supplying customer needs.

Companies are supplying increased marketing training to operating departments in topics such as brand awareness and are giving marketing departments training which consists of two parts. The first part focuses on normal technicalities such as research and promotional techniques. The second gives marketers a wider perspective on the rest of the company, focusing on issues such as systems, distribution, customer service and financial management. Motivating operating departments to become more innovative and centred on the customer is seen as being very important.

Action Programme 7

Devise a training programme for a new recruit who will be doing a job similar to yours.

5 Counselling and advice

In addition to appraisal people often require help. Advice is often unrequested, although it might be to do with a specific problem. **Counselling** is a more formal, long-term process with a specific objective.

To **advise** is to propose solutions to someone else's problems. To **counsel** is to assist someone through the process of finding his or her own solutions. The counselling approach involves a number of considerations.

- Discerning the need for counselling
- Ensuring privacy and time
- Encouraging openness and ensuring confidentiality
- Using specific examples to illustrate points discussed and avoiding abstract comments
- Emphasis on constructive interaction including personal rapport and trust
- Sensitivity to the subject's beliefs and values
- Guidance in evolving the subject's own solutions rather than giving advice
- Avoiding arguments but instead getting the subject to discuss reasons for disagreement
- Supporting the solution devised
- Monitoring the progress of the solution

You will note that **counselling** requires a systematic approach, with careful planning and a range of interpersonal skills being brought into play. Particularly important are listening skills. It requires the support of the organisation, to train counsellors, to back the solutions reached and to allow time for the counselling and monitoring period. Some organisations formalise this in a counselling programme, with qualified counsellors, while others prefer to support managers in particular counselling situations.

Advising is a much more common and on-going process. Because, unlike counselling, advising is not essentially a co-operative process, the **effectiveness of advice depends on the willingness of the recipient to accept suggestions**. It also depends on the **soundness of the advice itself**: unlike counselling, advising has very little beneficial effect **in itself**.

A counselling approach is now often applied to interviewing situations previously regarded as purely informative or judgmental, for example, disciplinary and grievance interviews, and appraisal interviews.

An open door management policy or supervisory style may encourage employees to come forward with a wide range of work and even personal problems which require counselling. Some organisations may have a welfare officer to provide counselling.

5.1 The role of counselling in organisations

Effective counselling is not merely a matter of pastoral care for individuals, but is very much in the organisation's interests.

- Appropriate use of counselling tools can prevent underperformance, reduce labour turnover and absenteeism and increase commitment from employees.

- Workplace counselling recognises that the organisation may be contributing to the employees' problems and therefore it provides an opportunity to reassess organisational policy and practice.

Action Programme 8

How do you react when people try to give you advice at work? Have you ever been counselled? If so, did you feel differently about that experience?

Who (if anyone) is responsible for formal counselling in your company: a specialist or line manager? Is the availability of counselling clearly communicated to staff, and in a way that will encourage them to come forward? Do people go to informal counsellors among their colleagues instead: if so, to whom and why?

6 Discipline and grievance

FAST FORWARD

Disciplinary proceedings are, sadly, sometimes necessary, for a variety of reasons relating to behaviour at work. People should know what is expected of them and discipline should be fair. Statutory disciplinary procedure should be followed.

6.1 Disciplinary principles

Maintaining discipline among employees is an integral part of leadership, and requires human relations and communication skills. Discipline is a condition of orderliness in which the members of the enterprise behave sensibly and conduct themselves according to the standards of acceptable behaviour as related to the goals of the organisation. Once employees know what is expected of them and feel that the rules are reasonable, **self-disciplined** behaviour becomes a part of group norms.

Self discipline must start at the top: the manager should comply with certain requirements, such as being on time, observing safety rules, no smoking and no drinking rules, and dressing and behaving in a manner expected of the position.

There are some employees in every organisation who will fail to observe the established rules and standards even after having been informed of them. These employees simply do not accept the responsibility of self discipline. Firm action is required to correct those situations which interfere with the accepted norms of responsible employee behaviour.

Disciplinary action can lead to significant legal problems. The employee may be dismissed or regard the disciplinary action as amounting to **substantive dismissal**. In either case, an **action for wrongful or unfair dismissal** may result. This can be very expensive for the employer. **Managers commencing any formal disciplinary procedure would be well advised to consult the HR department first**.

There are many types of disciplinary situations which require attention by the supervisor or manager.

- Excessive absenteeism
- Excessive lateness in arriving at work
- Poor attitudes which influence the work of others or harm the firm's image
- Improper personal appearance
- Breaking safety rules
- Open insubordination

In addition to these types of situations managers might be confronted with disciplinary problems stemming from employee behaviour **off the job** such as a drinking problem or involvement in some form of law breaking activity. In such circumstances, whenever an employee's off-the-job conduct has an impact upon the organisation the manager must be prepared to deal with such a problem within the scope of the disciplinary process.

Managers must not ignore disciplinary problems, however unpleasant they are for everyone. If a manager does not take firm and appropriate action, some other employees may be encouraged to break the rules because they think they can get away with it. It is also unfair to these members of staff who do observe the rules.

6.2 The manager-subordinate relationship in disciplinary situations

Any disciplinary action must be undertaken with sensitivity and sound judgement on the manager's part. Disciplinary action must have as its goal the improvement of the future behaviour of the employee and other members of the organisation.

Even if the manager uses sensitivity and judgement, imposing disciplinary action tends to generate resentment because it is an unpleasant experience.

Following the basic rules set out below will help the manager to reduce the resentment inherent in all disciplinary actions.

(a)   **Immediacy** means that the manager takes disciplinary action as speedily as possible; the full circumstances may not be known or there may be doubt as to the penalty which should be imposed. The nature of the incident may make it advisable to have the offender leave the premises quickly, but the ACAS Code of Practice requires that **investigation** be made **before action is taken**. Consideration should be given to the employee's record and all pertinent details of the situation in preparation for the disciplinary interview.

(b)   **Advance warning**. In order to have employees accept disciplinary action as fair, it is essential that they know in advance what is expected of them. Many companies find it useful to have a disciplinary section in an employee handbook, which every new employee receives. However, each new employee should also be informed orally about what is expected.

(c)   **Consistency**. Consistency of discipline means that each time an infraction occurs appropriate disciplinary action is taken. Inconsistency lowers morale, diminishes respect and creates doubt.

(d)   **Impersonality**. It is only natural for an employee to feel some resentment towards a manager who has taken disciplinary action against him or her. The supervisor can reduce the amount of resentment by making disciplinary action as impersonal as possible. Penalties should be connected with the act and not based upon the personality involved. Once a disciplinary action has been taken, the manager should treat the employee in the same way as before the infraction.

(e)   **Privacy**. As a general rule, unless the manager's authority is challenged directly and in public disciplinary action should be taken in private.

Action Programme 9

Outline a disciplinary incident in which you have been involved as the person imposing discipline – even if it is only an informal telling off you've given someone. What were the interpersonal difficulties involved: the attitudes and feelings that made the situation awkward? (If it wasn't awkward at all, stop and think: were you just insensitive to the other person's feeling at the time – or were there **real** reasons why the encounter was friendly and positive, in which case, what were they?)

6.3 Disciplinary action

The purpose of discipline is not punishment or retribution. Disciplinary action must have as its goal the improvement of the future behaviour of the employee and other members of the organisation. The purpose obviously is the avoidance of similar occurrences in the future.

6.3.1 ACAS code of practice

In the UK, discipline in civilian organisations is governed by the ACAS Code of Practice on disciplinary and grievance procedures. As far as disciplinary procedures are concerned, the code of practice lays down certain essential features.

… good disciplinary procedures should:

- be in writing

- specify to whom they apply

- be non-discriminatory

- provide for matters to be dealt with without undue delay

- allow for information to be kept confidential

- tell employees what disciplinary actions may be taken

- say what levels of management have the authority to take disciplinary action

- require employees to be informed of the complaints against them and supporting evidence before any hearing

- give employees a chance to have their say before management reaches a decision

- provide employees with the right to be accompanied

- provide that no employee is dismissed for a first breach of discipline, except in cases of gross misconduct

- require management to investigate fully before any disciplinary action is taken

- ensure that employees are given an explanation for any sanction

- allow employees to appeal against a decision

All disciplinary incidents should be thoroughly investigated and a written record made by the appropriate manager. It will then be necessary to decide how to proceed. Many minor cases of poor performance or misconduct are best dealt with by informal advice, coaching or counselling. An informal oral warning may be issued. None of this forms part of the formal disciplinary procedure, but workers should be informed clearly what is expected and what action will be taken if they fail to improve.

In cases involving gross misconduct, breakdowns in relationships or risk to persons or property, a brief suspension on pay may be ordered while the case is investigated. Such a suspension is not in itself a disciplinary sanction. A new **statutory disciplinary procedure** was introduced from 1 October 2004.

Step 1   The appropriate manager must write to the employee stating why disciplinary action is being taken and inviting him or her to a meeting to discuss the matter. The employee has the right to be accompanied at the meeting.

Step 2   At the meeting, the manager must explain the problem and allow the employee to respond. After the meeting, the manager should explain his or her decision and inform the employee that he or she has the right to appeal.

Step 3   The employee may appeal and has the right to be accompanied to the appeal meeting, which should be with a different or more senior manager.

This procedure should only be used if the manager is contemplating serious disciplinary action such as dismissal. For less serious offences, if informal methods have no effect, a first written warning should be issued.

First warning. A first warning could be either oral or written depending on the seriousness of the case.

(a)   An **oral warning** should include the reason for issuing it, notice that it constitutes the first step of the disciplinary procedure and details of the right of appeal. A note of the warning should be kept on file but disregarded after a specified period, such as 6 months.

(b)   A **first written warning** is appropriate in more serious cases. It should inform the worker of the improvement required and state that a final written warning may be considered if there is no satisfactory improvement. A copy of the first written warning should be kept on file but disregarded after a specified period such as 12 months.

A first written warning may also be appropriate if there has not been satisfactory improvement after an oral warning has been issued.

Final written warning. If an earlier warning is still current and there is no satisfactory improvement, a final written warning may be appropriate. Also, sufficiently serious infringements may lead directly to the issue of a final written warning.

Note that, depending on the offence, it is not necessary to progress through all of these levels of warning. One could go straight to the final written warning. This is thus a very flexible system, capable of dealing with disciplinary problems in a measured and proportionate way. It is however **always** necessary to investigate the allegations and to give the worker opportunity to reply to them.

6.4 Disciplinary sanctions

The final stage in the disciplinary process is the imposition of sanctions.

(a)   **Suspension without pay**

This course of action would be next in order if the employee has committed repeated offences and previous steps were of no avail. Disciplinary lay-offs usually extend over several days or weeks. Some employees may not be very impressed with oral or written warnings, but they will find a disciplinary lay-off without pay a rude awakening. This penalty is only available if it is provided for in the contract of employment.

(b)   **Demotion**

This course of action is likely to bring about dissatisfaction and discouragement, since losing pay and status over an extended period of time is a form of constant punishment. This dissatisfaction of the demoted employee may easily spread to co-workers, so most enterprises avoid downgrading as a disciplinary measure: like suspension without pay, this sanction may only be imposed if it is provided for in the contract of employment.

(c)   **Discharge**

Discharge is a drastic form of disciplinary action, and should be reserved for the most serious offences. For the organisation, it involves waste of a labour resource, the expense of training a new employee, and disruption caused by changing the make-up of the work team. There also may be damage to the morale of the group.

6.5 Disciplinary interviews

Preparation for the disciplinary interview

(a)   **Gathering the facts** about the alleged infringement

(b)   **Determination of the organisation's position:** how valuable is the employee, potentially? How serious are his offences/lack of progress? How far is the organisation prepared to go to help him improve or discipline him further?

(c)   **Identification of the aims of the interview**: punishment? deterrent to others? improvement? Specific standards of future behaviour/performance required need to be determined.

(d)   **Ensure that the organisation's disciplinary procedures have been followed**

    (i)   Informal oral warnings (at least) have been given.

    (ii)   The employee has been given adequate notice of the interview for his own preparation.

    (iii)   The employee has been informed of the complaint against him, of his right to be accompanied by a colleague or representative and so on.

The content of the disciplinary interview

Step 1   The manager will explain the purpose of the interview.

Step 2   The charges against the employee will be delivered, clearly, unambiguously and without personal emotion.

Step 3   The manager will explain the organisation's position with regard to the issues involved: disappointment, concern, need for improvement, impact on others. This can be done frankly - but tactfully, with as positive an emphasis as possible on the employee's capacity and responsibility to improve.

Step 4   The organisation's expectations with regard to future behaviour/performance should be made clear.

Step 5   The employee should be given the opportunity to comment, explain, justify or deny. If he is to approach the following stage of the interview in a positive way, he must not be made to feel 'hounded' or hard done by.

Step 6   The organisation's expectations should be reiterated, or new standards of behaviour set for the employee.

    (i)   They should be specific and quantifiable, performance related and realistic.

    (ii)   They should be related to a practical but reasonably short time period. A date should be set to review his progress.

    (iii)   The manager agrees on measures to help the employee should that be necessary. It would demonstrate a positive approach if, for example, a mentor were appointed from his work group to help him check his work. If his poor performance is genuinely the result of some difficulty or distress outside work, other help (temporary leave, counselling or financial aid) may be appropriate.

Step 7   The manager should explain the reasons behind any penalties imposed on the employee, including the entry in his personnel record of the formal warning. He should also explain how the warning can be removed from the record, and what standards must be achieved within a specified timescale. There should be a clear warning of the consequences of failure to meet improvement targets.

Step 8   The manager should explain the organisation's appeals procedures: if the employee feels he has been unfairly treated, there should be a right of appeal to a higher manager.

Step 9   Once it has been established that the employee understands all the above, the manager should summarise the proceedings briefly.

Records of the interview will be kept for the employee's personnel file, and for the formal follow-up review and any further action necessary.

Action Programme 10

Discipline is a particularly difficult matter for junior managers to deal with correctly. What common mistakes would you expect to encounter in the administration of discipline and what suggestions would you offer on the subject of disciplinary interviews?

6.6 Dealing with grievances

FAST FORWARD

Occasionally employees will have a **grievance**. In a grievance interview, the facts are checked and examined, and remedies are suggested. Statutory grievance procedure should be followed.

Organisations should have an established procedure for dealing with employees who think they have been wrongly treated. In the UK a **statutory grievance procedure** was established alongside the statutory disciplinary procedure on 1 October 2004.

Step 1   The employee sets out his or her grievance in writing

Step 2   The employer arranges a meeting, at which the employee has the right to be accompanied, to discuss the matter. At the end of the meeting the employer informs the employee of the decision and the employees' right of appeal.

Step 3   The employee tells the employer if he or she wishes to appeal. If an appeal is requested, a further meeting, at which the employee has the right to be accompanied, is held, preferably with a different or more senior manager. After the meeting the employee is told of the employer's decision.

6.7 Exit interviews

Employees may resign for any number of reasons, personal or occupational. Some or all of these reasons may well be a reflection on the structure, management style, culture or personnel policies of the organisation itself. When an employee announces the intention to leave, verbally and/or by letter, it is important for the manager to find the real reasons why they are leaving, in an exit interview. This may lead to a review of existing policies on pay, training, promotion, the work environment, the quality and style of supervision and so on.

7 Managing peripheral workers

FAST FORWARD

Many firms are experimenting with alternatives to full-time, office-based employment: a core workforce is surrounded by a periphery of temporary and/or part-time employees. Particular management problems relate to generating commitment. Technology enables many people to work from home. Supervisory problems include control.

You may have read about job insecurity and the decline of the permanent, full-time job. Whilst this development can be exaggerated, there are a number of new ways in which people are employed and managed. A firm might have a **core workforce** of permanent, full-time employees. This core might be supplemented by a **periphery** of people employed on a number of other bases, such as part-timers, people on short-term employment contracts which may or may not be renewed and freelances who are contracted to work when needed.

As a result of such arrangements, the organisation saves money and gains **flexibility**. However, there might be concerns as to the **commitment** of the peripheral workforce. After all, if management can dispose of them at will, why should they be committed to the long-term future of the organisation? Such problems are truer for some organisations than others.

(a)   Many part-timers welcome the opportunity to work part-time and the flexibility it provides.

(b)   People on short-term contracts might hope that their performance will result in a full-time job eventually. Even if not, they might welcome the opportunity for personal learning and skill development.

(c)   Freelances, will welcome the opportunity for more work – but they will also be hunting around elsewhere.

Another development is **telecommuting** or **teleworking**, which involves the use of IT to work at home but remain in close contact.

 Marketing at Work

One in 100 of *British Telecommunications'* 100,000 UK employees could find their home transformed into their office in Britain's most ambitious experiment in teleworking.

The UK's largest telecoms operator is hoping to persuade at least 10,000 of its office staff to work from home, communicating with customers and managers by fax machine, telephone and the internet.

BT estimates it would save at least £134m a year in costs and an unquantifiable amount in terms of reduced stress, commuting delays and fuel. *Financial Times* (12 May 1999).

Working at home (**homeworking**) is not new in itself: there are many pieceworkers in the textile industry who do certain jobs at home, but it is relatively new to the management of the office.

7.1 Advantages to the organisation of homeworking

(a)   **Cost savings on space**. Office rental costs and other charges can be very expensive. Firms can save money if they move some of their employees to homeworking.

(b)   **A larger pool of labour**. The possibility of working at home might attract more applicants for clerical positions, especially from people who have other demands on their time.

(c)   If the homeworkers are freelances, then the organisation need only pay them when they are actually working. However organisations should consider whether lack of benefits means that homeworkers are regarded as having second-class status.

(d)   **Improved customer service** may result from a better match between available and required hours.

7.2 Advantages to the individual of homeworking

- No time is wasted commuting to the office.

- The work can be organised flexibly around the individual's domestic commitments.

- Jobs which require concentration can sometimes be done better at home without the disruption of the office.

- It makes employment possible in remote areas.

Managers who practise close supervision will perhaps feels a worrying **loss of control**. Managers who take the Theory X view of human nature might view homeworking as an opportunity for laziness and slack work.

However, these problems of control are partly illusory. There are **real problems for the organisation**.

(a) **Co-ordination** of the work of different homeworkers. The job design should ensure that homeworkers perform to the required standard. They should have the opportunity to ask for help, and supervisors should visit on a regular basis.

(b) **Briefing**. If a homeworker needs a lot of help on a task, this implies that the task has not been properly explained. So, briefing must be thorough.

(c) **Culture**. A homeworker is relatively isolated from the office and therefore, it might be assumed, from the firm. However, questions of **loyalty and commitment** do not apply for an organisation's sales force, whose members are rarely in the office. There should be regular meetings of homeworkers, and other regular contacts with the office.

(d) **Health and safety**. Health and safety regulations apply to homeworkers as well as office-based staff.

7.3 Other management issues

(a) When introducing homeworking for the first time, it is best done voluntarily. Homeworking is likely to be a change in conditions of employment.

(b) When recruiting, employers need to check that the home environment is suitable, and the candidates will be suited to working at home.

(c) The induction process for new employees is likely to have to be more extensive for homeworkers, since they cannot pick things up whilst being in the office.

(d) Homeworkers will have the same training and development needs as office-based workers, but may not be able to attend training courses. Distance learning packages can be used. Homeworkers should also have regular appraisals.

7.4 Problems for homeworkers

(a) **Isolation**. Work provides people with a social life, and many people might miss the sense of community if they are forced to work at home. Some firms get round this by having meetings where groups of homeworkers can get together.

(b) **Intrusions**. A homeworker is vulnerable, by definition, to interruptions especially from members of his or her family forgetting that the worker is **working** at home, in time that the employer is paying for.

(c) **Adequate space**. It is not always possible to obtain a quiet space at home in which to work.

(d) In practice many homeworkers, especially if they are freelances, have **fewer employment rights**. They are not entitled to sick pay or holiday pay. They have limited security, as the firm can dispense with their services at whim.

(e) **Technology**. Successful homeworking using IT requires systems that the homeworkers are able to use, and the availability of support in case there are technical problems with hardware or software.

The most important question that has to be decided is how homeworkers should be paid. Homeworkers should be rewarded equally for work of equal value, but the organisation has to decide how that work is to be measured. Using timesheets to determine hours worked may not be satisfactory since work patterns may be irregular. It may be better to pay for **output**, with average pay equivalent to an office wage. There can be some standardisation of pay so that minor output variations do not change wages.

Evidence suggests that work processes which are ideal for homeworking tend to be individually driven, require few instructions, need not be performed at set times and produce outputs that can be measured precisely.

Exam tip

Questions on improving the performance of individuals or teams are very common in this exam, and you must have the basics at your fingertips. These are motivation, training, appraisal, and discipline.

Chapter Roundup

- Motivation is an essential ingredient in ensuring that the individual and the team perform efficiently and effectively.

- Management writers have devoted considerable time to understanding motivation because it is believed improvements here can generate competitive advantage.

- There are basically two types of motivational theory.

    - **Content theories**: motivation is driven by needs. Maslow's hierarchy of needs is the basic form of this approach

    - **Process theories**: motivation is a process of making choices about how best to satisfy needs..

- **Maslow** described a **hierarchy of needs** of relative strength. Herzberg's work was important because it encourages managers to recognise the **hygiene** factors, which can cause dissatisfaction if they are absent, but are unlikely to generate positive motivation.

- **Herzberg** also highlighted the motivational opportunities from job enlargement, enrichment and rotation, all of which are quite commonly used for both motivation and for training and development.

- **Victor Vroom** suggested that the strength of an individual's motivation to do something will depend on the extent to which he **expects** the results of his efforts to contribute towards his personal needs or goals, to reward him or to punish him.

- **Schein** summarises the historical development of thinking about motivation by describing **three sets of assumptions about people**. These correspond to the scientific management, human relations and Maslow/Herzberg schools of thought. Schein then describes his own model, which may be thought of as a **contingency approach**.

- **Drucker** suggested that job satisfaction comes from acceptance of responsibility.

- A wide variety of options are available to motivate the individual and the team. The important thing is to develop motivational strategies which suit both the situation and the individual. Schemes should be simple to administer, easy to understand and perceived to be fair, and any incentives should be clear.

- Participation in the decision-making process can be a powerful source of motivation and improved decisions. However, it must be genuine or it may be negative in its effects. Empowerment can improve efficiency and motivation and reduce management costs.

- Incentive schemes are an attempt to use pay as a motivator. This is very difficult to do, since pay is widely seen as a hygiene factor rather than a motivator.

- Appraisal can improve performance by providing a formal system of feedback which is also a useful benchmark for monitoring performance changes. Most appraisal systems require a manager to appraise a subordinate, but alternatives can be suggested.

- As with all interviews, an appraisal interview must be well planned and taken seriously. It should be part of an appraisal system or scheme which is seen to be of value to both appraiser and appraisee. It should encourage two-way communication.

- One of the common follow-up outcomes will relate to **training and development**, and identified training needs.

    - To tackle an identified weakness
    - To develop skills in anticipation of a change in the job, environment or technology
    - In preparation for promotion

Chapter roundup continued

- Training methods are many and varied. They must be selected with care to be best suited to the needs of the organisation in terms of cost, time, approach and the individual in terms of level, style, relevance and commitment needed.

- In addition to appraisal people often require help. Advice is often unrequested, although it might be to do with a specific problem. **Counselling** is a more formal, long-term process with a specific objective.

- **Disciplinary proceedings** are, sadly, sometimes necessary, for a variety of reasons relating to behaviour at work. People should know what is expected of them and discipline should be fair. Statutory disciplinary procedure should be followed.

- Occasionally employees will have a **grievance**. In a grievance interview, the facts are checked and examined, and remedies are suggested. Statutory grievance procedure should be followed.

- Many firms are experimenting with alternatives to full-time, office-based employment: a core workforce is surrounded by a periphery of temporary and/or part-time employees. Particular management problems relate to generating commitment. Technology enables many people to work from home. Supervisory problems include control.

Quick Quiz

1 What is motivation and why is it important?

2 What are the levels in Maslow's hierarchy?

3 Briefly describe Herzberg's 'two-factor' theory.

4 Identify and describe three types of psychological contract.

5 Drucker suggested that, in order to persuade employees to accept responsibility, four ingredients are needed. What are they?

6 What methods have been suggested for increasing motivation generally?

7 What are the benefits of non-financial incentives?

8 What is the purpose of appraisal?

9 What are training needs?

10 What is the difference between advice and counselling?

11 What is the purpose of exit interviews?

12 Distinguish between 'core' and 'peripheral' employees.

Answers to Quick Quiz

1 Motivation is reasons for behaviour, including behaviour and performance at work.

2 Physiological, safety, love/social, esteem, self-actualisation

3 Motivator factors can create **job satisfaction**; an absence of hygiene factors can create **dissatisfaction**.

4 Coercive, calculative and co-operative

5 Careful placement in jobs; high performance standards; provision of control information; participation in relevant decisions

6 Job design; participation; and incentive systems

7 They can have a higher **perceived value** than financial incentives do.

8 To improve organisational efficiency

9 Training needs are defined by the difference between job requirements and the ability of the job holders.

10 To advise is to propose solutions; to counsel is to assist to find solutions.

11 To ascertain the leaver's true reasons for leaving

12 Core workers are permanent, full-time employees, while peripheral workers are employed on a number of other bases, such as part-time and on temporary contracts.

Action Programme Review

2 Hygiene factors, which cause dissatisfaction at work

- Company policy and administration
- Salary
- The quality of supervision
- Interpersonal relations
- Working conditions
- Job security

3 Perhaps the narrator is contrasting economic man with self-actualising man. For some people the enjoyment of the job itself is satisfaction enough. People will accept less money to pursue an interest.

5 Typical features of enrichment are challenge; a whole job rather than part of one; responsibility for results; trust in small matters such as access to stores and making small purchases; and the power to take decisions, even if only small ones.

6 (a) **Coaching:** the trainee is put under the guidance of an experienced employee who shows the trainee how to do the job. The length of the coaching period will depend on the complexity of the job and the previous experience of the trainee.

(b) **Job rotation:** the trainee is given several jobs in succession, to gain experience of a wide range of activities. (Even experienced managers may rotate their jobs to gain wider experience; this philosophy of job education is commonly applied in the Civil Service, where an employee may expect to move on to another job after a few years.)

(c) **Temporary promotion:** an individual is promoted into his/her superior's position whilst the superior is absent due to illness. This gives the individual a chance to experience the demands of a more senior position.

(d)   **'Assistant to'** positions: a junior manager with good potential may be appointed as assistant to the managing director or another executive director. In this way, the individual gains experience of how the organisation is managed at the top.

(e)   **Committees:** trainees might be included in the membership of committees, in order to obtain an understanding of inter-departmental relationships.

7   Don't forget administrative items like where the lavatories are, nor health and safety issues. Allow time for the recruit to ask questions and make some allowance for checking that the training has achieved its objectives. You did start with objectives, didn't you?

10   (a)   **Common mistakes**

(i)   **Not following the right procedure**. Most firms have a disciplinary procedure, commencing with verbal warnings, followed by more formal written warnings if the 'offence' is repeated. Failure to follow this procedure can invalidate the process.

(ii)   **Failure to investigate the problem properly** and prejudging the issue. As it is a serious matter, the 'offence' should be properly investigated. Facts are often in dispute. This is especially a problem in the existence of a personality clash between manager and subordinate.

(iii)   **Confusing disciplinary with appraisal interviews**. An appraisal is an ongoing process to review past performance with a view to improving it, even though, if performance is not up to scratch, this can also result in dismissal. A disciplinary interview is generally the result of a specific issue.

(iv)   **Failure to keep records and to follow-up**. To be successful the disciplinary interview must have a result, even if this is only a mild rebuke or an acceptance that there has been a problem disciplinary interview.

(b)   **Guidelines to managers**

(i)   **Stay calm**. Although the offence might be intensely irritating, disciplinary action taken in bad temper may not follow the principles outlined above.

(ii)   Arrange a specific time and place for the interview, letting the employee know that the matter is up for discussion.

(iii)   **Explain the purpose** of the interview.

(iv)   Explain the organisation's views with regard to the disciplinary issue.

(v)   Clarify the organisation's expectations with regard to future behaviour. For example, there must be no repetition of a particular offence, or performance in a particular area must improve within a specific timescale.

(vi)   The reasons behind penalties must be explained. Clear warnings must be given about failure to improve against targets.

(vii)   The appeals procedure must be clearly explained.

(viii)   Records must be kept for the personnel file.

Now try Question 2 at the end of the Study Text

BPP)))
PROFESSIONAL EDUCATION

Part B
Managing change

Strategic marketing and change

Syllabus content

- Achieving a stronger market orientation
- Pressures for change and means of response
- The role and content of an internal marketing communications plan and its contribution to managing change

Introduction

Element 2 of your syllabus is concerned with change in organisations and particularly with the role of marketing in managing change. Change has implications for all parts of an organisation and managers at all levels have their parts to play in bringing it about. Strategic management is concerned with change, as is functional management within the marketing department.

We consider several aspects of change in this chapter. In Section 1 we look at the way marketing is often required to drive the re-orientation of the organisation to a closer focus on its markets and the reciprocal effect this has on the marketing function. Section 2 looks more closely at market-influenced drivers of change and how change management may be approached. Finally, in Section 3, we look at the role of internal marketing communications.

1 Strategic marketing orientation

A **market** is a group of customers. **Marketing** is a process or activity. As you probably know, the CIM defines marketing as 'the management process responsible for identifying, anticipating and satisfying customer requirements profitably.' The **American Marketing Association's** definition is: 'The process of planning and executing the conception, pricing, promotion, and distribution of ideas, goods and services to create exchanges that satisfy individual and organisational goals.'

Note that the AMA definition includes **ideas**. This has some important implications.

(a) **Ideas** can be intellectual property, such as software and so forth, which can be sold as products. Marketing is not limited to FMCG products.

(b) Many industries are **knowledge-based industries**. The ability to tap knowledge and create ideas might be instrumental in corporate success, as might be the ability to communicate these ideas.

(c) Ideas can include **information** that will help customers determine whether the product will, in fact, be able to satisfy their needs.

Marketing can also refer to a department within an organisation, with its own professional staff with specialist expertise, and **potential** interests in terms of other business functions.

1.1 Marketing-led and market-led orientation

FAST FORWARD

A **market-led firm** is a company in which everyone puts the customer at the centre of decision-making. The customer is not owned by the marketing department.

Elements of a **market-orientation** include culture, capabilities, organisation, and strategic thinking.

Marketing personnel are catalysts in generating a market-orientation and promoting market-led strategic change.

Barriers to being market-led mainly rest in the way the business is run.

Given that marketing is a process, an organisational function, and an academic discipline, it is worth going back to first principles. A market is a customer or a group of customers.

Key concept

Market orientation is 'an organisational culture where beating the competition through the creation of superior customer value is the paramount objective throughout the business'. (Piercy, *Market Led Strategic Change*, 2001)

A **marketing-led organisation is led by the marketing department**. Marketing orientation might just refer to increased power for marketing personnel. The customer, however, is not necessarily at the heart of **everyone's** thinking.

In a company with a market orientation, the aim of **providing superior customer value** dominates all thinking.

- What the business is
- Which markets to service
- Investments and acquisitions
- Which people to employ and how to promote them

In **market-led** organisations, the marketing department is not in a world of its own. Customer value is designed and created by **multi-function** product teams supporting **all the business functions**. Piercy suggests that marketing should be a philosophy that pervades the organisation so that 'marketing' would still go on even if the 'marketing department' were to disappear.

Focusing on customers and their needs is something which should be your meat and drink. Hooley *et al* (*Marketing Strategy and Competitive Positioning*) identify the following components of a market orientation.

- **Customers**: know them well enough to give superior value.
- **Competition**: what are their short– and long-term capabilities?
- **Inter-functional**: mobilise the entire company to create superior customer value.
- **Culture**: employee behaviour should be managed to ensure customer satisfaction.
- **Long term profit focus**: have a strategic but realistic vision.

Marketing expertise and personnel are important drivers in taking a firm to the customer, as the example below suggests.

Marketing at Work

Waterford Wedgwood/Royal Doulton

From *Financial Times*, 1 May 2001

Royal Doulton, one of the great names in British ceramics, is shrinking to survive. The contraction of Royal Doulton, which is based in Stoke-on-Trent, mirrors a decline in the whole Staffordshire ceramics industry.

Wedgwood, Royal Doulton's main rival, seems curiously insulated from the pain.

The business, a division of Waterford Wedgwood, the Irish luxury goods group chaired by Sir Anthony O'Reilly, made operating profits last year of €18.7m (£11.6m). This compared with a loss of £9.6m at Royal Doulton. Wedgwood's sales were a third higher than its rival, while its workforce was two-thirds smaller.

Redmond O'Donoghue, Waterford Wedgwood's genial president, frets that its shares trade on a prospective p/e of about 12 compared to multiples of some more than 20 for luxury goods business such as Bulgari, Tiffany and LVMH. That Mr O'Donoghue can afford such aspirational worries is partly the result of Waterford Wedgwood's revamp of its ceramics division in the late 1990s. At the time, it was sharply criticised by some analysts for investing about £30m in automating what many saw as a dying business.

But the move was justified by revival in sales, triggered by the reinvention of the previously fusty Wedgwood brand using experience and knowledge gained in the Waterford glassware business. Independent designers, such as Paul Costellow, brought their own followings to the brand, as well as fresh design thinking.

Marketing, not production, now drives the business. The Duchess of York, retained expensively for a few day's work a year, has proved an improbably potent ambassador for the brand in the US.

Waterford Wedgwood's glossy magazine includes interviews with Washington socialites and features on vacations in the Hamptons.

The next fundamental shift, says Mr O'Donoghue, is for Wedgwood to crank up its sales in giftware, as Waterford has already done.

Website addresses

www.wedgwood.co.uk   www.royal-doulton.com

1.2 Market-led strategic management

Market-led strategic management rests on the following assumptions (Piercy, 2001).

Assumptions	Application in Wedgwood and Royal Doulton
All organisations must follow the dictates of the market to survive.	Risk of relying on current tableware market. Company had to find new customers.
Organisational effectiveness can be pursued by being market-led, focusing on the customer.	Winning sales at all costs. The firm needed **marketing** knowledge and implementation skills, by reinventing Wedgwood Brand.
Barriers to being market-led come, not from ignorance of customer characteristics, but from the way organisations are run.	Experience in one part of the business was applied elsewhere. There must have been good communications to ensure knowledge transfer.
Becoming market-led often needs an upheaval.	New designers, and more resources focused on the customer communications.
Deep seated strategic change, not just hiring a marketing executive.	Change from providing tableware to offering giftware.

In short the pursuit of **customer satisfaction** is at the heart of the market-led company. *Piercy* makes a distinction between **marketing** and **going to market**. Markets are more important than marketing, *per se*, and markets and customers are important for everyone in a company (not just the marketing department). '**Going to market** is a process owned by everyone in the organisation … the context for marketing should be the **process** of going to market, not the marketing department.'

According to Piercy, the process of going to market needs to be **managed**.

(a)   **Strategies** are based on customers and markets.

(b)   **Internal programmes** and **external actions** are driven by such strategies.

(c)   The company must **deliver its strategy** into the market. This involves more than the marketing department.

(d)   **Cross-functional teams** cross organisational boundaries to get the job done.

(e)   New types of **relationships** are created.

(f)   New ways of doing business are supported by a new **information technology** infrastructure.

1.3 Challenges for the market-led organisation

Four broad issues arise for the market-led organisation (Piercy, 2001).

Issue	Comment
New customers	• **Rising expectations**: customers exposed to world class service will expect it everywhere • **Sophistication**: customers can see through marketing-speak, and want transparency • Increased **cynicism** about marketing
New competitors	• From **overseas** • **Reinventing** the business (eg Direct Line Insurance)
New types of organisation	• **Outsourcing** arrangements • **Collaboration** arrangements • **Alliances** (eg airlines) • **Stakeholder** influences
New ways of doing business	• **Customer-specific** marketing • **Databases** are used to develop profiles of individual customers to entice them into a **relationship** • **Internet marketing**: buyers and sellers can conduct a dialogue as the Internet is interactive • **Customer co-operatives**: Internet newsgroups and chatrooms enable customers to get together perhaps to negotiate discounts or to share experience of a brand

1.4 Role of marketing in market-led firms

FAST FORWARD

The role of marketing has changed from being an isolated, specialist staff department to being **integrated** with line management, **widespread** in the organisation and involved in strategic decision making.

What might be the role of marketing and marketing management in this particular context? *Kashani* (*Financial Times*, *Mastering Management* series) argues that the role of marketing has changed significantly but has also become much more important to the activities of many firms. The changes he notes are these.

(a) **From staff to line**. Marketing thinking and action are better integrated into the day-to-day decisions of managers running important parts of the business. In other words, instead of a separate, staff marketing department going its own way and putting a promotional gloss on what the organisation does, marketing is more involved in line decisions, such as segment or product management.

(b) **From specialist to strategic**. 'Marketing in the organisation has evolved beyond its traditional specialist focus. Tasks once exclusively associated with marketing, such as market and competitive assessment or end-user communication, are now only a part of a far more integrated marketing process that may include other functions such as upstream product development or downstream management of distribution.'

(c) **From isolated to widespread**. Marketing has become more diffused within the organisation, and is no longer the concern of the few. In short, Kashani argues, the market orientation is spreading.

(i)   'Companies are inculcating their managers in various back office functions with market and customer-mindedness – the very attributes that were the exclusive domain of marketing people.

(ii) A widespread appreciation of market forces and customer needs and how parts of an organisation may contribute to creating a superior customer value is a necessity if the entire organisation is to become market responsive.'

 Marketing at Work

Marketing Business described change in the financial services sector. In a service business such as the Halifax, group marketing staff report to a main board director who is head of personnel. This is because service businesses are people businesses, and 'in a corporate brand, the brand is everybody and the brand strategy is the corporate strategy'.

Website address: www.halifax.co.uk

Exam tip

It is worth emphasising that this paper is about strategy rather than the design of tactical marketing programmes. The list below, Piercy (2001), covers some of the issues.

• Customers: does the firm take customers seriously and work for customer satisfaction? How do you create a customer-focused organisation?

• How are markets defined and segmented around issues that matter to customers?

• How do we create a value proposition based on our mission and our ability to differentiate from competitors?

 Action Programme 1

An IMD survey put 'knowledge of other [business] functions beyond marketing' as fairly low on the list (4th from bottom). Given that this survey covered only marketing managers, how significant do you think it is that they seem relatively unconcerned with understanding other business functions such as the production department and the finance department? Do they know enough already, or do you think a failure to understand how the rest of the organisation works could be a weakness, especially given that a market-led company embodies everybody?

1.5 Role of marketing in strategic management: summary

Step 1   Identify customer requirements and disseminate information

Step 2   Determine competitive positioning (matching customer needs with organisational resources)

Step 3   Implement the strategy to deliver satisfaction. Internal marketing is needed here

1.6 Theory or practice?

There are many doubts as to whether the marketing concept is followed in practice and the degree to which firms are in fact market orientated.

The **marketing orientation checklist** (adapted from Wilson, Gilligan and Pearson) shows how a firm can assess how far it has a marketing orientation.

		High	Medium	Low
1	Understanding of customer needs throughout the organisation			
2	Profit-maximising, not sales-volume chasing			
3	Chief executive is the voice of the customer			
4	Market-driven mission			
5	Strategies reflect the market			
6	Marketing seen as more important than other functions			
7	Responsiveness to marketing opportunities			
8	Good MkIS			
9	Use of marketing research			
10	Analysis of marketing revenues/costs			
11	Link between marketing and NPD			
12	Are marketing staff market-orientated, not just sales orientated?			
13	Marketing seen as everyone's responsibility			
14	Co-ordinated and integrated marketing decisions			

1.7 A model of organisational effectiveness

FAST FORWARD

The **7S model** illustrates the various aspects of the organisation's functioning. Culture and **culture change** are particularly important in the development of a marketing orientation.

A useful model which will help integrate various aspects of the internal functioning of the organisation is the 7S framework, developed by *McKinsey*.

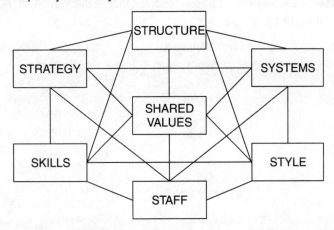

'S'	Description
Structure	How the organisation is arranged into departments
Systems	How the organisation carries out its operations and processes information
Style	Organisation culture, how it presents itself to the world
Staff/Skills	How individual skills are deployed to meet corporate objectives
Strategy	The organisation's business and competitive strategies
Shared values	How people feel about the organisation and its mission

Structure, strategy, systems are relatively 'hard' in that they are easy to define and quantify. The other Ss – shared values, skills, style and staff – are harder to quantify.

Developing a strategic marketing orientation can involve **changing the culture** of the organisation and requires the support of top management.

Step 1   Get top management commitment to introducing strategic marketing orientation (SMO)

Step 2   Specify mission, objectives and resources for introducing SMO

Step 3   Set up a task force

- Identify current orientation
- Identify **needs analysis** to change orientation
- Implement training and management development programmes

Step 4   Monitor marketing effectiveness to maintain momentum

We will return to the 7S model in a later chapter.

2 Marketing and change

Marketers need to attend to the **strategic triangle**: customers, competitors and the company (and its stakeholders). **Challenges** are new customer expectations, new competitors and ways of doing business, and new types of organisation.

2.1 Marketing and the strategic triangle

An IMD survey identified **competition** as a major worry for marketing managers. The reason why businesses and firms need a competitive orientation is that customers have a choice, and they can compare the firm's offering with what competitors are offering.

Given that the marketing orientation needs to be present in all the areas of the organisation, we are led to *Ohmae's* strategic triangle: **company**, **competitors** and **customers**.

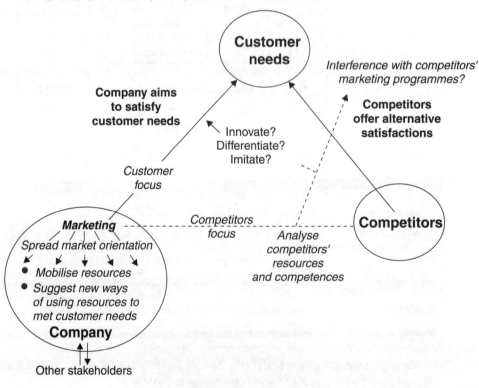

Exam tip

> Competition is explicit or implicit in many questions. For example, in June 2000, you had to identify strategic options in a developing price war. However head-to-head battling is not what is always needed. Developing a position away from competitors is as valid as beating them, hence attention should be paid to competitor positioning.

All organisations are subject to increasing change. It has been said that change is the only business certainty. It follows that the possibility of change should be incorporated in every business strategy. *Drummond and Ensor* (*Strategic Marketing Planning and Control,* 1999) pose the following questions about this.

(a) **What drives change?** An analysis of PEST forces is useful here (political, economic, social and technological).

(b) **How does change impact on our business environment?** Even the most mature and traditional markets may change with customer needs and expectations. *Marks & Spencer* has suffered from a shift in the middle market of fashion retailing, as customers become increasingly polarised between 'designer' and 'value' outlets. Intense competition and shorter product life cycles make it difficult to predict the future.

(c) **What is the result of change on the organisation's strategy?** Change brings opportunities for those companies that are willing and able to take them, and also implies that old ways of doing business (however well they served the company in the past) must be reassessed to reflect the new needs of the marketplace.

2.2 Looking at the future

It is worth having a look at how certain trends might affect how things will appear in a few years' time. When introducing the *Financial Times Mastering Marketing* series, *Kotler* made the following predictions for 2005.

Trend	Comment
Disintermediation	All products can be bought off in the Internet, meaning that there is less need for intermediaries
Retailers	Simple shopping is out, as people can buy supplies over the Internet. Shops become entertainment venues (eg bookshops with coffee shops)
Mass customisation	Customers can order bespoke products but these can be produced with the efficiency of mass production
Data mining	Firms get more information about customers and use it for cross selling
Management information	Real information about customer profitability can be obtained
Long-term supplies	Customers will be offered life-time supplies
Outsourcing	This will be the norm
Franchising	Most field sales people will become franchisees
End of mass TV	TV advertising takes on the characteristics of magazine advertising, with a proliferation of TV and Internet channels made possible with digital TV
Sustainable competitive advantages	Benchmarking, reverse engineering and technological leapfrogging

Have any of these predictions come about? Do you think progress is being made towards any of them? Do any seem to have been overtaken by events?

Exam tip

> New developments were covered explicitly in an essay question set in December 1997 in the old syllabus. However, such developments, especially in relation to IT, can be brought into any question. Before you get carried away, you must bear in mind that change, particularly in relation to technology, moves at different paces in different market segments. So, for example, despite the Internet, marketers will still have to address people who are afraid of, or not interested in, new technology.

2.3 Marketing in non-profit-making organisations

Governments and **non-profit-making organisations** might adopt a marketing orientation to achieve their objectives more effectively. The marketer's skills are relevant but the 'profit' aspect of marketing is absent.

(a)   Governments wish to promote or discourage certain activities or attitudes.

(b)   The main purpose of a non-profit-making organisation will be to satisfy the needs and wants of a group or section of a community.

Action Programme 2

What would be the effects of introducing a marketing approach to a charity?

Non-profit marketing differs from marketing for profit.

(a)   Whereas marketers in a profit-making organisation can focus mainly on customers, many non-profit-making organisations have two major publics that they must satisfy.

  • **Donors** (who provide the funds, the **customers**)
  • **Beneficiaries** (the **consumers**)

(b)   Whereas profit-making organisations can work primarily towards a profit objective, non-profit-making organisations are likely to have **complex multiple objectives**, which are hard to measure.

(c)   Non-profit-making organisations often come under more **public scrutiny** than profit-making organisations.

2.4 Managing change

FAST FORWARD

> **Management of change** is likely to be a continuing imperative for all managers, **human factors** are particularly influential in determining the degree of success achieved by any programme of change.

It is management's responsibility to prepare the organisation for the future. We have also seen that the future will inevitably bring change. Organisations have to adapt and modify if they are to survive in the environment of the future. We have already seen how **strategic management** and corporate planning are essential in identifying and meeting needs, both **for** change and those brought about **by** change. Change in the environment creates opportunities and threats: the organisation must respond with internal change in order to maximise its strengths and minimise its weaknesses.

BPP
PROFESSIONAL EDUCATION

2.4.1 Aspects of change

Aspect	Comment
The environment	These could be changes in what competitors are doing, what customers are buying, how they spend their money, changes in the law, changes in social behaviour and attitudes and economic changes.
The products the organisation makes, or the services it provides	These are made in response to changes in customer demands, competitors' actions and new technology.
How products are made (or services provided), by whom, working methods	These changes are also in response to environmental change, for example new technology and new laws on safety at work.
Management, working relationships and corporate culture	These include changes in leadership style, and in the way that employees are encouraged to work together. Changes in training and staff development are also relevant here.
Organisation structure or size	These might involve creating new departments and divisions, greater delegation of authority or more centralisation, changes in the way that plans are made, management information is provided and control is exercised.

2.4.2 Evaluating the effectiveness of change management

(a) The **impact of the change on attainment of organisational goals**: has the change contributed to the overall objectives of the organisation as defined by the corporate plan?

(b) The success of the change in meeting its **specified objective** (and short-term targets set for progress measurement): has the change solved the problem?

(c) The **behaviour of people in the organisation**: has the change programme resulted in the behavioural changes planned (for example, higher output, better teamwork, more attention to customer care)?

(d) The **reaction of the people** in the organisation: has the change programme been implemented without arousing hostility, fear or conflict, and their symptoms, such as absenteeism and increased labour turnover etc?

2.4.3 Reasons why an organisation might fail to manage change successfully

(a) **Failure to identify the need to change** (typically a failure to pay attention to change in the environment).

(b) **Failure to identify the objectives of change**, so that the wrong areas are addressed.

(c) **Failure to identify correctly the strategy required**, out of all the options, to achieve the objectives. The result is that change takes place, but not in the relevant direction. New technology, for example, is sometimes regarded as a universal solution to organisational problems, but it will not necessarily improve productivity or profitability if the product/market strategy or the workforce is the real problem.

(d) **Failure to commit sufficient resources** to the strategy.

(e) **Failure to identify the appropriate method of implementing change**, for the situation and the people involved (typically, failing to anticipate resistance to change).

(f)   **Failure to implement the change in a way that secures acceptance**, because of the leadership style of the person managing the change (typically, failure to consult and involve employees).

The first four of the above reasons for failure are to do with strategic planning generally: they are potential shortcomings in any planning exercise. The **peculiar difficulties of introducing change, however, are human factors**. When implementing plans or changes, managers must never lose sight of the fact that their success depends on people. **Before commencing their internal marketing of plans, managers must recognise the behavioural factors** which might influence people to welcome or resist change.

We will discuss change management in more detail in the next chapter.

3 Internal marketing

Internal marketing is an important part of the role of marketing, particularly where new ways of working are needed. The concept of the marketing mix may be applied to programmes of internal marketing.

Key concept

Internal marketing is the use of a marketing approach in the internal environment of an organisation, whose employees are seen as customers and have to be persuaded to buy into management ideas.

Internal marketing is particularly important in introducing strategic marketing organisation or in any change. In service industries, the employee is the deliverer of the service (interactive marketing). *Kotler* identifies a **marketing triangle**, which is adapted below.

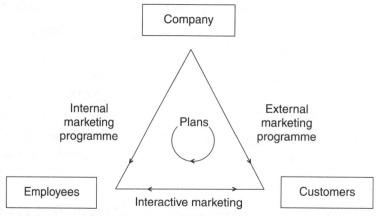

This shows that both the external customer and employees need to be marketed to, but that in a marketing-oriented company the natural planning cycle considers the needs of the external customer first.

Unfortunately, the term **internal marketing**, has been used in a variety of ways. It has, for instance, been adopted in the field of **quality management** where the concept of the internal customer is used to motivate staff towards achieving quality objectives. **In its most common usage, internal marketing means the promotion of a marketing orientation throughout the organisation** and, in particular, creating customer awareness among staff who are not primarily concerned with selling. Hotel housekeeping staff, for instance, may rarely be seen by the guests, but their work makes a major contribution to the guests' perception of their welcome.

The achievement of such a widespread marketing orientation may involve **major changes in working practices and organisational culture**. The successful management of organisational change depends to a great extent upon successful communication and communication is a major marketing activity. 'Internal marketing' has therefore also come to mean the communication aspect of *any* programme of change and, even more simply, **the presentation by management to staff of any information at all**.

3.1 Internal marketing as part of marketing management

If we concentrate on the use of the term to mean the use of marketing approaches and techniques to gain the support and co-operation of other departments and managers for the marketing plan, we will see that a number of challenges may exist. The first is that we may well be looking at a **major cultural shift**. Even in businesses which have highly skilled and motivated sales teams, **there may be areas of the organisation whose culture, aims and practices have nothing to do with customer satisfaction**. Engineering is a good example. The old nationalised industries like British Railways and Post Office Telecommunications saw engineering effectiveness as their major goal, with customer service nowhere. A business which takes this view is unlikely to succeed, but achieving a change of orientation can be a long, difficult and painful process. It will involve a major change in culture and probably entail significant changes to the shape of the organisation, as departments which contribute little to customer service lose influence and shrink or even disappear as the cost base is cut.

3.1.1 Organisational change

(a) Measuring activities against contribution to customer satisfaction means that some areas of the organisation are likely to shrink. The process of **delayering** may be necessary. This utilises modern information technology systems to replace the communications relaying function of middle management. As this activity forms a large part of middle management work, the result is a much reduced requirement for general managers and an increased span of control. A **Total Quality approach** can also lead to staff reductions: if the organisation succeeds in improving initial quality, the need for people to handle complaints, claims and rework is much diminished.

(b) At the same time as these changes are being made, front-line sales and marketing capability will probably have to be enhanced. This is likely to involve more than just an increase in numbers. New methods of working will be introduced, including working in cross-functional teams. In particular, the natural partner of delayering is **empowerment**. Front line staff will take greater responsibility for delivering customer satisfaction and will be given the necessary authority to do so. Relationship marketing databases and staff will be installed and key account managers appointed.

Such restructuring of the organisation has important human resources management (HRM) implications.

(a) There are likely to be **redundancies**. Staff who cannot adjust to the new methods must be released with proper attention to both the legal requirements relating to redundancy and the organisation's policies on social responsibility.

(b) **Recruitment** will continue, because of natural wastage, but it will probably be necessary to adjust recruitment policy and practice to reflect the new requirements. Recruits must be selected who will be able to absorb the new approach and respond to the necessary training.

(c) **Training** will become a major feature of the change management programme. As well as new recruits, existing staff must be educated in the new methods and approach. The Marketing Department may have an input here, or the task of inculcating the marketing orientation and ideal of customer service may be contracted out to consultants.

Research suggests that although the principles involved may be acknowledged by a large number of companies, **formalised internal marketing programmes in the UK are still fairly uncommon**. Initial findings make several other suggestions.

(a) Internal marketing is **implicit in other strategies** such as quality programmes and customer care initiatives, rather than standing alone as an explicit policy in its own right.

(b)   Where it is practised, internal marketing tends to involve a **core of structured activities** surrounded by less rigorously defined ad hoc practices.

(c)   To operate successfully, internal marketing relies heavily on **good communication** networks.

(d)   Internal marketing is a key factor in **competitive differentiation**.

(e)   Conflicts between functional areas are significantly **reduced** by internal marketing.

(f)   **Internal marketing depends heavily on commitment at the highest level of management, on general, active, widespread co-operation, and on the presence of an open management style.**

 Marketing at Work

Scandinavian Airlines Systems

Companies using this approach to great effect include *Scandinavian Airline Systems*, who have increased the involvement of employees in the decision-making process to achieve the highest levels of satisfaction, empowered them to make decisions appropriate to the requirements of particular customers, and trained them to feel a responsibility towards customers of all kinds. As a consequence, the company culture fosters a caring relationship internally and externally.

3.1.2 Segmenting the internal market

Pursuing the link between internal marketing and change, we may identify **three segments** in the internal market.

(a)   **Supporters** are likely to approve of and gain from proposed change.

(b)   **Opposers** will oppose change, perhaps because it is likely to threaten their position or possibly because of inherent consumerism.

(c)   **Neutrals** have no formed opinion but could go either way.

A similar segmentation may well be possible for internal marketing on other issues, including the development of a marketing orientation.

3.2 The marketing mix for internal marketing

Product under the internal marketing concept is the changing nature of the job.

Price is the balance of psychological **costs and benefits** involved in adopting the new orientation, plus those things which have to be given up in order to carry out the new tasks. Difficulties here relate to the problem of arriving at an accurate and adequate evaluation of psychological costs. As with any product, there may need to be regulation.

Many of the methods used for communication and **promotion** in external marketing may be employed to motivate employees and influence attitudes and behaviour. HRM practice is beginning to employ techniques, such as multi-media presentations and in-house publications. Presentational skills are borrowed from personal selling techniques, while incentive schemes are being employed to generate changes in employee behaviour.

Poor communication is probably the biggest single failure when instituting change. Communication should be two-way; meetings and discussions to take account of staff's views at an early stage will help implementation later.

Advertising is increasingly used to generate a favourable corporate image amongst employees as well as external customers. Federal Express has the largest corporate television network in the world, with 1,200 sites.

Place for internal marketing means the locations used for meetings or conferences, and physical means such as noticeboards which can be used to announce and deliver policies and training programmes. Appraisal systems are an important means of embedding customer commitment. There is a link with promotion.

Physical evidence is tangible items which facilitate delivery or communication of the product. Quality standards such as ISO 9000, for instance, place great emphasis on documentation. Other tangible elements might involve training material, which would constitute a manifestation of commitment to standards or policies.

Process, which is how a 'customer' actually receives a product, is linked to communication and the medium of training used to promote customer consciousness, as well as to the way in which change is delivered.

Participants are the people involved in producing and delivering the product, and those receiving the product (who may influence the external customer's perceptions) are clearly important within the internal marketing process. Communications must be delivered by someone of the right level of authority in order to achieve the aim. The way in which employees act is strongly influenced by fellow employees, particularly their immediate superiors. Inter-departmental or interfunctional communications are likely to be least effective, because they have equal status or lack the authority to ensure compliance.

Segmentation and marketing research can also be used in internal marketing. In addition to the analysis suggested earlier, employees may be grouped according to their service characteristics, needs, wants or tasks in order to organise the dissemination of a service orientation. Research will monitor the needs and wants of employees, and identify the impact of corporate policies.

3.3 Problems with the internal marketing concept

Even effective use of inwardly directed marketing techniques cannot solve all employee related quality and customer satisfaction problems. **Research clearly shows that actions by the personnel department, or effective programmes of personnel selection and training, are likely to be more effective than marketing based activities**. In the UK retail sector, for example, while many large scale operations have begun Sunday trading, there has been significant resistance from employee organisations. Internal marketing would argue that employees should be persuaded by means of a well-executed communications campaign and by the offer of proper incentives. Although these strategies have been tried, they have met with little success, or, in the case of incentives, have been too expensive. Employers have solved the problem by specifically recruiting employees who are required to work on Sunday, and who may be paid slightly higher wage rates for the time in question. **Rather than internal marketing, external recruitment proved to be the solution.**

Claims by marketers such as *George*, *Berry* and *Parasuraman*, that marketing can replace or fulfil the objectives of some other functions are clearly overstated. However, the internal marketing concept has a major role to play in making employees customer conscious. The most effective and widely adopted programme at the moment appears to be TQM, although there are very few models of how internal marketing should be implemented currently available.

Exam tip

Past exam questions on internal marketing have covered internal marketing in large service organisations – banks and accounting firms. This could be significant. In such businesses, internal marketing may be essential to achieve a successful 'people' element of the service marketing mix.

Chapter Roundup

- A **market-led firm** is a company in which everyone puts the customer at the centre of decision-making. The customer is not owned by the marketing department.

- Elements of a **market-orientation** include culture, capabilities, organisation, and strategic thinking.

- **Marketing personnel are catalysts** in generating a market-orientation and promoting market-led strategic change.

- **Barriers** to being market-led mainly rest in the way the business is run.

- The role of marketing has changed from being an isolated, specialist staff department to being **integrated** with line management, **widespread** in the organisation and involved in strategic decision making.

- The **7S model** illustrates the various aspects of the organisation's functioning. Culture and **culture change** are particularly important in the development of a marketing orientation.

- Marketers need to attend to the **strategic triangle**: customers, competitors and the company (and its stakeholders). **Challenges** are new customer expectations, new competitors and ways of doing business, and new types of organisation.

- **Management of change** is likely to be a continuing imperative for all managers, **human factors** are particularly influential in determining the degree of success achieved by any programme of change.

- **Internal marketing** is an important part of the role of marketing, particularly where new ways of working are needed. The concept of the marketing mix may be applied to programmes of internal marketing.

Quick Quiz

1   What is marketing?

2   What is a market orientation?

3   What drives both internal programmes and external actions in the market-oriented organisation?

4   What are the four broad issues for the market led organisation?

5   What changes are likely to occur in the role of marketing as market orientation increases?

6   What makes up Ohmae's strategic triangle?

7   Where is effective change management likely to make an impact?

8   What is internal marketing?

9   What are the probable HRM implications of organisational change involving restructuring?

10 Can internal marketing be substituted for other management activities?

Answers to Quick Quiz

1   The management process responsible for identifying, anticipating and satisfying customer requirements profitably

2   An organisation culture based on the creation of superior customer value

3   Strategies based on the customers and markets

4   New customers, new competitors, new types of organisation and new ways of doing business

5   From staff to line; from specialist to strategic; from isolated to widespread

6   Company, competitors and customers

7   On the attainment of organisational objectives or more specific change objectives; and on the behaviour and reactions of the people in the organisation

8   The use of a marketing approach to the internal organisational environment and, in particular, to the furtherance of management policy

9   Redundancies, recruitment and training

10 No. It is an adjunct to them.

Action Programme Review

1   If market-led strategy is necessary throughout the company, then understanding how other functions in the company work would seem significant – otherwise marketing will be conducted in a vacuum.

2   (a)   The reasons for the organisation's existence should be expressed in terms of the consumer or client.

    (b)   Marketing research should be used to find out:

          (i)   Who needs help, and in what ways, and how satisfactory is the current help provided

          (ii)   Where funds should be raised, and what the best approaches should be

          (iii) Which political figures are susceptible to lobbying and how such lobbying should best be conducted

    (c)   Target markets would be identified for charitable acts, fund-raising and influencing.

    (d)   The charity might also wish to promote an image to the public, perhaps by means of public relations work.

    (e)   The management of the charity will be aware that they are in competition for funds with other charities, and in competition with other ways of spending money in trying to obtain funds from the public. It should organise its 'sales and marketing' systems to raise funds in the most effective way.

          (i)   Many charities now engage in telemarketing.
          (ii)   Many charities have acquired logos – even NHS hospitals have acquired them.

Now try Question 3 at the end of the Study Text

Change management

4

Syllabus content

- Identification and evaluation of sources and technology for overcoming resistance to change
- Planning for change in a marketing department

Introduction

We introduced the idea of **change management** in the previous chapter. Because of its importance, we deal here with this idea in greater detail.

Change is often an outcome of the strategic process, particularly when the environment is dynamic and market conditions are themselves changing. Unfortunately, the human reaction to proposals for change is often one of fear and opposition. Much effort has been expended on attempts to create models for the management of change and some of these are discussed in this chapter.

We also look specifically at cultural change. This is because cultural features like the **paradigm** and management style are frequently obstacles to necessary change in other aspects of the organisation's life and work.

1 Strategic change

FAST FORWARD

Changes occur within the **environment**, **goods/services**, **technology**, **management**, **organisation structure**, and in an organisation's **capacity** to meet them. It may be **incremental** or **transformational** and management may take a **proactive** or **reactive** role.

Some change is **transformational**, that is, extensive and crucial to the organisation.

However, much change is incremental: there is steady development that may, over time, lead to the compete redesign of significant aspects of the organisation.

 Marketing at Work

William Grant and Sons

People Management (September 1996) described how whisky distiller *William Grant and Sons* called on Jack Black, a 'business preacher,' to help a workforce struggling to come to terms with a major **change programme**.

Whisky producers like to emphasise **tradition** in their advertising: the centuries old recipes, the oak casks, the rural landscape around the distillery, the company's colourful founding fathers and their forelock-tugging workers.

William Grant and Sons, the Scottish distiller, in the last three years has put itself through a major programme of change. Until then, the image of tradition would have been nearer the truth. As David Nisbet, HR director at William Grants, puts it: 'We were benignly autocratic and paternalistic. Now we are team-based and non-hierarchical, but getting from one to the other proved difficult.'

The journey started with a **physical move** by the bottling plant and administrative headquarters from Paisley, west Glasgow, to Motherwell, east of the city. At the same time, the company **derecognised most of its unions**, retaining a purely representational agreement with one union at each site. Meanwhile, the whole workforce was being organised into **teams** of between three and 30 people each.

In short, it was the **big bang** approach to the management of change. For the restrained, Calvinist culture that predominated among the workforce, it was a little too much to absorb. To many people, quality circles were infra dig. Nisbet recalls: 'It was like pulling teeth. They sat round in these meetings and nothing happened. They weren't contributing.' What was needed was a massive injection of enthusiasm, an overnight **culture change**. It came from a Scottish consultant who has been making a name for himself over recent years as a kind of business preacher, a saver of commercial souls and the slayer of cynicism.

Jack Black has been described as a cross between Billy Connolly and Billy Graham. It may seem strange that his 'mental fitness programme' could have enthused a workforce in a part of the world where the statement 'it's quite nice' is the ultimate accolade.

Black's programme, Mindstore, synthesises the ideas of many others – including Tony Buzan's mind-mapping techniques, neurolinguistic programming and the theories of Napoleon Hill, one of the first people to analyse leadership qualities – and delivers then in a humorous, chalk-and-talk style, interspersed with paper exercises which each participant does on their lap.

Since Mindstore, according to Nisbet, everyone in the organisation has been looking at their objective-setting. Each team has set three 'Smart goals' and is now moving to what they call 'Winner's goals'.

Initially, the **managers** took the course: then about a third of employees, from all levels, chose to go on it. But a drawback soon became apparent: 'some people still didn't have a positive **attitude to change** and didn't want to go on the course. They were finding it very difficult when their colleagues were coming back from it all fired up, positive and full of enthusiasm. They felt it put more pressure on them, and they were becoming more stressed and fearful.'

This manifested itself as absenteeism and an increase in visit to the occupational health department. The HR director made the decision to make it compulsory to attend Mindstore, despite the fact that the 'only way to really get it into the company culture is to make it mandatory.'

'You tend to find that when a company gives the workforce 'stretching' goals, they usually do that in an environment of fear, so people don't buy it. But if you train the people concerned to understand all this, which is what we do, they will set bigger goals than management would ever come up with.'

Strategy can be seen as a process of adapting the organisation to its environment. This implies that any strategy is likely to require change to take place in the organisation. Further, the necessary rate of change is likely to be determined by the rate of change occurring in the environment. This is not, however, a full picture. While change itself may be divided into two types, **incremental** and **transformational**, so too may the management approach to change be divided into **reactive** and **proactive**. *Johnson and Scholes* suggest the model of change shown below.

Nature of change

	Incremental	Transformational
Proactive	Tuning	Planned
Reactive	Adaptation	Forced

Management role

The importance of the **proactive management** role is that it implies that organisational change may be undertaken *before* it is imposed by events. It may, in fact, result from the process of forecasting and be response to *expected developments.* The organisation that does not take a proactive stance in the matter of change is likely to find itself in the **forced** quadrant of the diagram. **Forced change** is likely to be both painful and fraught with risk.

The failure of much **planned change** to achieve its objectives has led to the idea of **emergent change** in which attention is focused more on understanding the **complexity of the issues** promoting change than on planning and controlling it. This approach is likely to be most effective on the incremental side of the diagram above.

The need for change can affect any aspect of the organisation. The creation of new products and services is an obvious area for change, as is the development of the processes by which they are created and delivered. However, change can also become necessary in the **supporting activities** and **linkages** of the **value chain**, since **core competences** can be developed in these areas.

Inevitably, it is in these more amorphous areas, where human behaviour is of vital importance, that the management of change becomes most important and most difficult. **Cultural change** has been a preoccupation of senior managers for some time, reflecting the need to deliver significant improvements in quality, efficiency and service. We consider this in more detail later on in this chapter.

1.1 Drivers of strategic change

External developments, whether or not forecast, are the most usual drivers of change. These can be analysed using the PEST approach. Change may also be driven by factors **internal to the organisation** including technical, administrative, financial and social developments.

2 Change and the individual

FAST FORWARD

People resist change because of **uncertainty**, **fear**, **lack of confidence**, and a sense of **dissonance**. The success of change can be promoted by taking these factors into account.

2.1 Effect of change on individuals

(a) There may be **physiological changes** in a person's life, both as the natural product of ageing, and as the result of external factors (a change in the pattern of shift-working).

(b) **Circumstantial changes** – living in a new house, establishing new relationships, working to new routines – will involve letting go of things, and learning new ways of doing things.

(c) Change affects individuals **psychologically**.

   (i) **Disorientation** before new circumstances have been assimilated. A new set of models may have to be confronted, if the change involves a new roles set, new milieu, new relationships.

   (ii) **Uncertainty** may lead to **insecurity**, especially acute in changes involving work (staying in employment) and/or fast acclimatisation (a short learning curve may lead to feelings of incapacity).

   (iii) New expectations, challenges and pressures may generate **role stress** in which an individual feels discomfort in the role he or she plays.

   (iv) **Powerlessness**. Change can be particularly threatening if it is perceived as an outside force or agent against which the individual is powerless.

2.2 Resistance to change at work

Resisting change means attempting to preserve the existing state of affairs against pressure to alter it. Despite the possibly traumatic effects of change most people do *not* in fact resist it on these grounds alone. Many people long for change, and have a wealth of ideas about how it should be achieved.

2.2.1 Sources of resistance to change

(a) **Attitudes or beliefs**, perhaps arising from cultural, religious or class influences (for example resistance to changes in the law on Sunday trading)

(b) **Loyalty to a group and its norms**, perhaps with an accompanying rejection of other groups or 'outsiders'

(c) **Habit or past norms**

(d) **Politics** – in the sense of resisting changes that might weaken the power base of the individual or group or strengthen a rival's position. Changes involving increased delegation may be strongly resisted by senior management, for example

(e) **The way in which any change** is put forward and implemented

(f) **Personality**

2.2.2 Immediate causes of resistance in any particular situation

(a) **Self-interest**: if the status quo is perceived to be preferable

(b) **Misunderstanding and distrust**: if the reasons for, or the nature and consequences of, the change have not been made clear

(c) **Contradictory assessments**: disagreement over the likely costs and benefits of the change

(d) **Low tolerance of change itself**: differences in tolerance of ambiguity, uncertainty and challenge to self-concept

2.2.3 Reactions to proposed change

(a) **Acceptance** whether enthusiastic espousal, co-operation, grudging co-operation or resignation

(b) **Indifference**: usually where the change does not directly affect the individual evidence is apathy, lack of interest, inaction

(c) **Passive resistance**: refusal to learn, working to rule; pleas of ignorance or defensiveness; procrastination

(d) **Active resistance**: deliberate 'spoiling', go-slows, deliberate errors, sabotage, absenteeism or strikes

2.2.4 Sequence of adaptation

It has been suggested that the sequence of emotions, known as the 'grief cycle', can be used to analyse the process of **adaptation to change**. This sequence was originally described by *Elizabeth Kübler-Ross* as showing how people react to catastrophic news. The five stages are given below.

- Denial
- Anger
- Bargaining
- Depression
- Acceptance

It is normal for people to got through these stages before beginning the process of adaptation to new circumstances.

Marketing at Work

Whether caused by mergers and acquisitions or the market, change has been at the top of management consciousness in the public and private sectors for a decade. Yet it remains the case that many change programmes will be either a disaster or an expensive joke. A disaster because so often they destroy value, cause share prices to tumble, force talent to walk out of the door, spark destructive rumours in the press and wreck carefully constructed networks. A joke because so often nothing fundamental changes as executives mouth platitudes and make big announcements while everyone else lets them have their fun and carries on exactly as before.

Indeed, in many offices, resistance becomes one of the satisfactions of work. It is common enough to blame 'human forces' for the failure of these initiatives. People do not do what they should, they do not show enthusiasm in the right measure at the right time, they do not buy in. But Jeanie Daniel Duck, who as senior vice-president of The Boston Consulting Group carries a certain battle-bloodied authority about her subject, has taken the understanding of the dynamics of those forces several stages on while serving up a timely, well-judged argument that few executives will care for.

First, change is essentially an emotional proposition. Second, it is very difficult. Third, it involves personal change. Oh, and there's nothing touchy-feely about it, either. There is a kind of silent consensus in business that if anyone disagrees with a management strategy, they are negative, hostile freeloaders who would quarrel with the sun for shinning on them. Ms Duck is withering about such attitudes. Any business leader who seeks to blame failure on people deserves to fail. Managers can have all the commercial logic and strategic vision in the world but if they cannot get employees to understand what they are doing and why, and voluntarily elicit their excitement, forget it.

Stephen Overell, *Financial Times*, 2 May 2001

2.3 Technological change and the working environment

The consequences of **technological changes** are particularly felt in the world of work.

(a) Unskilled and **semi-skilled jobs** will be automated.

(b) **Degrading of old skills**. New skills will be needed, and there will be more pressure on managers to provide training or re-training for staff.

(c) As equipment becomes simpler to use, there could be opportunities for **greater flexibility** in manning, with one worker able to carry out more varied tasks.

(d) Since more jobs will be **part-time**, there will be less need for full-time employees.

(e) Better communications systems, portable computers etc reduce the need for people to work together in an office. There will be more **working at home**.

(f) Working at home is likely to speed up the progression towards 'sub-contracting', and some managers might become self-employed **consultants**.

(g) Improved information systems should help managers to **plan and control** work more effectively.

(h) Better information systems open up opportunities for more **centralisation** of decision making by top management and a **reduced need** for **middle managers**.

BPP
PROFESSIONAL EDUCATION

2.3.1 Areas of concern

Issue	Comment
Job security	The threat of being out of work would unsettle the entire office staff.
Status loss	A new system might result in a loss of status for the individual or department concerned.
Promotions	A new system might damage **career prospects** by reducing the opportunities for promotion.
Social change in the office	Individuals who are used to working together might be separated into different groups, and individuals used to working on their own might be expected to join a group.
Bewilderment	It is easy for individuals to be confused and bewildered by change.
Fear of depersonalisation	Staff may resent losing the ability to introduce the 'human touch' to the work they do.

Marketing at Work

E-mail

Reports in the papers suggest that e-mail enhances informal communications, so much so that use of e-mail for items not directly related to work is a matter for disciplinary procedures.

Other reports are that e-mail is used to avoid personal communications – people have been bullied and even dismissed by e-mail.

3 Models of the change process

FAST FORWARD

Management sometimes must introduce **change** to the organisation. A variety of forces will promote or resist the change. **Lewin's force field analysis** shows the forces driving and restraining change. It illustrates the idea that weakening the restraining forces is probably more appropriate than overwhelming them.

3.1 Managing change

3.1.1 Force field analysis

Kurt Lewin developed a simple technique of visualising the change process called **force field analysis**. In any group or organisational situation there is an interplay of driving and restraining forces. The balance between them keeps things as they are. The example below describes a public sector organisation whose management are introducing a performance review system.

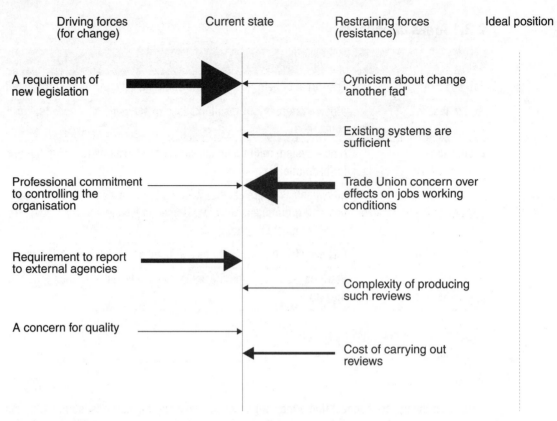

| Driving forces (for change) | Current state | Restraining forces (resistance) | Ideal position |

- A requirement of new legislation
- Cynicism about change 'another fad'
- Existing systems are sufficient
- Professional commitment to controlling the organisation
- Trade Union concern over effects on jobs working conditions
- Requirement to report to external agencies
- Complexity of producing such reviews
- A concern for quality
- Cost of carrying out reviews

Forces can be impersonal (eg a new law, new technology), personal (the commitment of a new leader), institutional (trade union), or environmental (competitors). Lines of varying thickness to represent the probable strength of different forces.

The force field model suggests two ways of dealing with change.

(a)   **Strengthening driving forces**. People associated with the driving forces can be co-opted to 'educate opponents'.

(b)   **Weakening the opposing forces**

- Persuasion (eg getting endorsement by a supposedly neutral consultant)
- Concessions – buying people off
- Involving people in diagnosing problem situations (eg in quality circles)
- Coercion

Generally, it will be more productive to weaken the opposing forces that to force change past them.

3.1.2 Planned change

A **systematic approach** should be established, for planning and implementing changes.

Step 1   **Exploration**. Determine need or desire for change in a particular area. The objectives must be clear. Allocate resources and establish change project team.

Step 2   **Planning**. Prepare a tentative plan. Brainstorming sessions are a good idea, since alternatives for change should be considered. Search for information. Analyse probable reactions to the change. Gain support of key decision makers. Make a final decision from the choice of alternative options. Establish a timetable for change

- Coerced changes can probably be implemented faster, without time for discussions.

- The speed of implementation that is achievable will depend on the likely reactions of the people affected.

- Identify those in favour of the change, and perhaps set up a pilot programme involving them. Talk with the others who resist the change.

Step 3   **Communication**. Communicate the plan for change. This is really a continuous process, beginning at Step 1.

Step 4   **Implementation**. Implement the change. Review the change.

Step 5   **Integration**. Carry out continuous evaluation and modification.

3.2 The change process

The **unfreeze-change-refreeze** model emphasises the need to abandon old ways.

In the words of *John Hunt* (*Managing People at Work*): 'Learning also involves re-learning – not merely learning something new but trying to unlearn what is already known.' This is, in a nutshell, the thinking behind *Lewin and Schein's* three stage approach to changing human behaviour, which may be depicted as follows.

UNFREEZE existing behaviour $\longrightarrow$ Attitudinal/ behavioural change $\longrightarrow$ REFREEZE new behaviour

Step 1   **Unfreeze** is the most difficult stage of the process, concerned mainly with 'selling' the change, with giving individuals or groups a **motive** for changing their attitudes, values, behaviour, systems or structures.

(a)   If the need for change is immediate, clear and necessary for the survival of the individual or group, the unfreeze stage will be greatly accelerated.

(b)   Routine changes may be harder to sell if they are perceived to be unimportant and not survival-based.

(c)   Unfreezing processes need four things

- A trigger (eg a crisis).
- Someone to challenge and expose the existing behaviour pattern.
- The involvement of outsiders.
- Alterations to power structure.

Step 2   **Change** is mainly concerned with identifying what the new, desirable behaviour should be, communicating it and encouraging individuals and groups to adopt it. The new ideas must be shown to work. People must be involved and take charge of their own contribution to the change process.

Step 3   **Refreeze** is the final stage, implying consolidation or reinforcement of the new behaviour. Positive reinforcement (praise, reward) or negative reinforcement (sanctions applied to those who deviate from the new behaviour) may be used.

Marketing at Work

In a *Harvard Business Review article*, *Pascale, Milleman and Groga* described change at *Shell Malaysia*. Its new chairman, who arrived in 1992, found an overstaffed organisation, facing declining revenues and increased competition, and offering poorer standards. The functional departments quarrelled a great deal but the culture did not encourage outright confrontation. Their way of dealing with impasses was 'smooth and avoid'.

'For more than a year, Knight (the new chief executive) tried to achieve authentic alignment among his eight-person executive team. Somehow the goal always eluded his grasp. In exasperation, he scheduled an event to which all 260 of Shell's mid-level and senior mangers were invited. At this unusual gathering:

(a) Knight proposed two new strategic changes.

(b) Managers were asked to deal with the issues in groups and come up with a response.

(c) Most lower level managers agreed with the plans, despite the fact they realised that their operating practices would have to change.

(d) This isolated the 'obstructionist' senior managers, one of whom was fired – 'a firing heard round the world'.

3.3 Strategies for change management

Peter Honey (quoted by *Robinson* in *Managing after the Superlatives*) suggests that each of the sources of resistance to change identified below can be dealt with in a different way.

Cause	How to deal with it
Parochial self-interest	**Negotiation** (eg offer incentives to those resisting on grounds of self-interest).
Misunderstanding	This is best dealt with by **educating and reassuring** people. Trust has to be earned.
Different viewpoints of the situation	Change can be promoted through participation and by **involving potential resisters**.
Low tolerance of change	Force the change through and then **support** the new behaviours it requires. In short, people have to be encouraged (by carrot and stick methods) to adopt the new methods.

3.4 Champion of change model: the role of the change agent

FAST FORWARD

It may be necessary to appoint a **change agent** who, with the public support of senior management, must promote the change to managers and workers, and ensure they implement it.

The **champion of change model** recognises the importance of change being led by a **change agent**, who may be an individual or occasionally a group.

Step 1 **Senior management** are the **change strategists** and decide in broad terms what is to be done. There is a need for **powerful advocacy** for change at the strategic apex. This will only occur if senior management are themselves agreed on the need for change. This is a role requiring a clear **vision** of what the change is to achieve.

Step 2 They appoint a **change agent** to drive it through. Senior management has three roles.

- Supporting the change agent, if the change provokes conflict between the agent and interest groups in the organisation

- Reviewing and monitoring the progress of the change

- Endorsing and approving the changes, and ensuring that they are publicised

Step 3   The change agent has to **win the support of functional and operational managers**, who have to introduce and enforce the changes in their own departments. The champion of change has to provide advice and information, as well as evidence that the old ways are no longer acceptable.

Step 4   The change agent **galvanises managers into action** and gives them any necessary support. The managers ensure that the changes are implemented operationally, in the field. Where changes involve, say, a new approach to customer care, it is the workers who are responsible for ensuring the effectiveness of the change process.

It is important to realise that successful change is not something exclusively imposed from above. There is a sense in which middle and junior managers are **change recipients** in that they are required to implement new approaches and methods. However, they are themselves also **change agents** within their own spheres of responsibility. They must be committed parts of the change process if it is to succeed.

New information systems developments often need management support and a management sponsor.

4 Overcoming resistance to change

FAST FORWARD

Managing **resistance** to change requires consideration of the **pace**, **manner** and **scope** of the change.

When dealing with resistance to change, managers should consider three aspects of the change.

- Pace
- Manner
- Scope

4.1 Pace of change

The more gradual the change, the **more time** is available for questions to be asked, reassurances to be given and retraining (where necessary) embarked upon.

Presenting the individual concerned with a *fait accompli* ('Let's get it over with – they'll just have to get used to it!') may short-circuit resistance at the planning and immediate implementation stages. It may cause problems later.

4.2 The manner of change

The **manner** in which a change is put across is very important.

(a)   **Confront resistance**. Talking through areas of conflict may lead to useful insights and the adapting of the programme of change to advantage.

(b)   **Keep people informed**. Information should be sensible, clear, consistent and realistic: there is no point issuing information which will be seen as a blatant misrepresentation of the situation.

(c)   **Explanation**. The change can be sold to the people: people can be convinced that their attitudes and behaviours need changing.

(d)   **Skills training**. Learning programmes for any new skills or systems necessary will have to be designed according to the abilities, previous learning experience etc of the individuals concerned.

(e)   **Empathy**. Getting to know the people involved in and affected by changes enables their reactions to be anticipated.

(f)   The degree to which **consultation or participation** will be possible (or genuine) will depend on management's attitude towards the competence and trustworthiness of its workforce.

PART B   MANAGING CHANGE

When to start participation	**How participation is achieved in practice**
(a) From the beginning, discuss ideas. Gradually, acceptable ideas will emerge.	The desire of the manager for participation must be genuine. It won't work if' participation is something the top orders the middle to do from the bottom'. (*Kanter* 1983)
(b) Make tentative plans for change, and then start to discuss them with subordinates.	1. Ask for input of ideas.
(c) Decide to make a change and then try to sell the idea to subordinates.	2. Seriously consider input and evaluate it objectively.
	3. Use good ideas.
Approaches (a) or (b) are preferred for real participation.	4. Reject bad ideas.
	5. Give credit/rewards to providers of good ideas.
	6. Convince the providers of bad ideas that their ideas were bad.

4.2.1 Coercion

Explicit or implicit **coercion**, that is, **autocratic** or **unilateral** imposition of change can be effective in some cases.

(a)   Behavioural change or **compliance** is all that is required, and where resistance in attitudes can have no significantly detrimental effect on performance.

(b)   The **balance of power** is heavily weighted in favour of the change agent.

(c)   The **prevailing culture** is one of acceptance of dictatorial change, and there is little expectation of anything else.

4.3 Scope of change

The **scope of change** should also be carefully reviewed.

(a)   **Total transformation** will create greater insecurity – but also greater excitement, if the organisation has the kind of innovative culture that can stand it – than moderate innovation.

(b)   There may be **hidden changes** to take into account: a change in technology may necessitate changes in work methods, which may in turn result in the breaking up of work groups.

(c)   Management should be aware of **how many different aspects** of their employees' lives they are proposing to alter – and therefore on how many fronts they are likely to encounter resistance.

 Marketing at Work

The famous research by *Coch and French* into resistance to change in a pyjama factory provides evidence in favour of consultation. The company faced resistance to frequent changes to jobs and work methods necessitated by the product and production method development. This resistance showed in pay complaints, absenteeism and leaving, low efficiency (despite financial incentives), restriction of output and hostility to management. The main problem was that changes and transfers led to loss of status and earnings, through reduced efficiency ratings.

Coch and French designed an experiment in which changes were introduced in three production groups with different levels of participation.

106

(a)   The *non-participative group* was informed about the change but not involved in the decision-making. Resistance was immediate; conflict flared, efficiency remained low, and some members left.

(b)   The *representative group* was given a hand in the change to the extent that after a preliminary meeting of explanation, representatives were given appropriate training and subsequently trained fellow members. The group was co-operative and submissive and efficiency rose rapidly.

(c)   The *total participation group* also had a preliminary meeting, but all members then took part in the design and standard-setting for the new job. The group recovered its efficiency rating very rapidly, and to a level much higher than before the change, without conflict or resignations.

(d)   The *non-participative members* were later re-grouped and followed the total participation procedure – with the beneficial results of the latter. Coch and French concluded that it was not the people or personality factors that mattered, but the *way in which change was implemented*.

4.4 Acceptance

It takes time for changes to get accepted, in other words the 'Refreeze' steps. *Conner and Patterson* identified three phases and eight stages in the process of accepting change by the people affected.

Phase 1: Preparation phase

Stage 1	Contact	First knowledge that a change is imminent
Stage 2	Awareness	Knowledge that change will happen

Phase 2: Acceptance phase

Stage 3	Understanding	Gaining an understanding of the nature and purpose of the change
Stage 4	Positive perception	Developing a positive view towards the change, and accepting the need for it

Phase 3: Commitment phase

Stage 5	Installation	The change becomes operational
Stage 6	Adoption	The change has been in force for long enough and its value has become apparent
Stage 7	Institutionalisation	The change has been in for long enough to become routine and the norm
Stage 8	Internalisation	Individuals are highly committed to the change because it is now congruent with their personal interests, goals and value systems.

Conner and Patterson argued that **commitment** to change is necessary for its successful implementation.

(a)   Getting commitment is **expensive**, and calls for an investment of time, effort and money, for instance providing information, involving subordinates in the planning and implementation process, rewarding them for their participation and so on.

(b)   Strategies for commitment ought to be developed. For any change, management needs to decide how far through the eight stages the acceptance process needs to go. Some changes can stop at Stage 5; other must go to Stage 7 or Stage 8, otherwise the benefits of the change will be lost.

5 Changing corporate culture

FAST FORWARD

Cultural change is difficult and likely to be time-consuming. It requires an understanding of what the prevailing culture is and why it exists. Leadership, communication and training are essential elements.

Any programme of cultural change involves identifying and exposing three things.

- The hidden assumptions of the new culture
- The conflicts hidden in the culture
- Cultural mechanisms for change

'Changing a culture to increase a corporation's effectiveness is a hazardous undertaking,' says *Hampden-Turner*. He recommends a number of steps that senior managers, perhaps with the advice of management consultants, should take.

Step 1   **Find the dangers**. The best way to find out about how a culture works is to violate it, by doing something culturally shocking.

Step 2   **Bring conflicts into the open**. Interviewing and observation are the principal tools of cultural investigation. Interviews identify what people believe as *individuals*, as opposed to what they affirm as *employees*.

Step 3   **Play out corporate dramas**. The manager or consultant then discusses the culture with its members. 'A repressive culture may simply deny that remarks qualifying or criticising it were ever made.' 'A narrow or low context culture may agree that such remarks were made, but treat them as the utterances of private persons, irrelevant to the common task.' This can result in heated, but hopefully constructive argument.

Step 4   **Reinterpret the corporate myths**. Corporate stories passed round to recruits indicates something about competing value systems. Sometimes these corporate myths have to change. Hampden-Turner cites the experiences of Volvo in France. The French sales force considered the cars they were selling to be boring: after a long trip to Sweden, when they were shown around the factories, they changed their views.

Step 5   **Look at symbols, images, rituals**. An example quoted by Hampden-Turner is 'PepsiCo', where every month there is a formal meeting comparing Pepsi's sales with Coca-Cola's. Rituals are used to celebrate achievement, or to mark changes (eg in a merger): 'changing a corporate culture can mean that new symbols, rituals and approaches are devised.'

Step 6   **Create a new learning system**. Cultures filter and exclude information. They need to be modified to accept new types of data.

The norms in a culture include attitudes toward performance, teamwork, communication, leadership, profitability, staff relations, customer relations, honesty and security, training and innovation. A consistent approach is needed. Here are some essential features for a programme of cultural change.

- Top management commitment
- Modelling behaviour: managers should practice what they preach
- Support for positive behaviour and confrontation of negative behaviour
- Communication of desired norms
- Recruitment and selection of the right people
- Induction programmes for new employees on the desired norms of behaviour
- Training and skills development

Most research has shown that, in a large organisation, shifting the value system or culture can take between **three and eight years** to bring about. Strong cultures discourage the questioning of their basic assumptions, especially where they have been implemented successfully and reinforced in the recruitment of clones.

Chapter Roundup

- Changes occur within the **environment**, **goods/services**, **technology**, **management**, **organisation structure**, and in an organisation's **capacity** to meet them. It may be **incremental** or **transformational** and management may take a **proactive** or **reactive** role.

- People resist change because of **uncertainty**, **fear**, **lack of confidence**, and a sense of **dissonance**. The success of change can be promoted by taking these factors into account.

- Management sometimes must introduce **change** to the organisation. A variety of forces will promote or resist the change. **Lewin's force field analysis** shows the forces driving and restraining change. It illustrates the idea that weakening the restraining forces is probably more appropriate than overwhelming them.

- The **unfreeze-change-refreeze** model emphasises the need to abandon old ways.

- It may be necessary to appoint a **change agent** who, with the public support of senior management, must promote the change to managers and workers, and ensure they implement it.

- Managing **resistance** to change requires consideration of the **pace**, **manner** and **scope** of the change.

- **Cultural change** is difficult and likely to be time-consuming. It requires an understanding of what the prevailing culture is and why it exists. Leadership, communication and training are essential elements.

Quick Quiz

1   List five areas where change may occur.

2   How may change affect an individual?

3   How do people react to proposed change?

4   What is the Lewin/Schein model?

5   How would you deal with parochial self-interest?

6   What is force field analysis?

7   Is coercion likely to work in a power culture?

Answers to Quick Quiz

1   Environment, products, manufacturing/service processes, management organisation structure/ size

2   Physiologically, psychologically, circumstantially

3   Acceptance, indifference, passive resistance or active resistance

4   Unfreeze-change-refreeze

5   Negotiation, possibly using incentives

6   A visualisation of the forces driving and restraining a change

7   Yes

Now try Question 4 at the end of the Study Text

Part C
Implementing business strategy

5

A framework for implementation

Syllabus content

- The link between marketing activities and shareholder value; and measurement using economic value added
- The contribution of marketing activities to shareholder value
- Methods of valuing brands and building brand equity
- Measuring the financial returns on specific investments in marketing activities
- Assessing the value that marketing activities generate

Introduction

This chapter is concerned to set marketing activity in the context of **creating shareholder value**, which is, or should be, the primary objective of any commercial organisation. 'Shareholder' is to some extent a short-hand term and includes the owners of unincorporated businesses such as sole traders.

Section 1 gives an introduction to **shareholder value analysis** and the need for value based management. This concept is of particular importance to marketing management, since much of their work is concerned with activities that create long-term value but are not recognised by traditional accounting based performance measures.

Section 2 examines in more detail the ways in which shareholder value may be created, while Section 3 looks briefly at the limitations of the approach.

The **building of a brand** is a very good example of the sort of marketing activity that can be assessed by means of SVA. It is also an example of the way that SVA can be used to demonstrate the value of marketing activities in general. Building a brand requires the **long-term commitment** of substantial resources. Normal financial accounting practice would be to charge the costs of these resources against profit in the period in which they were incurred, thus failing to recognise the potential long-term investment value. This approach is clearly detrimental to the development of competitive advantage through marketing activities. In Section 4 we look at the way brand value may be created and measured using the SVA approach.

Since the measurement of shareholder value depends heavily on the **discounting of future cash flows**, this financial arithmetic technique is discussed in detail in the Annex to this chapter.

1 Shareholder value analysis

FAST FORWARD

Shareholder value analysis attempts to measure management and marketing performance by measuring the probable success of proposed action in terms of **economic profit**. Economic profit is created when the return on capital employed exceeds the cost of that capital.

Shareholder value analysis (SVA) is a method of approaching the problem of business control by focussing on the **creation of value for shareholders**. Independent financial analysts measure the value offered by a company's shares by considering the **market value** of all the shares in existence (the **market capitalisation**), in the light of the **company's prospects** for generating both cash and capital growth in the future. If the current market capitalisation is less than the estimate of actual value, then the shares are undervalued. Investment is necessary to produce either assets that grow in value or actual cash surpluses, so the process of shareholder value analysis is essentially one of estimating the likely effectiveness of the company's **current investment decisions**. It is thus both a system for judging the worth of current investment proposals and for judging the performance of the managers who are responsible for the company's performance.

In the past, marketing managers have tended to pursue purely **marketing objectives**, such as sales growth, market share, customer satisfaction and brand recognition. None of these marketing objectives *necessarily* translates into increased shareholder value, and as a result, marketing has suffered from a **lack of perceived relevance** to true business value. An emphasis on profitability as a measure of success has led to a certain amount of short-termism in strategic management, with an emphasis on **containing and reducing current costs** in order to **boost current profits**. Unfortunately, this approach tends to underestimate the longer-term effect of such action and can lead to corporate decline. Investment in **intangible assets** such as brands can make a positive contribution to long-term shareholder value.

1.1 Computing value

Economic profit = NOPAT − (capital employed × cost of capital). Economic profit from future activity can be measured by discounting future cash flows to a **net present value**.

According to *Doyle* (2000), the extent of a company's success may be measured in two ways.

1.1.1 Economic profit

The first is by using the concept of **economic profit** (trademarked by Stern, Stewart and Company as **Economic Value Added®**). The expression *economic profit* is used to distinguish the measure from accounting profit, which is computed according to the strict rules of accountancy. These feature, in particular, the principle of **prudence**. This makes it impossible for **accounting profit** to recognise spending on pure research, for instance, as an investment in an asset, since there is no guarantee that it will ever produce anything worth having; the same would be true of much marketing spending on building long-term effectiveness.

Economic profit is created when the return on a company's capital employed exceeds the cost of that capital.

Economic profit = NOPAT − (capital employed × cost of capital)

where NOPAT is net operating profit after tax.

Cost of capital may be calculated as the **weighted average cost of capital**, which takes account of both the expectations of the shareholders who have provided share capital and the lenders who have provided loans. (Buying shares generally entails greater risk than making a loan, so shareholders generally demand higher returns than lenders. This is why a weighted average figure must be used.)

Economic profit is related to capital employed by **return on capital employed** (ROCE). This is a percentage and may thus be compared directly with cost of capital. When ROCE exceeds the cost of capital (r), economic value is created: under these circumstances (ROCE > r), the company is offering a greater return on capital than is available elsewhere.

1.1.2 Cash flow

Economic profit is useful for examining the company's current and past performance, but is less useful for assessing future prospects. For that purpose it is more appropriate to use the **cash flow approach**. Be aware that both the economic profit method and the cash flow method should produce the same result when applied to a particular company

The **cash flow approach** may be used to estimate the degree of economic value a company may be expected to create in the future. It is based on an estimation of likely future **cash flows**, both positive and negative, as indicated in the corporate plans. (A cash flow is simply a sum of money paid or received by the company.) This is easier to do than to compute future NOPAT, because it is far less complex and depends on far fewer variables.

1.2 Discounting cash flows

The cost of capital depends in part on the degree of risk inherent in the company's operations.

Because the SVA technique depends very much on the estimation of future cash flows arising from current investments, it is necessary to use **discounting arithmetic** in order to make the necessary judgements. Discounting is a fairly specialist financial management technique and you are unlikely to be asked to use it in your exam. However, you need to be aware of it and to understand the principle that it employs, so we provide an explanation in the Annex to this chapter.

Business risk. Some businesses are inherently **riskier** than others: the degree of risk can be measured by the degree of predictability that attaches to its expected cash flows. A low risk business will have steady income from period to period, without any unexpected highs and lows. A high-risk business will have returns that vary wildly and unexpectedly from period to period, though its total long-term return may be as great or greater than the low risk operation. Generally, **investors are risk averse** and, as a result, they demand higher returns from high-risk businesses than from low risk ones. The high-risk business must therefore use a **higher cost of capital** in its shareholder value analysis than the low risk business.

1.3 Value based management

Management should aim to create value and expect to be judged in terms of SVA. Marketing managers must be prepared to use their budgets to create measurable assets in terms of competitive advantage.

Doyle (2003), tells us that business success should be measured by shareholder value analysis because of the property rights of shareholders and the 'pressures to oust management that does not deliver competitive returns'. Purely marketing objectives are no longer acceptable to investors or the analysts whose reports they rely on. What Doyle calls **value based management** is based on three elements.

(a) A **belief** that maximising shareholder returns is the objective of the firm

(b) The **principles**, or strategic foundations of value are first, to target those market segments where profits can be made and second, to develop competitive advantage 'that enables both the customer and the firm to create value'.

(c) The **processes** 'concern how strategies should be developed, resources allocated and performance measured'.

SVA is particularly appropriate for **judging strategic investment decisions** and applies the same principles that have been used for appraising investment in such tangible assets as premises and plant for many years. It is necessary to consider both the **cash costs** of the strategic investment to be made, and the **positive cash flows** that are expected to be produced by it. These may then be discounted to a net present value (NPV) using an appropriate cost of capital, and a judgement made on the basis of the NPV. Any specifically marketing proposal, such as an enhanced advertising spend or a new discount structure may be assessed in this way, though it will almost certainly be necessary to take advice from the finance function on the process.

Estimating the value of such investments forms one part of basic shareholder value analysis. Doyle also recommends that when considering the total value of a business, it is also necessary to consider the probable **residual value** of the business. This is the present value of cash flows in the more distant future, outside the normal planning horizon, which Doyle suggests is five years. This assumes no special competitive advantage from current investments and simply uses the cost of capital as an estimate of the rate of return on investment.

1.4 Marketing assets

Value based management means that purely marketing investment proposals will be judged as described above. It will be necessary for marketing managers to justify their spending requests in such terms, on the basis that such spending is not a cost burden to be minimised but an investment in intangible assets such as the four that Doyle suggests.

- Marketing knowledge
- Brands
- Customer loyalty
- Strategic relationships with channel partners

The obstacle that lies in the path of this approach to marketing use of SVA is the common perception that marketing spending is merely a cost to be controlled and minimised. The onus is on marketing managers to demonstrate that their budgets do in fact create assets that provide competitive advantage for the business and that the benefits exceed the costs.

1.5 References

Value-Based Marketing, Doyle, P, John Wiley & Sons Ltd, Chichester, 2000

Strategy as Marketing, Doyle, P in *Images of Marketing* ed Cummings S and Wilson D, Blackwell Publishing Limited, 2003

2 Value drivers

Doyle suggests that it is possible to identify the factors that are critical to the creation of shareholder value. These he calls **value drivers**; he divides them into three categories.

- **Financial**
- **Marketing**
- **Organisational**

It is important to remember that the **financial drivers should not be targeted directly**: they are objectives, not the components of strategy. The company influences them by the proper management of the **marketing** and **organisational** drivers

2.1 Financial value drivers

FAST FORWARD

Financial value drivers are the volume, timing, riskiness and sustainability of positive cash flows.

There are four drivers of financial value.

- **Cash flow volume**
- **Cash flow timing**
- **Cash flow risk**
- **Cash flow sustainability**

2.1.1 Cash flow volume

Clearly, the higher that positive cash flows are and the lower negative cash flows are, the greater the potential for creating value.

Profitability. In the most simple terms, profit margin is measured by net operating profit after tax (NOPAT). NOPAT can be increased in three ways.

(a) **Higher prices**. Marketing strategies such as building strong brands can enable the charging of premium prices. A particularly powerful route to higher prices is innovation, since desirable new products will normally justify increased prices.

(b) **Reduced costs**. Cost reduction depends on increased efficiency in all aspects of the business operation.

(c) **Volume increases**. Other things being equal, volume growth increases the absolute profit margin and may increase the profit rate as well

Sales growth. If increases in sales volume can be achieved without disproportionate increases in costs or, in particular, excessive discounting, positive cash flows will naturally increase. Increased sales can also bring increased **economies of scale**, which will take the form of reduced costs of all types. Overheads are spread over greater volumes and purchasing discounts reduce the cost of sales.

Investment. Investment provides the resources necessary to do business. These include premises, equipment, stocks, transport and well-trained, experienced staff. However, ill-advised investment can destroy value faster than profitable investment can create it, so any proposal for investment must be judged on its potential for generating acceptable returns. The **net present value** (NPV) approach (described in the Annex to this chapter) is the investment appraisal method best suited to the shareholder value principle, in that any project that has a NPV greater than zero provides a return greater than the cost of capital used in the discounting arithmetic.

2.1.2 Cash flow timing

The further into the future a cash flow occurs, the lower its present value. If positive cash flows can be achieved in the near future and negative ones put off until later, the company benefits. This is why companies and individuals put off paying their bills for as long as possible. Buying on credit and selling for cash is another approach.

Doyle gives five examples of ways that marketing managers can accelerate cash flows.

(a)   **Faster new product development** processes, including the use of cross-functional teams and conducting projects concurrently rather than consecutively.

(b)   **Accelerated market penetration** through pre-marketing campaigns, early trial promotions and word-of-mouth campaigns using early adopters.

(c)   **Network effects**: that is, achieving market status as the industry standard. This is a self-reinforcing, feedback effect in which success leads to even greater success. It was seen, for instance, in the videotape market when *VHS* displaced the technically superior *Betamax*. Aggressive marketing measures to build the installed base are required.

(d)   **Strategic alliances** speed market penetration, normally by providing extra distribution effort.

(e)   **Exploiting brand assets**: new products launched under a suitable, established brand are likely to be more successful than others.

2.1.3 Cash flow risk

The higher the degree of **risk** associated with future cash flows, the greater the proportion of them that will not actually come to pass. High risk can produce low returns as easily as high ones. Apart from this overall averaging effect, there is the disadvantage associated with **infrequent large cash flows**: failure of such a cash flow to occur can have catastrophic consequences. Risk is also associated with timing: the further into the future that a cash flow is expected to occur, the greater the risk associated with it, since there is a greater likelihood of **changed conditions** affecting its eventual value and even whether or not it actually occurs.

Doyle suggests that the most effective marketing route to reduced cash flow risk is 'to increase customer satisfaction, loyalty and retention' by deploying such techniques as loyalty programmes and measures to increase satisfaction. Building **good channel relationships** also helps, both by building an element of loyalty based on good service and by sharing information on demand patterns to smooth stock fluctuations.

2.1.4 Cash flow sustainability

A single positive cash flow is useful. A positive cash flow that is repeated at regular intervals is much more useful. Quite apart from the extra cash involved, sustainable cash flows make it easier to plan for the future. Positive cash flows derive from the creation of competitive advantage and a sustainable advantage will lead to sustainable cash flows.

There are many **threats to sustainable profits**, including aggressive competition from copies and substitutes and, particularly in B2B markets, the bargaining power of customers. Part of the role of marketing management is to counter such threats using techniques such as those outlined above in connection with reducing risk.

Sustainable advantage also offers a benefit in the form of **enhanced options** for future development. Just as financial options to buy and sell securities and currency have their own value, so a strategy that creates **real options** for future activity has a value over and above any immediate competitive advantage it may offer. A simple example is the development of a completely new product for a given market that can also be made viable in other markets at low incremental cost. *Richard Branson's* ability to use his brand *Virgin* with almost any consumer product is another example. There are network effects here too, in that as more and more dissimilar *Virgin* products become available, the brand's suitability for use with even more types of product grows.

2.2 Marketing value drivers

Marketing value drivers are

-   **Choice of markets/SBUs**: a mix is required of today's businesses, tomorrow's businesses and options for growth.

-   **Target customers** should be strategic, significant, profitable and loyal.

-   **Differential advantage** arises in four ways: product leadership, operational excellence, brand superiority and customer intimacy.

Doyle analyses four marketing value drivers. The first, choice of markets, is only applicable to the large, diversified organisation, but the remaining three apply to all companies.

2.2.1 Choice of markets

A large organisation operating a number of strategic business units (SBUs) must apply a continuing **portfolio analysis** to them. You will be familiar with such portfolio analysis tools as the BCG matrix and the GE business screen from your earlier studies, but you may only have considered their use at **the product level**. Nevertheless, it is both feasible and proper to apply the concept at **the SBU level** in order to determine priorities for investment and policies for exploitation. Doyle suggests a very simple, one-dimensional classification of SBUs.

(a)   **Today's businesses** generate the bulk of current profits and cash, but probably have only modest growth potential. If successful, they attract modest investment for incremental developments; if performing badly they are put right rapidly or sold off.

(b)   **Tomorrow's businesses** have high potential and require major investment.

(c)   **Options for growth** are the seeds of more distant businesses; such as research projects, market trials and stakes in new, small businesses that are a long way from success. Recognising the worth of such ventures is a difficult task; in the world of venture capital, it is recognised that many good ideas will come to nothing in the end.

A large company needs a suitable mix of the three types of SBU each with its own appropriate strategic objectives, though there may be opportunities for **synergy**, such as the use of common brand names. SBUs that do not fit into one of the categories should be divested.

2.2.2 Target markets

Most customers are not worth selling to. The loyal, long-term customer that pays full price and requires little special service attention is the ideal – but very few fall into this category. Nevertheless, it is appropriate to target this class of customer specifically rather than simply to aim for a large customer base. Desirable customers display four important characteristics.

- They are **strategic** in that their needs match the company's core capabilities.
- They are **significant** in terms of their size or potential for growth.
- They are **profitable**.
- They are **loyal**.

2.2.3 Differential advantage

For other than convenience purchases, customers must have a reason for buying from a particular supplier. **Differential advantage** is created when target customers decide to buy and to remain loyal. Doyle proposes four types of customer, each of which is suited by a particular strategic approach to creating differential advantage.

A strategy of **product leadership** is based on innovation and speed to market. It is the differential advantage that enables a company to sell to **customers who want the latest, most fashionable products**. A good example is *Sony*, with its continuing development of well-designed, expensive customer electronics.

Operational excellence is needed to offer a combination of **customer convenience** and the **lowest prices**. *Wal-Mart* and *Toyota* are good examples of this approach.

Brand superiority is based on careful marketing research and strong and consistent marketing communication. This approach works with customers who identify with the **brand's values** or seek the **reassurance** that brands provide.

A growing segment is made up of customers seeking customised solutions to their specific wants. The appropriate strategy here is **customer intimacy**. This approach is becoming more feasible as information technology developments improve the ability of companies to store and access details of customer habits, needs and preferences.

Note that concentration on one particular strategy does not mean that the others can be neglected. A level of **threshold competence** must be achieved in all four, with one being established as the field of **core competence**.

2.2.4 Marketing mix

The fourth marketing value driver is the marketing mix. Marketing mix decisions, however, are subordinate to and must reflect earlier decisions about the other three marketing value drivers. For example, the nature of the target market segments will influence decisions about promotion.

2.3 Organisational value drivers

FAST FORWARD

Organisational value drivers are centred on core competences and culture. Hierarchical structures are being replaced with flatter, more flexible **internal networks** and **external networks** based on core competences.

The McKinsey 7S model shows how the various elements of a business relate to one another and, in particular, to **shared values**.

Doyle declares that 'in most situations organisational capabilities and culture are more important than strategy', and goes on to make several comparisons between pairs of companies that use similar strategies in the same industries but with markedly differing degrees of success. The differences arise from the extent to which the companies involved are able to develop and deploy appropriate **core competences** and this in turn is highly conditional upon the **culture** of the organisation and the **attitudes** of the people working in it.

Marketing at Work

One of the examples Doyle gives is the contrast between the relative performance of *Singapore Airlines* and *Sabena*. Both 'target business travellers travelling between major international hubs with a value proposition based on service. But Singapore Airlines has been much more successful in delivering high levels of customer service and achieving extraordinary customer satisfaction and loyalty.'

An important variable is **organisational structure**. In the days of mass marketing, a vertically organised hierarchical form was appropriate for achieving economies of scale and expertise. Companies now seeking to cut overheads, achieve fast response to changing markets and competition and exploit the advantages of a mass customisation approach need something better. Increasingly, advances in IT are producing organisations based on **networks**.

(a) **Internal networks** take the form of horizontally oriented, cross-functional teams with responsibility for processes that deliver customer satisfactions. Communication flows freely, making the best use of resources whatever their functional label. This style of working reduces costs, speeds response and improves motivation.

(b) **External networks** are created when companies withdraw from activities that are not fundamental to their specific value-creating strategy and **concentrate on their core competences**. They buy in the services they no longer perform for themselves, using the core competences of other companies to support their own. This type of organisation arises under the pressure of new technologies, new markets and new processes that make it difficult for any organisation to do everything well.

We introduced the **McKinsey 7S** model in an earlier chapter. It was designed to show how the various aspects of a business relate to one another. It is a useful illustration of the way culture fits into an organisation. In particular, it shows the links between the organisation's behaviour and the behaviour of individuals within it.

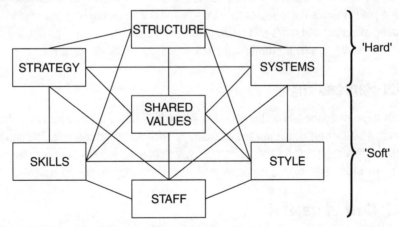

Three of the elements were considered 'hard' originally, but in today's context they are becoming more flexible.

(a) **Structure**. The organisation structure determines division of tasks in the organisation and the hierarchy of authority from the most senior to junior. As discussed above, today's company is likely to be made up of flat, empowered networks.

(b) **Strategy**. Strategy is way in which the organisation plans to outperform its competitors; it will be market-led.

(c) **Systems**. Systems include the technical systems of accounting, personnel, management information and so on, with particular emphasis on how market-related information is distributed and used.

The McKinsey model suggests that the 'soft' elements are equally important.

(a) **Shared values** lie at the heart of the organisation and are the guiding principles for the people in it. They are vital for developing the motivation to drive the organisation to achieve.

(b) **Staff** are the people in the organisation. They have their own complex concerns and priorities. The successful organisation will recruit the right staff and develop their motivation to pursue the right goals.

(c) **Style** is another aspect of the **corporate culture**, and includes the shared assumptions, ways of working and attitudes of senior management.

(d) **Skills** are the core competences that enable the company to create value in a particular way.

The importance of the 'soft' elements for success was emphasised by Peters and Waterman in their study of 'excellent' companies.

3 Limitations of SVA

FAST FORWARD

The **SVA** approach has its limitations.

- Need for accurate **forecasts**
- Difficulty of establishing the **cost of capital**
- Difficulty of establishing **terminal value**
- Difficulty of establishing **baseline business value**
- Difficulty of valuing **real options**
- Short-term disconnection between **economic value** and **market value**

Doyle says that the 'essence of the shareholder value approach is that managers should be evaluated on their ability to develop strategies that earn returns greater than their cost of capital'. He goes on to assert that this approach is superior to traditional performance measures because it avoids emphasis on short-term results and is more appropriate than financial accounting measures for valuing businesses when intangibles such as brands and relationships with customers and suppliers are the primary assets. However, **SVA has its limitations** and managers should be aware of them.

3.1 Forecasting

SVA depends absolutely on the accuracy with which future cash flows can be forecast and these in turn depend on the normal parameters of planning such as sales forecasts. The danger is always that the managers responsible for these forecasts will display conscious or unconscious **bias**, either building slack into their forecasts to produce easily attainable targets or being over-optimistic to please their seniors.

3.2 Cost of capital

Calculating an accurate cost of capital is very difficult and the subject of much debate and research by financial management professionals. While the level of **loan interest** is clearly easily available, it can vary from loan to loan and in the case of overdraft finance may vary from time to time. The **cost of share capital** is much more difficult to compute since it is really only accessible through an examination of stock market behaviour and that is extremely complex. A further complication is the issue of **risk premium**. We discussed this earlier. To some extent this is built into the cost of loan and share capital, but where money is allocated internally, management must make up their own minds. All these factors mean that choice of discount rate is very much a matter of judgement and the 'correct' rate may be unknowable to an accuracy of better than plus or minus several percentage points.

3.3 Estimating terminal value

When SVA is applied to a business strategy or project, two time periods are considered, divided by the **normal planning horizon**, which Doyle suggests should be five years. During the first five years, returns greater than the cost of capital are sought; thereafter, it is assumed that initial competitive advantage will have been eroded away and returns are expected to cover the cost of capital and no more. For this approach to work, it is necessary to estimate the present value of the cash flows from the five-year point onwards. There is no single, accepted way of doing this; business and financial judgement are needed and widely differing estimates can result.

3.4 Baseline business value

To calculate the **extra value** created by a given strategy it is necessary to compare two figures: the present value of the company if the strategy is pursued, and the present value if no change is made to current strategy. The latter is the baseline value. Once again, judgement is required in calculating this value, particularly since it may not be possible to maintain the current flow of profit simply by doing more of the same. Indeed, new strategies may be essential if the business is to avoid eventual liquidation.

3.5 Options for the future

Options to buy and sell securities, commodities and currencies have been a feature of financial markets for many years. Such options have prices and the way their value changes with time has also been the subject of much debate and research among finance professionals. Companies can create **real options** for themselves by their strategic decisions, but the valuation of such options is not currently possible using the techniques of SVA. A simple example of such an option would arise if a company decided to enter a new foreign market by means of direct exports. The market knowledge and contacts thus generated might well put the company in a strong position to undertake local manufacturing, should it wish to do so. The basic strategy of direct exporting could itself be valued by means of SVA, but it would not be possible to measure the extra value created in the form of the option to manufacture locally.

3.6 Market valuation

The aim of the shareholder value approach to strategic management is to reward shareholders for providing financial resources to the company. These rewards take two forms: **dividends** and **capital appreciation**. Dividends are directly affected by the positive cash flows generated by successful strategies; capital appreciation, however, in the form of a rising share price, is not so clearly subject to this effect in the short term. Longer term future prospects for positive cash flows explain about 80 per cent of market price movement, but in the shorter term, markets are heavily influenced by a variety of other extraneous environmental influences. To reduce short-term share price volatility, company senior management must both investigate strategic forecasts very carefully and communicate their longer-term plans to the market.

4 Branding strategy

FAST FORWARD

A **brand** is a collection of attributes that strongly influence purchase. It consists of an effective **product**, a distinctive **identity** and added **values**. It can bring benefits to marketers, customers and shareholders.

4.1 What is a brand?

Key concept

> A **brand** is a collection of attributes which strongly influence purchase. (Davidson)
>
> 'A name, term, sign, symbol or design or combination of them, intended to identify the goods or services of one seller or group of sellers and to differentiate them from those of competitors.' (Kotler)

Branding and a firm's reputation are linked. The important thing to remember is that a brand is something **customers** value: it exists in the customer's mind. A brand is the link between a company's marketing activities and the customer's perception.

 ## Marketing at Work

In suburban Philadelphia, not too many miles from Wharton's campus, is a retail establishment called *Ed's Beer Store*. It's a wonderfully prosaic name. Customers know what they can buy there, and if they have a complaint, they know whom to talk to.

But what about companies with names like *Agere, Agilent* or *Altria*? Or *Diageo, Monday* and *Verizon*? Or *Accenture, Cingular* and *Protiviti*?

Except for Monday, which may be a strange thing to call a company but it is nonetheless a real word, all these names are fabricated. What's more, none of them, even Monday, tells potential customers anything about the businesses they are in. Plus, they sound so contrived that you might conclude they will do nothing but elicit snickering and confusion in the market place.

According to marketing professors at Wharton, however, that is not necessarily the case. They say peculiar names, by themselves, may mean nothing to begin with. But if backed by a successful branding campaign, they will come to signify whatever the companies want them to mean.

Website: http://knowledge.wharton.upenn.edu

4.1.1 What makes up a brand?

- Effective **product**
- Distinctive **identity**
- Added **values**

} supported by {

Visible: Symbol, advertising, presentation (eg packaging)

Invisible: assets and competences, strong R&D, supply chain, effective selling, costs

4.1.2 Benefits of branding

Beneficiary	Benefit of branding
Customers	• Branding makes it easier to choose between competing products, if brands offer different benefits. Brands help consumers cope with information overload • Brands can support aspirations and self image • Branding can confer membership of reference groups
Marketers	• Enables extra value to be added to the product • Creates an impression in the consumer's mind; encourages re-purchase • Differentiates the product, especially if competing products are similar • Reduces the importance of price

Beneficiary	Benefit of branding
	• Encourages a pull strategy
	• Other products/services can exploit the brand image (eg Virgin)
Shareholders	• A brand is an intangible asset; even though it is not on the financial statements, a strong brand promises to generate future cash inflows and profits. This is called **brand equity**.
	• Brands build market share, which can generate high profits through:
	– Higher volume
	– Higher value (higher prices)
	– Higher control over distributors

Key concept

Brand equity is the asset the marketer builds to ensure continuity of satisfaction for the customer and profit for the supplier.

Evolution of brands. Brands have evolved over time, to the extent that they satisfy customer needs.

(a) **Classic brands** (post World War II) were linked to a single goal (eg cleaner clothes).

(b) **Contemporary brands** meet functional needs but give associated benefits (eg *Volvo* and safety).

(c) **Post-modern brands**? Consumers use brands to attain a broad array of goals, as a result of 'time famine'.

  (i) Some marketers suggest that brands have an emotional content. Certainly, this might be the case for fashion items (eg trainers) where they confer status.

  (ii) Strangest of all is *Mercedes* (a subsidiary of *Daimler Chrysler*), previously known for luxury cars. Mercedes now has product offering that embraces small cars.

4.2 Brand architecture

FAST FORWARD

Brand architectures include company, name, range, product and umbrella brands.

4.2.1 Brand architecture

(a) **Company brand**. The company name is the most prominent feature of the branding (eg Mercedes).

(b) **The company brand** combined with a **product brand** name (eg Kellogg's: *Corn Flakes*, *Rice Krispies*). This option both legitimises (because of the company name) and individualises (the individual product name). It allows **new names to be introduced quickly and relatively cheaply**. Sometimes known as **source branding**, firms might use this approach as a short-term way to save money.

(c) **Range brand**. Firms group types of product under different brands. For example, Sharwoods is a brand owned by *RHM Foods. Sharwoods* offers pickles, poppadums, sauces and so on. A brand restricted to a small range of goods may be called a **line brand**.

(d) **Individual name**. Each product has a unique name. This is the option chosen by *Procter & Gamble* for example, who even have different brand names within the same product line, eg

Bold, *Tide*. The main advantage of individual product branding is that an unsuccessful brand does not adversely affect the firm's other products, nor the firm's reputation generally.

(e) **Umbrella brands** are used to support several products in very different markets. This shares brand building costs but may weaken brand identity. An example is *Philips'* wide range of electrical and electronic products.

 Marketing at Work

Penguin is one of the oldest brands in UK paperback publishing and over the years has introduced brand extensions (Puffin for children, Pelican for academic) and sub-brands (Penguin Classics, Penguin Modern Classics) and indeed other products (Penguin Classic CDs).

A key issue for publishing is to identify the core of the brand.

(a) The imprint or publisher?

(b) The author? It appears to go without saying that people will buy a book by a recognised author, and that the author is at the heart of the brand.

In contrast, people buy '*Mills & Boon*' books – the core of the brand is the publisher, not the author.

The Folio Society publishes versions of classic literature, but markets its books partly as art objects, owing to the quality of the binding and paper, and the specially-commissioned illustrations.

4.2.2 Choice of brand architecture

(a) **Company and/or umbrella brand name**

Advantages	Disadvantages
• Cheap (only one marketing effort)	• Not ideal for segmentation
• Easy to launch new products under umbrella brand	• Harder to obtain distinct identity
• Good for internal marketing	• Risk that failure in one area can damage the brand
	• Variable quality

For example, *Virgin* is a company brand name, supported by advertising, PR and the celebrity status of Richard Branson. (To what extent will the problems of *Virgin Trains* adversely affect the other brands?)

(i) Service industries use umbrella marketing as customer benefits can cross product categories. *Marks & Spencer* diversified from clothes, to food and to financial services. *Tesco* and *Asda* have followed suit.

(ii) Communication media are more diffuse and fragmented.

(iii) One brand is supported by integrated marketing communications.

(iv) Umbrella branding supports **database marketing** across the whole product range.

(v) Distributor/retailer brands are umbrella brands in their own right, so brand owners have to follow suit.

(b) **Range brands** offer some of the advantages of an umbrella brand with more precise targeting.

(c) **Individual brand name**

Advantages	Disadvantages
• Ideal for precise segmentation	• Expensive
• Crowds out competition by offering more choice	• Risky
• Damage limitation to company's reputation	

4.3 Brand-created satisfaction

The extra **satisfactions** created by brand equity are largely subjective. They arise from such sources as usage experience; user associations and image; irrational belief; appearance and company reputation.

The added satisfactions conferred by brands are largely subjective. In blind testing many consumers cannot tell the difference between different products; however, they will exhibit a preference for a strong brand name when shown it.

Most consumer buying decisions, therefore, do not depend on the functionality of the product.

(a) Products are bought for emotional reasons. For example, most sports trainers are fashion products.

(b) Branding reduces the need to choose.

 Marketing at Work

Early in 1993, it was announced that the price of *Marlboro* cigarettes was to be cut in some of its US markets. Marlboro had been one of the USA's most heavily supported brands, but was losing ground to cheap discounted competitor brands. What do you think might be the significance of this?

The purpose of a brand is, in part, to reduce the consumer's sensitivity to price. It might promise an income stream in future and hence be worth valuing as a fixed asset. However, the price cut of Marlboro cigarettes sends a significant message to many brand-based businesses. US analysts believed that Marlboro was one of the strongest brands ever promoted, recognised world wide and supported by consistently heavy investment. Cutting the price of Marlboro indicated the fact that some brands are never impervious to price competition. The price cut led to a fall in the share price of companies dealing heavily in branded goods, indicating that the value of their main asset, their brand, was less than supposed.

4.3.1 Sources of brand satisfactions

Source	Comment
Experience	Customer's actual usage of a brand can give positive or negative associations.
User associations	Brands get an image from the type of people using them; brands might be associated with particular personalities.
Belief	This might be a placebo effect; **belief** in a brand may enhance its effectiveness.
Appearance	Design appeals to people's aesthetic sensibilities.
Manufacturer's name	The company reputation may support the brand.

4.3.2 Brand identity

> **Brand identity**: 'the message sent out by the brand through its product form, name, visual signs, advertising'. This is not the same as **brand image** which is how the target market perceives the brand.

4.3.3 Three aspects to a brand

Aspect	Comment
Core	Fundamental, unchanging aspect of a brand. (Cider is an alcoholic drink made from applies.)
Style	This is the brand's culture, personality, the identity it conveys and so on. Compare the: • Rustic personality of Scrumpy Jack • Almost club-orientated personality of Diamond White
Themes	These are how the brand communicates through physical appearance of the product.

Clearly, the **themes** are more easy to change than the **style**, which is more easy to change than the **core**.

4.4 How to build brands

> **Brand strategies** must be based on market analysis and a clear understanding of the brand. Future positions must be targeted and progress planned and controlled.

The process for building the brand is similar to that of building a product (core product, an expected product, an augmented product and a potential product). However, a product is, in some respects, purely functional, whereas a brand offers more.

4.4.1 A step approach to designing brands

Step 1   **Have a quality product** – but remember quality means **fitness for use** not the **maximum specification**. Functionality is only a starting point.

Step 2   **Build the basic brand**. These are the marketing mix criteria.

- They should support product performance
- They should differentiate the brand
- They should be consistent with positioning
- The basic brand delivers the core product in an attractive way.

Step 3   **Augmentations** include extra services, guarantees and so on. (Expensive guarantees provide evidence that the firm takes quality seriously.)

Step 4   **Reaching its potential**, so that customers will not easily accept substitutes.

Step 5   Maintain **brand value** by using the marketing mix to persuade customers to re-buy.

Step 6   **Build brand loyalty**. Customers who rebuy and are loyal are valuable because:

- Revenue from them is more predictable
- Existing customers are cheaper than new customers

Step 7   **Know where to stop in developing the brand**. (For example, an alcohol-free alcopop would be pointless.)

4.5 Implementing the brand strategy

Brands that **reach their potential** have five key characteristics.

- A quality product underpinning the brand
- Being first to market, giving early mover advantages
- Unique positioning concept: in other words they are precisely positioned
- Strong communications underpinning the brand
- Time and consistency

4.5.1 The brand planning process

Brand strategy is one of the steps in the brand planning process just as marketing strategy is one step in the marketing planning process. *Arnold* (1992) in *The Handbook of Brand Management* offers a five stage brand planning process.

Stage	Description
Market analysis	An overview of trends in the macro and micro environment and so includes customer and competitor analysis and the identification of any PEST factors which may affect our brand. For soft drinks, the explosion of competitive activity, particularly by own label, and new product introductions, such as Fruitopia, will be important.
Brand situation analysis	Analysis of the brand's personality and individual attributes. This represents the internal audit and questions such as, 'Is advertising projecting the right image?', 'Is the packaging too aggressive?', 'Does the product need updating?' need asking. This is a fundamental evaluation of the brand's character.
Targeting future positions	This is the core of brand strategy. Any brand strategy could incorporate what has been learnt in steps (i) and (ii) into a view of how the market will evolve and what strategic response is most appropriate. Brand strategy can be considered under three headings. (1) Target markets (2) Brand positions (3) Brand scope
Testing new offers	Once the strategy has been decided the next step is to develop individual elements of the marketing mix and test the brand concept for clarity, credibility and competitiveness with the target market.
Planning and evaluating performance	The setting of the brand budget, establishing the type of support activity needed and measurement of results against objectives. Information on tracking of performance feeds into step (i) of the brand management process.

 Marketing at Work

Sunny Delight

This is an example of what can go well – and – not well in planning, introducing and managing a new product. (Extracts from *The Guardian*, 11 April 2001.)

Sunny Delight burst upon Britain with its sunshine logo in April 1998. By August 1999, it was the country's third-largest-selling soft drink. Three years later, sales were down 36% by value and 28% by volume (moving annual totals to February 2001).

It was a textbook launch. Delight had been available in the US since 1964, it was sold as a downmarket drink competing for space alongside squashes and long-life drinks on ordinary shelves. The approach in the UK was to be different. *P&G*, one of the world's most powerful grocery manufacturers, had acquired it at the end of the 80s and in 1996 began a long and thorough process of test marketing it for the UK in Carlisle.

Delight is 5% citrus juice, and a lot of sugar and water, with vegetable oil, thickeners, added vitamins and flavourings, colourings and other additives that make it look like fresh orange juice but appeal to the immature tastebuds of young children.

The ingredients were cheap but the price was set at a premium. P&G invested in a new filling plant costing about £12m, according to industry estimates, so that the drink could be packaged in the sort of frosted plastic bottles that fresh orange juice is usually sold in chill cabinets, next to fresh fruit juices.

P&G is one of the handful of companies that has the muscle to dictate where products are sold in supermarkets. All this was backed up by a huge direct marketing campaign and a £9.2m advertising campaign.

P&G's brands include *Pampers*, and it is thought to have built up a powerful database from offers over the years, which tells the company who we are and how old our children are ... it is also reported to have worked with retailers' data from loyalty cards to identify young, lower-income families. Teenagers were targeted with sponsorship of basketball.

This combined onslaught led to instant success. But the backlash came equally fast. The Food Commission condemned Sunny Delight as a con, accusing P&G of putting it in chill cabinets to mislead. Newspapers, the BBC's *Watchdog* programme and Radio 4 all carried attacks on the brand and dubbed it 'The unreal thing'.

Then came the comic twist in the drama. In December 1999, a paediatrician, Dr Duncan Cameron, reported a new and alarming condition in the medical journals: Sunny Delight syndrome. A girl of five had turned bright yellow and orange after drinking 1.5 litres of the stuff a day. She was overdosing on betacarotene, the additive that gives the sugar-and-water drink its orange colour.

By a marketing man's nightmare of coincidence, the TV ads for the brand at the time showed two white snowmen raiding the fridge for Sunny Delight and turning bright orange. To add to the embarrassment, a leading consultant dermatologist, Professor John Hawks, said too much betacarotene could cause tummy upsets. As if to confirm its status as spawn of the devil, P&G was forced to join that happy band of cigarette manufacturers who put voluntary warnings on their products.

4.6 Specific strategies for brands

> **Brand stretching** uses the brand equity established in one market to enter another. Careful consideration must be given to the use of **global** or **local** brands.

4.6.1 Brand stretching

Key concept

> **Brand extension** involves using the same brand name, successfully established in one market or channel, to enter other. It is often termed **brand stretching** when the markets are very different.

4.6.2 Examples of brand extension

- **Retailers** such as *Dixons* and *Tesco* launching themselves as **Internet Service Providers**
- *Penguin Books* launching its own 'brand' of compact discs
- *Swatch* becoming involved in motor vehicles

4.6.3 Conditions for brand stretching/extension

(a) The **core values** of the brand must be **relevant to the new market**. EasyJet has transferred to car rental and internet cafes.

(b) The new market area must not affect the core values of the brand by association. Failure in one activity can adversely affect the core brand.

4.6.4 Advantages of brand extension

Advantage	Comment
Cheap	It is less costly to extend a brand then to establish a new one from scratch.
Customer-perception	Customer expectations of the brand have been built up, so this lower risk for the customer encourages 'trial'.
Less risky	Failure rate of completely new brands.

4.6.5 Disadvantages of brand extension

Disadvantage	Comment
Segments	The brand personality may not carry over successfully to the new segment. The brand values may not be relevant to the new market.
Strength	The brand needs to be strong already.
Perception	The brand still needs a differential advantage over competitors.
Over-dilution	Excessive extensions can dilute the values of the brand.

4.7 Revitalising brands

At times, the performance of a brand will falter and managers will attempt to rectify the situation by:

- Enhancing sales volume
- Improving profits in other ways

Revitalisation means increasing the sales volume through:

- New markets (eg overseas)
- New segments (eg personal computers are being sold for family, as opposed to business, use)
- Increased usage (encouraging people to eat breakfast cereals as a snack during the day)

Repositioning is more fundamental, in that it is a **competitive strategy** aimed to change position to increase market share.

Type of position	Comment
Real	Relates to actual product features and design
Psychological	Change the buyer's beliefs about the brand
Competitive	Alter beliefs about competing brands
Change emphasis	The emphasis in the advertising can change over time

4.8 Success criteria for branding

4.8.1 Beneficial qualities of a brand name

- Suggest **benefits**, eg *Schweppes' Slimline* tonic
- Suggest qualities such as **action** or **colour** (eg easyJet, with an orange colour)
- Be **easy to pronounce**, recognise and remember
- Be **acceptable in all markets**, both linguistically and culturally
- Be **distinctive**
- Be **meaningful**

 Marketing at Work

Compare the following mobile phone brands.

- *Orange*
- *Vodafone*

- *Cellnet*
- *One-to-One*

Orange appropriates the colour orange, whereas Vodafone and Cellnet suggest aspects of the product, and One-to-One suggests the actual consumer benefit.

4.8.2 Global or local brand?

The key differences between a standardised global brand approach and an approach based upon identifying and exploiting global marketing opportunities are as described below.

(a)   The **standardised global brand approach** requires:

   (i)   A standardised product offering to market segments which have exactly similar needs across cultures

   (ii)   A common approach to the marketing mix and one that is as nearly standardised as may be, given language differences

(b)   An approach based upon **local marketing opportunities** reflects:

   (i)   A recognition that the resources of the company may be adapted to fulfil marketing opportunities in different ways taking into account local needs and preferences but on a global basis

   (ii)   A willingness to sub-optimise the benefits of having a single global brand (eg advertising synergy) in order to optimise the benefits of meeting specific needs more closely

For the **international company** marketing a brand, there are two further policy decisions to be made. These are:

(a)   The problem of deciding if and **how to protect the company's brands** (and associated trademarks)

(b)   Whether there should be **one global brand** or many different national brands for a given product

Marketing at Work

Television formats

- *Who Wants to be a Millionaire?*

  Developed in the UK, this format has been successfully exported to the US and India. In the Indian version, the programme is in Hindi and hosted by a major film star (Amitabh Bachhan); otherwise the music and lighting is very similar. Is this a global brand?

- *The Weakest Link vs AbFab*

  When Absolutely Fabulous was remade for the US market, cigarettes and excess alcohol consumption were deemed not appropriate, and so these features were removed, perhaps destroying the programme's appeal.

  With The Weakest Link, however, the rudeness and aggression of the British presenter, Anne Robinson, has been replicated in the American version, with successful impacts on audience share.

The most successful examples of worldwide branding occur where the brand has become **synonymous with the generic product** (eg Sellotape, Aspirin), though this, of course, has its disadvantages.

4.9 Valuing brands

FAST FORWARD

The effort put into building a brand can create a valuable asset that can be valued, though the value of such an intangible asset may only be shown on the balance sheet if it has been purchased.

A brand can be an important business asset. Customers learn to trust the brand to deliver greater satisfaction than the generic product. This satisfaction can be realised by the supplier in the form of increased revenue. Investment in building a brand thus has the potential to increase the value created by the supplier. However, success is not guaranteed and even when achieved it may not last long. Successful brands must be defended and maintained if their value is not to be eroded by competition, neglect and even mismanagement.

Marketing at Work

Tommy Hilfiger

It has been quite a decade for Tommy Hilfiger. During the 90s, it seems his brand could do no wrong. The business experienced meteoric growth and, by 2000, was generating $2bn in worldwide sales.

But then came the new century, and Hilfiger struggled to maintain the momentum. Last week, the brand was brought by Apax Partners, a global private equity firm, for $1.6bn (£850m). Perhaps the first step under the new regime will be to look back on some of the major errors that the brand made in the 90s, because Tommy Hilfiger learned some of the key lessons of brand management the hard way.

First, growth and success are the two biggest enemies of all the strong brands. Hilfiger's global sales grew tenfold during the 90s. It is a classic conundrum for most niche brands that experience market success. Their scale increases, they lose focus and, eventually, all the elements that made the brand successful are lost.

Second, watch out for retail 'partners'. Hilfiger, like most fashion brands, relies both on its own outlets and selling through major department stores. The latter are not necessarily motivated to protect and care for brand equity over the long haul. Hilfiger experienced first-hand the classic one-two-three of retail sales.

'The problem was the department stores in the US', he said. 'First of all they copy you, then they under-price you and then they discount the brand. They don't take care of your shop areas in stores'.

Third, the financial markets are run by brand morons with unreasonably short-term profit goals.

Hilfiger himself accepts the pressure of the market made his life a very difficult and had a negative impact on the brand. Everything you do is looked at under a microscope, so you make decisions based on Wall Street agendas, and maybe those aren't always the right decisions to make'.

Fourth, pressure from Wall Street often leads to a focus on short-term sales at the expense of long-term marketing focus. There is a bid difference between marketing and sales. When you are sales-orientated, all customers are equally valuable additions to your quarterly sales figures. Marketers, however, know that all customers are not created equally.

To succeed over the long term, a fashion brand must aim high and deliberately avoid appealing to customers lower down the fashion hierarchy. According to the company's new chief executive Fred Gehring, this is something that he will attempt to redress. 'Over the part couple of years, everything was top-lined focused', he said. 'In a (non-publicly listed) situation, we don't have to have an obsession with the top line anymore and can focus on quality, not quantity'.

Fifth, beware sales promotions. The single fastest way to kill any brand is to over-produce and then discount heavily through sales promotions. Price-based promotions kill brand equity and, when the former is more prominent then the latter, disaster is rarely far away.

Creating a successful brand can be very expensive in money and effort. When a company makes a significant investment in creating and enhancing a brand, it is appropriate to measure the degree of success that it achieves. This is the process of **brand valuation**.

You must be careful to distinguish between **brand *value*** and **brand *values***. Brand *values* are the intangible factors that make up the identity or image of the brand. They are usually quoted as a list of adjectives, such as *young, active, exclusive, fun, reliable, secure, safe* and so on. Brand *value*, on the other hand, is value in an economic sense: the monetary worth of the brand, or the cash value it represents. We have discussed brand *values* extensively; we must now consider brand *value*.

The valuation of brands is an important aspect of the application of SVA to marketing management. Shareholders rightly expect to see a return on their investment. The greater the value achieved from a given cash investment, the better the performance of the company and its management is assessed to be. This applies as much to investment in intangible assets, such as brands, as to investment in tangible ones such as machinery or premises. The problem is that intangible assets are much more difficult to value than tangible ones.

It is also necessary to value brands if they are to be sold or licensed.

4.9.1 Should brands be valued at all?

When considering the valuation of brands (or any other intangible asset) you should be aware of the differences in **philosophy** that exist, particularly between financial and marketing staff. Accountants are cautious and even pessimistic as a matter of professional habit. It is their job to be **realistic**. Marketing people, on the other hand, tend to be **optimistic** and not averse to risk. And they want their brand-building efforts to be recognised. As a result of these two orientations, there will often be a problem with brand valuation, with marketers talking about *investment* and attempting to justify high values to accountants, who talk in terms of *cost* and would rather write it all off against profit.

An important consideration is that the rules of financial accounting produce an overall value for the company that tends to be very different from its **real market value**. The difference is made up of **intangible value** residing in such things as brands and the expertise of the employees. This is accepted as a problem, but accounting rules have not moved very far towards acceptance of brands as balance sheet assets since they are so difficult to value.

Currently, there are two circumstances in which a brand may be shown as an asset on the balance sheet. The first is if it has been **purchased**, since it is then possible to state an unequivocal value, which is based on its cost. Then, like all assets, it must be **amortised**, that is, written down in value each year to recognise its diminishing value.

The second occasion is when there is an identifiable market into which a brand could be sold and it is possible to estimate, on a prudent basis, a reasonable market value. Note carefully that this procedure is only available if the brand is truly saleable as a **separate asset**, as was the case with the Tommy Hilfiger brand as outlined above.

In both cases, the annual write down of value by amortisation is not required if, instead, the brand's value is carefully re-evaluated on the market price basis.

4.9.2 Reasons for valuing brands

(a)   To make the **balance sheet** reflect more accurately the value of the business. This is particularly useful for comparisons over time and with other companies.

(b)   To improve **financial market efficiency**. This follows from point (a) above: proper valuation is important if investment is to be carried on in an informed way.

(c)   To set a price for **disposing of a brand**. This can only be useful when the brand and its associated manufacturing and service activities and so on are truly **separable**.

(d)   **Improved brand management** should flow from proper valuation and regular re-valuation, since the effectiveness of promotion can be assessed and resources can be allocated where they are most likely to be effectively used.

(e)   **Internal effects** may be important, in that brand success will probably be good for morales and motivation.

4.10 Methods of valuing brands

FAST FORWARD   Doyle dismisses all brand valuation methods except the SVA approach.

Doyle mentions several methods of computing a brand's value. He dismisses all but the SVA approach as inappropriate.

(a)   **Cost**. The past costs incurred in building the brand are indexed to current values and summed. The problem with using historical cost is that its relevance to current value can be extremely limited; this applies to all assets, tangible and intangible.

(b)   **Royalties**. Attempting to estimate what the brand would cost to license is quite a sensible approach and allows for the use of experience in current market conditions. Notional future charges are discounted to give a present value for the brand. Unfortunately, in the absence of plentiful hard data on actual current royalty rates, this technique is no more than guesswork.

(c)   **Market value**. Recent sales of comparable brands or businesses may be used as a guide to value. When a branded business is sold, part of the sale price is related to tangible assets and part to intangibles. It will probably be quite difficult to arrive at a value for the tangible assets, and even if this can be done, there remains the problem of analysing out the values of the individual intangible assets: there may be several brands as well as other intangibles such as established dealer relationships.

(d) **Economic use value**. Extra profits attributable to the ownership of the brand are averaged over, say, the last three years and multiplied by, say, 10. This is a popular method and can be used to compare brands, but the choice of multiple is highly subjective and past performance is a poor guide to the future.

4.10.1 Proprietary brand valuation models

WPP Group subsidiaries offer three contrasting methods of brand valuation.

Research International's Equity Engine estimates brand equity by measuring **affinity** and **performance**.

(a) **Affinity** is an emotional response that depends on three factors.

(i) Brand **authority** includes trust, heritage and innovation.

(ii) **Identification** with the brand depends on its empathic aspects, such as care for the customer.

(iii) Approval depends on prestige and endorsement by leaders of opinion.

(b) **Performance** depends on product features and functionality.

The **Young and Rubicam BrandAsset Valuator** is based on four aspects of the brand.

(a) **Differentiation** builds the brand initially.

(b) **Relevance** is the brand's actual importance to the consumer.

(c) **Esteem** depends on quality and popularity and varies from culture to culture.

(d) **Knowledge** depends on awareness of brand values.

Together, differentiation and relevance make up **brand strength**, which is an indicator of the brand's future potential. Esteem and knowledge, however, are lagging indicators that decline as a brand declines in strength. Together, they indicate **brand stature**.

Millward Brown's BRANDZ™ is based on an annual survey of more than 650,000 consumers and professionals in 31 countries and covering more than 21,000 brands. Analysis of the results provides a combined diagnostic and predictive tool that evaluates brand strength and growth potential. Scores are generated for bonding with a brand, its advantage over rivals, brand performance and relevance to consumer needs. A **brand voltage score** indicates the brand's potential, while a **brand presence** score indicates areas for development.

4.10.2 The SVA approach to brand valuation

Doyle proposes that brands should be valued by the standard shareholder value approach; that is, on the basis of the **extra value they will create**. To do this it is necessary to forecast the *extra* future cash flows they are expected to bring over and above what an unbranded product would provide. These sums are then discounted to a present value, which is the value represented by ownership of the brand. As with all SVA applications, this is subject to the problems outlined earlier in this chapter and, in particular, to the difficulty of establishing a suitable **discount rate** and estimating future **earnings**.

Discount rate. The discount rate takes account of **risk**.

(a) The *Interbrand* **brand strength index** is based on the brand's market qualities. The method used is to score the brand on seven attributes including stability, legal protection and growth. The total score is out of 100 points.

Source	Weighting	Comment
Leadership	25%	How dominant is the brand in its sector? High scores are earned for dominance.
Market	10%	What are the growth characteristics of the market?
Stability	15%	Well established brands that enjoy consumer loyalty will receive higher strength scores.
Internationality	25%	International brands are generally worth more than national ones, as they are not vulnerable to one market, and a brand might be in another stage of its life cycle in an overseas market.
Trend	10%	A trend indicates a brand's ability to sustain itself. Reductions in sales volume reduce profit, but also make price increases harder to justify.
Support	10%	Marketing expenditure can support a brand, but it must be of the right quality (eg a successful re-positioning).
Protection	5%	(eg Patent protection, copyright, imitation)

A discount rate can be found from a graph using the total score as the entering argument. It's also possible to use a non-SVA brand valuation method based on the interbrand strength score: a multiplier based on the score is applied to average earnings from the board. The highest possible multiplier is 20.

(b) *Haigh's* **brand beta analysis** is based on the capital asset pricing market analysis model and takes account of four elements of risk.

- A risk-free return based on government securities
- The extra risk associated with investment in shares
- A market sector risk adjustment
- The brand risk profile

Brand earnings. Future cash flows attributable to the brand are estimated in two steps.

(a) Total earnings from intangible assets are calculated by deducting earnings traceable to tangible assets from economic value added (calculated as NOPAT – capital charge: see above). Earnings from tangible assets are calculated by taking the assets' realisable value and applying the risk-free rate of return.

(b) The intangibles return must then be analysed into its components, such as brands, patents and trademarks. The Interbrand method uses two steps.

- Establish the value drivers applicable in the market, such as location, price and promotion.

- Estimate the extent to which each value driver depends on the brand.

Chapter Roundup

- **Shareholder value analysis** attempts to measure management and marketing performance by measuring the probable success of proposed action in terms of **economic profit**. Economic profit is created when the return on capital employed exceeds the cost of that capital.

- Economic profit = NOPAT − (capital employed × cost of capital). Economic profit from future activity can be measured by discounting future cash flows to a **net present value**.

- The cost of capital depends in part on the degree of risk inherent in the company's operations.

- Management should aim to create value and expect to be judged in terms of SVA. Marketing managers must be prepared to use their budgets to create measurable assets in terms of competitive advantage.

- **Financial value drivers** are the volume, timing, riskiness and sustainability of positive cash flows.

- **Marketing value drivers** are

    - **Choice of markets/SBUs**: a mix is required of today's businesses, tomorrow's businesses and options for growth.

    - **Target customers** should be strategic, significant, profitable and loyal.

    - **Differential advantage** arises in four ways: product leadership, operational excellence, brand superiority and customer intimacy.

- **Organisational value drivers** are centred on core competences and culture. Hierarchical structures are being replaced with flatter, more flexible **internal networks** and **external networks** based on core competences.

- **The McKinsey 7S** model shows how the various elements of a business relate to one another and, in particular, to **shared values**.

- The **SVA** approach has its limitations.

    - Need for accurate **forecasts**
    - Difficulty of establishing the **cost of capital**
    - Difficulty of establishing **terminal value**
    - Difficulty of establishing **baseline business value**
    - Difficulty of valuing **real options**
    - Short-term disconnection between **economic value** and **market value**

- A **brand** is a collection of attributes that strongly influence purchase. It consists of an effective **product**, a distinctive **identity** and added **values**. It can bring benefits to marketers, customers and shareholders.

- **Brand architectures** include company, name, range, product and umbrella brands.

- The extra **satisfactions** created by brand equity are largely subjective. They arise from such sources as usage experience; user associations and image; irrational belief; appearance and company reputation.

- **Brand strategies** must be based on market analysis and a clear understanding of the brand. Future positions must be targeted and progress planned and controlled.

- **Brand stretching** uses the brand equity established in one market to enter another. Careful consideration must be given to the use of **global** or **local** brands.

- The effort put into building a brand can create a valuable asset that can be valued, though the value of such an intangible asset may only be shown on the balance sheet if it has been purchased.

- Doyle dismisses all brand valuation methods except the SVA approach.

Quick Quiz

1   Should investment in intangible assets be regarded as representing a contribution to long-term shareholder value?

2   What is the formula for economic profit?

3   Suggest a normal planning horizon.

4   What three categories does Doyle split value drivers into?

5   What is a product leadership strategy based on?

6   What are the elements of the McKinsey 7S model?

7   What makes up a brand?

8   How does an umbrella brand differ from a range brand?

9   What are the conditions for successful brand stretching?

10   How should brands be valued?

Answers to Quick Quiz

1   Broadly, yes, but the prospects for enhanced future positive cashflows must be carefully assessed.

2   Economic profit = NOPAT − (capital employed × cost of capital)

3   Doyle suggests five years

4   Financial, marketing and organisational

5   Innovation and speed to market

6   Shared values, strategy, structure, systems, skills, staff, style

7   Effective product, distinctive identity, added values

8   A brand used with a range of products in a single market is a range brand; if the same brand is used in several distinct markets, it is an umbrella brand

9   Brand core values must be relevant to the new market and the new market must not adversely affect the brand core values

10   According to the principles of SVA: analyse out the future cashflows attributable to the brand and discount them to a NPV using a discount rate that reflects the degree of risk associated with the brand

Now try Question 5 at the end of the Study Text

Annex: Discounting cash flows

Discounting is a basic tool of financial analysis that is also widely used in other business techniques, so we will start off by showing you how it works.

The **basic principle of compounding** is that if we invest £X now for n years at r% interest per annum, we should obtain £S in n years time, where £S = £X$(1+r^n)$.

Thus if we invest £10,000 now for four years at 10% interest per annum, we will have a total investment worth £10,000 × 1.10^4 = £14,641 at the end of four years (that is, at year 4 if it is now year 0).

Key concept

> The basic principle of **discounting** is that if we wish to have £S in n years' time, we need to invest a certain sum *now* (year 0) at an interest rate of r% in order to obtain the required sum of money in the future.

For example, if we wish to have £14,641 in four years' time, how much money would we need to invest now at 10% interest per annum? This is the reverse of the situation described above and, fairly obviously, the answer is £10,000. We can prove this.

Using our formula, $S = X(1 + r)^n$

where X = the original sum invested
        r = 10%
        n = 4
        S = £14,641

£14,641 = $X(1 + 0.1)^4$

£14,641 = X × 1.4641

∴ X = $\dfrac{£14,641}{1.4641}$ = £10,000

£10,000 now, with the capacity to earn a return of 10% per annum, is the equivalent in value of £14,641 after four years. We can therefore say that £10,000 is the present value of £14,641 at year 4, at an interest rate of 10%.

Key concept

> The **present value** of a future sum is obtained by discounting the future sum at an appropriate discount rate.

The discounting formula is

$$X = S \times \frac{1}{(1+r)^n}$$

where S is the sum to be received after n time periods
        X is the present value (PV) of that sum
        r is the rate of return, expressed as a proportion
        n is the number of time periods (usually years).

The rate r is sometimes called a cost of capital.

Example: discounting

(a) Calculate the present value of £60,000 at year 6, if a return of 15% per annum is obtainable.

(b) Calculate the present value of £100,000 at year 5, if a return of 6% per annum is obtainable.

(c) How much would a person need to invest now at 12% to earn £4,000 at year 2 and £4,000 at year 3?

Solution

The discounting formula, $X = S \times \dfrac{1}{(1+r)^n}$ is required.

(a)
$S = £60,000$
$n = 6$
$r = 0.15$
$PV = 60,000 \times \dfrac{1}{1.15^6}$
$= 60,000 \times 0.432$
$= £25,920$

(b)
$S = £100,000$
$n = 5$
$r = 0.06$
$PV = 100,000 \times \dfrac{1}{1.06^5}$
$= 100,000 \times 0.747$
$= £74,700$

(c)
$S = £4,000$
$n = 2 \text{ or } 3$
$r = 0.12$
$PV = \left(4,000 \times \dfrac{1}{1.12^2}\right) + \left(4,000 \times \dfrac{1}{1.12^3}\right)$
$= 4,000 \times (0.797 + 0.712)$
$= £6,036$

This calculation can be checked as follows.

	£
Year 0	6,036.00
Interest for the first year (12%)	724.32
	6,760.32
Interest for the second year (12%)	811.24
	7,571.56
Less withdrawal	(4,000.00)
	3,571.56
Interest for the third year (12%)	428.59
	4,000.15
Less withdrawal	(4,000.00)
Rounding error	0.15

Project appraisal

Discounted cash flow techniques can be used to evaluate expenditure proposals such as the purchase of equipment or marketing budgets.

Key concept

Discounted cash flow (DCF) involves the application of discounting arithmetic to the estimated future cash flows (receipts and expenditures) from a project in order to decide whether the project is expected to earn a satisfactory rate of return.

The net present method value (NPV) method

Key concept

> The **net present value (NPV)** method works out the present values of all items of income and expenditure related to an investment at a given rate of return, and then works out a net total. If it is positive, the investment is considered to be acceptable. If it is negative, the investment is considered to be unacceptable.

Example: the net present value of a project

Dog Ltd is considering whether to spend £5,000 on an item of equipment. The excess of income over cash expenditure from the project would be £3,000 in the first year and £4,000 in the second year.

The company will not invest in any project unless it offers a return in excess of 15% per annum.

Required

Assess whether the investment is worthwhile.

Solution

In this example, an outlay of £5,000 now promises a return of £3,000 **during** the first year and £4,000 **during** the second year. It is a convention in DCF, however, that cash flows spread over a year are assumed to occur **at the end of the year**, so that the cash flows of the project are as follows.

	£
Year 0 (now)	(5,000)
Year 1 (at the end of the year)	3,000
Year 2 (at the end of the year)	4,000

The NPV method takes the following approach.

(a)   The project offers £3,000 at year 1 and £4,000 at year 2, for an outlay of £5,000 now.

(b)   The company might invest elsewhere to earn a return of 15% per annum.

(c)   If the company did invest at exactly 15% per annum, how much would it need to invest now to earn £3,000 at the end of year 1 plus £4,000 at the end of year 2?

(d)   Is it cheaper to invest £5,000 in the project, or to invest elsewhere at 15%, in order to obtain these future cash flows?

If the company did invest elsewhere at 15% per annum, the amount required to earn £3,000 in year 1 and £4,000 in year 2 would be as follows.

Year	Cash flow £	Discount factor 15%	Present value £
1	3,000	$\frac{1}{1.15} = 0.870$	2,610
2	4,000	$\frac{1}{(1.15)^2} = 0.756$	3,024
			5,634

The choice is to invest £5,000 in the project, or £5,634 elsewhere at 15%, in order to obtain these future cash flows. We can therefore reach the following conclusion.

- It is cheaper to invest in the project, by £634.
- The project offers a return of over 15% per annum.

The net present value is the difference between the present value of cash inflows from the project (£5,634) and the present value of future cash outflows (in this example, £5,000 × $1/1.15^0$ = £5,000).

An NPV statement could be drawn up as follows.

Year	Cash flow £	Discount factor 15%	Present value £
0	(5,000)	1.000	(5,000)
1	3,000	$\frac{1}{1.15} = 0.870$	2,610
2	4,000	$\frac{1}{(1.15)^2} = 0.756$	3,024
	Net present value		+634

The project has a positive net present value, so it is acceptable.

Project comparison

The NPV method can also be used to compare two or more investment options. For example, suppose that Daisy Ltd can choose between the investment outlined in Question 2 above *or* a second investment, which also costs £28,000 but which would earn £6,500 in the first year, £7,500 in the second, £8,500 in the third, £9,500 in the fourth and £10,500 in the fifth. Which one should Daisy Ltd choose?

The decision rule is to choose the option with the highest NPV. We therefore need to calculate the NPV of the second option.

Year	Cash flow £	Discount factor 11%	Present value £
0	(28,000)	1.000	(28,000)
1	6,500	0.901	5,857
2	7,500	0.812	6,090
3	8,500	0.731	6,214
4	9,500	0.659	6,261
5	10,500	0.593	6,227
			NPV = 2,649

Daisy Ltd should therefore invest in the second option since it has the higher NPV.

Limitations of using the NPV method

There are a number of problems associated with using the NPV method in practice.

(a) The **future discount factors** (or interest rates) which are used in calculating NPVs can only be **estimated** and are not known with certainty. Discount rates that are estimated for time periods far into the future are therefore less likely to be accurate, thereby leading to less accurate NPV values.

(b) Similarly, NPV calculations make use of estimated **future cash flows**. As with future discount factors, cash flows which are estimated for cash flows several years into the future cannot really be predicted with any real certainty.

(c) When using the NPV method it is common to assume that all cash flows occur **at the end of the year**. However, this assumption is also likely to give rise to less accurate NPV values.

There are a number of computer programs available these days that enable a range of NPVs to be calculated for different circumstances (best-case and worst-case situations and so on). Such programs allow some of the limitations mentioned above to be alleviated.

6

Ethical considerations

Syllabus content

- Building sustainability and ethics into business and marketing activities (including the mix) through planning, the instillation of values and day-to-day values
- Measuring the value generated by sustainability or ethics and the progress of the organisation towards achieving its desired position

Introduction

Organisations are part of human society and, like individual people, are subject to rules that govern their conduct towards others. Some of these rules are **law** and enforced by legal sanction. Other rules fall into the realm of **ethics** or morality and are enforced only by the strength of society's approval or disapproval. Under a system of government that enjoys a measure of political legitimacy, law is generally a matter of consensus. Legal rules are therefore largely a matter of enforcing broadly acceptable standards of behaviour in a practical way. Ethics is more concerned with **absolute standards** of **right and wrong** and, human nature being what it is, individuals have widely divergent views on what those standards should be. Inevitably, therefore, ethical conduct is a matter of continuing debate. The first section of this chapter is concerned with the strategic impact of ethical ideas on organisations.

The behaviour of organisations may also be considered in the light of notions of **corporate social responsibility**. This is a rather poorly defined concept and the subject of continuing debate. However, there does now seem to be widespread acceptance that commercial organisations should devote some of their resources to the promotion of wider social aims that are not necessarily mandated by either law or the rules of ethics.

The final section of this chapter is concerned with **corporate governance** and the mechanisms that may be installed to promote fair and honest behaviour at the strategic apex.

1 Ethics and the organisation

FAST FORWARD

Ethics is concerned with the nature of right and wrong but it is not the same thing as law or the rules of religion.

1.1 Fundamentals of ethical theory

Ethics is concerned with **right and wrong** and how conduct should be judged to be good or bad. It is about how we should live our lives and, in particular, how we should behave towards other people. It is therefore relevant to all forms of human activity.

Business life is a fruitful source of **ethical dilemmas** because its whole purpose is material gain, the making of profit. Success in business requires a constant, avid search for potential advantage over others and business people are under pressure to do whatever yields such advantage.

1.1.1 Non-cognitivism, ethical relativism and intuitionism

The approach called **non-cognitivism** denies the possibility of acquiring objective knowledge of moral principles. It suggests that all moral statements are essentially subjective and arise from the culture, belief or emotion of the speaker.

Non-cognitivism recognises the differences that exist between the rules of behaviour prevailing in different cultures. The view that right and wrong are culturally determined is called **ethical relativism** or **moral relativism**. This is clearly a matter of significance in the context of international business. Managers encountering cultural norms of behaviour that differ significantly from their own may be puzzled to know what rules to follow.

1.1.2 Cognitivism

Cognitivist approaches to ethics are built on the principle that objective, universally applicable moral truths exist and can be known. There are four important cognitivist theories to consider after we have looked at **law** and **religion** in relation to ethics.

1.1.3 Ethics and religion

Religions are based on the concept of universally applicable principle. However, they not only provide endless examples to support the moral relativist approach, both in their rules and their statements of fundamental belief; they are also vulnerable to criticism on logical rounds. Specifically, how does God decide what is right and what is wrong? Presumably, it is not mere whim and **moral principles** are involved. The implication is that it is proper to seek to understand these reasons for ourselves and to use them as the basis of our moral code.

1.1.4 Ethics and law

Cognitivist ethics and law can be seen as parallel and connected systems of rules for regulating conduct. Both are concerned with right conduct and the principles that define it. However, ethics and law are not the same thing.

Law must be free from ambiguity. However, unlike law, ethics can quite reasonably be an arena for debate, about both the principles involved and their application in specific rules. The law must be certain and therefore finds it difficult to deal with problems of conduct that are subject to opinion and debate.

Another difference is that many legal rules are only very remotely connected with ethics, if at all, and some laws in some countries have been of debateable moral stature, to say the least.

1.2 Consequentialist ethics: utilitarianism

FAST FORWARD

The **consequentialist** approach to ethics is to make moral judgements about courses of action by reference to their outcomes or **consequences**. Right or wrong becomes a question of benefit or harm.

Utilitarianism is the best-known formulation of this approach and can be summed up in the **'greatest good'** principle. This says that when deciding on a course of action we should choose the one that is likely to result in the greatest good for the greatest number of people.

There is an immediate problem here, which is how we are to define what is good for people. *Bentham* considered that **happiness** was the measure of good and that actions should therefore be judged in terms of their potential for promoting happiness or relieving unhappiness. Others have suggested that longer lists of harmful and beneficial things should be applied.

The utilitarian approach may also be questioned for its potential effect upon minorities. A situation in which a large majority achieved great happiness at the expense of creating misery among a small minority would satisfy the 'greatest good' principle. It could not, however, be regarded as ethically desirable. A linked problem arises when we consider the nature of happiness and unhappiness, in that pain can be very much more intense than pleasure. We must therefore be very cautious in our netting-off of total happiness against total unhappiness.

However, utilitarianism can be a useful guide to conduct. It has been used to derive wide ranging rules and can be applied to help us make judgements about individual, unique problems.

1.3 Deontological ethics

FAST FORWARD

Deontological ethical theory assumes that there are universal, objective moral rules that must always apply.

Deontology is concerned with the application of universal ethical principles in order to arrive at rules of conduct, the word deontology being derived from the Greek for 'duty'. Whereas the consequentialist approach judges actions by their outcomes, deontology lays down *a priori* criteria by which they may be judged in advance. The definitive treatment of deontological ethics is found in the work of *Immanuel Kant*.

Kant's approach to ethics is based on the idea that facts themselves are neutral: they are what *is*; they do not give us any indication of what *should be*. If we make moral judgements about facts, the criteria by which we judge are separate from the facts themselves. Kant suggested that the criteria come from within ourselves and are based on a sense of what is right; an **intuitive awareness** of the nature of good.

Kant spoke of motivation to act in terms of 'imperatives'. A **hypothetical imperative** lays down a course of action to achieve a certain result. For instance, if I wish to pass an examination I must study the syllabus. A **categorical imperative**, however, defines a course of action without reference to outcomes. For Kant, moral conduct is defined by categorical imperatives. We must act in certain ways because it is right to do so – right conduct is an end in itself.

Kant arrived at two formulations of the categorical imperative with which we should be familiar.

(a)   'So act that the maxim of your will could hold as a principle establishing universal law.'

In other words, never act in a way that you would condemn in others. This is very close to the common sense maxim called the 'golden rule' that is found in many religious teachings. It appears in the Bible as

'Therefore all things whatsoever ye would that men should do to you, do ye even so to them: for this is the law and the prophets' (Matthew 7:12)

(b)   'Do not treat people simply as means to an end but as an end in themselves.'

The point of this rule is that it distinguishes between **people** and **objects**. We use objects as means to achieve an end: a chair is for sitting on, for instance. People are different. Human dignity requires that we regard people differently from the way we regard objects, since they have unique intellects, feelings, motivations and so on of their own. Note, however, that this does not preclude us from using people as means to an end as long as we, at the same time, recognise their right to be treated as autonomous beings. Clearly, organisations and even society itself could not function if we could not make use of other people's services.

1.4 Duty and consequences

FAST FORWARD

Ethical theory is not integrated: consequentialist, deontological and natural law based rules are capable of pointing to different conclusions. Partly as a result of this, **ethical dilemmas** can exist at all levels in the organisation.

In their pure form, neither the duties of natural law nor Kant's categorical imperative will admit consideration of the consequences of our actions: we act in a certain way because we are obeying inflexible moral rules. Unfortunately, such an approach can have undesirable results. If people have **absolute rights** that we must respect whatever the circumstances, we may find that our actions in doing so harm the **common good**. An example is the accused person who commits an offence while on bail. The potential threat to public safety has to be balanced against the right of the individual to liberty. There is thus a **great potential for conflict** between courses of action based on the consequentialist approach and those based on deontology or natural law.

While individual cases are bound to provoke debate, it would be reasonable to suggest that an inflexible approach to rules of conduct is likely to produce ethical dilemmas. Deciding what to do when the arguments point in opposite directions is always going to be difficult. However, generally **we do not have the option of doing nothing**, and this is particularly true of business. We discuss some specific business related dilemmas later in this chapter.

1.5 Natural law

Natural law approaches to ethics are based on the idea that a set of 'natural' moral rules exists and we can come to know what they are.

At one time natural law theory time was concerned with the rights of the citizen against arbitrary acts by powerful rulers. This was subsequently developed into a more democratic concept of government by consent, with a prominent position occupied by what are now called 'human rights'.

In terms of business ethics, the natural law approach deals mostly with **rights and duties**. Where there is a right, there is also a duty to respect that right. Clearly, this idea is not limited in its application to matters of law and government. It implies that we all must respect one another's rights of all kinds. For those concerned with business ethics there are undeniable implications for behaviour towards **individuals**. Unfortunately, the implications about duties can only be as clear as the rights themselves and there are wide areas in which disagreement about rights persists.

1.6 Virtue ethics

The idea of pursuing a harmonious or virtuous life was first expressed by *Aristotle*. His approach was based on gentlemanly behaviour and a rational judgement about what constitutes good. To some extent this consists of **avoiding extremes** of any kind, since moderation will lead to virtue. For example, courage lies between cowardice at one end of the scale and foolhardiness at the other.

We need not concern ourselves too closely with the detail of Aristotle's approach, except to note that the cultivation of **appropriate virtues** has been proposed as a route to ethical behaviour in business. For example, managers might cultivate a range of virtues such as those listed below.

- Courage
- Fairness
- Empathy
- Persistence
- Honesty

- Politeness
- Receptivity to new ideas
- Determination
- Firmness

1.7 The scope of corporate ethics

FAST FORWARD

Corporate ethics has three contexts.

- Interaction with national and international society
- Effects of routine operations
- Behaviour of individuals

Mission should incorporate recognition of the ethical dimension.

Corporate ethics may be considered in three contexts.

- The organisation's interaction with **national** and **international society**
- The effects of the organisation's **routine operations**
- The behaviour of **individual members** of staff

Influencing society. Businesses operate within and interact with the political, economic and social framework of wider society. It is both inevitable and proper that they will both influence and be influenced by that wider framework. Governments, individual politicians and pressure groups will all make demands on such matters as employment prospects and executive pay. Conversely, businesses themselves will find that they need to make their own representations on such matters as monetary policy and the burden of regulation. International variation in such matters and in the framework of **corporate governance** will affect organisations that operate in more than one country. It is appropriate that the organisation develops and promotes its own policy on such matters.

Corporate behaviour. The organisation should establish **corporate policies** for those issues over which it has direct control. Examples of matters that should be covered by policy include health, safety, labelling, equal opportunities, environmental effects, political activity, bribery and support for cultural activities.

Individual behaviour. Policies to guide the behaviour of individuals are likely to flow from the corporate stance on the matters discussed above. The organisation must decide on the extent to which it considers it appropriate to attempt to influence individual behaviour. Some aspects of such behaviour may be of strategic importance, especially when managers can be seen as representing or embodying the organisation's standards. Matters of financial rectitude and equal treatment of minorities are good examples here.

Corporate ethical codes. Organizations often publish corporate codes of ethical standards. Fundamentally, this is a good idea and can be a useful way of disseminating the specific policies we have discussed above. However, care must be taken over such a document.

(a) It should not be over-prescriptive or over-detailed, since this encourages a legalistic approach to interpretation and a desire to seek loopholes in order to justify previously chosen courses of action.

(b) It will only have influence if senior management adhere to it consistently in their own decisions and actions.

1.7.1 Ethics and strategy

In this Study Text we have emphasised that what the organisation wishes to achieve – its **mission** – is fundamental to any focused control of its activities. When we discussed the concept of mission we made passing reference to **policies and standards of behaviour**.

It is important to understand that if ethics is applicable to corporate behaviour at all, it must therefore be a fundamental aspect of **mission**, since everything the organisation does flows from that. Managers responsible for strategic decision making cannot avoid responsibility for their organisation's ethical standing. They should consciously apply ethical rules to all of their decisions in order to filter out potentially undesirable developments.

 Marketing at Work

Shell

'I am becoming sick and tired about lying.' Those are not the words shareholders want to hear from a senior executive. They are certainly not words anybody ever expected from an heir-apparent at Royal Dutch/Shell, one of the world's largest – and until recently, one of its most admired – oil companies.

And yet, as a new report is revealed this week, those words of exasperation did indeed come from a senior Shell executive. Walter van de Vijver, until recently the firm's head of exploration and production (E&P), wrote them in an angry e-mail to Sir Phillip Watts, then the firm's chairman, in November 2003 – fuming that he was tired of covering up for shortfalls in the firm's reserves that resulted from 'far too aggressive/optimistic bookings.' Also, the overzealous booker was none other than Sir Phillip, who preceded him as head of E&P.

The overbooking finally caught up with both men when, in January, Shell was forced to reclassify a whopping fifth of its 'proved' reserves. When preliminary investigations pointed the finger at the two men, both were forced out.

The Economist, 24 April 2004

The changing ethical environment

The surreal dilemmas sound like they could be drawn from a magazine advice column for paranoid lawyers: can I provide sacrificial goats for my customers in the Middle East? What if the client asks us to procure internal organs for his sick relative? Is it ok for me to donate cash at a Korean funeral?

These are real life scenarios under discussion by senior executives responsible for setting policies for corporate hospitality and gifts in an increasingly strict US regulatory environment.

The conclusion of the executives, who recently gathered in New York for a summit on the problem, was that the fine grey line that separates acceptable generosity from the darker world of bribery and corruption has narrowed substantially.

What lies behind their nervousness is the growing impact of Sarbanes-Oxley corporate governance legislation on the already strict rules of the US Foreign Corrupt Practices Act. Combine this with increasingly active enforcement agencies and the rapid globalisation of US business and there is a recipe for multinational angst on a grand scale.

Where minor local transgressions might once have been swept under the carpet, they are now likely to emerge as so-called 'material weaknesses' in internal control reports requiring sign-off from a chief executive and finance director worried about their own liability.

Some rules are clear-cut. *Schering Plough* makes a rule not to pay for spouses to attend medical conferences, for example. Other policies can be difficult. Rule one is no cash – yet there are countries in Asia where token payments in envelopes are still expected at certain social situations such as funerals or Chinese New Year.

In contrast, *Northrop Grumman*, the US defence manufacturer, takes a more rule-bound approach – perhaps in keeping with the military background of many of its employees.

Trace International, which advises its member companies on differing international standards, recently conducted a survey of corporate lawyers that found a wide range of in-house policies. Thirteen per cent of companies had no policy for gifts and hospitality, 17 per cent left it to the discretion of local managers and 34 percent simply required prior approval for any 'reasonable' expenditure. Only 3 per cent demanded approval if the monetary value was above a pre-determined threshold, while three per cent applied a blanket ban on anything above their threshold.

This is likely to change quickly as companies realise the impact of the changing regulatory climate. Provisions to protect whistleblowers and ensure full disclosure are also likely to increase the number of cases that come to the surface.

The trend in fines is also going up. Last July, two divisions of *ABB's* oil, gas and petrochemicals business pleaded guilty to charges of bribing Nigerian government officials – including with cash and pedicures – and agreed with the Department of Justice to pay fines of $10.5m (£5.4m). Separately, ABB, the Swiss-Swedish engineering group, resolved civil charges brought by the SEC and agreed to pay an additional $5.9m fine.

The Changing Ethical Environment. Dan Roberts. *Financial Times, 20 April 2005*

2 Social responsibility

2.1 Corporate social responsibility

FAST FORWARD

There is a fundamental split of views about the nature of corporate responsibility.

–   The **stakeholder view** that a range of goals should be pursued
–   The view that the business organisation is a purely **economic force**, subject to law

Businesses, particularly large ones, are subject to increasing expectations that they will exercise **social responsibility**. This is an ill-defined concept, but appears to focus on the provision of specific benefits to society in general, such as charitable donations, the creation or preservation of employment, and spending on environmental improvement or maintenance. A great deal of the pressure is created by the activity of minority action groups and is aimed at businesses because they are perceived to possess extensive resources. The momentum of such arguments is now so great that the notion of social responsibility has become almost inextricably confused with the matter of ethics. It is important to remember the distinction. Social responsibility and ethical behaviour are not the same thing.

In this context, you should remember that a business managed with the sole objective of maximising shareholder wealth can be run in just as ethical a fashion as one in which far wider stakeholder responsibility is assumed. On the other hand, there is no doubt that many large businesses have behaved irresponsibly in the past and some continue to do so.

2.2 Against corporate social responsibility

Milton Friedman argued against corporate social responsibility along the following lines.

(a)   Businesses do not have responsibilities, only people have responsibilities. Managers in charge of corporations are responsible to the owners of the business, by whom they are employed.

(b)   These employers may have charity as their aim, but 'generally [their aim] will be to make as much money as possible while conforming to the basic rules of the society, both those embodied in law and those embodied in ethical custom.'

(c)   If the statement that a manager has social responsibilities is to have any meaning, 'it must mean that he is to act in some way that is not in the interest of his employers.'

(d)   If managers do this they are, generally speaking, spending the owners' money for purposes other than those they have authorised; sometimes it is the money of customers or suppliers that is spent and, on occasion, the money of employees. By doing this, the manager is, in effect, both raising taxes and deciding how they should be spent, which are functions of government, not of business. There are two objections to this.

(i)   Managers have not been democratically elected (or selected in any other way) to exercise government power.

(ii)   Managers are not experts in government policy and cannot foresee the detailed effect of such social responsibility spending.

Friedman argues that the social responsibility model is politically collectivist in nature and deplores the possibility that collectivism should be extended any further than absolutely necessary in a free society.

A second argument against the assumption of corporate social responsibility is that the **maximisation of wealth is the best way that society can benefit from a business's activities**.

(a)   Maximising wealth has the effect of increasing the tax revenues available to the state to disburse on socially desirable objectives.

(b)   Maximising shareholder value has a 'trickle down' effect on other disadvantaged members of society.

(c)   Many company shares are owned by pension funds, whose ultimate beneficiaries may not be the wealthy anyway.

2.3 The stakeholder view

The **stakeholder view** is that many groups have a stake in what the organisation does. This is particularly important in the business context, where shareholders own the business but employees, customers and government also have particularly strong claims to having their interests considered. This is fundamentally an argument derived from **natural law theory** and is based on the notion of individual and collective **rights**.

It is suggested that modern corporations are so powerful, socially, economically and politically, that unrestrained use of their power will inevitably damage other people's rights. For example, they may blight an entire community by closing a major facility, thus enforcing long term unemployment on a large proportion of the local workforce. Similarly, they may damage people's quality of life by polluting the environment. They may use their purchasing power or market share to impose unequal contracts on suppliers and customers alike. And they may exercise undesirable influence over government through their investment decisions. Under this approach, the exercise of corporate social responsibility constrains the corporation to act at all times as a good citizen.

Another argument points out that corporations exist within society and are dependent upon it for the resources they use. Some of these resources are obtained by direct contracts with suppliers but others are not, being provided by government expenditure. Examples are such things as transport infrastructure, technical research and education for the workforce. Clearly, corporations contribute to the taxes that pay for these things, but the relationship is rather tenuous and the tax burden can be minimised by careful management. The implication is that corporations should recognise and pay for the facilities that society provides by means of socially responsible policies and actions.

Henry Mintzberg (in *Power In and Around Organisations*) suggests that simply viewing organisations as vehicles for shareholder investment is inadequate.

(a)   In practice, he says, organisations are rarely controlled effectively by shareholders. Most shareholders are passive investors.

(b)   Large corporations can manipulate markets. Social responsibility, forced or voluntary, is a way of recognising this.

(c)   Moreover, as mentioned above, businesses do receive a lot of government support. The public pays for roads, infrastructure, education and health, all of which benefits businesses. Although businesses pay tax, the public ultimately pays, perhaps through higher prices.

(d)   Strategic decisions by businesses always have wider social consequences. In other words, says Mintzberg, the firm produces two kinds of outputs: **goods and services** and the **social consequences of its activities** (eg pollution).

2.4 Externalities

FAST FORWARD

There is particular concern over **externalities**, or the social and environmental costs of corporate activities.

If it is accepted that businesses do not bear the total social cost of their activities, then the exercise of social responsibility is a way of compensating for this. An example is given by the environment. Industrial pollution is injurious to health: if someone is made ill by industrial pollution, then arguably the polluter should pay the sick person, as damages or in compensation, in the same way as if the business's builders had accidentally bulldozed somebody's house.

In practice, of course, while it is relatively easy to identify statistical relationships between pollution levels and certain illnesses, mapping out the chain of cause and effect from an individual's wheezing cough to the dust particles emitted by Factory X, as opposed to Factory Y, is quite a different matter.

Of course, it could be argued that these external costs are met out of general taxation: but this has the effect of spreading the cost amongst other individuals and businesses. Moreover, the tax revenue may be spent on curing the disease, rather than stopping it at its source. Pollution control equipment may be the fairest way of dealing with this problem. Thus advocates of social responsibility in business would argue that business's responsibilities then do not rest with paying taxes.

Is there any justification for social responsibility outside remedying the effects of a business's direct activities. For example, should businesses give to charity or sponsor the arts? Several arguments have been advanced suggesting that they should.

(a) If the **stakeholder concept** of a business is held, then the public is a stakeholder in the business. A business only succeeds because it is part of a wider society. Giving to charity is one way of encouraging a relationship.

(b) Charitable donations and artistic sponsorship are a useful medium of **public relations** and can reflect well on the business. It can be regarded, then, as another form of promotion, which like advertising, serves to enhance consumer awareness of the business, while not encouraging the sale of a particular brand.

The arguments for and against social responsibility of business are complex ones. However, ultimately they can be traced to different assumptions about society and the relationships between the individuals and organisations within it.

Marketing at Work

Corporate social responsibility

As William Allen, then chancellor of the Delaware Court of Chancery, said in a brilliant lecture to the Cardozo School of Law in 1992, the argument about the purpose of companies has been around for more than a century. Underlying the debate, he said, were 'two quite different and inconsistent ways to conceptualise the public corporation'. Prof Allen called these two ideas 'the property conception' and the 'social entity conception'. The first saw the company's aim as being to advance the financial interests of the owners. The second viewed the company as having 'a duty of loyalty, in some sense, to all those interested in or affected by the corporation'.

For most of the century, these two ideas managed to rub along. Courts, managers and commentators reconciled them by arguing that looking after employees and the community was good for the shareholders in the long run. Happy staff would provide better service, a contented community would furnish loyal customers – and profits would rise, along with the share price and dividend payments. This is the argument underlying the current case for corporate social responsibility.

There are times, however, when the inherent conflict between these two concepts bursts into the open. Prof Allen noted that takeovers often pitted shareholders, who benefited by selling their shares at a premium, against employees who stood to lose their jobs.

Today, the availability of cheap labour in Asia, allied with consumer insistence on low prices, has brought the two concepts of the company into conflict once more. While good for shareholders, offshoring is disastrous for many existing employees.

Who should prevail – shareholders or staff? Some argue that employee commitment is more important to companies than shareholder investment. Modern shareholders are vast institutional funds with no loyalty to the company. In an article published this month in *Learning & Education* journal the late Sumantra Ghoshal of London Business School made the case for putting staff flrst.

'Most shareholders can sell their stocks far more easily than most employees can find another job. In every substantive sense, employees of a company carry more risks than do the shareholders. Also, their contributions of knowledge, skills and entrepreneurship are typically more important than the contributions of capital by shareholders, a pure commodity that is perhaps in excess supply.'

There is much to this, but there are three reasons why we should not dismiss shareholders so easily. First, many people's hopes for a comfortable retirement depend on those faceless institutional investors. The beneficiaries of the institutional shareholders are often employees too, either of that company or another one.

Second, with the collapse of trade unions, institutional investors are the only force able to stand up to over-powerful management. This is particularly true when shareholders act through representative associations.

Third, share-price performance is a fair guide to corporate success – eventually. Shareholders often follow the herd. They can go collectively mad, as during the dotcom silliness. But the market cannot fool itself forever. Judged over five or ten or fifty years, a successful company's worth will be recognised by the stock markets.

Financial Times, 2 March 2005

2.5 The ethical stance

FAST FORWARD

An organisation's **ethical stance** is the extent to which it will exceed its minimum obligations to stakeholders. There are four typical stances.

– Short-term shareholder interest
– Long-term shareholder interest
– Multiple stakeholder obligations
– Shaper of society

Key concept

An organisation's **ethical stance** is defined by *Johnson and Scholes* as the extent to which it will exceed its minimum obligation to stakeholders.

Johnson and Scholes illustrate the range of possible ethical stances by giving four illustrations.

- **Short-term shareholder interest**
- **Long-term shareholder interest**
- **Multiple stakeholder obligations**
- **Shaper of society**

2.5.1 Short-term shareholder interest

An organisation might limit its ethical stance to taking responsibility for **short-term shareholder interest** on the grounds that it is for **government** alone to impose wider constraints on corporate governance. This minimalist approach would accept a duty of obedience to the demands of the law, but would not undertake to comply with any less substantial rules of conduct. This stance can be justified on the grounds that going beyond it can **challenge government authority**; this is an important consideration for organisations operating in developing countries.

2.5.2 Long-term shareholder interest

There are two reasons why an organisation might take a wider view of ethical responsibilities when considering the **longer-term interest of shareholders**.

(a)   The organisation's **corporate image** may be enhanced by an assumption of wider responsibilities. The cost of undertaking such responsibilities may be justified as essentially promotional expenditure.

(b)   The responsible exercise of corporate power may prevent a build-up of social and political **pressure for legal regulation**. Freedom of action may be preserved and the burden of regulation lightened by acceptance of ethical responsibilities.

2.5.3 Multiple stakeholder obligations

An organisation might accept the **legitimacy of the expectations of stakeholders other than shareholders** and build those expectations into its stated purposes. This would be because without appropriate relationships with groups such as suppliers, employers and customers, the organisation would not be able to function.

A distinction can be drawn between **rights** and **expectations**. The *Concise Oxford Dictionary* defines a right as 'a legal or moral entitlement'. One is on fairly safe interpretative ground with legal rights, since their basis is usually clearly established, though subject to development and adjustment. The concept of *moral* entitlement is much less well defined and subject to partisan argument, as discussed above in the context of **natural law**. There is, for instance, an understandable tendency for those who feel themselves aggrieved to declare that their *rights* have been infringed. Whether or not this is the case is often a matter of opinion. For example, in the UK, there is often talk of a 'right to work' when redundancies occur. No such right exists in UK law, nor is it widely accepted that there is a moral basis for such a right. However, there is a widespread acceptance that governments should make the prevention of large-scale unemployment a high priority.

Clearly, organisations have a duty to respect the **legal rights** of stakeholders other than shareholders. These are extensive in the UK, including wide-ranging **employment law** and **consumer protection law**, as well as the more basic legislation relating to such matters as contract and property. Where **moral entitlements** are concerned, organisations need to be practical: they should take care to establish just what *expectations* they are prepared to treat as *obligations*, bearing in mind their general ethical stance and degree of concern about bad publicity.

Acceptance of obligations to stakeholders implies that **measurement of the organisation's performance** must give due weight to these extra imperatives. For instance, as is widely known, Anita Roddick does not care to have the performance of *Body Shop* assessed in purely financial terms.

2.5.4 Shaper of society

It is difficult enough for a commercial organisation to accept wide responsibility to stakeholders. The role of **shaper of society** is even more demanding and largely the province of public sector organisations and charities, though some well-funded private organisations might act in this way. The legitimacy of this approach depends on the framework of corporate governance and accountability. Where organisations are clearly set up for such a role, either by government or by private sponsors, they may pursue it. However, they must also satisfy whatever requirements for financial viability are established for them.

2.6 The strategic value of stakeholders

The firm can make strategic gains from managing stakeholder relationships. This was highlighted by a recent report by the Royal Society of Arts on **Tomorrow's Company**. 'Failure to manage such relationships can carry heavy penalties.' Studies have revealed:

(a)   **Correlation between employee retention and customer loyalty** (eg low staff turnover in service firms generally results in more repeat business).

(b)   **Continuity and stability** in relationships with employees, customers and suppliers is important in enabling organisations to **respond to certain types of change**.

These soft issues are particularly pertinent for industries where creativity is important and for service businesses. Knowledge based and service industries are likely to be the growth industries of the future.

2.7 Ethical dilemmas

There are a number of areas in which the various approaches to ethics and conflicting views of a business's responsibilities can create **ethical dilemmas** for managers. These can impact at the highest level, affecting the development of policy, or lower down the hierarchy, especially if policy is unclear and guidance from more senior people is unavailable.

Dealing with **unpleasantly authoritarian governments** can be supported on the grounds that it contributes to economic growth and prosperity and all the benefits they bring to society in both countries concerned. This is a consequentialist argument. It can also be opposed on consequentialist grounds as contributing to the continuation of the regime, and on deontological grounds as fundamentally repugnant.

Honesty in advertising is an important problem. Many products are promoted exclusively on image. Deliberately creating the impression that purchasing a particular product will enhance the happiness, success and sex-appeal of the buyer can be attacked as dishonest. It can be defended on the grounds that the supplier is actually selling a fantasy or dream rather than a physical article.

Dealings with **employees** are coloured by the opposing views of corporate responsibility and individual rights. The idea of a job as property to be defended has now disappeared from UK labour relations, but there is no doubt that corporate decisions that lead to redundancies are still deplored. This is because of the obvious impact of sudden unemployment on aspirations and living standards, even when the employment market is buoyant. Nevertheless, it is only proper for businesses to consider the cost of employing labour as well as its productive capacity. Even employers who accept that their employees' skills are their most important source of competitive advantage can be reduced to cost cutting in order to survive in lean times.

Another ethical problem concerns **payments by companies to officials** who have power to help or hinder the payers' operations. In *The Ethics of Corporate Conduct, Clarence Walton* discusses to the fine distinctions which exist in this area.

(a)   **Extortion**. Foreign officials have been known to threaten companies with the complete closure of their local operations unless suitable payments are made.

(b)   **Bribery**. This is payments for services to which a company is not legally entitled. There are some fine distinctions to be drawn; for example, some managers regard political contributions as bribery.

(c)   **Grease money**. Multinational companies are sometimes unable to obtain services to which they are legally entitled because of deliberate stalling by local officials. Cash payments to the right people may then be enough to oil the machinery of bureaucracy.

(d)   **Gifts**. In some cultures (such as Japan) gifts are regarded as an essential part of civilised negotiation, even in circumstances where to Western eyes they might appear ethically dubious. Managers operating in such a culture may feel at liberty to adopt the local customs.

Business ethics are also relevant to competitive behaviour. This is because a market can only be free if competition is, in some basic respects, fair. There is a distinction between competing aggressively and competing unethically. The dispute between British Airways and Virgin centred around issues of business ethics.

2.8 The societal marketing concept

Kotler (*Social Marketing,* 2002) suggests that a **societal marketing concept** should replace the marketing concept as a philosophy for the future.

Key concept

> 'The **societal marketing concept** is a management orientation that holds that the key task of the organisation is to determine the needs and wants of target markets and to adapt the organisation to delivering the desired satisfactions more effectively and efficiently than its competitors in a way that preserves or enhances the consumers' and society's well-being.'

Exam tip

> In a past *Analysis and Decision* case study question, candidates were asked to consider what to do with a 'town centre': effectively being asked to advise a local authority. In this case a variety of stakeholder groups were interested: the general public, shopkeepers, drivers and so on.

3 Corporate governance

FAST FORWARD

> **Corporate governance** is the conduct of the organisation's senior officers. Abuses have led to a range of measures to improve corporate governance. Non-executive directors have a particular role to play.

Key concept

> The conduct of an organisation's senior officers constitutes its **corporate governance**.

Lynch says that the field of corporate governance includes the **selection** of the organisation's senior officers and 'their relationships with owners, employees and other stakeholders'. He points out that the influence of those officers over the future direction of the organisation makes corporate governance a matter of **strategic importance**.

Senior managers' influence amounts, in fact, to considerable **power**, and it is a matter of wide concern that power is wielded responsibly. Within the organisation, whatever the formal **ethical stance**, management decisions affect interests other than the purely financial. The effect on employment of short-term cost cutting is an example. Externally, the public interest may be affected. Lynch gives the example of the directors of privatised UK utility companies that awarded themselves large rewards, effectively at the taxpayer's expense.

Other recent examples include the deception and fraud committed by Robert Maxwell and, in the USA, the corrupt accounting policies pursued at *Enron Corporation*.

Extensive abuses have led to a variety of measures intended to improve the quality of corporate governance.

    (a)   The development of **accounting standards** has been driven in part by the need to prevent abuses in financial reporting.

    (b)   The various professional bodies all have their own **codes of professional conduct**.

    (c)   A series of major financial scandals has led to government intervention in the UK in the form of **commissions on standards of behaviour**, each producing its code of conduct.

Many companies have established, and promoted their own **corporate codes of ethical behaviour**.

Marketing at Work

Corporate codes of ethics

What can be done to make an ethics code work? It is an important question, given that this once voluntary tool is now a virtual obligation, especially for multinationals. New York Stock Exchange listing rules require companies to have a publicly displayed code of business conduct and ethics. Codes can cover everything from obeying the law and accurate financial disclosure to conflicts of interest, bribery and sexual harassment.

In the UK, it has been best practice since the 1992 Cadbury report on corporate governance for boards to draw up and publicise a code of ethics or statement of business principles. More than 90 of the FTSE 100 companies now have codes.

Judgment about the effectiveness of a code depends on what its primary purpose is. This varies. In the US, having a code can give legal protection: the federal sentencing guidelines allow for reductions in penalties for corporate crimes if companies already have programmes to detect and prevent misconduct. Elsewhere, reasons for having codes include protecting reputation, reinforcing an ethical culture and supporting staff who blow the whistle.

Human nature is a further complicating factor. Companies may be disappointed if they think that simply having a code in place will alter behaviour. Someone who disagrees with a view expressed in a code is unlikely to change behaviour unless there are appropriate penalties, say Bruce Gaumnitz and John Lere. The two professors say: 'Statements in codes of ethics are most likely to have an impact when they address new situations or when they take positions with which one mildly disagrees'.

In a study published in the *Journal of Business Ethics*, Mark Schwartz, assistant professor of business ethics at Toronto's York University, asked 57 managers, employees and ethics officers at four large Canadian companies what it was about their codes and the way they were implemented that made them effective or ineffective.

Some respondents pointed to requirements that they found unfair, implying they were less likely to follow these.

Mr Schwartz also found that: concrete examples were very important in helping employees understand codes; codes that were negative in tone were considered clearer than those that sounded positive; and it mattered who did the training. Most staff thought training by managers rather than outsiders was more credible and relevant, but some strongly disagreed. 'My manager probably can't say the word [ethics],' one commented.

All four companies' codes required staff to report violations. Would they do so?, Mr Schwartz asked. That depended on a lot of things, including the nature of the offence, the person who had violated the code and fear of retribution. Even some ethics officers indicated that they might have difficulty reporting their supervisors.

The study confirmed the importance of senior management backing if codes are to be taken seriously. There are signs that companies are recognising this. The study shows that the board or the chief executive takes responsibility for administering the code in 26 per cent of companies – up from 16 per cent four years ago.

Of course, no code of ethics can be effective in the face of a hostile corporate culture, as Enron demonstrated. If the culture allows, or encourages, the pursuit of maximum financial reward at any cost, a code of ethics contradicting this will fall on deaf ears.

Alison Maitland, *Financial Times, 7 March 2005*

Marketing at Work

The Chartered Institute of Marketing's *Code of Professional Standards* is reproduced below.

1   A member shall at all times conduct himself with integrity in such a way as to bring credit to the profession of marketing and The Chartered Institute of Marketing.

2   A member shall not by any unfair or unprofessional practice injure the business, reputation or interest of any other member of the Institute.

3   Members shall, at all times, act honestly in their professional dealings with customers and clients (actual and potential), employers and employees.

4   A member shall not, knowingly or recklessly, disseminate any false or misleading information, either on his own behalf or on behalf of anyone else.

5   A member shall keep abreast of current marketing practice and act competently and diligently and be encouraged to register for the Institute's scheme of Continuing Professional Development.

6   A member shall, at all times, seek to avoid conflict of interest and shall make prior voluntary and full disclosure to all parties concerned of all matters that may rise to any such conflict. Where a conflict arises a member must withdraw prior to the work commencing.

7   A member shall keep business information confidential except: from those persons entitled to receive it, where it breaches this code and where it is illegal to do so.

8   A member shall promote and seek business in a professional and ethical manner.

9   A member shall observe the requirements of all other codes of practice which may from time to time have any relevance to the practice of marketing insofar as such requirements do not conflict with any provisions of this code, or the Institute's Royal Charter and Bye-laws; a list of such codes being obtainable from the Institute's head office.

10   Members shall not hold themselves out as having the Institute's endorsement in connection with an activity unless the Institute's prior written approval has been obtained first.

11   A member shall not use any funds derived from the Institute for any purpose which does not fall within the powers and obligations contained in the Branch or Group handbook, and which does not fully comply with this code.

12   A member shall have due regard for, and comply with, all the relevant laws of the country in which they are operating.

13   A member who knowingly causes or permits any other person or organisation to be in substantial breach of this code or who is a party to such a breach shall himself be guilty of such breach.

14   A member shall observe this Code of Professional Standards as it may be expanded and annotated and published from time to time by the Ethics Committee in the manner provided for below.

Lynch points out that an important check on the abuse of power by senior managers is the **free flow of information to stakeholders**: 'wrongdoing will go unchecked as long as it remains unknown or unreported'. However, there are legitimate concerns about commercial confidentiality to be addressed here. The **auditor** has an important role to play, reviewing internal information on a confidential basis.

3.1 Two approaches to managing ethics

FAST FORWARD

A compliance-based approach highlights conformity with law and regulation. An integrity-based approach suggests a wider remit, incorporating ethics in the organisation's values and culture.

Lynne Paine (*Harvard Business Review*, March–April 1994) suggests that ethical decisions are becoming more important as penalties, in the US at least, for companies which break the law become tougher. (This might be contrasted with UK, where a fraudster whose deception ran into millions received a sentence of community service.) Paine suggests that there are two approaches to the management of ethics in organisations.

- **Compliance**-based
- **Integrity**-based

3.1.1 Compliance-based approach

A compliance-based approach is primarily designed to ensure that the company **acts within the letter of the law**, and that violations are prevented, detected and punished. Some organisations, faced with the legal consequences of unethical behaviour take legal precautions such as those below.

- Compliance procedures to detect misconduct
- Audits of contracts
- Systems for employees to report criminal misconduct without fear of retribution
- Disciplinary procedures to deal with transgressions

Corporate compliance is limited in that it relates only to the law, but legal compliance is 'not an adequate means for addressing the full range of ethical issues that arise every day'. This is especially the case in the UK, where **voluntary** codes of conduct and self-regulation are perhaps more prevalent than in the US.

An example of the difference between the **legality** and **ethicality** of a practice is the sale in some countries of defective products without appropriate warnings. 'Companies engaged in international business often discover that conduct that infringes on recognised standards of human rights and decency is legally permissible in some jurisdictions.'

The compliance approach also overemphasises the threat of detection and punishment in order to channel appropriate behaviour. Arguably, some employers view compliance programmes as an insurance policy for senior management, who can cover the tracks of their arbitrary management practices. After all, some performance targets are impossible to achieve without cutting corners: managers can escape responsibility by blaming the employee for not following the compliance programme, when to do so would have meant a failure to reach target.

Furthermore, mere compliance with the law is no guide to **exemplary** behaviour.

3.1.2 Integrity-based programmes

'An integrity-based approach combines a concern for the law with an **emphasis on managerial responsibility** for ethical behaviour. Integrity strategies strive to define companies' guiding values, aspirations and patterns of thought and conduct. When integrated into the day-to-day operations of an organisation, such strategies can help prevent damaging ethical lapses, while tapping into powerful human impulses for moral thought and action.

It should be clear to you from this quotation that an integrity-based approach to ethics treats ethics as an issue of organisation culture.

Ethics management has several tasks.

- To define and give life to an organisation's defining values
- To create an environment that supports ethically sound behaviour
- To instil a sense of shared accountability amongst employees

The table below indicates some of the differences between the two main approaches.

	Compliance	Integrity
Ethos	Knuckle under to external standards	Choose ethical standards
Objective	Keep to the law	Enable legal and responsible conduct
Originators	Lawyers	Management, with lawyers, HR specialists etc
Methods (both includes education, and audits, controls, penalties)	Reduced employee discretion	Leadership, organisation systems
Behavioural assumptions	People are solitary self-interested beings	People are social beings with values
Standards	The law	Company values, aspirations (including law)
Staffing	Lawyers	Managers and lawyers
Education	The law, compliance system	Values, the law, compliance systems
Activities	Develop standards, train and communicate, handle reports of misconduct, investigate, enforce, oversee compliance	Integrate values *into* company systems, provide guidance and consultation, identify and resolve problems, oversee compliance

In other words, an integrity-based approach **incorporates** ethics into corporate culture and systems.

 Marketing at Work

Charles Hampden-Turner (in his book *Corporate Culture*) notes that attitudes to safety can be part of a corporate *culture*. He quotes the example of a firm called (for reasons of confidentiality) *Western Oil*.

Western Oil had a bad safety record. 'Initially, safety was totally at odds with the main cultural values of productivity (management's interests) and maintenance of a macho image (the worker's culture) ... Western Oil had a culture which put safety in conflict with other corporate values.' In particular, the problem was with its long-distance truck drivers (which in the US have a culture of solitary independence and self reliance) who drove sometimes recklessly with loads large enough to inundate a small town. The company instituted *Operation Integrity* to improve safety, in a lasting way, changing the policies and drawing on the existing features of the culture but using them in a different way.

The culture had five dilemmas.

(a)   **Safety-first vs macho-individualism.** Truckers see themselves as 'fearless pioneers of the unconventional lifestyle ... "Be careful boys!" is hardly a plea likely to go down well with this particular group'. Instead of trying to control the drivers, the firm recommended that they become *road safety consultants* (or design consultants). Their advice was sought on improving the system. This had the advantage that 'by making drivers critics of the system their roles as outsiders were preserved and promoted'. It tried to tap their heroism as promoters of public safety.

(b)   **Safety everywhere vs safety specialists.** Western Oil could have hired more specialist staff. However, instead, the company promoted cross functional safety teams from existing parts of the business, for example, to help in designing depots and thinking of ways to reduce hazards.

(c) **Safety as cost vs productivity as benefit.** 'If the drivers raced from station to station to win their bonus, accidents were bound to occur ... . The safety engineers rarely spoke to the line manager in charge of the delivery schedules. The unreconciled dilemma between safety and productivity had been evaded at management level and passed down the hierarchy until drivers were subjected to two incompatible injunctions, work fast and work safely'. To deal with this problem, safety would be built into the reward system.

(d) **Long-term safety vs short-term steering.** The device of recording 'unsafe' acts in operations enabled them to be monitored by cross-functional teams, so that the causes of accidents could be identified and be reduced.

(e) **Personal responsibility vs collective protection.** It was felt that if 'safety' was seen as a form of management policing it would never be accepted. The habit of management 'blaming the victim' had to stop. Instead, if an employee reported another to the safety teams, the person who was reported would be free of *official* sanction. Peer presence was seen to be a better enforcer of safety than the management hierarchy.

It has also been suggested that the following institutions can be established.

(a) An **ethics committee** is a group of executives (perhaps including non-executive directors) appointed to oversee company ethics. It rules on misconduct. It may seek advice from specialists in business ethics.

(b) An **ethics ombudsperson** is a manager who acts as the corporate conscience.

Whistle-blowing is the disclosure by an employee of illegal, immoral or illegitimate practices on the part of the organisation. In theory, the public ought to welcome the public trust: however, confidentiality is very important in the accountants' code of ethics. Whistle-blowing frequently involves **financial loss** for the whistleblower.

(a) Whistle-blowers may lose their jobs.

(b) A whistle-blower who is a member of a professional body cannot, sadly, rely on that body to take a significant interest, or even offer a sympathetic ear. Some professional bodies have narrow interpretations of what is meant by ethical conduct. For many the duties of **commercial confidentiality** are felt to be more important.

In the UK, the Public Interest Disclosure Act 1999 offers some protection to whistle-blowers, but both the subject of the disclosure and the way in which it is made must satisfy the requirements of the Act.

Exam tip

> The ethics codes described above can be related to mission, culture and control strategies. A compliance-based approach suggest that bureaucratic control is necessary; an integrity based approach relies on cultural control.

Marketing at Work

Ethical investment

In April 2004, the Australian Ethical Investment Association reported 23 percent growth in the ethical sector over the previous six months. This pushed the performance of ethical investment indexes slightly above that of their mainstream rivals.

Hunter Hall, the largest ethical funds manager in Australia uses a negative screening process to block investment in activities it feels are harmful, such as uranium mining, armaments production and intensive animal husbandry.

Chapter Roundup

- **Ethics** is concerned with the nature of right and wrong but it is not the same thing as law or the rules of religion.

- The **consequentialist** approach to ethics is to make moral judgements about courses of action by reference to their outcomes or **consequences**. Right or wrong becomes a question of benefit or harm.

- **Deontological ethical theory** assumes that there are universal, objective moral rules that must always apply.

- Ethical theory is not integrated: consequentialist, deontological and natural law based rules are capable of pointing to different conclusions. Partly as a result of this, **ethical dilemmas** can exist at all levels in the organisation.

- Corporate ethics has three contexts.

   - Interaction with national and international society
   - Effects of routine operations
   - Behaviour of individuals

   Mission should incorporate recognition of the ethical dimension.

- There is a fundamental split of views about the nature of corporate responsibility.

   - The **stakeholder view** that a range of goals should be pursued.
   - The view that the business organisation is a purely **economic force**, subject to law.

- There is particular concern over **externalities**, or the social and environmental costs of corporate activities.

- An organisation's **ethical stance** is the extent to which it will exceed its minimum obligations to stakeholders. There are four typical stances.

   - Short-term shareholder interest
   - Long-term shareholder interest
   - Multiple stakeholder obligations
   - Shaper of society

- **Corporate governance** is the conduct of the organisation's senior officers. Abuses have led to a range of measures to improve corporate governance. Non-executive directors have a particular role to play.

- A compliance-based approach highlights conformity with law and regulation. An integrity-based approach suggests a wider remit, incorporating ethics in the organisation's values and culture.

Quick Quiz

1   What is an organisation's ethical stance?

2   Why might an organisation act to secure long-term shareholder interests?

3   What is a right?

4   When should ethical considerations be included in performance measures?

5   What is bribery?

6   What is corporate governance?

7   What is the role of the auditor in corporate governance?

8   What is an externality?

9   What is whistle-blowing?

Answers to Quick Quiz

1   The extent to which it will exceed its minimum obligation to shareholders

2   To improve corporate image and forestall legal regulation

3   A legal or moral entitlement

4   When moral expectations are accepted as obligations

5   Payment for services for which there is no entitlement

6   The conduct of the organisation's senior officers

7   The independent review of confidential information

8   A social or environmental cost of the organisation's activities not borne by the organisation

9   Informing outside agencies about transgressions by one's organisations

Now try Question 6 at the end of the Study Text

Integrating marketing communications

7

Syllabus content

- Developing and managing integrated marketing and communications programmes
- Contingency planning for crises and threats to the brand

Introduction

Communication is a major marketing activity and can absorb large budgets. It is important that communication efforts are properly **integrated**: that is, they support one another and, even more important, that they support the overall marketing and business strategies. The importance of this aspect of marketing was until recently reflected in the old post-graduate diploma syllabus, under which integrated marketing communication was the subject of an entire exam in its own right.

We reflect the need for proper integration of communications effort by opening this chapter with a section on **goals**. We then move on to a consideration of the psychology of marketing communications. There is a clear link here with **perception** and, hence, our next topic is **product positioning**.

Section 4 is taken up with an overview of **communications tools**. You should already have a basic acquaintance with these tools from your earlier studies, so this is not an exhaustive treatment. However, when considering PR, we take the opportunity to deal with the topic of crisis and threats to the brand, since dealing with such things will normally require considerable PR expertise and effort.

An awareness of the **financial implications of marketing decisions** is a high priority for marketing managers, as you should be aware by now. Section 5 is concerned with budgeting for communications activities; budgeting is, of course, the usual first step in the process of controlling and managing an activity. In the case of communications budgets it is complicated by the extreme difficulty of establishing clear links between what is spent and what is achieved.

Section 6 is a brief consideration of some minor strategic issues and we conclude the chapter by examining the special aspects of cross border marketing communication. This is an important topic for your exam, given the need to integrate the international dimension into your thinking for all four of your exams at this level.

1 Promotional goals

FAST FORWARD

Marketing communications effort must be planned and controlled in such a way that it supports rational communications objectives that themselves support over-arching strategic plans.

Marketing objectives, such as increasing market share, translate into communications objectives. In order to deliver an effective plan, it is important to establish marketing communications objectives. These will involve variables such as **perception**, **attitudes**, developing **knowledge and interest** or creating new levels of prompted and spontaneous **awareness**.

Action Programme 1

Select a television or print advertisement and think about the goals it attempted to achieve.

One of the first things that you might have thought of was that to increase sales was the main goal. What other elements might the advertisers be seeking to achieve?

Is it fair to expect marketing communications to achieve all the marketing plan's objectives?

1.1 Promotional objectives

Objectives should be **specific** in that they must be capable of communicating to a target audience (**who**), a distinct message (**what**), over a specified time frame (**when**). Promotional objectives must therefore include five elements.

- Identification of the **target audience**
- A **clear message**
- **Expected outcomes** in terms of trial purchase, awareness and so on
- A measurement of **results**
- Mechanisms for **monitoring and control**

The objectives should be **measurable and therefore quantifiable**. Statements such as 'increase consumer awareness' are vague, whereas 'increase awareness of the 55 – 65 year age group from 40% to 80%' is more precise and capable of measurement.

Objectives should be **achievable**. Purely from an internal company perspective, if sales are targeted to increase by 25% over a designated time period then manufacturing capacity will have to be secured to meet this target. Likewise, attempting to gain additional shelf space within a retail outlet will require that additional resources are devoted to the sales force, to sales promotions and to advertising.

Objectives should be set with a degree of **realism** rather than on the basis of wild imagination. Otherwise, a company would be better off having no targets at all. An unrealistic target would tend to ignore the **competitive and environmental forces** affecting the company, the available **resources** at the company's disposal and the **time frame** in which the objectives have to be achieved.

Finally, objectives should be scheduled and reviewed over a relevant time period. Although a plan of action may be drawn up for a year, it will be the case that the plan will be reviewed against target, for example monthly or quarterly, so as to enable corrective action to be taken.

The principle of SMART objectives applies not only to the overall communication strategy but also to the setting of objectives for each tool within the **promotional mix**. Once the overall communication strategy has been set, then individual, integrated plans should be devised for each of the promotional tools. Using the SMART principle objectives can be set for advertising, sales promotion, public relations, direct marketing and personal selling.

2 How marketing communications works

FAST FORWARD

AIDA is no longer regarded as useful for understanding how communication works. **Sales, persuasion, involvement, saliency and awareness, trial, reinforcement, nudge** are more modern approaches.

The purpose of marketing communications is to **inform**, **persuade** or **remind/reassure** audiences in order to **differentiate** a product, service or organisation. To accomplish these tasks it is necessary to deliver messages that enable audiences to understand and act upon information received.

Before considering the different types of messages it is necessary to consider briefly the ways in which marketing communications (and advertising in particular) is considered to work. There is no set model or framework. For a long time the **AIDA model** was considered to be an appropriate interpretation. Through this model, it was considered that prospective buyers moved through successive stages from learning about the existence of a product to actual purchase. However, AIDA and similar 'hierarchy of effects' models are now considered to be too rigid, inflexible and an inappropriate explanation of the communication process.

The **Sales, Persuasion, Involvement** and **Saliency** frameworks are considered by some to be more acceptable.

Frameworks	Comment
Sales	Advertising works on the basis that it **affects sales directly**, and nothing else is worth considering.
Persuasion	Advertising works by **persuading people to act** (to buy products and services) in ways that they might not have acted had they not seen/heard the advertising message.
Involvement	Advertising works by **drawing people into an advertisement** and making associations between the advertisement and the product/brand.
Saliency	Advertising works by **standing out and being different** from other advertisements, especially those in the same category.

Action Programme 2

Find two further examples for each of the persuasion, involvement and saliency interpretations of advertising.

Underpinning many of these views is the notion that advertising can persuade people to purchase products. This has been termed a **strong force**.

Marketing at Work

Although this may seem astonishing by European standards, only 35% of the under thirties in the US have a mobile phone. Richard Branson believes that he can change that. The brand-obsessed US could be a goldmine – insiders at *Virgin* believe *Virgin Mobile* will have a turnover of $3 billion within three years, dwarfing even *Virgin Atlantic*.

- Guerrilla marketing, targeted at university campuses, will highlight the brand, reinforced by a commercial link with MTV.

- The company is offering a simple pay-as-you-go price plan with no small print.

- The venture will be supported by a network of 11,000 shops.

Plans are afoot to launch Virgin Mobile in South Africa and Canada.

Adapted from *The Observer, 28 July 2002*

Ehrenberg counters this view with an **Awareness, Trial, Reinforcement** and **Nudge** model, which interprets advertising as a **weak force**. This says that advertising **reinforces** previous purchase decisions and serves to **defend** them and **maintain market share**.

Awareness

Trial

Reinforcement

Nudge

The ATRN model of advertising (after Ehrenberg 1997)

Both models accept that **awareness is a necessary prerequisite** for purchase, although it may not always be through advertising.

(i) If a potential purchaser shows some interest in a product, perhaps because it is new or significant to them at that particular time, then they might try or **experiment** with the product.

(ii) If this is successful then a **repeat purchase** may be made.

(iii) With **reinforcement**, the purchaser might be encouraged to add the product to their **evoked set** (a small cluster of brands in each product category from which purchase decisions are made).

Advertising can assist any of these stages and can nudge people into buying one particular brand from their repertoire.

There is no fixed model of advertising. However, research suggests that advertising might be more effective when **combined with brands**, so that potential purchasers are enabled to develop links or associations between a brand and its advertising and related communications.

2.1 Messages

Messages have greater impact if their sources are **attractive** and **credible**. **High involvement** purchases tend to require messages based on **reason**, but messages based on **emotions** and, especially, **image**, work for low involvement purchases.

2.1.1 Source

The source of the communication directly influences the consumer's acceptance and interpretation of a message. **Credibility** and **attractiveness** are two major source factors influencing customers.

Key concept

> **Source credibility** is defined as the level of expertise and trustworthiness customers attribute to the source of the message.

For example, some spokespersons may be regarded with high **credibility** in a particular field, but the **trustworthiness** of their product endorsements may be questioned because they are being paid by the advertiser. Indeed, product messages sponsored by the advertiser are seen as less trustworthy than product messages from sources that are perceived as impartial, such as the Consumers' Association. Research appears to show that the **greater the perceived credibility of the source, the greater is the likelihood that the receiver will accept the message**.

Source attractiveness is determined by its **likeability** and its similarity to the consumer. Research has shown that when consumers perceive salespeople as similar to themselves, they are more likely to accept and be influenced by the sales messages.

2.1.2 Balance of the message

Our understanding of the **level of involvement** that may exist in the target audience can be used to determine the **overall balance of the message**. If there is **high involvement** then interested members of the target audience will **actively seek information**. Messages therefore tend to be **rational**, proclaiming **product benefits** and the **key attributes**.

Where there is **low involvement** the audience are not really interested and **need to be drawn to the communication message**. In these cases, **image-based** appeals tend to be more successful and the use of **emotion** rather than logic predominates.

The strategic implication is that if integration and consistency is to be achieved then **adherence to an emotional or rational approach has to be maintained** throughout all the promotional tools.

3 Positioning

Positioning is about **customer perception** and **evaluation** relative to competing brands. Positioning may be based on:

–   Attribute, feature or customer benefit
–   Price and quality
–   Use or application
–   Product user image
–   Product class dissociation
–   Competitor

The target marketing process is a process of **positioning**.

Key concept

Positioning is how the product is perceived and evaluated by the target audience relative to competing products. This is why perception is an important and integral part of the context analysis.

Positioning has developed in importance because of **increasing competition** and the **increasing sophistication of consumers**, who are able to perceive the similarities of physical form and function of competitive products. Therefore, it is important to position organisations as brands in the minds of customers.

The basic thesis of positioning is that companies **must differentiate their products or services** if they are to avoid **commoditisation**, that is, becoming providers of generic products or services sold at the lowest price.

According to the basic principles of marketing, products and services are created to solve customer problems (that is, to satisfy needs and wants) and provide benefits. Thus, to be effective, **positioning must promise the benefit the customer will receive**, create the expectation, and offer a solution to the customer's problem. If at all possible, the solution should be different from and better than the competition's solution, especially if the competitors are already offering their own solutions.

3.1 Positioning statement

A positioning strategy statement can be as simple as a one-page document that will act as a guideline to measure the consistency of all marketing programmes.

A carefully crafted business positioning strategy can be used as a guideline for judging the appropriateness of all marketing programmes, especially for promotion, advertising, and PR events. It will ensure that the business image is consistent with the target buyers/end users and help to build an enduring, memorable (and hopefully unique) message to sell the business's products.

 Marketing at Work

Positioning for growth in the drinks market

In the early to mid 90s, the alcoholic drinks market was based on three principal sectors; beer, wine and spirits. Consumer research suggested to *Bacardi-Martini* that they wanted great tasting, 'portable' alcoholic products. Premium packaged beers satisfied the portability factor but did not offer a wide range of differing tastes. Spirits offered a range of tastes but not the portability. The research further highlighted a blurring of the boundaries between drink categories. This provided the platform for Bacardi to develop and launch ready to drink products, most significantly the *Breezer* brand of fruit flavoured Bacardi spirit. Sales have doubled year on year in the UK since the launch in 1994 to current levels around £450 million. Others have readily joined in with brands such as *Smirnoff Ice*, *Hoopers Hooch*, *Metz* and *WKD* the dominant brands.

Not only were Bacardi competing against direct rivals such as Smirnoff but also against beer brands such as Budweiser. Early distribution battles were overcome as a result of demand created from advertising showing the product being consumed in bars and clubs. Their owners could not ignore this and fridge space had to be given over to the new brands alongside beer. The 'Latin spirit in everyone' theme has established Bacardi's brand values and distinguish it from other premium packaged spirits.

The positioning has very definitely reflected the value inherent in the principal Bacardi brand and as such represents brand extension just as Smirnoff has achieved with the Ice brand.

Bacardi – Martini are continuing to look for further opportunities by undertaking a marketing mapping exercise to test consumer needs for different products and purchase situations.

From Marketing Business, October 2000

3.2 Positioning strategies

Marketers may decide to select the most appropriate of the following strategies, depending on the information gathered during market and psychological positioning. (There is some overlap between the strategies: for instance superb after-sales service could be offered simply as a customer benefit or as something that a competitor does *not* offer.)

- **Attribute**, **feature** or **customer benefit**
- **Price** and **quality**
- **Use** or **application**
- Product user **image**
- Product class **dissociation**
- **Competitor**

Action Programme 3

For each of the positioning strategies mentioned below, identify a product and/or a service that fits into the category.

3.2.1 Attribute, feature or benefit

Positioning by **attribute or feature** involves positioning the product by clearly identifying it **with a distinct set of attributes which distinguish the product within the market**. *BMW*, the German car manufacturer, while positioned within the luxury end of the car market, make constant reference to the engine performance and design as part of their positioning statement. Likewise, *Volvo* the Swedish car manufacturer have for many years positioned themselves on safety features incorporated into the design of the car.

Another way to differentiate yourself from the competition is by providing a **unique range of services**. Depending on the characteristics of your local market, unique capabilities could include 24-hour operations, free pickup and delivery, or electronic commerce (online file transfer and on-demand output).

Exceptional customer service can be another differentiator. For obvious reasons, customers prefer vendors who follow their instructions and offer a simple ordering system, on-time delivery, easy problem-resolution, timely and accurate invoicing, and personalised service.

3.2.2 Price and quality

Price and quality are becoming increasingly important as companies attempt to offer more features, better value and improved quality at competitive prices.

Price. Some companies go for the bottom line: they attract customers by being the lowest cost service providers in the market. They do this by having highly efficient operations, so their cost-per-unit of output is the lowest. This does not necessarily mean those businesses spend less money than their competitors. For example, the price leader in a given market will probably do the most advertising, but because of the high volume of work the advertising helps bring in, the business will achieve the lowest cost per unit. However, a low-price positioning strategy always requires a high volume of business.

Quality. A company that provides exceptional quality to its customers can command a higher price for its services than its less quality-conscious competitors. However, quality is a variable that customers may take for granted after a while.

If a company intends to sell its quality program in order to charge higher prices for its services, then it must be willing to invest the time and money required to live up to the higher expectations of its customers. If it creates expectations of superior quality but fails to deliver, few customers will give the company a second chance.

3.2.3 Use or application

In the third case, the company attempts to position its product or service by deliberately associating it with a specific **use or application**. *Kellogg's*, the cereal manufacturer, in striving to defend their market position and increase sales, have positioned their main product *Corn Flakes* as an 'any time of day food', and not just to be eaten at breakfast.

3.2.4 Product user image

Positioning by virtue of **product user** associates the product with a particular class of user. *SmithKline Beecham* have positioned *Lucozade Sport* with the sporting fraternity, and have strengthened this through endorsement advertising using major sporting personalities.

3.2.5 Product class dissociation

It is possible to position a company brand against a product class or an associated product class, claiming that yours is different from the rest. *Kraft* foods, who produce *Golden Crown*, have positioned their product with respect to the associated product class, butter. *Heinz*, who produce a range of *Weight Watcher* foods, are positioning these against traditional but more calorific foods.

3.2.6 Competitors

A **competitor's position** within a market may be used as a frame of reference in order to create a distinct positioning statement. *Avis* car rental use the slogan 'We're number 2, so we try harder'. Here the market leader is being used as a reference point to create a competitive statement. The key determinant for the marketer is whether claims made within a promotional campaign which use blatant comparisons can be substantiated through better quality, service, value, cost and so on.

This approach is used when it is necessary to meet the competition head-on; to bring out differences between products. For example, *Visa* credit cards compete with *American Express* by showing examples of places from around the world that do not accept American Express but do accept Visa.

Marketing at Work

Ice cream success is in the difference

The premium ice cream sector had been dominated by the sophistication of the *Haagen-Dazs* brand, and previous challenges had come to ground after challenging head on with similar approaches to branding and communications. Having established brand presence via limiting distribution and selective use of PR, *Ben and Jerry's* finally took on *Haagen-Dazs* but chose a very different approach. Rather than promote luxuriousness via sexual connotations which had been the Haagen-Dazs theme, B&J's built a position based on humour.

The communications aim to remain true to the original brand positioning of the niche, loveable underdog. The success of the brand has led to its acquisition by the giant food group Unilever who intend to maintain the difference in the approach and not seek to apply 'big brother' principles.

From an article in Marketing Business, July/August 2000

4 An overview of promotional tools

The **range of promotional tools continues to grow**. These tools represent the deployment of **deliberate and intentional methods** calculated to bring about a favourable response in the customer's behaviour. The diagram represents the most obvious promotion methods, though other parts of the marketing mix, including the product itself, pricing, policy and distribution channels, will also have decisive effects.

Action Programme 4

(a)   Actually read your junk mail, wander around the supermarket, read the paper, watch TV, and start collecting those leaflets that are constantly posted through your letterbox. How many examples of the tools shown above can you find? Be on the alert constantly for real-life examples and illustrations that you could use in your examination answers.

(b)   Were you influenced by any of the examples that you found? Did you respond? You should be able to analyse your reasons.

(c)   Can you think of (or better, find examples of) any other promotional tools, not shown above?

Discussions of buyer behaviour have shown that there is not just one process that influences the customer but a whole series. It follows therefore that **each promotional tool will have a variety of roles**.

In terms of making management decisions and allocating budgets it is possible to consider promotional tools in two broad categories of **primary** and **support** roles. For example in a consumer campaign it may be that television is used as the main vehicle for launching the campaign, which is then sustained by a longer-lasting poster campaign.

Action Programme 5

One-to-One, the mobile phone company, ran a campaign of TV ads featuring a romance along the lines of the *Nescafé Gold Blend* couple. Then they ran a competition showing viewers extracts from the first series of ads and offering a prize to those who could put the extracts in the order in which they originally appeared. This (we were told) was a prelude to the second series of ads.

What are the primary and supporting promotional activities here? What do you think the prize was? Can you classify other campaigns that you have witnessed in a similar way?

4.1 Advertising

FAST FORWARD

Advertising is non-personal, paid for mass communications. It should have clear objectives.

Key concept

Advertising may be defined as non-personal paid-for communications targeted through mass media with the purpose of achieving set objectives. Advertising is a means of reaching large audiences in a cost-effective manner. Personalised feedback from an advertising message is not usually obtained.

The purpose of advertising is to achieve set objectives. These objectives will vary depending on the following factors.

- The result of the **context analysis**
- The nature of the **product** or **service** to be advertised
- The stage it has reached in its **life cycle**
- The **marketplace** in which it operates
- The **role** advertising is to play

Action Programme 6

Choose some television or print advertisements and try to work out what each one might be trying the achieve. What type of goals might there be?

4.2 Personal selling

FAST FORWARD

Personal selling involves team work over a wide range of activities undertaken within the context of the overall marketing strategy.

Key concept

Personal selling has been defined as 'the presentation of products and associated persuasive communication to potential clients, which is employed by the supplying organisation. It is the most direct and longest established means of promotion within the promotional mix' (*Baron et al, Macmillan Dictionary of Retailing* 1991).

All organisations have employees with responsibility for contacting and dealing directly with customers and potential customers. These employees provide a vital function to the organisation as they form a direct link to the buyers.

The sales force needs the support of other groups within the organisation if it is to operate efficiently and effectively. *Kotler* identifies the following groups whose activities impact upon the effectiveness of the sales force.

(a) **Top management** can be increasingly involved in the selling process, particularly with big orders or key accounts.

(b) **Technical sales personnel** who supply technical information and service to the customer before, during or after the sale of the product.

(c) **Customer service representatives** who provide installation, maintenance and other services to the customer.

(d) **Office staff** including sales analysts, administrators and secretarial staff.

Indeed, Kotler maintains that selling should increasingly be regarded as a **team effort** involving all these groups.

The art of selling in its narrowest sense is only one of a number of tasks that the salesperson could perform. A salesperson could perform many different activities.

Activity	Comment
Prospecting	Gathering additional **prospective customers** in addition to sales leads generated by the company on his behalf.
Communicating	**Communicating information** to existing and potential customers about the company's products and services.
Selling	**'The art of salesmanship'**, encompasses approaching the customer, presenting, answering objections and closing the sale.
Servicing	A salesperson may provide **various services** to the customer, such as consulting about their problems, rendering technical assistance, arranging finance and expediting delivery.
Information gathering	The salesperson can be a very useful source of **marketing intelligence** because of his or her links with the end customer. Many salespeople are responsible for supplying regular **reports on competitive activity** within their particular sales area.
Allocating	The salesperson may assist in evaluating **customer profitability** and creditworthiness, and may also have to control the allocation of products to customers in times of product shortages.
Shaping	An increasingly important role is to help build and sustain **relationships** with major customers.

While a salesperson may engage in all these tasks from time to time, **the mix of tasks will vary according to the purchase decision process, company marketing strategy and the overall economic conditions of the time**.

Sales force activity must be undertaken within the context of the organisation's overall marketing strategy.

(a) For example, if the organisation pursues a **pull strategy**, relying on massive consumer advertising, then the **role of the sales force may primarily be a servicing one**, ensuring that retailers carry sufficient stock, allocate adequate shelf space for display and co-operate in sales promotion programmes.

(b) Conversely, with a **push strategy**, the organisation will rely primarily on the sales force to **sell the brands to the marketing intermediaries** who will then assume the main responsibility for selling on the brands to the end customer.

4.3 Sales promotion

Sales promotion techniques involve providing a material incentive to buy.

Key concept

> The Institute of Sales Promotion (ISP) defines **sales promotion** as 'a range of tactical marketing techniques, designed within a strategic marketing framework, to add value to a product or service, in order to achieve a specific sales and marketing objective.'

(a) Sales promotion encompasses a range of techniques appropriate for targeting **consumers**, for instance via price reductions, competitions or gifts with purchases. However, **trade and sales force incentives** are also included under the general heading of sales promotion.

(b) The majority of companies will use sales promotion as a means of achieving a **short-term sales objective**, such as an increase in sales volume or to encourage trial and brand switching by a rival manufacturer's consumers.

(c) Although it is used as a tactical tool, sales promotion works within a strategic marketing framework and should support **the strategic objectives for the brand**.

(d) Sales promotion always seeks to **add value** to a product or service. Thus, consumers are offered something extra for their purchase, or the chance to obtain something extra.

Sales promotion includes both **pull** and **push** techniques. As we have seen, sales pull techniques incentivise the consumer to buy. Sales push techniques ensure that the distribution pipeline is well loaded, and sales are pushed along the distribution chain.

Exam tip

> Be aware of the potential for confusion between the terms promotion (used as a synonym for communication techniques in general) and sales promotion (which is a specialist term reserved for the specific techniques described above). In examinations some candidates read the question paper very quickly and mistake a question on sales promotion for one on promotional techniques in general. This unfortunate slip can result in a candidate scoring virtually no marks for a question.

4.3.1 Sales promotion objectives

Examples of consumer sales promotion objectives. Sales promotion objectives will link into overarching marketing and marketing communications objectives.

(a) Increase **awareness and interest** amongst target audiences

(b) Achieve a **switch in buying behaviour** from competitor brands to your company's brand

(c) Incentivise consumers to make a **forward purchase** of your brand, thus shutting out competitor purchase opportunities

(d) Increase **display space** allocated to your brand in store

(e) Smooth **seasonal dips** in demand for your product

(f) Generate a **consumer database** from mail-in applications

Action Programme 7

Tesco and *Sainsbury* issue a type of loyalty card which shoppers present when they reach the check-out. Points are awarded for sums spent over a minimum amount and these are added up each quarter. Money-off vouchers to be used against future grocery bills are sent to the shopper's home. What do you think is the value of this? In 2000, Safeway decided to pull out of its loyalty scheme.

Why do you think these firms have used different strategies?

4.4 Public relations

PR is largely about goodwill and image. Under the **two-way symmetric model** the practitioner mediates between the organisation and its publics. This model is best able to deal with PR arises and similar threats.

Key concept

The Institute of Public Relations has defined **PR** as 'the planned and sustained effort to establish and maintain goodwill and mutual understanding between an organisation and its publics'.

The Public Relations Consultants Association (PRCA) says that:

Public relations is the name given to the managed process of communication between one group and another. In its purest form it has nothing to do with marketing, advertising or 'commercialism'. It will, however, often promote one group's endeavours to persuade another group to its point of view and it will use a number of different methods, other than (although often alongside) advertising to achieve this aim.

4.4.1 The scope of PR

The scope of public relations activity is very broad. The specific practice of the discipline of public relations will vary from sphere to sphere and from organisation to organisation, but **public relations activity**, if implemented effectively, should **embrace the whole organisation**.

(a) Programmes should be managed **strategically**.

(b) There should be a single **integrated** public relations department.

(c) Public relations managers should **report directly to senior management**.

(d) Public relations should be a **separate function from marketing**.

(e) The senior public relations person should be a member of the organisation's **dominant coalition**.

(f) Communication should adhere to the **two-way symmetrical model**.

4.4.2 Four models of PR

This last factor relates to the way in which public relations is practised. Given the diversity of the role of PR as emphasised above, it is logical to consider different ways in which PR could be practised. A framework for considering this has been propounded by *Grunig and Hunt, Managing Public Relations* (1984), who suggest that there are **four models of public relations practice**. Each model will be considered in turn.

Press agency/publicity. The role of PR is primarily one of **propaganda**, spreading the faith of the organisation, often through incomplete, half-true or distorted information. **Communication is one-way**, from the organisation to its publics: essentially telling the publics the information the organisation wants them to hear.

Public information. In this model the role of PR is the dissemination of **information**, not necessarily with a persuasive intent. As Grunig and Hunt state, 'the public relations person functions essentially as a journalist in residence, whose job it is to report objectively information about his organisation to the public'.

Two-way asymmetric. Grunig and Hunt describe the main function of the two-way asymmetric model as **scientific persuasion**, using social science theory and research about attitudes and behaviour to persuade publics to accept the organisation's point of view and to behave in a way that supports the organisation. The aim is to achieve the maximum change in attitudes and behaviour.

Two-way symmetric. In the two-way symmetric model the **PR practitioner serves as a mediator between the organisation and its publics** with the aim of facilitating mutual **understanding** between the two. If persuasion occurs it is as likely to persuade the organisation's management to change its attitude as it is to persuade the publics to change theirs.

Public relations is, therefore, the **management of an organisation's reputation with its publics** and this management involves a close consideration of the relationships involved. The organisation can be either reactive or proactive in its management of these relationships.

(a)   **Reactive PR** is primarily concerned with the communication of what has happened and responding to factors affecting the organisation. It is primarily defensive, with little or no responsibility for influencing policies.

(b)   In contrast, **proactive public relations practitioners** have a much wider role and thus have a far greater influence on overall organisational strategy.

4.4.3 PR crises

A proactive approach to PR is probably of most use for dealing with publicity crises. These can blow up at any time and can be extremely damaging to a company's reputation and ultimately therefore to the value it creates for its shareholders.

 Marketing at Work

Shell and Brent Spar

When *Shell* announced that it intended to dispose of its obsolete oil platform Brent Spar by sinking it in the Atlantic, the green lobby succeeded in generating so much public concern that Shell was forced to cancel its plan. The most effective tactic of their opponents was to organise a boycott of Shell petrol that created a major threat to the company's revenues.

It is now widely accepted that the Shell plan was the most environmentally appropriate and that the alternative forced upon it (piecemeal demolition in a Norwegian fiord) was a poor choice. Nevertheless, despite having been completely wrong, the green lobby still enjoys considerable public confidence, while Shell is widely seen as displaying poor corporate citizenship. The general public were therefore unsurprised when, in early 2004, a scandal blew up over the financially and technically complex topic of valuing Shell's reserves of crude oil.

It is doubtful whether Shell or any other well-known oil company can ever enjoy the sympathy of public opinion, given the common perception of their contribution to pollution and the nature of the regimes they must deal with in many of their extractive operations. For less vilified companies, however, the proper use of PR techniques may help to at least **minimise the effect of bad publicity**. This is done by promoting the company's reputation **in advance** and **responding appropriately when a crisis arises**. For this to work, there must be a **close relationship of trust** between the executives at the strategic apex of the company and their PR advisers. While it would be inappropriate for a company to follow the recent example of the British government and determine policy entirely in terms of what can be given positive spin, it should at least **consider** the effect on public opinion of action it may be planning.

 Marketing at Work

Product contamination

Tylenol

In 1982 an extortionist tried to obtain money from pharmaceutical company *Johnson and Johnson* by contaminating capsules of their pain relief product *Tylenol* with cyanide. Seven people died as a result.

Johnson & Johnson acted swiftly. Before the government could take action and before the media had started to exploit the story, the company recalled all Tylenol products. This action cost the company $100m and caused a dip in sales. However, consumer confidence in the company increased and it quickly regained its sales lead in the pain relief market.

Coca Cola

In 1999, dozens of children in Belgium and Luxembourg were taken to hospital with stomach cramps, vomiting and dizziness after drinking *Coca Cola* products. Coca Cola's investigation indicated that a small number of cans had been contaminated with a fungicide used on wooden pallets and that some products had been injected with tainted carbon dioxide. The company aimed for a discreet targeted withdrawal of the affected products.

Unfortunately for the Company, it had moved rather slowly and had downplayed the seriousness of the problem. Governments, distributors and consumers were unimpressed. Despite the fact that a very small quantity of a few products seemed to be affected, the governments of Belgium and Luxemburg banned the sale of *all* Coca Cola products and in France, major distributors withdrew them *all* from sale. There was extensive hostile press coverage of the affair.

Dasani

Coca Cola's bottled water product *Dasani*, though competing with natural mineral water, is merely a highly filtered and purified version of the normal domestic water supply. Nevertheless, the brand was extremely successful in the USA and grew in the UK until its banal origin and extremely high profit margin became common knowledge in early 2004. UK consumers are prepared to pay a high price for a brown fizzy variation of tap water but not for a clear still one, it seems. This could have probably been foreseen.

The fate of Dasani was sealed when it was learned that, despite the extensive purification it was subjected to, it contained a high level of bromate, a chemical though to be carcinogenic. The product was withdrawn from the UK market and a European launch was shelved.

From the examples above it is clear that careful action is needed if damage to the brand and the organisation are to be avoided under such circumstances.

The first step is to have a **plan**. This may extend no further than having a PR expert on call and able to determine the facts of any story that breaks. This will normally entail contact with the strategic apex of the company concerned. It is then appropriate to **err on the side of caution**. Even if it is felt that nothing has really gone wrong, it will be difficult to proceed on this basis. It is far better to take immediate action to **calm public concern**, such as by issuing an immediate product recall. It is also necessary to **be open with consumers** and to **show contrition** if the company is in any way at fault. In this way many a potential crisis may be defused.

Consistency of communication is very important. Journalists are likely to pounce on any inconsistencies or apparent hesitations. Consistency is achieved by having a single corporate point of contact for all parties interested in the story. When this is not possible and it becomes necessary for senior executives to appear in person, they must be thoroughly briefed beforehand.

As well as the media and the general public they represent, the company's internal and connected stakeholders must be kept informed. They may be given more information, but the overall story must be the same as that told to the press. Confidential background information should be protected as far as possible, but bad news is likely to leak and the company and its PR advisers must be prepared for this.

A very fine judgement is required as to whether to seek **legal protection** for confidential information. Recent governments, *Robert Maxwell* and others abused the law of libel to such an extent that in the UK, recourse to law is now viewed by the public as proof that the litigant has something unsavoury to hide.

4.4.4 The crisis life cycle

A more sophisticated approach might be based on the **crisis life cycle** concept. This model was proposed in the early 1980s and based on the well-known product life cycle. Several writers have been involved in developing the idea and there is now widespread acceptance of a model that includes five phases.

(a) **Signal detection**: continuing monitoring of stakeholders and communications media identifies potential crisis themes. At this stage it is important to act on controllable matters, ensure stakeholders are fully informed in order to prevent misunderstanding and plan for deterioration in the situation.

(b) **Preparation or probing**: the mass media begin to focus on a trigger theme. This is the opportunity to kill the crisis. Proactive communication to target stakeholders, both external and internal is enhanced and crisis action teams are assembled and briefed.

(c) **Acute or containment**: the mass media isolate a trigger theme to explain the crisis. The organisation focuses on crisis management activity. PR effort is directed at opportunities to present positive aspects to prioritised stakeholders using external evidence available. There is continuous monitoring of media and stakeholder groups.

(d) **Chronic or learning**: the media focus in assigning responsibility or blame. PR activity continues as above and the organisation audits the events and activities to date.

(e) **Resolution**: the aim is to rebuild trust and stakeholder relationships. Apology, compensation and practical response to criticism may all be appropriate. Rebuilding brand values will be a major concern.

4.5 Direct marketing

FAST FORWARD

Direct marketing is based on the establishment of direct relationships with customers. **Direct mail** is the main medium and has been extended by the power of ICT units **database marketing**.

Key concept

The Institute of Direct Marketing in the UK defines **direct marketing** as 'The planned recording, analysis and tracking of customer behaviour to develop relational marketing strategies'.
The Direct Marketing Association in the US defines direct marketing as 'An interactive system of marketing which uses one or more advertising media to effect a measurable response and/or transaction at any location'.

Direct marketing helps create and develop direct relationships between the company and each of its prospects, on an individual basis. It is a form of direct supply, embracing both a variety of alternative **media channels** (like direct mail), and a choice of **distribution channels** (like mail order). Because direct marketing **removes all channel intermediaries** apart from the **advertising** medium and the **delivery** medium, there are no resellers, therefore avoiding loss of control and loss of revenue. In developing a comprehensive direct marketing strategy, organisations will often utilise a range of different yet complementary techniques.

Direct mail tends to be the main medium of direct response advertising. Newspaper ads can include coupons to fill out and return, and radio and TV can give a phone number to ring. However, direct mail has a number of strengths as a direct response medium.

(a)   The advertiser can target down to **individual level**.

(b)   The communication can **be personalised**.

(c)   The medium is good **for reinforcing interest stimulated by other media** such as TV. It can supply the response mechanism (a coupon) which is not yet available in that medium.

(d)   The opportunity to use **different creative formats** is almost unlimited.

(e)   **Testing potential is sophisticated**: a limited number of items can be sent out to a 'test' cell and the results can be evaluated. As success is achieved, so the mailing campaign can be rolled out.

The cornerstone upon which the direct mailing is based, however, is the **mailing list**. It is far and away the most important element in the list of variables, which also include the offer, timing and creative content.

An extension of the mailing list is the development of **database marketing**. A **database** is a collection of available information on past and current customers together with future prospects, structured to allow for the implementation of effective marketing strategies. **Database marketing** is a customer-oriented approach to marketing, and its special power lies in the techniques its uses to harness the capabilities of computer and telecommunications technology. Building accurate and up-to-date profiles of existing customers enables the company to:

• Extend help to a company's target audience

• Stimulate further demand

• Stay close to them. Recording and keeping an electronic database of customers and prospects, and of all communications and commercial contacts, helps to improve all future contacts.

 Marketing at Work

Database applications

Computers now have the capacity to operate in three new ways which will enable businesses to operate in a totally different dimension.

'Customers can be tracked individually. Thousands of pieces of information about each of millions of customers can be stored and accessed economically.

Companies and customers can interact through, for example, phones, mail, E-mail and interactive kiosks. ... for the first time since the invention of mass marketing, 'companies will be hearing from individual customers in a cost-efficient manner'.

Computers allow companies to match their production processes to what they learn from their individual customers – a process known as 'mass customisation' which can be seen as 'the cost-efficient mass production of products and services in lot sizes of one'.

There are many examples of companies which are already employing or experimenting with these ideas. In the US *Levi Strauss*, the jeans company, is taking measurements and preferences from female customers to produce exact-fitting garments. The approach 'offers the company tremendous opportunities for building learning relationships'.

The *Ritz-Carlton* hotel chain has trained staff throughout the organisation to jot down customer details at every opportunity on a 'guest preference pad'.

The result could be the following: 'You stay at the Ritz-Carlton in Cancun, Mexico, call room service for dinner, and request an ice cube in your glass of white wine. Months later, when you stay at the Ritz-Carlton in Naples, Florida, and order a glass of white wine from room service, you will almost certainly be asked if you would like an ice cube in it.'

Financial Times

Telemarketing is the planned and controlled use of the telephone for sales and marketing opportunities. Unlike all other forms of direct marketing it allows for immediate two-way communication.

5 Communication budgets

There is no one uniform method of deciding what to spend on marketing communications. This is not so surprising. The following are some of the **considerations that can affect the amount of expenditure**.

- What variety of marketing communications is to be used?
- What tasks are to be undertaken?
- How competitive is the market place?
- How well known is the organisation?
- Are there any special requirements?

Costs to be budgeted

- Air time and broadcast media
- Space and printed media
- Production costs
- Staff salaries
- Overheads and expenses

5.1 Theoretical approaches to budgeting

FAST FORWARD

Communications budgets are difficult to set because of the difficulty of measuring the marginal effect of spending. The **objective and task** method is popular since it is logical and based on achieving the overall marketing objectives.

Theoretical approaches to setting budgets have not found favour in industry because the effects of **any marginal increase on expenditure are likely to be swamped**, or at least hidden, by many other marketing variables. The effects of any expenditure will have both long-term and short-term effects. It is worthwhile emphasising the view here that **marketing communications should be treated as an essential long-term investment**.

Methods of deciding budgets have, however, been developed over a period of time and, in the absence of clearer guidance, are useful in approaching a budget decision for the first time. After several years' operations it is possible to use experience to make decisions. One, or a combination of more than one, of the following methods can be used to approach the problem.

BPP
PROFESSIONAL EDUCATION

- Completely arbitrarily
- All you can afford
- Historical basis
- Matching the competition
- Percentage of sales
- Experiment and testing
- Modelling and simulation
- Objective and task method

Recent research has indicated a growing trend towards database methods and especially favours the **objective and task method**.

5.1.1 Completely arbitrarily

There are many examples of budgets being set in an apparently **arbitrary way by senior management**. There may be a link between the **personality** of the **decision maker and the level of expenditure**. This link may not be obvious to people elsewhere in the organisation. Subsequent arbitrary cuts in expenditure if trading becomes difficult and the profit margins begin to suffer are more worrying.

5.1.2 All you can afford

This often applies to a new company starting up or to an existing company advertising for the first time. The conscious decision has to be taken to forgo immediate profits or to forgo an investment in another area in favour of an investment in marketing communications. This often means **investing at a minimum level**. This will necessarily limit the **scope** of the work, however, and limit the **results** to be achieved.

5.1.3 Historical basis

We have already indicated that with **experience**, managers are able to form their own judgement of the effectiveness or otherwise of particular expenditure levels and different promotional methods. Year-on-year figures provide the basis for **following trends** and making decisions accordingly.

(a) The **danger of inertia**: a temptation just to keep it the same, in which case all the elements of the environment and the costs associated with the task facing the organisation are ignored.

(b) A slight improvement is to use a **media multiplier**, which at least recognises that media rate card costs may have increased.

5.1.4 Matching the competition

In many cases an organisation is trying to reach exactly the **same customers** through exactly the **same channels**. In order to obtain a certain market share it is then necessary to **match the competition** and particularly the market leader.

5.1.5 Percentage of sales

The **percentage of sales** is a commonly used method of determining a marketing communications budget because:

- It is easy to calculate
- It is precise
- It can be quickly monitored
- It can be varied in progressive steps
- It appears logical
- It is financially safe

Action Programme 8

What do you think is the logical flaw associated with the percentage of sales method as an effective technique for budget allocation?

If all companies in an industry use a similar calculation then **expenditure** will approximate to **market share positions**. However, it must be clear that the real position is very complex and sales are the result of marketing communications and not the other way round. The method is in reality over-simplistic but does form a good basis of calculation.

Once a sales forecast has been made then the approximate budget level can be obtained. It can then be moderated for special circumstances such as the **degree of competition** experienced in the previous year or expected in the next year.

5.1.6 Experiment and testing

This method involves selecting a **set of matched markets**. Different final promotional budgets can be set for each of these markets and the results carefully monitored. The resulting levels of **awareness and sales delivered** can be compared. For example, this method can be used to **evaluate alternative media schedules**. Problems associated with this method include:

- The **cost** of conducting the experiment
- The **time** it takes to get results
- The premature **informing of competitors**
- The fact that markets can never be completely **matched**

5.1.7 Modelling and simulation

With advancing use of computer databases and more precise promotional media it is possible to build **models** to forecast the likely performance of different media schedules. There are likely to be an increasing number of PC based modelling programs available which will allow a number of business variables to be examined including:

- Sales levels
- Purchase frequency
- Awareness levels
- Profits achievable

5.1.8 The objective and task

The **objective and task method** is probably the one which is most **logical and appropriate** to the complex situation found in planning marketing communications programmes. Basically the logic of the method is as follows.

Determine the marketing communications objectives

↓

Determine tasks necessary to achieve these objectives

↓

Determine the cost of each element

This approach is simple to understand and uses carefully considered and linked objectives and tasks. It is necessary to be **realistic about the objectives** and **accurate in the costing** of the tasks. This is an extremely difficult process in reality because of the large number of unknowns.

Action Programme 9

To demonstrate the logic and difficulty of this method choose a marketing communications problem with which you are familiar.

(a)   Define the precise marketing communication objectives.

(b)   Determine the tasks necessary to achieve these objectives.

(c)   Cost out the problem both in terms of the individual tasks and in total.

A systematic approach to applying the objective and task method will pay dividends because of its rigorous nature. Although it will not necessarily produce perfect results it will lead to disciplined thinking and provide an excellent communication and decision device.

5.1.9 Ten steps in applying the objective and task method

Step 1   Define marketing and promotion objectives

Step 2   Determine the tasks to be undertaken

Step 3   Build up expenditure by costing the tasks

Step 4   Compare the results against industry averages

Step 5   Compare the results as a percentage of sales

Step 6   Reconcile differences between steps 3, 4 and 5

Step 7   Modify estimates to meet company policies

Step 8   Specify when expenditures are to be made

Step 9   Maintain an element of flexibility

Step 10   Monitor actual results against these forecasts

6 Strategic considerations

You may notice, say, that you see *British Telecom* ads far more frequently than ads for most of its competitors such as the cable companies' telephone services. BT is, of course, the largest player in the market. But then, French car ads are more often to be seen than ads for Japanese cars, yet the Japanese have a larger share of the market. How can we **analyse** these strategies?

6.1 Advertising to sales ratios (A/S Ratios)

FAST FORWARD

The A/S ratio can be used to make comparisons with competitors.

One of the important factors that always needs to be considered is the **amount spent on communications by competitors**. It can be difficult determining the amount spent by competitors on below-the-line activities, although reasonable guesstimates can often be made by those actively involved in the market.

Above-the-line activities can be measured (data bought from various marketing research agencies) and can be used to gain an insight into possible strategies.

The **A/S ratio** for an industry provides a **benchmark** against which it is possible to determine **how much should be spent** or stimulate consideration of **why certain amounts have been spent**.

Key concept

> The **A/S ratio** is different for each market sector. It is calculated by working out the total amount spent on advertising (usually at rate card cost) as a proportion of the sales in the market. Therefore, if sales in a market are valued at £150 million per year and the amount spent on advertising is £14 million then the A/S ratio is said to be 9.33%.

Part of the strategic decision is to decide whether an individual company's A/S ratio should be higher, lower or the same as the industry average.

(a)   **Reasons to spend more** might be that a **new product or variant** is being introduced to the market so greater effort is require to **develop awareness** (reach) and then perhaps knowledge and or establish brand values.

(b)   **Reasons to underspend** the industry average might include trying to maintain an established market position or **directing spend to other products** in the portfolio or deciding to **put more work below-the-line**.

6.2 Share of voice

FAST FORWARD

> **Share of voice** must be considered alongside **share of market**. Spending can be used to maintain equilibrium or to create disequilibrium.

Key concept

> **Share of voice**. Within any market the total of all advertising expenditure (adspend), that is, all the advertising by all the players, can be analysed in the context of the proportions each player has made to the total.

If one advertiser spends more than any other then more of their messages will be received and therefore stand a better chance of being heard and acted upon. If a brand's **share of market (SOM)** is equal to its **share of voice (SOV)** an equilibrium can be said to have been reached.

It is possible that organisations can use their advertising spending either to maintain **equilibrium (SOV = SOM)** or to create disequilibrium.

The following matrix (*Shroer*, 1990) shows how **different spending strategies are appropriate** depending on your competitors' **share of voice** and your own **share of market**.

	Your share of market	
	Low	High
Competitors' share of voice — High	Adjust spending to the amount needed to defend your niche	Increase spending defend your brand
Competitors' share of voice — Low	Attack: spend more so that your SOV is greater than your current SOM	Maintain spending slightly, above equilibrium level

Note that **careful monitoring of the fortunes of competitors is needed**: if you know that a competitor is spending large sums on restructuring, say, they may not be in a position to retaliate to a sudden advertising burst by your company.

6.3 Controlling the budget

Communicators budgets must be subject to normal control measures to avoid either overspend or underspend. At the same time, **effectiveness** must be considered, even if informal judgement is the only technique available.

Marketing communication budgets may be very substantial and have a major effect on profitability. Controlling the effectiveness of the budget may be difficult if not impossible. What is possible is to use normal budgetary control techniques and to **review its effectiveness regularly** even if this is only by means of informed judgement. A simple way of representing this twin track is shown below.

Controlling the budgets and effectiveness

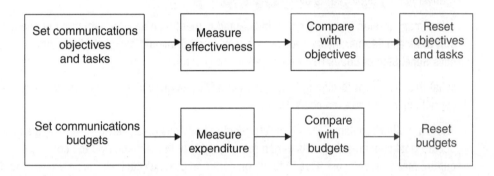

7 Cross border marketing communications

7.1 A global village?

As far back as 1983, *Levitt* argued that consumers the world over were converging in tastes and that the globalisation of markets was at hand. Levitt saw the emerging global village as presenting a huge opportunity for multinational companies to standardise products and attract large numbers of consumers through low costs brought about by economies of scale.

Factors contributing towards the globalisation of markets include the following.

(a) More **sophisticated consumers** who holiday outside their home country and are willing to experiment with non domestic products and services.

(b) The trend towards **elimination of political, trade and travel barriers** worldwide.

(c) The **internationalisation of broadcast and print media** (for example, cross border satellite transmission means consumers receive common programming).

(d) The **saturation of domestic markets**, leading companies to search for growth for their goods and services in new markets.

Levitt's globalisation argument has been criticised for adopting a production rather than a marketing orientation. **Standardisation may suit companies, but may not be what consumers are seeking**. An alternative view is that **consumer markets are fragmenting rather than converging**. Consumers are seeking to express themselves as individuals and do not want to be treated as part of a homogeneous mass. Products and services should therefore be **adapted** to individual country markets.

These two conflicting opinions provide a starting point for any consideration of international marketing management.

(a) It is unlikely that the majority of companies competing outside their own home market will be able to standardise their marketing mix completely.

(b) Nor is it likely that they will choose to adapt their marketing mix totally for each country in which they operate.

(c) The nature of the product or service, consumer buyer behaviour and competitive market environment will all dictate the appropriate strategy to adopt.

 Marketing at Work

Consumers in India are acutely price sensitive. They will think nothing of spending an entire morning scouting around to save five rupees. As a result, India has the largest 'used goods' market in the world. Most washing machines in the Punjab are used to churn butter, and the average washing machine (conventionally deployed) is over 19 years old.

"What many foreign investors don't understand is that the Indian consumer is not choosing between one soft drink and another; he's choosing between a soft drink and a packet of biscuits or a disposable razor" says Suhel Seth of Equus Red Cell, an advertising company.

What this means for foreign investors is that they must price cheaply, and therefore source almost everything locally, to keep costs down.

There are other problems. Standard refrigeration becomes pretty useless when acute power shortages occur. Most consumable goods perish pretty quickly in the climate. And the country's fragmented regional culture means advertisers have to focus on common ground (such as music, Bollywood and cricket).

Is it worth the effort? Investors say that overcoming such obstacles has equipped them for success in any market in the world.

Adapted from the *Financial Times, April 2002*

7.2 Cultural considerations

A variety of **cultural factors** must be considered when dealing with international communications. Legal matters may be even more important.

Key concept

> **Culture** is a term used to describe the set of values, beliefs, norms and artefacts held in common by a social group.

7.2.1 Various dimensions of culture are relevant to the international marketing communicator

- Verbal and non verbal **communications**
- **Aesthetics**
- **Dress** and **appearance**
- **Family roles** and **relationships**
- **Beliefs** and **values**
- **Learning**
- **Work habits**

7.2.2 Language

Common-sense dictates that care must be taken when **translating copy** from one language to another. A catchy phrase in the home market may not work so well elsewhere.

It may be difficult to decide exactly which language to choose for translation purposes. The official language of China is Mandarin, but a large proportion of Chinese living in the south of the country have Cantonese as their native tongue. In Canada, although the majority of the population speak English, packaging must include a French translation.

An additional consideration is that of the **space required for foreign language text**.

Brand and product names must be assessed for their suitability in international markets. *Mars* changed the name of their *Marathon* chocolate bar to *Snickers* in 1990 to facilitate their global communications strategy. A different approach is demonstrated by companies who choose to go with different names in different markets. For instance *Ford's Mondeo* name works well in European markets, where the 'world' association comes across powerfully. In the US market however, the car is called the *Contour*.

7.2.3 Aesthetics

Attitudes towards different design and colour aesthetics vary around the world. A fragrance or toiletries carton decorated with chrysanthemum flower graphics would not be a success in France, where the flowers are traditionally associated with funerals. Similarly, the colour white, which carries connotations of freshness, purity and fragility in the UK is the colour of mourning in China.

Different cultures will have grown up with their own rules about visual representation. The idea of showing a figure partially out of frame is well known in Europe. In much of Africa by contrast, figures that go over the edge of their frame transgress the cultural rule about how pictures should look.

7.2.4 Dress and appearance

Dress, be it formal or social, is very much constrained by culture. Advertisers need to be aware of cultural dress codes when deciding if an execution prepared in one market will be acceptable in another. In Europe, for instance, adverts for shower and bath products will often depict a semi-nude model. Such executions would be out of the question in the Middle East where women can only appear in advertisements if carefully attired.

7.2.5 Family roles and relationships

Family roles can differ greatly from country to country. Recent television adverts in the UK have shown fathers shopping in the supermarket with their children (*Bisto*); fathers washing children's clothes while their wives are out (washing powder commercial); and men cooking happily in the kitchen (*Sainsbury's*). In countries with more rigid gender codes, these executions might be either absurd or offensive.

7.2.6 Beliefs and values

Beliefs and values evolve from religious teachings, family structures and the pattern and nature of economic development in that society. In our culture, material well being is important, people tend to be defined (and define themselves) by their work roles, individualism and equal opportunities are held dear and time is a precious commodity. Different cultures may put a different emphasis on these values. Any communications imagery designed to be used internationally should therefore be scanned for **underlying values or beliefs that are culture specific**.

7.2.7 Learning

The level of education within a culture is an important factor for the international marketing communicator. Low **literacy levels** will mean that verbal methods of communication take precedence.

Press advertising and direct marketing may have to be ruled out. Packaging may need to be simplified, and point of sale and sales promotion techniques handled with care.

7.2.8 Work habits and lifestyles

Not all societies conform to the Monday to Friday, 9.00am till 5.00pm work routine. In Hong Kong, the working week extends until Saturday lunchtime. In some parts of South Europe, it is usual to work from very early in the morning until early afternoon. Workers then go home for a siesta.

7.2.9 Advertising culture

It has been suggested that in addition to being sensitive to a country's culture in general, **marketers should be aware of the level of a country's advertising literacy**. She argues that advertising in any national culture develops in a predictable way, and according to its position on this development curve, it can be described as having either high or low advertising literacy. Thus, imported advertising can be inappropriate because the advertising of country A is at a different stage of development from that of country B.

7.2.10 Five levels of advertising development

Level	Comment
Least sophisticated	The emphasis is on the **manufacturer's description** of the product. Messages are factual and rational with much repetition. Product or pack shots take prominence.
Unsophisticated	Consumer choice is acknowledged so emphasis switches to the **product's superiority** over the competition (eg products that wash whiter, feel softer).
Mid point	**Consumer benefits are emphasised**, rather than product attributes. Executional devices may include the use of celebrity endorsements or role models may give demonstrations, for example a dentist endorsing toothpaste products.
More sophisticated	Brands and their attributes are well known, so need only **passing references** (perhaps by way of a brief pack shot or logo). The message is communicated by way of **lifestyle narrative** (eg Gold Blend couple; Bisto family).
Most sophisticated level	The **focus is on the advertising** itself. The brand is referred to only obliquely, perhaps at a symbolic level (eg Silk Cut; Benson & Hedges). Consumers are believed to have a **mature understanding of advertising**, and are able to think laterally in order to decode messages.

Action Programme 10

Choose a country which is quite dissimilar to your own. You could perhaps choose somewhere that you have visited on holiday, or that a friend, relative or colleague has visited and told you about. Using the headings listed in Paragraph 7.2.1, compile a list of similarities and differences between the culture of the foreign country and that of your own.

Ideally, this should be conducted as a class exercise, so that you can pool your experiences.

7.3 Legal considerations

Laws and regulations governing marketing communications must obviously be observed. Each country will have its own set of restrictions which apply to advertising, packaging, sales promotion or direct marketing.

In the EU alone, there are a number of significant differences regarding the regulation of advertising between member states. A recent *Gossard TV* commercial came under scrutiny in the UK for its risqué execution. In France, the problem was not the generous display of cleavage, but the fact that the advert was set in a bar where alcohol was being consumed. There is a ban on TV alcohol adverts and the Gossard ad needed to be re-edited to fall in line with French restrictions.

In some countries, restrictions apply to the use of non native models and actors. This can mean that advertising has to be reshot for specific countries.

Packaging regulations can vary. In a number of European markets, the push towards environmentally-friendly packaging has resulted in far more stringent rules than apply in the UK. In Denmark, soft drinks may not be sold in cans, only in glass bottles with refundable deposits.

7.4 Standardisation vs adaptation

FAST FORWARD

A major strategic problem centres on the degree of **adaptation** or **standardisation** to apply to both **product** and **communication**.

7.4.1 Strategies appropriate for companies operating in international markets

(a) **Standardise product/standardise communication** (for example, Coca-Cola).

(b) **Standardise product/adapt communication** (Horlicks is promoted as a relaxing bedtime drink in the UK and as a high protein energy booster in India).

(c) **Adapt product/standardise communication** (washing powder ingredients may vary from country to country depending on water conditions and washing machine technology. However, the communication message of clean clothes is the same).

(d) **Adapt product/adapt communication**.

(e) **Invent a new product** to meet the needs of the market.

Action Programme 11

Over the next few months, scan the marketing and advertising trade press alongside the quality papers for examples of products and services which adopt the different strategies listed above. You will be able to generate your own list of current examples to illustrate points you make in the examination. Examiners welcome up to date relevant examples which demonstrate that you keep abreast of current practice.

Advantages of standardising communications include the following.

(a) **Economies of scale** can be generated. A single worldwide advertising, packaging or direct mail execution will save time and money.

(b) A **consistent and strong brand image** will be presented to the consumer. Wherever users see the brand, they will be reassured because the messages received will be the same.

(c)   A **standardised communications policy** allows for **easier implementation** and control by management.

(d)   Good **communications ideas are rare** and should be exploited creatively across markets.

 Marketing at Work

Pirelli

A *Pirelli* ad featured Marie-Jo Perec, a double Olympic gold medal winner, outrunning an avalanche, a tidal wave and a river of volcanic lava. The ad is thought to have cost over £1m to make, but it ran in up to 40 countries from China to South Africa. This needs to be compared with the cost of making multiple commercials, a different one for each country: it is thought to cost at least £250,000 to make a decent 30-second ad.

'There are certain clues which showed that this ad was designed to run internationally. There was no dialogue, as that would mean expensive and potentially difficult translation. And the images were universally recognisable – human against nature. The only potential problem was that Perec's sprinting costume could be considered too skimpy for some Islamic countries'.

Arguments against standardising communications include the following.

(a)   Any standardisation policy **assumes consumer needs and wants are identical** across markets. This may be a false assumption.

(b)   Centrally-generated communications concepts may prove to be **inappropriate for the specific culture** of the local market.

(c)   **Media channel availability and infrastructure varies** widely from country to country.

(d)   A country's level of **educational development** may prevent a standardised approach. For instance, a press campaign featuring detailed copy would be a non starter if literacy levels were low.

(e)   **Legal restrictions** may prove to be a stumbling block. For example, France does not allow any advertising of alcohol on television; cashback sales promotion offers are not allowed in Italy or Luxembourg.

(f)   Standardisation may encourage the **'not invented here' syndrome**, so that local management become lacklustre about creative ideas and communications policies imposed from above.

(g)   Different countries have economies which may be much more or much less **developed** than others. Factors that need to be considered are as follows.

- What is the level and trend in per capita income?
- Is the balance of payments favourable or unfavourable?
- Is inflation under control?
- Are the exchange rates stable?
- Is the currency easily convertible?
- Is the country politically stable?
- How protectionist is the country?
- Who controls distribution channels?

Chapter Roundup

- **Marketing communications** effort must be planned and controlled in such a way that it supports rational communications objectives that themselves support over-arching strategic plans.

- AIDA is no longer regarded as useful for understanding how communication works. **Sales, persuasion, involvement, saliency and awareness, trial, reinforcement, nudge** are more modern approaches.

- Messages have greater impact if their sources are **attractive** and **credible**. **High involvement** purchases tend to require messages based on **reason**, but messages based on **emotions** and, especially, **image**, work for low involvement purchases.

- **Positioning** is about **customer perception** and **evaluation** relative to competing brands. Positioning may be based on:
  - Attribute, feature or customer benefit
  - Price and quality
  - Use or application
  - Product user image
  - Product class dissociation
  - Competitor

- **Advertising** is non-personal, paid for mass communications. It should have clear objectives.

- **Personal selling** involves team work over a wide range of activities undertaken within the context of the overall marketing strategy.

- **Sales promotion techniques** involve providing a material incentive to buy.

- **PR** is largely about goodwill and image. Under the **two-way symmetric model** the practitioner mediates between the organisation and its publics. This model is best able to deal with PR arises and similar threats.

- **Direct marketing** is based on the establishment of direct relationships with customers. **Direct mail** is the main medium and has been extended by the power of ICT units **database marketing**.

- **Communications budgets** are difficult to set because of the difficulty of measuring the marginal effect of spending. The **objective and task** method is popular since it is logical and based on achieving the overall marketing objectives.

- The A/S ratio can be used to make comparisons with competitors.

- **Share of voice** must be considered alongside **share of market**. Spending can be used to maintain equilibrium or to create disequilibrium.

- **Communicators budgets** must be subject to normal control measures to avoid either overspend or underspend. At the same time, **effectiveness** must be considered, even if informal judgement is the only technique available.

- A variety of **cultural factors** must be considered when dealing with international communications. Legal matters may be even more important.

- A major strategic problem centres on the degree of **adaptation** or **standardisation** to apply to both **product** and **communication**.

Quick Quiz

1   What does saliency consist of, in advertising?

2   What is the threat to a spokesperson's credibility?

3   What is positioning?

4   List three positioning strategies.

5   What is likely to be the main role of the sales force when a pull strategy is used?

6   What is the name of the model of PR in which the practitioner mediates between the organisations and its publics?

7   What is the most logical approach to setting a communications budget?

8   What is an appropriate spending strategy when share of market is high and competitors' share of voice is low?

9   List three cultural factors that influence international marketing communications.

10   How does mid-point advertising differ from that aimed at unsophisticated markets?

Answer to Quick Quiz

1   Standing out, being different

2   The fact that the message is paid for by the advertiser

3   The perception and evaluation of the product by the target audience

4   Three from: attribute, feature or customer benefit; price and quality; use or application; product user image, product class dissociation; competitor

5   Service: ensuring that retailers carry sufficient stock, provide shelf space and co-operate in sales promotion activity

6   Two-way symmetric

7   Objective and task

8   Maintain spending slightly above equilibrium level

9   Three from: verbal and non-verbal communications; aesthetics; dress and appearance; family roles and relationships; beliefs and values; learning; work habits

10   Emphasis is on consumer benefits rather than product attributes

Now try Question 7 at the end of the Study Text

Action Programme Review

1   Marketing communications can most effectively be expected to achieve objectives related to increasing awareness levels, changing attitudes and behaviour patterns. Increasing sales or market share is dependent on other marketing factors such as product acceptability, price and distribution.

3   Try and further identify similar kinds of products or services from competing companies. How does their approach to positioning vary? A skim through one of the Sunday newspaper supplements will show a range of different advertisements for motor cars that are all aimed at the same target audience but from a variety of positioning platforms.

4   You will find it useful to maintain files of these examples. Try and find examples relating to differing market sectors including consumer products, services, public sector and not-for-profit. At your place of work collect examples based on business-to-business marketing communications. Collect examples for the same companies over a period of time. This will illustrate different use of communication tools and identify changes in strategy and tactics over time.

5   How does this approach differ from other companies in this sector. How was this integrated with other communications activities by One-to-One?

6   Consider the goals in relation to business, marketing and communications strategies.

7   On the launch of its 'Clubcard' Tesco said that it was a way of saying thank you to customers and that it wanted to 'recreate the kind of relationship that existed between consumers and local shops half a century ago'.

In practice, however, the schemes give supermarkets the chance to build up a massive database containing customers' names, addresses and detailed information on individual shopping habits. But did they really encourage loyalty? No. Safeway decided that the considerable expenditure in the loyalty card scheme could be better spent on sales promotions targeted at local level (eg leafleting of local households). Safeway reported substantial increases in sales – but this has to be set against the fact that Tesco, still using the Clubcard, is the UK's most successful retailer.

8   The main deficiency of the percentage of sales method is that it turns the traditional cause and effect relationship on its head.

Promotion causes sales. Hence, the amount of sales is a function of the amount spent on promotion. The strict implementation of the percentage of sales method means that the promotional spend becomes a function of the level of sales. Therefore, if sales decrease, then the amount spent on promotion is also decreased, whereas it might be wiser to keep the promotional spend constant in the face of declining sales.

The problem in forecasting future sales is the uncertainty of knowing what resources will be available to achieve the sales targets. Hence, this method should only be used to determine how much needs to be spent if conditions remain static. Beyond that, the budget needs adjusting in view of the new objectives.

9   This could involve looking at your own organisation or use a past examination paper mini case study.

10 Once you have completed this, consider the implications for differences in approach to marketing communications.

11 This will be invaluable in giving supporting examples in your exam.

Managing services

Chapter topic list

1 Services marketing
2 Characteristics of services marketing
3 The extended marketing mix for services marketing
4 The importance of people
5 Service quality
6 The nature of the customer
7 Privacy and data protection

Syllabus content

- 'Moments of truth' in delivering a service and activities that may add further value and their impact on customers and intermediaries
- Improving customer service by developing or enhancing customer care programmes
- Techniques for managing and monitoring service quality, including the use of specific measures
- Supporting relationships with customers, clients and intermediaries using appropriate information systems and database and adhering to relevant privacy and data protection legislation

Introduction

> The service sector has grown rapidly in recent years in the UK, both as an employer and in terms of its contribution to GDP. There are certain basic characteristics of service industries (Sections 1 and 2) that differentiate them from other business operations. These characteristics mean that the successful marketing and delivery of services requires attention to areas not really covered by the 4 Ps: who gives the service (people); how the service is given (process); the environment in which the service is given (physical evidence). The nature of **quality in services** is complex. Section 5 discusses what it is and how to measure it.
>
> Improvements in service quality are relevant to the marketing of all forms of product that include an element of service. In Section 6 we examine some of the ideas that have been developed around the idea of **relationship marketing**, including the use of customer databases and key account management. The extensive use of IT in this context leads us naturally to the topic of **privacy and data protection**, and this forms the subject matter of Section 7.

1 Services marketing

FAST FORWARD

The extension of the **service sector**, and the application of market principles across many public sector and ex-public sector organisations, has made a large number of service providers much more marketing-conscious.

There are a number of reasons why services marketing is more important today than in the past. These include the following.

(a)   **The growth of service sectors in advanced industrial societies**. More people now work in the service sector than in all other sectors of the economy and the major contributors to national output are the public and private service sectors. Invisible earnings from abroad are of increasing significance for Britain's balance of trade.

(b)   **An increasingly market-oriented trend within service-providing organisation**. This has been particularly apparent within the public sector with the advent of internal markets, market testing and the chartermark.

The public sector in Britain includes service provision in the legal, medical, educational, military, employment, transportation, leisure and information fields. Increasingly, there is a focus on profits in many of these areas. The private sector embraces not-for-profit areas such as the arts, charities and religious and educational organisations and includes business and professional services in travel, finance, insurance, management, the law, building, commerce and entertainment.

Services: some definitions

(a)   ' ... those separately identifiable but intangible activities that provide want-satisfaction, and that are not, of necessity, tied to, or inextricable from, the sale of a product or another service.'
Donald Cowell, The Marketing of Services

(b)   ' ... any activity of benefit that one party can offer to another that is essentially intangible and does not result in the ownership of anything. Its production may or may not be tied to a physical product.'
P Kotler, Social Marketing

Marketing services faces a number of distinct problems, and as a consequence, the approach adopted must be varied, and particular marketing practices developed.

2 Characteristics of services marketing

Services marketing differs from the marketing of other goods in a number of crucial ways, and five specific characteristics of services marketing have been proposed: intangibility, inseparability, heterogeneity, perishability and ownership.

Characteristics of services which make them distinctive from the marketing of goods have been proposed. These are five major differences.

- **Intangibility**
- **Inseparability**
- **Heterogeneity**
- **Perishability**
- **Ownership**

2.1 Intangibility

Services have no physical substance. Clearly, this creates difficulties and can inhibit the propensity to consume a service, since customers are not sure what they have.

> 'Ultimately the customer may have no prior experience of a service in which he or she is interested, nor any conception of how it would satisfy the requirements of the purchase context for which it was intended.'
> *Morden, The Marketing of Services*

Shostack has suggested viewing insubstantiality as a continuum, as shown in the diagram below.

The Goods - Services Continuum

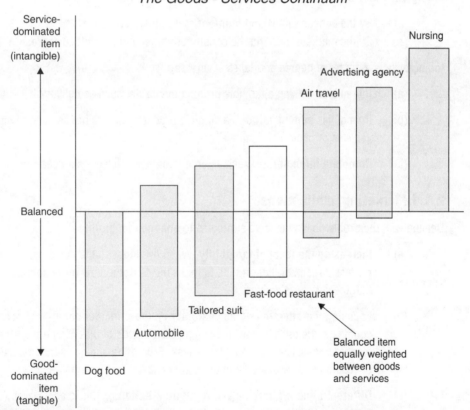

Shostack has also proposed that marketing entities are combinations of elements, which are tangible or intangible. A product then comes to be conceived as a blend of various elements, combining **material entities** (the aeroplane we are flying in, the airport lounge) with various sorts of **processes** (the courtesy of the airline staff, the frequency of services).

Clearly, for each service, the number, complexity and balance of the various elements involved will vary a great deal. What is experienced remains insubstantial, although many parts of the process (the machines, buildings and staff of an airline, for instance) are very substantial.

The consumer needs **information** to form some grounds for **judgement**, and to cut down **risk**. The marketer wishes to make the choice of the product safer and make consumers feel more comfortable about paying for something that has no physical form.

 Marketing at Work

Radio 5 Live

BBC Radio 5 Live is to embark on its first major TV advertising campaign since the station launched six years ago. It is part of a new marketing strategy for the station.

A month-long TV and poster campaign breaks in mid-February and will attempt to woo new listeners to R5 Live, according to BBC Radio head of marketing Vanessa Griffiths.

Griffiths says: 'The station has strong loyalty among its core audience but minimal awareness outside of it. But R5 Live has massive potential to talk to millions more listeners.'

The station has 5.6 million listeners and a 4.2 per cent share of listening, according to Rajar figures for the quarter ending September 1999.

Marketing Week, 20 January 2000

Intangibility may be countered in two ways.

(a) By the consumer seeking **opinions** from other consumers

(b) By the marketer offering the consumer something tangible to **represent the purchase**

Intangibility is a matter of degree and takes several forms.

(a) Intangibles making a tangible product **available**, such as delivery

(b) Intangibles **adding value** to a tangible product, such as house decorating, hairdressing, vehicles or plant maintenance

(c) **Complete intangibility**, such as entertainment or leisure services

2.1.1 Marketing implications

Dealing with the problems may involve strategies to **enhance tangibility**.

(a) **Increasing the level of tangibility**. When dealing with the customer, staff can use physical representations or illustrations to make the customer feel more confident as to what it is that the service is delivering.

(b) **Focusing the attention of the customer on the principal benefits of consumption**. This could take the form of communicating the benefits of purchasing the service so that the customer visualises its appropriateness. Promotion and sales material could provide images or records of previous customers' experience.

(c) **Differentiating the service and reputation-building**. This is achieved by enhancing perceptions of service and value through offering excellence in the delivery of the service and by promoting values of quality, service reliability and value for money. These must be attached as **values** to brands, which must then be managed to secure and enhance their market position.

2.2 Inseparability

A service often cannot be separated from the provider of the service. The **performance of a service often occurs at the same instant as its consumption**. Think of having dental treatment or going on a journey. Neither exists until actually consumed by the purchaser.

2.2.1 Marketing implications

Provision of the service may not be separable from the provider. Consequently, increasing importance is attached to **values of quality and reliability** and a customer service ethic which can be transferred to the service provision. This emphasises the need for customer orientation, high quality people and high quality training for them.

2.3 Heterogeneity

Many services face a problem of **maintaining consistency in the standard of output**. Variability of quality in delivery is inevitable, because of the number of factors which may influence it. This may create problems of operations management. For example, it may be difficult or impossible to attain:

(a) **Precise standardisation of the service offered**. The quality of the service may depend heavily on who delivers the service and when it takes place. Booking a holiday using standard procedures, may well be quite different on a quiet winter afternoon and on a hectic spring weekend, and may well vary according to the person dealing with the client.

(b) **Influence or control over perceptions of what is good or bad customer service**. From the customer's perspective, it is very difficult to obtain an idea of the quality of service in advance of purchase.

2.3.1 Marketing implications

As a result, it is necessary to monitor customer reactions constantly and to maintain an attitude and organisational culture which emphasises three things.

- Consistency of quality control
- Consistency of customer service
- Effective staff selection, training and motivation

Other important matters

(a) Clear and objective quality measures

(b) Standardising as much as possible within the service

(c) The **Pareto principle** (80 percent of difficulties arise from 20 percent of events surrounding the provision of the service). Therefore, identify and respond most closely to these potential troublespots.

2.4 Perishability

Services cannot be stored. They are innately **perishable**. Performances at a theatre or the services of a chiropodist consist in their availability for periods of time, and if they are not occupied, the service they offer cannot be used later.

2.4.1 Marketing implications

This presents specific marketing problems. **Meeting customer needs in these operations depends on staff being available when they are needed**. This must be balanced against the need to minimise unnecessary expenditure on staff wages. Anticipating and responding to levels of demand is, therefore, a key planning priority. There are two risks.

- Inadequate level of demand is accompanied by substantial fixed cost.
- Excess demand may result in lost custom through inadequate service provision.

Policies must seek to match demand with supply by price variations and promotions to stimulate off-peak demand.

2.5 Ownership

Services do not result in the transfer of property. In the case of purchasing a product, there is permanent transfer of title and control over the use of an item. An item of service provision is often defined by the length of time it is available.

This may very well lessen the perceived customer value of a service, and consequently make for unfavourable comparisons with **tangible** alternatives. Attempts have been made to overcome this problem by providing **symbolic** tangible items which can be taken away and kept. Car brochures, theatre programmes and the plethora of corporate giftwares such as golf umbrellas, pens and keyrings, are all examples of this.

Action Programme 1

What are the marketing implications of the lack of ownership of a service received?

Marketing at Work

Quality in stockbroking

The following table shows the type of factors on which judgements are based in stockbroking.

Dimension and definition	Examples of specific questions raised by stock brokerage customers
Tangibles. Appearance of physical facilities, equipment, personnel and communication materials.	• Is my stockbroker dressed appropriately?
Reliability. Ability to perform the promised service dependably and accurately.	• Does the stockbroker follow exact instructions to buy or sell?
Responsiveness. Willingness to help customers and provide prompt service.	• Is my stockbroker willing to answer my questions?
Competence. Possession of the required skills and knowledge to perform the service.	• Does my brokerage firm have the research capabilities accurately to track market developments?
Courtesy. Politeness, respect, consideration, and friendliness of contact personnel.	• Does my broker refrain from acting busy or being rude when I ask questions?
Credibility. Trustworthiness, believability, and honesty of the service provider.	• Does my broker refrain from pressuring me to buy?
Security. Freedom from danger, risk, or doubt.	• Does my brokerage firm know where my stock certificate is?
Access. Approachability and ease of contact.	• Is it easy to get through to my broker over the telephone?

Dimension and definition	Examples of specific questions raised by stock brokerage customers
Communication. Keeping customers informed in language they can understand, and listening to them.	• Does my broker avoid using technical jargon?
Understanding the customer. Making the effort to know customers and their needs.	• Does my broker try to determine what my specific financial objectives are?

Zeithaml, Parasuraman and Berry, *Delivering Quality Service*

3 The extended marketing mix for services marketing

FAST FORWARD

An **extended marketing mix** has been suggested for services marketing. Booms and Bitner suggested an additional 3Ps. These are people, process and physical evidence.

Booms and Bitner suggest that the standard 4P approach to the marketing of products should be extended for services by the addition of **three more Ps**.

- **People**
- **Process**
- **Physical evidence** (or ambience)

Services are provided by **people** for people. If the people providing the service are wrong, the service is spoiled. In the case of a bus service, a cheap fare, a clean vehicle and a frequent service can be spoiled by a surly driver.

Services are usually provided in a number of sequential steps. This is **process. The service can be spoiled or enhanced at any step in the sequence**.

Finally, there is the **physical evidence** or **ambience** which can be a maker or spoiler of experience of the service.

An alternative approach identifies four extra Ps.

- **Personal selling**
- **Place of availability** (operations management)
- **People and customer service**
- **Physical evidence**

3.1 Personal selling

Personal selling is very important in the marketing of services, because of the **greater perceived risk** involved and greater uncertainty about quality and reliability. The reputation of the supplier may be of greater importance, and the customer places greater reliance on the honesty of the individual salesperson. When consumers seek reassurance, personal contact with a competent, effective representative may provide the necessary confidence. Conversely, inappropriate selling may generate increased anxiety.

3.2 Place of availability

Place of availability is really covered by the distribution system, but there are special problems for services in **operations management**. The place and frequency of availability are key service variables but service resources must be used economically.

The level and quality of service are sensitive to the efficiency of the processes by which services are delivered. There are three key factors.

(a) **Capacity utilisation**: matching demand sequences to staff utilisation to avoid both the costs of overstaffing and the lost revenue of underprovision

(b) **Managing customer contact**, to avoid crowding and customer disruption, meet needs as they arise, and increase employee control over interactions

(c) **Establishing objectives within the not-for-profit sector**, for example, standards for teachers or medical staff

Interactions **between customers** are a key strategic issue. Customers often interact to gather information and form views about the service they are contemplating purchasing. Minimising exposure to negative feedback, and promoting the dissemination of positive messages about the service are important objectives.

3.3 People and customer service

For some services, the **presence of people performing the service is a vital aspect of customer satisfaction**. For example, staff in catering establishments are performing or producing a service, selling the service and liaising with the customer to promote the service, gather information and respond to customer needs. Customer orientation is needed in all sectors of organisational activity.

Customers will tend to use cues to establish a view about the organisation from the demeanour and behaviour of staff. The higher the level of customer contact involved in the delivery of a service, the more crucial is the staff role in adding value. In many cases, the delivery of the service and the physical presence of the personnel involved are completely inseparable; here, **technical competence and skill in handling people are of equal importance** in effective delivery of the service.

Action Programme 2

All levels of staff must be involved in customer service. To achieve this end, it is vital for senior management to promote the importance of customer service. How do you think that this might be achieved?

3.4 Physical evidence

Physical evidence is an important remedy for the intangibility of the product. This may be **associated with the service itself**, (for example, credit cards which represent the service available to customers); **built up by identification with a specific individual** (a 'listening' bank manager); or **incorporated into the design and specification of the service environment,** involving the building, location or atmosphere.

Action Programme 3

What do you think that design can achieve in services marketing?

4 The importance of people

4.1 'Moments of truth' – the service encounter

> Even the briefest service encounter is a 'moment of truth' for the organisation concerned. This emphasises the great importance of people and the need to recruit, select, train, motivate and manage them effectively.

In many service industries, the service encounter lasts only a few seconds. The service provider thus has a very limited time in which to make an impression. *Jan Carlzon*, formerly CEO of SAS Airlines calls these contacts '**moments of truth**' and says they can make the difference between success and failure. He describes how each of the airline's 10 million customers came into contact with approximately five employees for an average of 15 seconds each time. These 50 million 'moments of truth' are crucial to the airline in convincing customers that it is the best alternative for their needs. The **inseparability** of services means that such moments cannot be avoided: services are produced and consumed at the same time; they cannot be checked for quality conformance before being provided to the customer.

The importance of such encounters is that each one is in effect a **marketing communication** and contributes to the overall impression that the customer forms. People at all levels in the organisation thus have direct influence over its image and its value proposition. It is not possible to exercise direct control over these communications, but marketing managers must be aware of them, appreciate their importance and do what they can to control – or at least influence – them indirectly. This is done by setting up **systems and procedures** to govern interactions with the customer and by **motivating people** to give a high quality of service.

As a consequence of the importance of **people**, service marketing organisations have certain common areas of emphasis.

(a) **Selection** and **training**

(b) Internal marketing to promulgate the **culture of service** within the firm

(c) Ensuring conformance with **standards**

- Behaviour
- Dress and appearance
- Procedures
- Modes of dealing with the public

(d) **Mechanising** procedures where possible

(e) Constantly **auditing** personnel performance and behaviour

(f) **Extending** the promotion of the service and its qualities into the design of service environments and the engineering of interactions between staff and customers and among the customers themselves.

4.2 Types of service encounter

It is possible to identify three types of service encounter.

(a) **Remote** using technology such as a website or ATM
(b) **Telephone**
(c) **Face to face**

Remote encounters can be programmed to provide a high degree of satisfaction for routine business, but human contact is necessary for more complex requirements and when things go wrong.

4.3 Features of good service

4.3.1 Adaptability and spontaneity

Emphasis is given in well run service operations to standardisation of processes so that a constant level of good service is attained. However, service staff should be prepared to adapt and to make **spontaneous improvements**.

(a) **Adaptability** is needed so that adherence to fixed procedure does not frustrate customers with unusual or urgent requests.

(b) **Spontaneity** can add delight to the routine service encounter by adding to the standard process. The extra value might take the form of supplementary advice or help with an extraneous problem, for example.

(c) **Coping strategies** are needed for difficult and demanding customers in order to avoid conflict and resolve problems within resource constraints.

(d) **Service recovery** is required after a failure. Prompt action can enhance customer satisfaction and loyalty.

 Marketing at Work

Complaints

Complaints are among the best things that can happen to a company. They give managers the chance to rectify the situation over and above customer expectations; they give low cost feedback on how your products and services are perceived and handled properly, they create 'goodwill ambassadors' for your brand. In June, TMI, along with the Institute of Customer Service, the trade body, published research into how and why people in the UK complain and how they are dealt with. Among other findings, it confirmed the old management cliché that people tend not to complain they simply walk away. It is the expense of replacing customers that makes handling complaints well so cost-effective. 'We estimate that it costs five times as much to recruit a new customer as it does to keep an existing one,' says Julie Robinson, director of service delivery at *Virgin Atlantic*, the airline. 'As part of our staff training we need to show people that giving compensation when something goes wrong is not giving away the company's profits. Quite the opposite.' So what is the 'right' way to handle a complaint? Almost everyone agrees on step one: listen. 'You must listen to the customer,' says Ms Robinson, 'and not interrupt until you have under stood the problem.' But what then? Mr Brennan's company advocates an eight-step process. After saying 'thank you' comes explaining why you appreciate the complaint; apologising; promising you will do something about it straight away; asking for more information; correcting the mistake; checking customer satisfaction and, finally, preventing future mistakes. Mr Brennan is quick to point out the order of these steps. 'Many people ask for information first, such as name and address, making the customer feel as if they are somehow under suspicion. A complaint is a gift from a customer.' This unexpected generosity from the woman at the counter is confirmed by Stephen Walker, head of customer service at *Marks and Spencer*, the retailer, a UK company that is almost synonymous with handling complaints effectively. 'The information people give you when they complain,' he says, 'is invaluable to the organisation. We run a central database where complaints are logged, from which we can feed information back to the relevant buyer and suppliers, often on the same day. Customers are looking for a quick resolution of the problem and an assurance that we will do what we can to ensure it doesn't happen again.' Managers of big companies can also use complaints to develop one-to-one relationships with customers. 'Complaints offer an excellent chance to deal with customers face to face,' says Mr Walker. 'If you take a complaint seriously, and deal with it in a generous way, you can buy them for life.'

David Baker, *Financial Times, 2 August 2000*

PROFESSIONAL EDUCATION

The role of people in services marketing is especially important. What human characteristics improve the quality of client service?

5 Service quality

Service quality can be defined as the difference between what customers expect and what they perceive themselves to be receiving. This corresponds to Gap 5 in the Parasuraman, Zeithaml and Berry 5 gap quality model. The SERVQUAL questionnaire measures this gap. Improved service quality leads to higher profits and is a key task for service marketers. Technical quality is what the customer is left with; functional quality resides in the way it was delivered.

Service quality is a significant basis which customers use for differentiating between competing services. Second only to market share in the PIMS research (*Buzzell and Gale*, 1980), relative quality is a key contributor to **bottom line profit performance**.

Quality can only be defined by customers. It occurs where a firm supplies products to a specification that satisfies their needs. Customer expectations serve as standards against which subsequent service experiences are compared. When service performance falls short of customer expectations, dissatisfaction occurs.

There are two ways firms can gain from improving their quality of service.

(a) **Higher sales revenues** and improved marketing effectiveness brought about by improved customer retention, positive word-of-mouth recommendations and the ability to increase prices.

(b) **Improved productivity and reduced costs** because there is less rework, higher employee morale and lower employee turnover.

Grönroos introduced the concept of 'perceived service quality' in 1982 and extended this in the development of his widely cited model of service quality in 1984.

Grönoos (1984) Service Quality Model

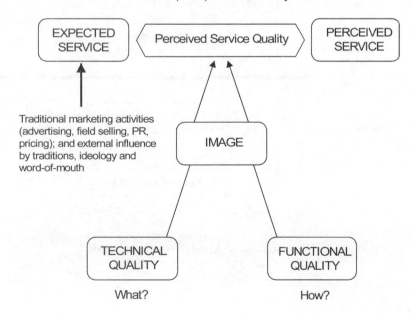

The model suggests that the quality of a given service is the outcome of an evaluation process where **consumers compare what they expected to receive with what they perceive that they actually received**. Consumer expectations are influenced by marketing mix activities, external traditions, ideology and word-of-mouth communications. Grönroos also suggests previous experience with the service will influence expectations.

In terms of perceived service quality, Grönroos suggests there are two principal components of quality, **technical** and **functional**, with a third, **image**, acting as a mediating influence.

(a)   **Technical quality** is what the customer is left with, when the production process is finished. For example, in higher education this would be perceived as the level of attainment and understanding achieved at the end of the course. This can be much more easily measured by the consumer.

(b)   **Functional quality**, on the other hand, is more difficult to measure objectively because it involves an evaluation of **how the consumer receives the technical quality** in the interactions between customer and service provider and other customers. Grönroos' suggestion that **service quality is dependent both on what you receive and how you receive it** emphasises the importance of service interactions, contact employees and managing in the service experience.

Image. Grönroos also suggests that both expectations and perceptions are affected by the consumer's view of the company and by its image. If a consumer has a **positive image** of a university or lecturer but has a negative experience, for example a rather confused lecture, the consumer may still **perceive** the service to be satisfactory because he or she will find excuses for the negative experience. Correspondingly, Grönroos suggests that a **negative image** may increase perceived problems with service quality.

5.1 Quality gaps

Parasuraman, Zeithaml and Berry developed the most widely applied model of service quality in 1985. The researchers developed their model via interviews with fourteen executives in four service businesses and twelve customer focus groups. The executive interviews resulted in the idea of **five gaps** which are potential hurdles for a firm in attempting to deliver high quality service.

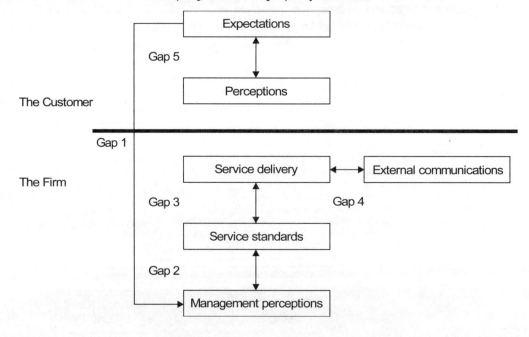

Gap 1   **Consumer expectations and management perceptions gap**
Essentially managers may not know what features connote high quality, what features a service must have or what levels of performance are required by customers.

Action
- Market research programmes
- Improvements based on customer comment and complaints
- Strategies for service recovery
- Improvements based on front line staff experience and suggestion

Gap 2   **Management perceptions and service quality specification gap**
Resource constraints, market conditions and/or management indifference may result in this gap.

Action
- New concepts of service rather than merely improving old ones
- Attention to physical evidence
- Customer focused activity goals

Gap 3   **Service quality specifications and service delivery gap**
Guidelines may exist but contract employees may not be willing or able to perform to the specified standards. Roles may be poorly organised, technology, supervision and team work may be unsatisfactory.

Action
- Define job roles and priorities clearly
- Provide proper training
- Build teams and team working
- Empower frontline staff
- Improve technology
- Recruitment, training and reward policy improvements

Gap 4   **Service delivery and external communications gap**
Exaggerated promises or lack of information will affect both expectations and perceptions.

Action
- Improve communications between staff and departments
- Educate customers
- Develop service rules but do not over-promote to customers
- Marketing communications emphasise what is actually delivered

Gap 5   **Expected service and perceived service gap**
This gap was defined as **service quality**. The authors argue that gap five is influenced by the preceding four gaps so if management want to close the gap between performance and expectations it becomes imperative to design procedures for measuring service performance against expectations.

In 1988, the researchers developed the SERVQUAL questionnaire which purports to be a global measure of Gap 5 across all service organisations. This measures the five generic criteria that consumers use in evaluating service quality.

1	*Tangibles*: physical facilities, equipment, appearance of personnel
2	*Reliability*: ability to perform the promised service dependably and accurately
3	*Responsiveness*: willingness to help customers and provide prompt service
4	*Assurance*: knowledge and courtesy of employees and their ability to convey trust and confidence
5	*Empathy*: caring, individualised attention

Respondents are asked first to give their expectations of the service on a seven point scale, then to give their evaluation of the actual service on the same scale. Service quality is then calculated as the difference between perception and expectations, weighted for the importance of each item.

Once a firm knows how it is performing on each of the dimensions of service quality it can use a number of methods to try to improve its quality.

(a)   Development of customer orientated mission statement and clear senior management support for quality improvement initiatives

(b)   Regular customer satisfaction research including customer surveys and panels, mystery shoppers, analysis of complaints and similar industry studies for benchmarking purposes

(c)   Setting and monitoring standards and communicating results

(d)   Establishment of systems for customers complaints and feedback

(e)   Encouragement of employee participation, ideas and initiative, often through the use of quality circles and project teams

(f)   Rewarding excellent service

Customer perception of service quality can vary even when the five generic criteria are successfully managed to achieve a high standard. This is the result of the influence of four further factors.

(a)   **Product quality** where there is a physical aspect
(b)   **Price**
(c)   **Situational factors** such as the urgency of the customer's need
(d)   **Personal factors** such as cultural and demographic influences

6 The nature of the customer

FAST FORWARD

> Customers vary in their needs and attitudes but a company should make efforts to retain **profitable** ones. A high degree of competition means this is only likely if the customer is very satisfied.

The customer is central to the marketing orientation, but so far we have not considered this important concept in detail. Customers make up one of the groups of **stakeholders** whose interests management should address. **The stakeholder concept suggests a wider concern than the traditional marketing approach of supplying goods and services which satisfy immediate needs**. The supplier-customer relationship extends beyond the basic transaction. The customer needs to **remain** satisfied with his purchase and positive about his supplier long after the transaction has taken place. If his satisfaction is muted or grudging, future purchases may be reluctant or non-existent and he may advise others of his discontent. Customer tolerance in the UK is fairly high, but should not be taken for granted.

Not all customers are the same. Some appear for a single cash transaction and are never seen again. Others make frequent, regular purchases in large volumes, using credit facilities and building up a major relationship. Yet another type of customer purchases infrequently but in transactions of high value, as for instance in property markets. This variation will exist to a greater or lesser extent in all industries, though each will have a smaller typical range of behaviour. However, even within a single business, customers will vary significantly in the frequency and volume of their purchases, their reasons for buying, their sensitivity to price changes, their reaction to promotion and their overall attitude to the supplier and the product. **Segmentation** of the customer base can have a major impact on profitability, perhaps by simply tailoring promotion to suit the most attractive group of customers.

Many businesses sell to intermediaries rather than to the end consumer. Some sell to both categories; they have to recognise that **the intermediary is just as much a customer as the eventual consumer**. Examples are manufacturers who maintain their own sales organisation but appoint agents in geographically remote areas and companies who combine autonomous operations with franchising. While it is reasonable to give the highest priority to the needs of the ultimate consumer and insist on some control over the activities of the intermediary, it must be recognised that he will only perform well if his own needs are addressed. For instance, a selling agent who has invested heavily in stock after being given exclusive rights in an area should be consulted before further demands are made on his cash flow by the launch of a new product.

6.1 Customer retention

Variation in customer behaviour was mentioned above. The most important aspect of this variation is whether or not the customer comes back for more. Customers should be seen as potentially providing a lifetime of purchases so that **the turnover from a single individual over time might be very large indeed**. It is widely accepted that there is a non-linear relationship between customer retention and profitability in that **a fairly small amount of repeat purchasing generates significant profit**. This is because it is far more expensive in promotion and overhead costs to convert a non-buyer into an occasional buyer than to turn an occasional buyer into a frequent buyer. The repeat buyer does not have to be persuaded to give the product a try or be tempted by special deals; he needs less attention from sales staff and already has his credit account set up. New customers usually have to be won from competitors.

Today's highly competitive business environment means that customers are only retained if they are **very satisfied** with their purchasing experience. **Any lesser degree of satisfaction is likely to result in the loss of the customer**. Companies must be active in monitoring customer satisfaction **because very few will actually complain**. **They will simply depart**. Businesses which use intermediaries must be particularly active, since research shows that even when complaints are made, the principals hear about only a very small proportion of them.

 Marketing at Work

Customer care

In the increasingly competitive service sector, it is no longer enough to promise customer satisfaction. Today, customer 'delight' is the stated aim for companies battling to retain and increase market share.

British Airways, which lists delighting customers among its new goals, says ensuring the safety of passengers and meeting all their needs drives everything it does. 'Other airlines fly the same routes using similar aircraft. What BA must do is provide a superior standard of efficiency, comfort and general service which persuades passengers to fly with us again and again,' says Mike Street, director of customer services at BA.

Kwik-Fit, the car repair group, is another company that has included customer delight in its mission statement. Its forecourt promises to deliver '100 per cent customer delight' in the supply and fitting of vehicle brakes, tyres and exhausts leaves little margin for mistakes – and none at all for making any customer unhappy. Staff attend courses at company-run centres covering 'all practical aspects of their work, customer care and general management techniques'. Commitment is encouraged by 'job security', opportunities for promotion and a reward package that includes profit-related pay and shares in the company.

Customer satisfaction is monitored via reply-paid questionnaires distributed after work is carried out and through a freephone helpline that is open 24 hours a day. Kwik-Fit also says its customer survey unit 'allows us to make contact with 5,000 customers a day, within 72 hours of their visit to a Kwik-Fit Centre.'

Financial Times, 25 November 1999

The most satisfactory way to retain customers is to offer them products which they perceive as providing superior benefits at any given price point. However, there are specific techniques which can increase customer retention. Loyalty schemes such as frequent flyer programmes, augment the product in the customer's eyes. The club concept, as used by *Sainsbury* and *Tesco*, offers small discounts on repeated purchases. The principal benefit of both these types of scheme, however, is the enhanced knowledge of the customer which they provide. Initial registration provides name, address and post code. Subsequent use of the loyalty card allows a detailed purchasing profile to be built up for individual customers. This enables highly targeted promotion and cross-selling later.

Research indicates that **the single largest reason why customers abandon a supplier is poor performance by front-line staff**. Any scheme for customer retention must address the need for careful selection and training of these staff. It is also a vital factor in **relationship marketing**.

6.2 Relationship marketing

FAST FORWARD

Relationship marketing is based on the fostering of a customer-oriented service culture. One approach involves

– Building a customer database
– Developing customer-oriented service systems
– Extra direct contacts with customers

The behaviour of **people** is crucial to the relationship marketing approach.

Key concept

Relationship marketing is defined very simply by *Grönroos* as the management of a firm's market relationships.

Much has been written in recent years on **relationship marketing**. *Gummesson* suggests it is a 'paradigm shift' requiring a **dramatic change** in marketing thinking and behaviour, not an add-on to traditional marketing.' In his book *Total Relationship Marketing*, he suggests that the core of marketing should no longer be the 4Ps, but 30Rs, which reflect the large number of **complex relationships** involved in business. *Kotler* says 'marketing can make promises but only the whole organisation can deliver satisfaction'. *Adcock* expands on this by remarking that relationship marketing can only exist when the marketing function fosters a customer-oriented **service culture** which supports the network of activities that deliver value to the customer. The metaphor of **marriage** has been used to describe relationship marketing, emphasising the nature of the necessary long term commitment and mutual respect.

Relationship marketing is thus as much about attitudes and assumptions as it is about techniques. The marketing function's task is to inculcate habits of behaviour at all levels and in all departments which will enhance and strengthen the alliance. It must be remembered, however, that the effort involved in long-term relationship building is more appropriate in some markets than in others. Where customers are purchasing intermittently and switching costs are low, there is always a chance of business. This tends to be the pattern in commodity markets. Here, it is reasonable to take a **transactions approach** to marketing and treat each sale as unique. A **relationship marketing approach** is more appropriate where switching costs are high and a lost customer is thus probably lost for a long time. Switching costs are raised by such factors as the need for training on systems, the need for a large common installed base, high capital cost and the incorporation of purchased items into the customer's worn designs.

The conceptual or philosophic nature of relationship marketing leads to a simple principle, that of **enhancing satisfaction by precision in meeting the needs of individual customers**. This depends on extensive two-way communication to establish and record the customer's characteristics and preferences and build a long-term relationship. *Adcock* mentions three important practical methods which contribute to this end.

- Building a customer database
- Developing customer-oriented service systems
- Extra direct contacts with customers

Modern **computer database systems** have enabled the rapid acquisition and retrieval of the individual customer's details, needs and preferences. Using this technology, relationship marketing enables telephone sales staff to greet the customer by name, know what he purchased last time, avoid taking his full delivery address, know what his credit status is and what he is likely to want. It enables new products to be developed that are precisely tailored to the customer's needs and new procedures to be established which enhance his satisfaction. It is the successor to **mass marketing**, which attempted to be customer-led but which could only supply a one-size-fits-all product. The end result of a relationship marketing approach is a mutually satisfactory relationship which continues indefinitely.

Relationship marketing *extends* the principles of **customer care**. Customer care is about providing a product which is augmented by high quality of service, so that the customer is impressed during his transaction with the company. This can be done in ignorance of any detail of the customer other than those implicit in the immediate transaction. The customer is anonymous. **Relationship marketing is about having the customer come back for further transactions by ending the anonymity**. Adcock says 'To achieve results, it will be necessary to involve every department ... in co-ordinated activity aimed at maximising customer satisfaction'. The culture must be right; the right people must be recruited and trained; the structure, technology and processes must all be right.

It is inevitable that **problems** will arise. A positive way of dealing with errors must be designed into the customer relationship. *Deming*, the prominent writer on quality, tells us that front line sales people cannot usually deal with the causes of mistakes as they **are built into the products, systems and organisation structure**. It is therefore necessary for management to promote vertical and horizontal interaction in order to spur changes to eliminate the **sources** of mistakes.

It is inevitable that there will be multiple contacts between customer and supplier organisations. Each contact is an opportunity to enhance or to prejudice the relationship, so staff throughout the supplier organisation must be aware of their marketing responsibilities. Two way communication should be encouraged so that the relationship can grow and deepen. There is a link here to the database mentioned above: extra contacts provide more information. Confidential information must, of course, be treated with due respect.

 Marketing at Work

Customer loyalty

The problem with profitable customers is retaining them, because they will attract the attention of your competitors. Building customer relationships may be the answer to both types of problem.

Relationship marketing is grounded in the idea of establishing a learning relationship with customers. At the lower end, building a relationship can create cross-selling opportunities that may make the overall relationship profitable. For example, some retail banks have tried selling credit cards to less profitable customers. With valuable customers, customer relationship management may make them more loyal and willing to invest additional funds. In banking, these high-end relationships are often managed through private bankers, whose goals are not only to increase customer satisfaction and retention, but also to cross-sell and bring in investment.

In determining which customers are worth the cost of long-term relationships, it is useful to consider their lifetime value. This depends on:

- Current profitability computed at the customer level
- The propensity of those customers to stay loyal
- Expected revenues and costs of servicing such customers over the lifetime of the relationship

Building relationships makes most sense for customers whose lifetime value to the company is the highest. Thus, building relationships should focus on customers who are currently the most profitable, likely to be the most profitable in the future, or likely to remain with the company for the foreseeable future and have acceptable levels of profitability.

The goal of relationship management is to increase customer satisfaction and to minimise any problems. By engaging in 'smarter' relationships, a company can learn customers' preferences and develop trust. Every contact point with the customer can be seen as a chance to record information and learn preferences. Complaints and errors must be recorded, not just fixed and forgotten. Contact with customers in every medium, whether over the Internet, through a call centre, or through personal contact, is recorded and centralised.

Many companies are beginning to achieve this goal by using customer relationship management (CRM) software. Data, once collected an centralised, can be used to customise service. In addition, the database can be analysed to detect patterns that can suggest better ways to serve customers in general. A key aspect of this dialogue is to learn and record preferences. There are two ways to determine customers' preferences: transparently and collaboratively.

Discovering preferences transparently means that the marketer learns the customers' needs without actually involving them. For example, the *Ritz Carlton Hotel* makes a point of observing the choices that guests make and recording them. If a guest requests extra pillows, then extra pillows will be provided every time that person visits. At upmarket retailers, personal shoppers will record customers' preferences in sizes, styles, brands, colours and price ranges and notify them when new merchandise appears or help them choose accessories.

Barbara Kahn, *Financial Times, 9 October 2000*

6.2.1 Differences between transactional and relationship marketing

Transactional	Relationship
Importance of single sale	Importance of customer relation
Importance of product features	Importance of customer benefits
Short time scale	Longer time scale
Less emphasis on service	High customer service
Quality is concern of production	Quality is concern of all
Competitive commitment	High customer commitment
Persuasive communication	Regular communication

(Marketing, Principles and Practice: Adcock, Bradford, Halborg and Ross)

Adcock *et al* point out that the most important issue in customer retention is focussing marketing effort on activities that promote a strong relationship rather than a single transaction.

The relationship marketing mix. By now you are familiar with the 4Ps of the basic marketing mix. Relationship marketing is highly dependent upon a fifth P: **people**. The features of the basic 4Ps must support the commitment to developing mutually beneficial customer relationships. The **behaviour of the people** involved in the customer relationship is even more important, because relationship marketing success depends on their motivation to achieve it. In turn, that motivation depends to a great extent upon the leadership exercised by marketing managers. It is not enough to expect self-motivation because *all* staff are involved, not just those with a sales role.

6.3 Key accounts

Key accounts are profitable and have potential for long-term development.

So far we have considered the retention of customers as an unquestionably desirable objective. **However, for many businesses a degree of discretion will be advisable**. 'Key' does not mean large. A customer's **potential** is very important. The definition of a key account depends on the circumstances. Key account management is about managing the future.

Customers can be assessed for desirability according to such criteria as the profitability of their accounts; the prestige they confer; the amount of non-value adding administrative work they generate; the cost of the selling effort they absorb; the rate of growth of their accounts and, for industrial customers, of the turnover of their own businesses; their willingness to adopt new products; and their credit history. Such analyses will almost certainly conform to a Pareto distribution and show, for instance that 80% of profit comes from 20% of the customers, while a different 20% generate most of the credit control or administrative problems. Some businesses will be very aggressive about getting rid of their problem customers, but a more positive technique would be to concentrate effort on the most desirable ones. These are the **key accounts** and the company's relationship with them can be built up by appointing **key account managers**.

Key account management is often seen as a high level selling task, but should in fact be a business wide team effort about relationships and customer retention. It can be seen as a form of co-operation with the customer's supply chain management function. The key account manager's role is to integrate the efforts of the various parts of the organisation in order to deliver an enhanced service. This idea has long been used by advertising agencies and was successfully introduced into aerospace manufacturing over 40 years ago. It will be the key account manager's role to maintain communication with the customer, note any developments in his circumstances, deal with any problems arising in the relationship and develop the long term business relationship.

The **key account relationship** may progress through several stages.

(a) At first, there may be a typical adversarial sales-purchasing relationship with emphasis on price, delivery and so on. Attempts to widen contact with the customer organisation will be seen as a threat by its purchasing staff.

(b) Later, the sales staff may be able to foster a mutual desire to increase understanding by wider contacts. Trust may increase.

(c) A mature partnership stage may be reached in which there are contacts at all levels and information is shared. The Key account manager becomes responsible for integrating the partnership business processes and contributing to the customer's supply chain management. High 'vendor ratings', stable quality, continuous improvement and fair pricing are taken for granted.

7 Privacy and data protection

Customer databases must conform with relevant privacy legislation. In the UK this is the *Data Protection Act 1998*. The Act lays down eight data protection principles.

Key concept

Privacy is the right of the individual to control the use of information about him or her, including information on financial status, health and lifestyle (ie prevent unauthorised disclosure).

7.1 Why is privacy an important issue?

In recent years, there has been a growing fear that the ever-increasing amount of **information** about individuals held by organisations could be misused.

In particular, it was felt that an individual could easily be harmed by the existence of computerised data about him or her which was inaccurate or misleading and which could be **transferred to unauthorised third parties** at high speed and little cost.

In the UK the current legislation covering this area is the **Data Protection Act 1998**.

7.2 The Data Protection Act 1998

The Data Protection Act 1998 is an attempt to protect the **individual**. The terms of the Act cover data about individuals – **not data about corporate bodies**.

7.3 Definitions of terms used in the Act

In order to understand the Act it is necessary to know some of the technical terms used in it.

Key concepts

> **Personal data** is information about a living individual, including expressions of opinion about him or her. Data about organisations is not personal data.
>
> **Data users** are organisations or individuals who control personal data and the use of personal data.
>
> A **data subject** is an individual who is the subject of personal data.

7.4 The data protection principles

The UK Data Protection Act includes eight Data Protection Principles with which data users must comply.

> **DATA PROTECTION PRINCIPLES**
>
> Schedule 1 of the Act contains the data protection principles.
>
> 1   Personal data shall be processed fairly and lawfully and, in particular, shall not be processed unless:
>
> (a)   At least one of the conditions in Schedule 2 is met (see 7.5.3 (c) later in this chapter).
>
> (b)   In the case of sensitive personal data, at least one of the conditions in Schedule 3 is also met (see 7.5.3 (d)).
>
> 2   Personal data shall be obtained only for one or more specified and lawful purposes, and shall not be further processed in any manner incompatible with that purpose or those purposes.
>
> 3   Personal data shall be adequate, relevant and not excessive in relation to the purpose or purposes for which they are processed.
>
> 4   Personal data shall be accurate and, where necessary, kept up to date.
>
> 5   Personal data processed for any purpose or purposes shall not be kept for longer than is necessary for that purpose or those purposes.
>
> 6   Personal data shall be processed in accordance with the rights of data subjects under this Act.
>
> 7   Appropriate technical and organisational measures shall be taken against unauthorised or unlawful processing of personal data and against accidental loss or destruction of, or damage to, personal data.
>
> 8   Personal data shall not be transferred to a country or territory outside the European Economic Area unless that country or territory ensures an adequate level of protection for the rights and freedoms of data subjects in relation to the processing of personal data.

The Act has two main aims:

(a)   To protect **individual privacy**. Previous UK law only applied to **computer-based** information. The 1998 Act applies to **all personal data, in any form.**

(b)   To **harmonise data protection legislation** so that, in the interests of improving the operation of the single European market, there can be a **free flow of personal data** between the member states of the EU.

7.5 The coverage of the Act

Key points of the Act can be summarised as follows.

(a)   **Data users** have to **register** under the Act with the **Data Protection Registrar**.

(b)   **Individuals** (data subjects) are awarded certain **legal rights**.

(c)   **Data holders** must adhere to the **data protection principles**.

7.5.1 Registration under the Act

The Data Protection Registrar keeps a Register of all data users. Only registered data users are permitted to hold personal data. The data user must only hold data and use data for the registered **purposes**.

7.5.2 The rights of data subjects

The Act establishes the following rights for data subjects.

(a)   A data subject may seek **compensation** through the courts for damage and any associated distress caused by the **loss**, **destruction** or **unauthorised disclosure** of data about himself or herself or by **inaccurate data** about himself or herself.

(b)   A data subject may apply to the courts for **inaccurate data** to be **put right** or even **wiped off** the data user's files altogether. Such applications may also be made to the Registrar.

(c)   A data subject may obtain **access** to personal data of which he or she is the subject. (This is known as the 'subject access' provision.) In other words, a data subject can ask to see his or her personal data that the data user is holding.

(d)   A data subject can **sue** a data user for any **damage or distress** caused to him by personal data about him which is **incorrect** or **misleading** as to matter of **fact** (rather than opinion).

7.5.3 Other features of the legislation

(a)   Everyone has the right to go to court to seek redress for **any breach** of data protection law.

(b)   Filing systems that are structured so as to facilitate access to information about a particular person now fall within the legislation. This includes systems that are **paper-based** or on **microfilm** or **microfiche**. Personnel records meet this classification.

(c)   Processing of personal data is **forbidden** except in the following circumstances.

(i)   With the **consent** of the subject. Consent cannot be implied: it must be by freely given, specific and informed agreement.

(ii)   As a result of a **contractual arrangement.**

(iii)   Because of a **legal obligation.**

(iv)   To **protect the vital interests** of the subject.

(v)   Where processing is in the **public interest.**

(vi)   Where processing is required to exercise **official authority.**

(d) The processing of **'sensitive data'** is forbidden, unless express consent has been obtained. Sensitive data includes data relating to **racial origin, political opinions, religious beliefs**, physical or mental **health, sexual orientation** and **trade union** membership.

(e) If data about a data subject is **obtained from a third party** the data subject must be given.

(i) The identity of the **controller** of the data.
(ii) The **purposes** for which the data are being processed.
(iii) **What data** will be disclosed and **to whom.**
(iv) The existence of a right of subject **access** to the data.

(f) Data subjects have a right not only to have a **copy of data** held about them but also the right to know **why** the data is required.

Chapter Roundup

- The extension of the **service sector**, and the application of market principles across many public sector and ex-public sector organisations, has made a large number of service providers much more marketing-conscious.

- Services marketing differs from the marketing of other goods in a number of crucial ways, and five specific characteristics of services marketing have been proposed: intangibility, inseparability, heterogeneity, perishability and ownership.

- An **extended marketing mix** has been suggested for services marketing. Booms and Bitner suggested an additional 3Ps. These are people, process and physical evidence.

- Even the briefest service encounter is a 'moment of truth' for the organisation concerned. This emphasises the great importance of people and the need to recruit, select, train, motivate and manage them effectively.

- **Service quality** can be defined as the difference between what customers expect and what they perceive themselves to be receiving. This corresponds to Gap 5 in the Parasuraman Zeithaml and Berry 5 gap quality model. The SERVQUAL questionnaire measures this gap. Improved service quality leads to higher profits and is a key task for service marketers. Technical quality is what the customer is left with; functional quality resides in the way it was delivered.

- Customers vary in their needs and attitudes but a company should make efforts to retain **profitable** ones. A high degree of competition means this is only likely if the customer is very satisfied.

- **Relationship marketing** is based on the fostering of a customer-oriented service culture. One approach involves

  - Building a customer database
  - Developing customer-oriented service systems
  - Extra direct contacts with customers

- The behaviour of **people** is crucial to the relationship marketing approach.

- **Key accounts** are profitable and have potential for long-term development.

- **Customer databases** must conform with relevant privacy legislation. In the UK this is the *Data Protection Act 1998*. The Act lays down eight data protection principles.

Quick Quiz

1   What are the five marketing characteristics of services?

2   What are the marketing implications of the intangibility of services?

3   What issues arise from the perishability of services being marketed?

4   How can the problems of lack of ownership be overcome in service marketing?

5   What are the additional 'Ps' in the service marketing mix?

6   In what areas should rigorous procedures be applied to take account of the importance of people in services marketing?

7   In what two ways can firms gain by improving their quality of service to customers?

8   What is 'quality' in marketing terms?

9   What is the single largest reason why customers abandon a supplier?

10 How does relationship marketing deal with failures of service?

Answers to Quick Quiz

1   Intangibility, inseparability, heterogeneity, perishability, ownership

2   Increase the tangibility; focus on benefits; differentiate the service

3   Staff must be available when they are needed

4   Provide tangible symbols

5   People, process and physical evidence *or* personal selling; place of availability; people and customer service; and physical evidence

6   Selection and training; culture of service; standards of dress and behaviour; mechanisation; audit of service

7   Higher revenues and reduced costs

8   Quality is defined by the customer; poor quality arises from five gaps in expectations

9   Poor performance by front-line staff

10 A positive way of dealing with errors must be built into the customer relationship

Action Programme Review

1   Possible marketing implications.

(a)   Promote the advantages of non-ownership. This can be done by emphasising, in promotion, the benefits of paid-for maintenance, and periodic upgrading of the product. Radio Rentals have used this as a major selling proposition with great success.

(b)   Make available a tangible symbol or representation of ownership (certificate, membership of professional association). This can come to embody the benefits enjoyed.

(c)   Increasing the chances or opportunity of ownership (eg time-shares, shares in the organisation for regular customers).

2   There must be continuous development of service-enhancing practice.

- Policies on selection
- Programmes of training
- Standard, consistent operational practices ('MacDonaldisation')
- Standardised operational rules
- Effective motivational programmes
- Managerial appointments
- The attractiveness and appropriateness of the service offer
- Effective policies of staff reward and remuneration

3   Things design can do:

- Convey the nature of the service involved
- Transmit messages and information
- Imply aesthetic qualities, moral values, or other socio-cultural aspects of a corporate image
- Reinforce an existing image
- Reassure
- Engender an emotional reaction in the customer, through sensory and symbolic blends

4   The following are all dimensions of client service quality.

- **Problem solving creativity:** looking beyond the obvious and not being bound by accepted professional and technical approaches

- **Initiative:** anticipating problems and opportunities and not just reacting

- **Efficiency:** keeping client costs down through effective work planning and control

- **Fast response:** responding to enquiries, questions, problems as quickly as possible

- **Timeliness:** starting and finishing service work to agreed deadlines

- **Open-mindedness:** professionals not being 'blinkered' by their technical approach

- **Sound judgement:** professionals such as accountants dealing with the wider aspects of their technical specialisations

- **Functional expertise:** need to bring together all the functional skills necessary from whatever sources to work on a client project

- **Industry expertise:** clients expect professionals to be thoroughly familiar with their industry and recent changes in it

- **Managerial effectiveness:** maintaining a focus upon the use of both the firm's and the client's resources

- **Orderly work approach:** clients expect salient issues to be identified early and do not want last minute surprises before deadlines

- **Commitment:** clients evaluate the calibre of the accountant and the individual attention given

- **Long-range focus:** clients prefer long-term relationships rather than 'projects' or 'jobs'

- **Qualitative approach:** accountants should not be seen as simple number crunchers

- **Continuity:** clients do not like firms who constantly change the staff that work with them – they will evaluate staff continuity as part of an ongoing relationship

- **Personality:** clients will also evaluate the friendliness, understanding and co-operation of the service provider

Now try Question 8 at the end of the Study Text

Part D
Managing the marketing function

Quality in marketing

Syllabus content

- Key concepts of quality management including structured approaches to continuous improvement and problem solving
- Planning for compliance of a marketing function's activities with an organisation's quality management system
- The concept of process and techniques for process management and their use in marketing activities
- Deciding the activities to be undertaken by external suppliers, including agencies and outsourcing, and gaining approval for the relevant expenditure

Introduction

Operations are the link between the strategy and the customer. They appear lower in status than strategy formulation, but are critical in delivering customer satisfaction and profits. In **service industries**, in particular, the operational interface with the customer is the crux of the business.

The organisation's **mission** is only really meaningful if, at operational level, the mission is embodied in **policies and behaviour standards** that promote the achievement of a consistent quality standard.

The theme of this chapter is **quality**. Quality has many aspects and reaches into all parts of the organisation. Modern practice in the **management of quality** is dealt with in Sections 3 and 4. In Sections 1 and 2 we deal with two important related topics, by way of introduction.

Business process re-engineering was something of a management fad a few years ago, but to see it this way only is to miss an important principle. Organisations cannot operate without systems and processes but they must not be allowed to hinder the proper pursuit of shareholder value. The tendency is for processes to become more certain as they develop over time, but this is at the price of increasing complexity. It is part of management's tasks to ensure that the costs inherent in secure processes to not outweigh the benefits of the reliability they bring.

Benchmarking is a useful technique in the search for efficient processes. However, note carefully the dangers we see in it.

We conclude this chapter with a section on **outsourcing**. This is a complex topic that involves consideration of not only quality but also cost/benefit analysis, decision-relevant costs, strategic thinking and the promotion of efficiency. It is also a specific topic in your syllabus.

1 Business process re-engineering

FAST FORWARD

Operations planning involves the detailed procedures for creating and delivering products and services. Business processes can be re-engineered from a zero base.

Many organisations have sought to improve performance by re-engineering their business processes.

Key concept

Business process re-engineering (BPR)

'the fundamental rethinking and radical redesign of business processes to achieve dramatic improvements in critical contemporary measures of performance, such as cost, quality, service and speed.' (*Hammer and Champy*)

Re-engineers start from the future and work backwards. They are unconstrained by existing methods, people or departments. In effect, they ask, 'If we were a new company, how would we run the place?'

1.1 Processes

'A collection of activities that takes one or more kinds of input and creates an output that is of value to the customer.' For example, order fulfilment is a process that takes an order as its input and results in the delivery of the ordered goods.

1.2 Principles of BPR

(a)   **Processes should be designed to achieve a desired outcome** rather than focusing on existing tasks.

(b) **Personnel who use the output from a process should perform the process**. For example, a company could set up a database of approved suppliers; this would allow personnel who actually require supplies to order them themselves, perhaps using on-line technology, thereby eliminating the need for a separate purchasing function.

(c) **Information** processing should be **included in the work which produces** the information.

(d) **Geographically dispersed resources should be treated as if they are centralised**, for example, economies of scale through central negotiation of supply contracts, without losing the benefits of decentralisation, such as flexibility and responsiveness.

(e) **Parallel activities should be linked rather than integrated**. This would involve, for example, co-ordination between teams working on different aspects of a single process.

(f) **'Doers' should be allowed to be self-managing**. This is empowerment. Decision aids such as expert systems can be provided where they are required.

(g) Information should be captured **once, at source**.

BPR cannot be planned meticulously and accomplished in small and cautious steps.

(a) It tends to be an **all-or-nothing proposition**, often with an uncertain result. It is therefore a **high risk** undertaking.

(b) Many organisations trying BPR do not achieve good results because they **fail to think it through**, do not engage **hearts and minds** sufficiently, act on **bad advice** or cannot override established departmental/functional power groups which have a vested interest in the **status quo**, or in incremental change rather than radical revolution.

2 Benchmarking

Operational effectiveness is vital in the delivery of customer satisfaction and maintaining profitability. This is why firms **benchmark** others in the same industry – although this may give an inappropriate emphasis on imitation where differentiation would be more appropriate.

Benchmarking generally involves comparing your operations to somebody else's.

Key concept

Benchmarking

'The establishment, through data gathering, of targets and comparators, through whose use relative levels of performance (and particularly areas of underperformance) can be identified. By the adoption of identified best practices it is hoped that performance will improve.

2.1 Types of benchmarking

(a) **Internal benchmarking**, is a method of comparing one operating unit or function with another within the same organisation.

(b) **Functional benchmarking** compares functions with those of the best external practitioners of those functions, regardless of the industry they are in (also known as operational, process or generic benchmarking).

(c) **Competitive benchmarking**, gathers information about direct competitors, through techniques such as reverse engineering.

(d) **Strategic benchmarking** is a type of competitive benchmarking aimed at strategic action and organisational change.

Marketing at Work

British Airways

British Airways used benchmarking from 1987 to help transform itself from a stodgy, state-controlled enterprise to a leading world airline. Apparently BA managers analysed their own business processes to identify the weakest elements, and then visited other airlines with checklists and questions. Problems are often found to be shared and competitors are willing to pool information in pursuit of solutions.

2.1.1 Advantages

(a) **Position audit**. Benchmarking can **assess a firm's existing position**.

(b) The comparisons are carried out by the **managers who have to live with any changes** implemented as a result of the exercise.

(c) Benchmarking **focuses on improvement in key areas** and sets targets which are challenging but **achievable**. What is really achievable can be discovered by examining what others have achieved: managers are thus able to accept that they are not being asked to perform miracles.

(d) **If all firms provide the same standard of quality, it ceases to be a source of competitive advantage.**

2.1.2 Dangers of benchmarking

(a) It **implies there is one best way** of doing business – arguably this boils down to the difference between efficiency and effectiveness. A process can be efficient but its output may not be useful. Other measures such as developing the value chain may be a better way of securing competitive advantage.

(b) The benchmark may be **yesterday's solution to tomorrow's problem**. For example, a cross-channel ferry company might benchmark its activities (eg speed of turnround at Dover and Calais, cleanliness on ship) against another ferry company, whereas the real competitor is the Channel Tunnel.

(c) It is a **catching-up exercise** rather than the development of anything distinctive. After the benchmarking exercise, the competitor might improve performance in a different way.

(d) It **depends on accurate information** about competitors, in the case of competitor benchmarking, or an **appropriate analogies** in other industries, in the case of process benchmarking.

To make benchmarking work, it is important to **compare like with like**.

2.1.3 Steps in a benchmarking process

Step 1   Identify items to be benchmarked.

Step 2   Identify suitable organisations for comparison.

Step 3   Collect data by an appropriate method.

Step 4   Determine the current performance gap.

Step 5   Project future performance levels.

Step 6   Tell people about benchmark findings.

Step 7   Establish goals for each business function.

Step 8   Develop action plans.

Step 9   Implement action plans.

Step 10   Re-set benchmarks to a higher level to encourage continuous improvement.

3 Quality

FAST FORWARD

Quality is the totality of features which bears on a product's ability to meet stated needs. **Design quality** includes the degree to which customer satisfactions are built into a product. **Conformance quality** is an absence of defects in the finished goods. Ideally, quality is designed into the product. Inspection and rectification are not value-adding activities.

Taguchi's quality/cost model is important as it identifies the necessity of **reducing variation** in production processes as a means of reducing losses.

Key concept

> **Quality** has been defined by Ken Holmes *(Total Quality Management)* as 'the totality of features and characteristics of a product or service which bears on its ability to meet stated or implied needs.' It is fitness for use.

Quality is concerned with fitness for use, and quality management (or control) is about ensuring that products or services meet their planned level of quality and conform to specifications.

Example

The postal service might establish a standard that 90% of first class letters will be delivered on the day after they are posted, and 99% will be delivered within two days of posting. Procedures would have to be established for ensuring that these standards could be met (eg frequency of collections, automated letter sorting, frequency of deliveries and number of staff employed). Actual performance could be monitored, perhaps by taking samples from time to time of letters that are posted and delivered. If the quality standard is not being achieved, the management of the postal service could take control action (eg employ more postmen or advertise again the use of postcodes) or reduce the standard of quality of the service being provided.

3.1 Traditional approaches to quality

In the past, quality control meant **inspection** of finished output (or goods inward). Quality was something assured **at the end** of the manufacturing process rather than being considered at the beginning.

3.1.1 Problems with inspection

(a)   The **inspection process itself does not add value**. If no defective items were produced, there would be no need for an inspection function.

(b)   The **production of substandard products is a waste** of materials and time.

(c)   The **inspection department takes up expensive land** and warehousing space.

(d)   **Working capital is tied up** in stocks which cannot be sold.

Quality costs. Quality imposes its own costs.

(a)   **Prevention costs** are the 'cost of any action taken to investigate or reduce defects and failures'.

(b) **Appraisal costs** are 'the costs of assessing quality achieved'.

(c) **Internal failure costs** are 'costs arising within the organisation of failing to achieve quality'.

(d) **External failure costs**. These are 'costs arising outside the manufacturing organisation of failure to achieve specified quality (after *transfer* of ownership to the customer)'.

3.2 Developments in quality

Fitness for use comes from two things.

- **Quality of design**: the customer satisfactions incorporated into the product.
- **Quality of conformance**: a lack of defects in the finished goods.

(Juran)

3.2.1 Zero defects and right first time

(a) **Zero defects concept**. There should never be any *defects* in a finished product. Some hold it to be an impossible ideal, and invoke the concept of diminishing returns. Alternatively it can be seen as a slogan to employees.

(b) **Right first time**: a product should not have to be corrected once it is built. It is thus a corollary of the zero defects concept.

(Crosby)

Design systems and products to reduce variation. *Genichi Taguchi* focuses on the importance of functions and activities undertaken **before** the manufacturing process in determining product quality. The aim might be to ensure conformance quality and to reduce variation.

3.2.2 Example

Compare two fast food outlets each selling hamburgers. Both *Gristle Prince* and *Greasy Mike's* sell burgers for £1 each and both outlets aim to serve *each* customer about 90 seconds after the customer has placed an order. Obviously certain times of the day are busier than others, so queues and hence serving times are slightly longer. There are no differences in the quality of the burgers served or in the layout of each shop. Both manage, on *average,* to serve a customer in the target 90 seconds, yet Gristle Prince is beginning to attract more customers. Greasy Mike's employ a quality consultant, who analyses both outlets using a Taguchi model. Here are the consultant's findings.

(a) 100 customers entered *Gristle Prince.* 50 of them were served in *less* than the 90 second target, and 50 of them in more. In fact 50 were served in 80 seconds and fifty in 100 seconds, leading to an average serving time of 90 seconds.

(b) At *Greasy Mike's* on the other hand the story was different. Again 100 customers entered the restaurant.

- Ten had to wait five minutes (300 seconds)
- Ten had to wait three minutes (180 seconds)
- Sixty had to wait one minute (60 seconds)
- Twenty had to wait 30 seconds

Again the average service time is 90 seconds.

The result of course is that *Gristle Prince's* service is much more predictable, which is why customers might prefer it. They know they will *never* have to wait more than 100 seconds for their meal.

3.2.3 Quality circles and employees' responsibilities

Ishikawa proposed **quality circles** (and the development of a few simple tools for quality improvement). Quality circles are groups of selected workers delegated with the task of analysing the production process, and coming up with ideas to improve it. Success requires a commitment from the circle's membership, and a management willingness to take a back seat.

3.3 Quality assurance and standards

Quality assurance is increasingly demanded of suppliers, usually in conformation with ISO 9000. Certification is granted to companies which have an adequate system of quality assurance.

The essentials of **quality assurance** are that the *supplier* guarantees the quality of goods supplied and allows the customers' inspectors access while the items are being manufactured. Usually agreed inspection procedures and quality control standards are worked out by customer and supplier between them, and checks are made to ensure that they are being adhered to.

(a)   The **customer can eliminate goods inwards inspection** and items can be directed straight to production. This can give large savings in cost and time in flow production, and can facilitate JIT production.

(b)   The **supplier produces to the customer's requirement**, thereby reducing rejects and the cost of producing substitutes.

Suppliers' quality assurance schemes are being used increasingly. The scheme known as ISO 9000 is fast becoming the global standard, only awarded after audit and inspection of a company's operations.

The **standard does not dictate the quality of individual goods and services**, but aims to ensure that **quality management systems of a suitable standard are in place**.

(a)   The standards 'set out how you can establish, document and maintain an effective quality system which will demonstrate to your customers that you are committed to quality and are able to satisfy their quality needs'.

(b)   While it provides feedback about performance, it cannot guarantee that control action is taken. It is 'an indicator of potential, not of achievement'.

(c)   Certification can be withdrawn, if a firm does not live up to the requirement.

(d)   ISO 9000 increasingly will become a factor in selecting suppliers. Customers wish to avoid the cost of inspecting goods inwards.

4 Total quality management

TQM is a concept that applies quality to the whole organisation. Relevant techniques concepts are statistical process control (for conformance quality) and quality function deployment (for design quality). Important aspects are continuous improvement, the fact that production has employees take part in controlling and improving quality, internal marketing and linking business activities in quality chains.

Key concept

Total quality management (TQM)

'A way of managing a business to ensure complete customer satisfaction internally and externally' (*Oakland*).

TQM takes on board many of the principles identified in the previous sections.

TQM programmes are aimed at identifying and then reducing or eliminating causes of wasted time and effort.

(a)   **Core activities** are the reason for the existence of the work group and add value to the business.

(b)   **Support activities** support core activities but do not themselves add value.

(c)   **Discretionary activities** such as checking, progress chasing and dealing with complaints are **all symptoms of failure** within the organisation. These should be reduced.

Statistical process control is used in manufacturing operations to ensure that systems are achieving their design level of quality. It is thus a technique for promoting **conformance quality**.

4.1 Quality function deployment (QFD): design quality

Quality function deployment (QFD) is a term to analyse how quality techniques can be used to cut across functional boundaries. QFD is aimed at getting quality right at an earlier time, and concentrates on design issues up front.

(a)   **'Translate the voice of the customer'**. This means applying the marketing concept in assessing in detail the customer's needs and including them in a design specification, so that they are accurately translated **into relevant technical requirements.**

(b)   **Obey the customer's voice**. Customer demands (eg that paper will not tear) are converted into quality requirements (paper must be of a minimum thickness). There is a matrix of relationships between customer demand and technical requirements.

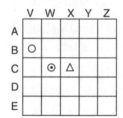

Quality characteristics

Customers' demands

⊙ = strong relationship

○ = medium relationship

△ = weak relationship

Customer demand C has a strong relationship to quality characteristic W but a weak one to X.

(i)   This matrix can determine where effort should be most expended

(ii)   Furthermore, certain customer requirements might contradict each other, so the matrix identifies possible trade offs.

4.2 Assessing and auditing quality

Proper quality management depends on information.

Key concept

> **Quality assessment** is the 'process of identifying business practices, attitudes, and activities that are either enhancing or inhibiting the achievement of quality improvement' (*Total Quality* Ernst and Young Quality Improvement Consulting Group).

4.2.1 Quality assessment exercises

(a)   **Supply proof** that quality improvement measures are needed.

(b)   **Provide a baseline for future measurement**, in other words to make a starting point from which you can measure your progress.

(c)   **Build management** support for quality measures, by the power of the evidence collected.

(d)   **Convince management**, particularly senior management, that the issue is important in the first place.

4.3 Continuous improvement

TQM is not a one-off process, but is the **continual examination** and improvement of existing processes. Continuous improvement applies both to the finished product, but also to the processes which make it.

(a) A philosophy of continuous improvement **avoids complacency**.

(b) **Customer needs change** so a continuous improvement enables these changes to be taken into account in the normal course of events.

(c) **New technologies or materials** might be developed, enabling cost savings or design improvements.

(d) Rarely do businesses know every possible fact about the production process. Continuous improvement **encourages experimentation** and a scientific approach to production.

(e) It is a way of **tapping employees' knowledge**.

(f) **Reducing variability** is a key issue for quality, if this is assessed on Taguchi's quality-cost model.

(g) Improvement on a continual, step by step basis is **more prudent** in some cases than changing things at one go.

4.3.1 Model for improving quality

Step 1   **Find out the problems** (eg from customer and employees).

Step 2   **Select action targets** from the number of improvement projects identified in *Step 1*, on the basis of cost, safety, importance, feasibility (with current resources).

Step 3   **Collect data** about the problem.

Step 4   **Analyse data** by a variety of techniques to assess common factors behind the data, to tease out any hidden messages the data might contain.

Step 5   **Identify possible causes** (eg using brainstorming sessions). No ideas are ruled out of order.

Step 6   **Plan improvement action**. Significant help might be required.

Step 7   **Monitor the effects of the improvement**.

Step 8   **Communicate the result**.

4.4 Total quality and customers (internal and external)

A **customer orientation** requires the firm to recognise that customers buy products for the benefits they deliver.

What constitutes a quality product or service must, it seems, be **related to what the customer wants.** Indeed, quality would have no commercial value unless it delivered benefits to the customer. The customer must be the final arbiter of the quality which a product possesses.

From a strategic point of view, then, **quality is in the eye of the consumer**. If quality is meeting the requirements of the consumer, then it should be recognised that throughout and beyond all enterprises, whatever business they are in, is a series of **quality chains**.

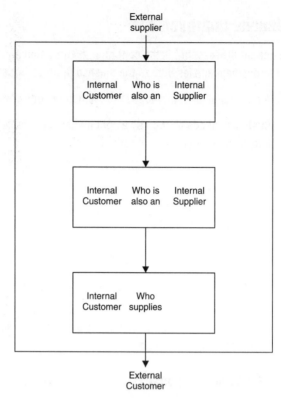

Oakland argues that meeting customer requirements is the main focus in a search for quality. (If the customer is outside the organisation, then the supplier must seek to set up a marketing activity to gather this information, and to relate the output of their organisation to the needs of the customer.)

Internal customers for services are equally important, but seldom are their requirements investigated. The quality implementation process requires that all the supplier/customer relationships within the **quality chain** should be treated as marketing exercises, and that each customer should be carefully consulted as to their precise requirements from the product or service with which they are to be provided.

Each link in the chain should prompt the following questions, according to Oakland.

Of customers
Who are my immediate customers?
What are their true requirements?
How do or can I find out what the requirements are?
How can I measure my ability to meet the requirements?
Do I have the necessary capability to meet the requirements? (If not, then what must change to improve the capability?)
Do I continually meet the requirements? (If not, then what prevents this from happening, when the capability exists?)
How do I monitor changes in the requirements?

Of suppliers
Who are my immediate suppliers?
What are my true requirements?
How do I communicate my requirements?
Do my suppliers have the capability to measure and meet the requirements?
How do I inform them of changes in the requirements?

4.5 Introducing TQM: organisational implications

Introducing TQM involves a significant shake up. TQM involves:

(a) **Giving employees a say** in the process (eg in the **quality survey**) and in getting them to suggest improvements.

(b) **Greater discipline** in the process of production and the establishment of better linkages between the business functions.

(c) **New relationships with suppliers**, which requires them to improve their output quality so that less effort is spent rectifying poor input. Long-term relationships with a small number of suppliers might be preferable to choosing material and sub-components on price.

(d) **Work standardisation** (with techniques perhaps introduced by the technostructure) and **employee commitment**.

(e) **Commitment over the long term.** It will fail if it is seen as just another fad.

(f) **All the organisation,** as the material on quality chains above suggests.

 Marketing at Work

TQM

TQM is not just a body of techniques; it is a philosophy and movement that attracts followers. There are many alternative definitions of TQM, but the central concept is that quality is the key strategic variable in business and it is a variable that is amenable to organisational culture. The idea is that quality should be rooted in the structure of the organisation. It should influence the way the organisation is run and the way that staff are recruited, assessed, promoted and rewarded. The view that quality is something imposed on staff by inspectors is anathema to the TQM movement.

The main principles of a TQM-orientated organisation are:

• Top priority is given to satisfying customers and the organisation is structured to ensure that owners, employees, suppliers and management are all working to achieve this. Managers should act as facilitators rather than controllers.

• People are considered the key internal guarantors of success. Decision-making processes are participative. Management is both visible and accessible.

• Constant change is considered a way of life and the organisation is structured in a way that readily embraces change. That structure is flat, requiring employees to use initiative and communicate directly with customers and suppliers.

• The organisation pursues continuous improvement, not static optimisation. The concept of an optimum defects level is entirely alien to TQM. Performance is measured against an external benchmark and not against an internal standard.

• The emphasis is on prevention of problems and faults rather than on detection. Employees have a wide span of activity, but a short span of control.

Bob Scarlett, *CIMA Insider, September 2001*

5 Outsourcing

FAST FORWARD

Outsourcing may be used to control costs and release resources to concentrate on **core competences**. Core competences are the source of **competitive advantage** and should not be outsourced.

Outsourcing of goods and services may be thought of as an extension of the normal practice of buying-in raw materials, components, stock for resale and specialist services such as legal advice. In the case of raw materials and components and stock for resale there is an obvious **marketing implication** in that some **control over the product** offering is surrendered to the supplier. The modern tendency to extend the buying-in process to wider categories of more complex services has major implications at the **strategic** level.

Outsourcing is often undertaken as a strategic move to contain the growth of costs. Specialists, such as designers, may be able to achieve **economies of scale** that enable them to provide services at a cost lower than that of retaining the function in-house. This is frequently seen in the area of premises services such as catering, cleaning and security. Similarly, 'off-shoring' of both manufacturing and back office services allows Western companies to benefit from the lower wages prevalent in developing countries.

Those responsible for business strategy, including marketers, must be aware of the considerations relevant to outsourcing in their own industries. While facing the customer, the company cannot ignore the **management of its inputs**, particularly in terms of cost and quality.

5.1 What not to outsource

A strong view has emerged that companies should base strategy on their **core competences**. This **asset-based** view of strategy suggests that the **adaptive model** of strategy typified by the rational model does not offer the prospect of achieving a unique competitive advantage. Any company, given adequate finance, could carry out a SWOT analysis and make a suitable market offer. This model thus leads only to severe competition with similar offerings. The asset-based approach offers a route out of this dead-end, via the cultivation and exploitation of core competences.

Under this model, the company's greatest assets are held to be those things it can do better than any other company; to a great extent, these depend in turn on the personal qualities, training and experience of its people. These **core competences** can be formed into the essential aspects of product offerings that generate superior competitive advantage. Note, however, that core competences alone are not enough. *IBM* had superb core competences even while it was being demolished by the rise of the PC. Environmental awareness and SWOT analysis must continue to be undertaken.

If the core competence model is accepted by a company, it is likely to consider whether it is worthwhile undertaking *any* activity in which it does not deploy such a competence. Judgement is required here. There is a strong case to be made for outsourcing any activity that is *not* a core competence, but considerations such as commercial secrecy, customer relations and the costs associated with change may produce pressure to retain at least some of these activities in-house.

Clearly, the converse is even more important. If a company has a core competence, it should exploit it: core activities should *not* be outsourced. That would lead to a loss of unique competitive advantage and the erosion of the competence itself. Eventually it would be lost forever.

Decisions about outsourcing are thus highly likely to be **strategic** in nature and, in principle, are taken at the **strategic apex**. It is part of the role of strategic management to foster the company's core competences and make strategy in a way that exploits them.

As far as non-core activities are concerned, the decision (and budget) to outsource them (or not) may well be delegated to more junior mangers. The well-established financial technique of relevant cost analysis

BPP
PROFESSIONAL EDUCATION

may be used to assist decision-making. This is usually encountered in terms of making or buying in a part-manufactured component, but the principles may also be applied to services.

5.2 Relevant costs

FAST FORWARD

> The decision to outsource non-core activities should be preceded by an analysis of **relevant costs**, but other aspects such as quality, reliability, spare capacity and control may be of greater importance in deciding not to outsource.

An analysis of costs is the first stage of deciding whether to outsource or provide in-house. However, it is important to consider only those costs that are **relevant** to the decision in hand.

Key concept

> **Relevant costs** are 'Costs appropriate to a specific management decision. These are represented by future cash flows whose magnitude will vary depending upon the outcome of the management decision made'.
> (CIMA *Official Terminology*)

Some rules based on this definition will help you to decide which costs are relevant

(a) **Relevant costs are future costs.**

   (i) A decision is about the future; it cannot alter what has been done already. A cost that has been incurred in the past is totally irrelevant to any decision that is being made now.

   (ii) Costs that have been incurred include not only costs that have already been paid, but also **costs that are the subject of legally binding contracts**, even if payments due under the contract have not yet been made. (These are known as **committed** costs.)

(b) **Relevant costs are cash flows.**

   Costs or charges which do not reflect additional cash spending should be ignored for the purpose of decision making. These include the following.

   (i) **Depreciation**, as a fixed overhead incurred.

   (ii) **Notional rent or interest**, as a fixed overhead incurred.

   (iii) **All overheads absorbed**. Fixed overhead absorption is always irrelevant since it is overheads to be incurred in the future that affect decisions.

(c) **Relevant costs are incremental costs.**

   A relevant cost is one which **arises as a direct consequence of a decision**. Thus, only costs which will differ under some or all of the available opportunities should be considered; relevant costs are therefore sometimes referred to as incremental costs.

Relevant costs are therefore **future, incremental cash flows**.

5.2.1 Differential costs

Key concept

> **Differential/incremental cost** is 'The difference in total cost between alternatives; calculated to assist decision-making'.
> (CIMA *Official Terminology*)

Such costs are therefore simply the additional costs incurred as a consequence of a decision.

5.3 Non-relevant costs

A number of terms are used to describe costs that are irrelevant for decision making because they are either not future cash flows or they are costs that will be incurred anyway, regardless of the decision that is taken.

5.3.1 Sunk costs

Key concept

> **Sunk costs** are 'Costs that have been irreversibly incurred or committed prior to a decision point and which cannot therefore be considered relevant to subsequent decisions. Sunk costs may also be termed irrecoverable costs'.
> (CIMA *Official Terminology*)

An example of this type of cost is money already spent on a project. It is very common to argue along these lines: 'We have spent so much already, we can't give up on this now'. This is false reasoning. *Nothing* we do can bring that money back. Any decision we take must be based on the costs and benefits that will accrue **in the future**. If that leads us to abandon a project that has already cost a great deal of money, so be it. Unfortunately, such decisions usually have unpleasant consequences for someone and the tendency of managers is to carry on regardless. Do not fall into this trap!

5.3.2 Committed costs

Key concept

> **Committed costs** are 'Costs arising from prior decisions, which cannot, in the short run, be changed. Committed cost incurrence often stems from strategic decisions concerning capacity, with resulting expenditure on plant and facilities'.
> (CIMA *Official Terminology*)

Committed costs may exist because of contracts already entered into by the organisation, which it cannot get out of.

Although **historical costs** are irrelevant for decision making, historical cost data will often provide the best available basis for predicting future costs.

If an organisation has the freedom of choice about whether to provide internally or buy in (and has no scarce resources that put a restriction on what it can do itself), the **relevant costs** for the decision will be the **differential costs between the two options**. Here is an example.

5.3.3 Example

Stunnaz plc is considering a proposal to use the services of a press cuttings agency. At the moment, press cuttings are collected by a junior member of the marketing department, who is also responsible for office administration (including filing), travel bookings, a small amount of proof reading and making the tea. The total annual cost of employing this person is £20,000 pa.

There is concern that the ability of this person to produce a comprehensive file of cuttings is limited by the time available. She has calculated that she needs to spend about two hours of her seven and a half hour day simply reading the national and trade press, but usually only has about five hours a week for this job.

Press subscriptions currently cost £850 pa and are paid annually in advance.

The assistant makes use of a small micro-fiche device for storing cuttings. The cuttings are sent to a specialist firm once a month to be put onto fiche. Stunnaz pays £45 each month for this service. The micro-fiche reader is leased at a cost of £76 per calendar month. This lease has another 27 months to run.

The cuttings service bureau has proposed an annual contract at a cost of £2750. Several existing users have confirmed their satisfaction with the service they receive.

Should Stunnaz plc outsource its press cuttings work?

Solution

Current annual costs amount to:

	£
Staff	£15,000 x 1/7.5 = 2000
Micro fiche service	£45 x 12 = 540
Subscriptions	850
	3390

The monthly leasing charge is a **committed cost** that must be paid whatever the decision. It is not therefore a decision-relevant cost.

Engaging the services of the press cuttings agency therefore has the *potential* to save Stunnaz plc £640 pa. However, this is not the final word: there are other considerations.

(a) The **'in-house' option** should give management **more direct control** over the work, but the **'outsource' option** often has the benefit that the external organisation has a **specialist skill and expertise** in the work. Decisions should certainly not be based exclusively on cost considerations.

(b) Will outsourcing create **spare capacity**? How should that spare capacity be profitably used?

(c) Are there **hidden benefits** to be obtained from subcontracting?

(d) Would the company's workforce resent the loss of work to an outside subcontractor, and might such a decision cause an **industrial dispute**?

(e) Would the subcontractor be **reliable with delivery times** and **quality**?

(f) Does the company wish to be **flexible** and **maintain better control** over operations by doing everything itself?

Chapter Roundup

- **Operations planning** involves the detailed procedures for creating and delivering products and services. Business processes can be re-engineered from a zero base.

- Operational effectiveness is vital in the delivery of customer satisfaction and maintaining profitability. This is why firms **benchmark** others in the same industry – although this may give an inappropriate emphasis on imitation where differentiation would be more appropriate.

- **Quality** is the totality of features which bears on a product's ability to meet stated needs. **Design quality** includes the degree to which customer satisfactions are built into a product. **Conformance quality** is an absence of defects in the finished goods. Ideally, quality is designed into the product. Inspection and rectification are not value-adding activities.

- Taguchi's quality/cost model is important as it identifies the necessity of **reducing variation** in production processes as a means of reducing losses.

- **Quality assurance** is increasingly demanded of suppliers, usually in conformation with ISO 9000. Certification is granted to companies which have an adequate system of quality assurance.

- **TQM** is a concept that applies quality to the whole organisation. Relevant techniques concepts are statistical process control (for conformance quality) and quality function deployment (for design quality). Important aspects are continuous improvement, the fact that production has employees take part in controlling and improving quality, internal marketing and linking business activities in quality chains.

- **Outsourcing** may be used to control costs and release resources to concentrate on **core competences**. Core competences are the source of **competitive advantage** and should not be outsourced.

- The decision to outsource non-core activities should be preceded by an analysis of **relevant costs**, but other aspects such as quality, reliability, spare capacity and control may be of greater importance in deciding not to outsource.

Quick Quiz

1   What is the link of operations to mission?

2   Define operations plans.

3   What is business process re-engineering?

4   Identify four types of benchmarking.

5   What is the difference between technical quality and functional quality in service operations?

6   Define quality.

7   Distinguish between design and conformance quality.

8   What is a quality circle?

9   Define TQM.

10   What is a relevant cost?

BPP
PROFESSIONAL EDUCATION

Answers to Quick Quiz

1   Mission should be embedded in policies and behaviour standards at operational level

2   Specifications for individuals to enable sectional objectives to be achieved

3   Fundamental rethinking and radical redesign of business processes to achieve dramatic improvements

4   Internal, functional, competitive, strategic

5   Technical quality lies in the nature of the service provided. Functional quality lies in the customer's subjective assessment of the service encounter

6   Fitness for use

7   **Design** quality lies in the customer satisfactions incorporated into the product; **conformance** quality lies in the defect rate in the finished article

8   Groups of workers selected to analyse and discuss the production process with the aim of improving quality

9   Managing quality to ensure customer satisfaction both internally and externally

10   A cost appropriate to a specific management decision

Now try Question 9 at the end of the Study Text

Project management

Syllabus content

- Key concepts and techniques of project management and their use in conducting marketing and other business activities
- Exploiting innovation and creativity in products and processes
- Developing techniques to exploit innovations in marketing

Introduction

Project management appears in your syllabus because so much marketing activity takes place in discrete chunks: product launches, research programmes and communication campaigns are all examples. The sensible use of established project management techniques is therefore an important part of marketing management.

Loosely associated is the topic of innovation. Innovation should be encouraged on a continuing basis, but much innovation is the result of programmes undertaken to address a perceived need and this is as much true of marketing as of any other business activity.

1 What is project management?

FAST FORWARD

A **project** is an undertaking with a defined beginning and end, directed towards the achievement of a specified goal (eg building a house). **Project management** always involves dealing with the unexpected. Each project is in some respects new.

The **objectives** of project management are to ensure that the end product conforms with customer specification and is produced on time and within budget.

Key concept

A **project** is 'an undertaking that has a beginning and an end and is carried out to meet established goals within cost, schedule and quality objectives' (Haynes, *Project Management*).

Characteristics of projects

- Specific start and end points
- Well-defined objectives
- Unique nature
- Cost and time constraints
- Cuts across organisational and functional boundaries

1.1 Unique features of project management

Key concept

Project management is directed at an end. It is not directed at maintaining or improving a continuous activity. It thus has a limited objective within a limited time span. According to Lock, 'the job of project management is to foresee as many dangers as possible, and to plan, organise and control activities so that they are avoided.'

1.1.1 Project management problems

Problem	Comment
Teambuilding	The work is carried out by a team of people usually assembled for one project, who must immediately be able to communicate effectively with each other.
Expected problems	**Expected** problems should be resolved by careful design and planning prior to commencement of work.
Unexpected problems	There should be mechanisms within the project to enable these problems to be resolved during the time span of the project without detriment to the objective, the cost or the time span.

Problem	Comment
Delayed benefit	**There is normally no benefit until the work is finished**. The 'lead in' time to this can cause a strain on the eventual recipient who is also faced with increasing expenditure for no immediate benefit.
Specialists	Contributions made by specialists are of differing importance at each stage.
Stakeholders	If the project involves several parties with different interests in the outcome, there might be disputes between them.

Many projects go wrong: this is usually manifested as a failure to complete on time, but this outcome can arise for a variety of reasons.

(a) **Unproven technology**. The use of new technological developments is likely to be a feature of any project. The range of such developments extends from fairly routine and non-critical improvements, through major innovations capable of transforming working practices, costs and time scales, to revolutionary techniques that make feasible projects that were previously quite impracticable. As the practical potential of a technical change moves from minor to major, so too moves its potential to cause disruption if something goes wrong with it. A classic example is *Rolls Royce's* attempt to use carbon fibre in the design of the RB211 engine in the early 1970s. Not only did the project fail to meet its objectives, its failure led to the company's financial failure, which necessitated its rescue by government.

(b) **Changing specifications**. It is not unusual for the ultimate customers' notions of what they want to evolve during the lifetime of the project. However, if the work is to come in on time and on budget, they must be aware of what is technically feasible, reasonable in their aspirations, prompt with their decisions and, ultimately, prepared to freeze the specification so that it can be delivered. The failure of the TSR2 aircraft project forty years ago was in large part caused by major, unrealistic changes to specification.

(c) **Politics**. This problem area includes politics of all kinds, from those internal to an organisation managing its own projects, to the effect of national (and even international) politics on major undertakings. Identification of a senior figure with a project; public interest and press hysteria; hidden agendas; national prestige; and political dogma can all have deleterious effects on project management. **Lack of senior management support** is an important political problem.

(d) **Poor project management**. This comes in several guises.

    (i) **Over optimism**. This can be particularly troublesome with new technology. Unrealistic deadlines may be accepted, for instance, or impossible levels of performance promised.

    (ii) **Over-promotion of technical staff**. It is common for people with a high level of technical skill to be promoted. Only then is it made clear that they lack management and leadership ability. This is a particular problem with IT projects.

    (iii) **Poor planning**. Realistic timescales must be established, use of shared resources must be planned and, most fundamental of all, jobs must be done in a sensible sequence.

    (iv) **Poor control**. Progress must be under continuous review and control action must be taken early if there are problems. The framework of control must provide for review at all levels of management and prompt reporting of problems.

1.1.2 The objectives of project management

The objectives, broadly speaking, of project management arise out of the deficiencies noted in Paragraph 1.1.1.

Objective	Comment
Quality	The end result should conform to the project specification. In other words, the result should achieve what the project was supposed to do.
Budget	The project should be completed without exceeding authorised expenditure.
Timescale	The progress of the project must follow the planned process, so that the result is ready for use at the agreed date. As time is money, proper time management can help contain costs.

1.2 The project life cycle

FAST FORWARD

The **project life cycle** can be broken down into the stages of project definition, planning, implementation, completion and review.

A typical project has a **project life cycle**.

- Conceiving and defining the project
- Planning the project
- Carrying out the plan (project implementation) and control
- Completing and evaluating the project

1.2.1 Conceiving and defining the project

A project often arises out of a perceived problem or opportunity. However, it is often not clear precisely what the problem is.

Step 1   **Analyse the problem**. The project team should study, discuss and analyse the project, from a number of different aspects (eg technical, financial).

Step 2   **Write the project definition**. There will be several stages, with each definition being more detailed and refined than before. The project might be defined in a:

- Contract
- Product specification
- Customer's specification

Step 3   **State the final objective of the project**. This clarifies what the project is trying to achieve (eg a sales system).

Step 4   **List the success criteria for a project**. These are the project's *basic* requirements and perhaps desirable enhancements. For the Channel Tunnel to be considered a success, the tunnel had to link the UK and France. If this was not done, the project would be a *total* failure.

Step 5   **Alternative strategies are identified** to find the best way to reach the project objective.

Step 6   **Evaluate alternatives** on the basis of technical and practical feasibility.

Step 7   **Assess the chosen strategy:** more detailed review and testing is carried out. A feasibility study examines the technical and financial aspects of the project, costing its critical assumptions and exposing possible flaws or unrealistic expectations.

1.2.2 Planning the project

A **project plan** aims to ensure that the project objective is achieved within the objectives of quality, cost and time. This involves three steps, once the basic project objective and the underlying activities have been agreed.

Step 1 **Break the project down into manageable units**. As a simple example, if your objective is to cook a dinner party for your friends, you will break down this task into preparing the starter, the main course, and then the dessert. If you were a stickler for planning, you could break these down further into detailed tasks (chop onions, peel potatoes). This is sometimes called establishing a **work breakdown structure**

Step 2 **For each unit, estimate the resources needed** (in materials, money and time).

Step 3 **Schedule and plan resource requirements and timings of each sub-unit. Gantt charts, network analysis** and so forth are ways by which this can be achieved. **Costing** is also part of the project planning stage.

1.2.3 Carrying out the plan: implementation and control

The project implementation stage is when the plans are put into action. Frequently a project is directed by a **project manager** (see below).

Step 1 **Review progress**

(i) Control point, identification charts indicate the sort of things that might go wrong, and the action taken to rectify them.

(ii) Project control charts use budget and schedule plans to give a status report on progress (eg cumulative time and cost) so that variances can be calculated.

Step 2 **Monitor performance**

- Inspection
- Progress reviews (at regular stages)
- Quality testing
- Financial audit

Step 3 **Take corrective action**. Falling behind schedule, because of some circumstance unforeseen at the planning stage, might require the rescheduling of the project or a change in resource configuration. If the project is over budget, cost savings can be found, or alternatively, more funds might be available from the client.

1.2.4 Completing and evaluating the project: post-audit

Finally, the project must be delivered to the customer, of course after final testing and review. Note that delivery might include subsidiary matters such as preparation of instruction manuals.

Project evaluation asks two questions.

(a) **Did the end result of the project meet the client's expectations?**

- The actual design and construction of the end product
- The timetable achieved: was the project achieved on time?
- The cost: was the project more or less within budget?

(b) Was the management of the project as successful as it might have been, or were there bottlenecks or problems?

- Problems that might occur on future projects with similar characteristics
- The performance of the team individually and as a group.

In other words, any project is an opportunity to learn how to manage future projects more effectively.

1.3 The role of the project manager

The project manager has to co-ordinate resources of time, money and staff.

Duty	Comment
Outline planning	Project planning (eg targets, sequencing) • Developing project targets such as overall costs or timescale needed (eg project should take 20 weeks). • Dividing the project into activities and placing these activities into the right sequence, often a complicated task if overlapping. • Developing a framework for the procedures and structures, manage the project (eg decide, in principle, to have weekly team meetings, performance reviews etc).
Detailed planning	**Work breakdown structure**, resource requirements, network analysis for scheduling.
Teambuilding	Brief superiors and team members.
Communication	The project manager must let superiors know what is going on, and ensure that members of the project team are properly briefed.
Co-ordinating project activities	Between the project team and users, and other external parties (eg suppliers of hardware and software).
Monitoring and control	The project manager should estimate the causes for each departure from the standard, and take corrective measures.
Problem-resolution	Even with the best planning, unforeseen problems may arise.
Quality control	There is often a short-sighted trade-off between getting the project out on time and the project's quality.

1.4 Section summary

- A project is not a continuous activity.
- Project objectives are quality, time and budget.
- Each project has a life cycle.
- Projects fail because of poor planning, poor management, political problems and vague or changing client specifications.
- Most projects are run by a project manager.

2 Planning and resourcing techniques

FAST FORWARD ▷ **Estimating** is always hazardous. Relatively small estimating errors can dent profits significantly.

An accurate estimate of project costs provides a proper basis for management control.

(a) **Ball-park estimates** are made before a project starts. They might be accurate to within 25%.

(b) **Comparative estimates** accurate to within 15% are made if the project under consideration has some similarities with previous ones.

(c) **Feasibility estimates** (probably accurate to within 10%) arise from preliminary aspects of the design. Building companies use feasibility estimates.

(d) **Definitive estimates** (accurate to within 5%) are only made when *all* the design work has been done.

Any **estimate** must be accompanied by a proviso detailing its expected **accuracy**. It is unreasonable to expect exact accuracy, but the project manager should be able to keep within estimates, particularly for projects with no margin of safety and tight profits. Estimates can be improved in four ways.

- Learn from past mistakes.
- Ensure sufficient design information, is adequate.
- Ensure as detailed a specification as possible from the customer.
- Analyse the job into its constituent units properly.

2.1 Work breakdown structure (WBS)

Work breakdown structure is the analysis of work into tasks. This can be used to estimate costs (by defining the resources needed for each task), and to schedule activities by determining which activities depend on which.

Key concept

Work breakdown structure is the analysis of the work of a project into different units or tasks. It identifies the work that must be done, determines the resources required, sequences the work done, and allocates resources in the optimum way.

For example, building a house can be **sub-divided** into ground work, masonry, wiring, and roofing. Dealing with the foundations involves digging, filling, area marking and disposal of soil.

The process of work breakdown continues until the smallest possible sub-unit is reached. Digging the foundations for example would be analysed so that the number of labour hours needed, and hence the cost, could be determined. *Lock* recommends giving each sub-unit of work a code number to enable resources to be obtained and the work to be planned.

2.2 Cost estimation

WBS may be used in devising estimates.

(a) From the WBS it is possible to 'compile a complete **list of every item** that is going to attract expenditure.'

(b) **Checklists** can be used to ensure that all factors are be taken into account.

(c) **Estimation forms** can be designed to be based on the work breakdown structure, so that by each work unit number, there are columns for labour, materials and so forth.

Costs should be analysed.

(a) **Direct costs** of a project include labour, raw materials and sub-components.

(b) **Overhead costs** include heating, lighting and so forth, and can be fixed and/or variable. Overhead allocation can be difficult in some project environments, as a large element of the project costs might be fixed or sunk. (For example, a building company is unlikely to buy a brand new crane for every house it builds. An element of a crane's depreciation charge might be charged to a project.)

(c) **In-house costs** and **subcontracted** costs.

Collating the various costs identified with each unit of the work breakdown structure:

(a)   Provides a useful cost analysis for various business functions.

(b)   Assists cost control.

(c)   Provides evidence, in any dispute with the client, that the costs are reasonable. (**Technical cost investigations** occur when the client sends technical cost officers to examine the books. The right to do so might be incorporated in the original contract.)

2.2.1 Labour time estimates

A project manager relies on the *personal* opinions of the individuals in each department.

(a)   'Estimates for any work will more frequently be understated than overstated'.

  (i)   Many people are **eager to please** the project manager.

  (ii)   People do **not** learn to estimate better. (In some companies, a rule of thumb is to add 50% on to the estimated time given by production or design staff.)

(b)   On occasions when people's estimates are **over-pessimistic**, a cause might be a desire to **inflate departmental budgets**.

(c)   Finally, some estimators are **inconsistent**. This is worst of all.

2.2.2 Materials estimates

(a)   **Total materials cost**. Design engineers should prepare lists of materials required for each task. The purchasing department should indicate the costs.

(b)   **Lead times for receipt**. Failure to receive materials on time can result in unexpected delay.

(c)   **Estimating problems**

  (i)   **Contingencies**. Projects can be delayed because of design errors, production mistakes, material and component failures. An allowance is sometimes built in.

  (ii)   Additional work can be included in the contract price on a **provisional basis**.

  (iii)   **Increases in prices** will increase costs over the contract's life.

2.3 Section summary

- A project should be broken down into its constituent tasks (work breakdown structure).

- Cost, labour and materials estimates can be obtained, sometimes with difficulty, for each task.

3 Project planning tools

FAST FORWARD

Project planning tools include **network analysis**, **Gantt charts** and **resource histograms**.

The project manager needs to **schedule the activities** identified in the WBS in the most efficient way given:

(a)   The **dependency** of some activities on others. In other words, job B may need to be done before job C.

(b)   **Constraints on resources.** Some resources will not be available at the ideal time or at the lowest price. For example, a computer project manager may have to compete with other project managers for the availability of skilled staff.

The project manager will have been given a broad time estimation for any activity based on three things.

- The **duration** of each sub-unit of work
- The **earliest time** work in a particular unit must be started
- The **latest time** it must be started

3.1 Gantt charts

A simple plan for a project is based on a **bar line chart** or **Gantt chart**.

(a) It can be used as a **progress control chart** with the lower section of each bar being completed as the activity is undertaken.

(b) A delay in a particular piece of work and its effect on other work can be shown in a **linked bar chart**. This shows the links between an activity and preceding activities which have to be completed before this particular activity can start.

(c) The requirement of each stage of the project for resources such as people and plant can also be shown on the Gantt chart. This can be done by entering numbers or by constructing a series of bar diagram along the bottom edge of the chart. This is similar to the resource histogram shown later in this section.

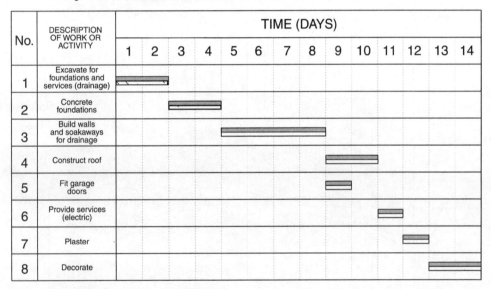

- **Advantage:** easy to understand
- **Disadvantage:** limited when dealing with large complex projects in that they can only display a restricted amount of information and the links between activities are fairly crude.

To overcome these problems we use a more sophisticated technique known as network analysis.

3.2 Critical path analysis (CPA) or network analysis

CPA describes the **sequence** of activities, and how long they are going to take. These diagrams are drawn left to right.

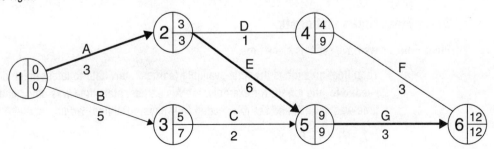

(a) **Events** (1 and 2) are represented by circles. **Activities** (eg A) connect events.

(b) The **critical path** is represented by drawing double line or a thicker line between the activities on the path. It is the **minimum amount of time** that the project will take.

(c) It is the convention to note the earliest start date of any activity in the top right hand corner of the circle.

(d) We can then work backwards identifying the latest dates when activities have to start. These we insert in the bottom right quarter of the circle.

The **critical path** in Paragraph 4.5 is AEG. Note the **float time** of five days for Activity F. Activity F can begin any time between days 4 and 9, thus giving the project manager a degree of flexibility.

This is a very simple example. Note that CPA for real world projects probably require specialised expertise (as may useable and useful Gantt charts and resource histograms). On the other hand, applications of the basic principles involved will help with the planning of simpler projects.

3.3 Resource histograms

If all activities are started as soon as possible, the labour requirements can be shown on a bar chart. Bar charts such as these are sometimes called **resource histograms**.

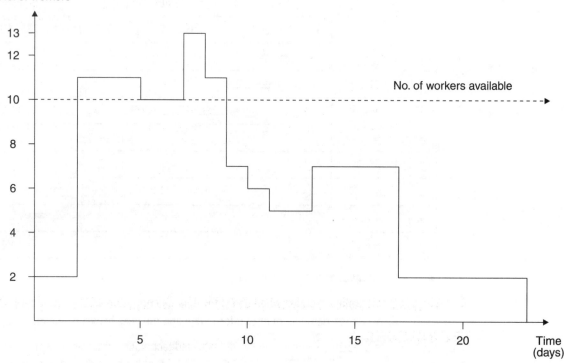

The number of workers required on the seventh day is 13. Can we re-schedule the non-critical activities to eliminate any excessive requirement? The various floats show whether we can move any activity. We might be able to re-arrange activities so that we can make use of the workers available from day 9 onwards.

3.3.1 Float times and costs

Float time, as we have seen, is slack time.

(a) Total float on a job is the time available (earliest start date to latest finish date) *less* time needed for the job. If, for example, job A's earliest start time was day 7 and its latest end time was day 17, and the job needed four days, total float would be:

$(17 - 7) - 4 = 6$ days

(b) **Free float** is the delay possible in an activity on the assumption that all preceding jobs start as early as possible and all subsequent jobs also start at the earliest time.

(c) **Independent float** is the delay possible if all preceding jobs have finished as late as was permissible, and all succeeding jobs start as early as possible.

Perhaps more important than cash flow consideration are the total expense and the expense involved in **crashing** a project.

(a) The **crash time** is the **minimum** time that an activity takes to be completed with **extra resources**.

(b) Crashing also has the affect of changing the critical path as extra resources can change the activity's duration.

It is possible therefore to draw up **two** sets of estimates identifying the cost, with or without crashing.

3.4 Criticisms of critical path/network analysis

(a) It is not always possible to devise an effective WBS for a project.

(b) **It assumes an essentially linear and sequential relationship** between activities: in other words it assumes that once Activity A is finished, Activity B proceeds, and that Activity B has no impact on Activity A. There may be complex and conditional relationships between what seem to be distinct and sequential activities, necessitating a much greater degree of analysis.

(c) There are inevitable **problems in estimation**. Where the project is completely new, the planning process may be conducted in conditions of relative ignorance.

(d) **Costs are based only on labour hours**, and all the problems relating to absorption of indirect overheads apply. Labour hours may only be a small proportion of the money involved in the project.

(e) Although network analysis plans the use of resources of labour and finance, it **does not appear to develop plans for contingencies, other than crashing time**.

(f) CPA **assumes a trade-off between time and cost** – but this does not really hold where a substantial portion of the cost is **indirect overheads** or where the direct labour proportion of the total cost of limited.

4 Management implications of project management techniques

Network analysis is a means of finding the best way to schedule activities, by highlighting the interrelationships between them. Central to the ideas are that work is broken down into units which can be analysed **independently** of each other.

4.1 Parallel engineering

Certain companies have taken this approach to product development. **Parallel engineering techniques** aim to speed the time taken to get a product to market. Once the overall idea of a design is agreed, individual development teams go ahead on **different aspects** of the project, in designing both the product and the production process and machinery.

4.2 Management by exception

Network planning facilitates management by exception, in which management attention is concentrated on items which deviate from plans. 'Critical operations usually make up about 20% of the project activities that can affect the overall progress'. Project management techniques enable management by exception by identifying, from the outset, those activities which might delay the others.

5 Innovation

Innovation can be a major source of competitive advantage but brings a burden of cost and uncertainty. **Intrapreneurship** is entrepreneurship carried on within the organisation at a level below the strategic apex.

For many organisations, product innovation and being the **first mover** may be a major **source of competitive advantage**.

(a) A **reputation for innovation** will attract **early adopters**, though it depends in part on promotional effort.

(b) Customers may find they are **locked in** to innovative suppliers by unacceptable **costs of switching** to competitors.

(c) The **learning** (or experience) **curve** effect may bring cost advantages .

(d) The first mover may be able to **define the industry standard**.

(e) A **price skimming** strategy can bring early profits that will be denied to later entrants.

(f) Legal protection, such as patents, for intellectual property may bring important revenue advantages. This is particularly important in the pharmaceutical industry.

However, the first mover also has particular **problems**.

- Gaining **regulatory approval** where required
- **Uncertain demand**
- **High levels of R&D costs**
- **Lower cost imitators**
- **Costs of introduction** such as training sales staff and educating customers.

In particular, it is common for later entrants into a market to learn from the first mover's mistakes and achieve market dominance. A good example is the way *Microsoft's Windows* operating system has overtaken *Apple's* offering.

Technology and the value chain. *Porter* points out in *Competitive Advantage* that 'every value activity uses some technology to combine purchased inputs and human resources to produce some output.' He goes on to discuss the varied role of **information technology** and emphasises the often-overlooked importance of **administrative** or **office technology**. The significance of this for strategy lies in the area of **core competences**. Just as **R&D** is as much concerned with processes as with products, so improvement in the linkages of the value chain will enhance competitive advantage.

Intrapreneurship. Intrapreneurship is entrepreneurship carried on within the organisation at a level below the strategic apex. The encouragement of intrapreneurship is an important way of promoting innovation. Such encouragement has many aspects.

(a) Encouragement for individuals to achieve results in their own way without the need for constant supervision

(b) A culture of risk-taking and tolerance of mistakes

(c) A flexible approach to organisation that facilitates the formation of project teams

(d)   Willingness and ability to devote resources to trying out new ideas

(e)   Incentives and rewards policy that support intrapreneurial activity

The chief object of being innovative is to ensure organisational success in a changing world. It can also have the following advantages.

(a)   Improvements in quality of **products** and **service**
(b)   A **leaner structure** – layers of management or administration may be done away with
(c)   Prompt and imaginative **solutions to problems**
(d)   **Less formality** in structure and style, leading to better communication
(e)   **Greater confidence** inside and outside the organisation in its ability to cope with change

Innovation and new product development (NPD) is therefore essential for many firms to survive and prosper. It is an increasingly important area.

Key concept

> **Innovation audit**: a critical assessment of the firm's innovation record, the internal obstacles to innovation and how performance can be enhanced.

A firm needs to assess how well it is able to deliver the level and type of innovation necessary to continue to meet customer needs and expectations. Drummond and Ensor (1999) identify **four key areas** for the innovation audit.

- The current **organisational climate**
- Measures of the organisation's **current performance** with regard to innovation
- Review of **policies and practices** supporting innovation and facilitating it
- The balance of **styles** of the management team

Exam tip

> The innovation audit featured in a June 2000 mini-case, in the case of a breakfast cereals producer. Improving the speed and quantity of innovation featured in June 2001. Innovation in a wider sense was also a major theme in a June 2002 mini-case.

5.1 Organisational climate

FAST FORWARD

> Barriers to innovation can be overcome using top management commitment and training and personal development.
>
> Innovation performance can be measured by the **rate** of new product launches or by customer satisfaction ratings.

5.1.1 Barriers to innovation in marketing

(a)   **Resistance to change**

Any new method of management thinking can experience some resistance from established managers. This resistance may be due to concern to protect the status quo, or because managers are ignorant of the new thinking. Integrating marketing communications seems so obvious that it may be overlooked or seen as a superficial approach.

(b)   **Old planning systems**

Old planning systems have sometimes downgraded marketing decisions to the tactical level. Advertising expenditure is decided on the basis of what the company can afford rather than what is strategically required. Promotion is seen as a series of short-term actions rather than as a long-term investment.

(c)   **Old structures/functional specialists**

Complementing traditional planning systems are traditional organisation structures. These structures freeze out new thinking on integrated marketing strategy. Individuals have limited specific responsibilities – just for advertising, say, or just for public relations – and this inhibits new thinking on integration.

(d)   **Centralised control**

If the chief executive keeps tight control of the organisation and of its planning and is unconvinced of the benefits of innovation then it will not happen.

(e)   **Cost considerations**

Innovation usually requires investment.

5.1.2 Methods of overcoming these barriers

(a)   **Top management commitment**

The most effective way of overcoming these barriers to change is through the commitment of top management. The chief executive in particular needs to be convinced of the appropriateness of the new thinking and be enthusiastic about its implementation throughout the organisation.

(b)   **Marketing reorganisation**

One way in which the chief executive can take advice is through a reorganisation of the marketing function in the organisation.

(c)   **Training and development**

It is one thing to change attitudes. It is another thing to be in a position to know exactly what to do. It needs the services of individuals trained in strategic thinking. The individuals chosen to implement any new programme must be enthusiasts capable of overcoming resistance to change.

(d)   **Marketing as a competitive advantage**

Those with responsibility for implementing an integrated marketing programme must do so with the objective of developing it as a sustainable, long-term competitive advantage.

(e)   **Producing the results**

Nothing succeeds like success. Producing the business results as a consequence of effective marketing communications will boost confidence and gain management converts to the new thinking on an integrated approach.

5.2 Policies to encourage innovation

To encourage innovation the objective for management should be to create a more outward-looking organisation.

- People should be encouraged to look for new products, markets, processes and designs
- People should seek ways to improve productivity

An innovation strategy calls for a management policy of **giving encouragement** to innovative ideas.

(a)   Giving **financial backing** to innovation, by spending on R & D and market research and risking capital on new ideas.

(b)   Giving employees the **opportunity** to work in an environment where the exchange of ideas for innovation can take place. Management style and organisation structure can help here.

(i)   Management can actively encourage employees and customers to put forward new ideas.

(ii)   **Development teams** can be set up and an organisation built up on project team-work.

(iii)   **Quality circles** and brainstorming groups can be used to encourage creative thinking about work issues.

(c)   Where appropriate, **recruitment policy** should be directed towards appointing employees with the necessary skills for doing innovative work. Employees should be trained and kept up-to-date.

(d)   Certain managers should be **made responsible for obtaining information** from outside the organisation about innovative ideas, and for **communicating** this information throughout the organisation.

(e)   **Strategic planning** should result in targets being set for innovation, and successful achievements by employees should if possible be rewarded.

5.3 Measures of performance

The **balanced scorecard** includes the **innovation and learning perspective**; this is because innovation is very important in the development and maintenance of competitive advantage. Appropriate devices to measure the degree of success a company has in innovation are therefore required. These may include measures such as the rate of successful **new product development** and related sales over the past years, or **customer satisfaction ratings**.

Customer satisfaction ratings. An important input to innovation is the degree of customer satisfaction, both from the product itself and service levels.

(a)   Customer satisfaction can be measured on a scale (eg from **highly satisfied** to **highly dissatisfied**).

(b)   Customers can also be asked to identify which features of a service/product they found most useful.

(c)   Firms should **actively measure** customer satisfaction, rather than simply **react to complaints**.

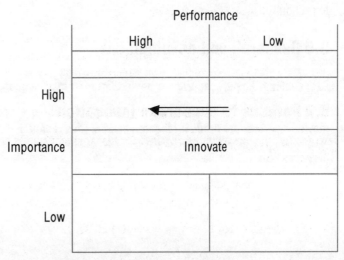

Clearly, a firm should be most concerned about matters of high importance with 'low' performance. Innovation may be necessary to ensure that high performance is achieved on matters of high importance.

5.3.1 Innovation/value matrix

(a)   A similar methodology can apply to innovation and its **value** to the customer. Clearly, the best sort of innovation gives highest customer value for the lowest cost or effort. Businesses can be categorised between those that offer the normal level of innovation and market value, those that offer some improvement on the offerings of competition, and finally those that offer significant innovations and value for the customer.

(b)   There is a danger that too many innovations can, in fact, confuse the customer. Recent research has encouraged some companies (such as Procter & Gamble) to reduce the variety of goods on offer.

(c)   The innovation process should consider both the **technology** and **customer needs**.

(d)   For example, once the limitations of the silicon chip are reached, optical computers might be invented. In some cases, instead of technical developments being used to predict future technologies, future social developments can be predicted, in order to **predict future customer needs**. The likely technologies which will satisfy these needs can then be considered.

5.4 The management team

The management team are key in setting the scene for innovation. The management team is also a critical influence on corporate culture.

The dynamics of the management team affects how it perceives the work environment.

Although the **environment poses strategic questions,** it is **people who make sense of it** and devise strategies. Whilst the recipe provides cultural coherence it can impede strategic renewal. If the corporate strategy is failing, a company will:

Step 1   Place tighter **controls** over implementation (eg give tougher performance targets to sales staff); but if **this** fails …

Step 2   Develop a new strategy (eg sell in a new market); but if this fails as well …

Step 3   Only now will the company abandon the recipe (eg realise that the product is obsolete).

This is significant if it impacts on the management team's attitude to innovation. A management team might be unbalanced if it has too many 'ideas' people and not enough implementers able to bring projects to fruition.

5.5 Research and development

FAST FORWARD

Research may be **pure**, **applied** or **development**. It may be intended to improve **products** or **processes**.

R&D should support the organisation's strategy and be closely co-ordinated with marketing. Research may be analysed into **product research** and **process research**. Product research is as much concerned with existing products as with new ones.

Here are some definitions culled from *Statement of Standard Accounting Practice 13.*

Key concepts

> **Pure research** is original research to obtain new scientific or technical knowledge or understanding. There is no obvious commercial or practical end in view.
>
> **Applied research** is also original research work like (a) above, but it has a specific practical aim or application (eg research on improvements in the effectiveness of medicines etc).
>
> **Development** is the use of existing scientific and technical knowledge to produce new (or substantially improved) products or systems, prior to starting commercial production operations.

The strategic role of R&D. R&D should support the organisation's chosen strategy. To take a simple example, if a strategy of **differentiation** has been adopted, it would be inappropriate to expend effort on researching ways of minimising costs. If the company has a competence in R&D, this may form the basis for a strategy of product innovation. Conversely, where product lifecycles are short, as in consumer electronics, product development is fundamental to strategy.

Many organisations employ **specialist staff** to conduct research and development (R&D). They may be organised in a separate functional department of their own. In an organisation run on a product division basis, R&D staff may be employed by each division.

There are two main categories of R&D.

Key concepts

> **Product research** is based on creating new products and developing existing ones, in other words the organisation's 'offer' to the market.
>
> **Process research** is based on improving the way in which those products or services are made or delivered, or the efficiency with which they are made or delivered.

5.5.1 Product research

New **product research** involves developing, testing and prototyping. A proposed new product will go through an extensive **screening process** whereby the idea is assessed for:

    (a)   Conformance to the firm's strategic objectives (eg it might only be a short-term money spinner but might attract attention).

    (b)   Attractiveness to enough customers.

    (c)   Technical feasibility.

(Thus, there will be a lot of marketing research before the product is introduced.)

Product research is not confined to dealing with new products. It has an important role in connection with **existing products**.

    (a)   **Value engineering** may be used to continue the development of existing products so that they use less costly components or processes without compromising the perceived value of the market offer.

    (b)   As products near the end of their **life cycle**, it may be possible to develop them for launch in a different market, or simply to extend their lives.

    (c)   Where products are being replaced by new versions it may be advantageous to ensure that the new products are **backwards compatible** with the installed base. This is an important consideration in software engineering, for example.

5.5.2 Process research

Process research involves attention to how the goods/services are produced. Process research has these aspects.

(a)   **Processes** are crucial in service industries (eg fast food), where processes are part of the services sold.

(b)   **Productivity**. Efficient processes save money and time.

(c)   **Planning**. If you know how long certain stages in a project are likely to take, you can plan the most efficient sequence.

(d)   **Quality management** for enhanced quality.

An important aspect of process research is that advances are much more difficult to imitate then are product developments. Competitors can purchase and **reverse engineer** new products. With good physical security in place, they will find it much more difficult to imitate new processes.

5.5.3 Problems with R&D

(a)   **Organisational**. Problems of authority relationships and integration arise with the management of R&D. The function will have to liase closely with marketing and with production, as well as with senior management responsible for corporate planning: its role is both strategic and technical.

(b)   **Financial**. R&D is by nature not easily planned in advance, and financial performance targets are not easily set. Budgeting for long-term, complex development projects with uncertain returns can be a nightmare for management accountants.

(c)   **Evaluation and control**. Pure research or even applied research may not have an obvious pay off in the short term. Evaluation could be based on successful application of new ideas, such as patents obtained and the commercial viability of new products.

(d)   **Staff problems**. Research staff are usually highly qualified and profession-orientated, with consequences for the style of supervision and level of remuneration offered to them.

(e)   **Cultural problems**. Encouraging innovation means trial and error, flexibility, tolerance of mistakes in the interests of experimentation, high incentives etc. If this is merely a subculture in an essentially bureaucratic organisation, it will not only be difficult to sustain, but will become a source of immense 'political' conflict. The R&D department may have an 'academic' or university atmosphere, as opposed to a commercial one.

R&D should be closely co-ordinated with marketing.

(a)   Customer needs, as identified by marketers, should be a vital input to new product developments.

(b)   The R&D department might identify possible changes to product specifications so that a variety of marketing mixes can be tried out and screened.

 Marketing at Work

An example of the relationship of R&D to marketing was described in an article in the *Financial Times* (14 July 1992) about the firm *Nestlé*, which invests £46m a year in research (and approximately £190m on development). Nestlé had a central R&D function, but also regional development centres. The central R&D function was involved in basic research. 'Much of the lab's work was only tenuously connected with the company's business... When scientists joined the lab, they were told "Just work in this or that area. If you work hard enough, we're sure you'll find something"'. The results of this approach were:

(a)   The research laboratory was largely cut off from development centres.

(b)   Much research never found commercial application.

As part of Nestlé's wider reorganisation, which restructured the business into strategic business units (SBUs), formal links have been established between R&D and the SBUs. This means that research procedures have been changed so that a commercial time horizon is established for some projects.

Chapter Roundup

- A **project** is an undertaking with a defined beginning and end, directed towards the achievement of a specified goal (eg building a house). **Project management** always involves dealing with the unexpected. Each project is in some respects new.

- The **objectives** of project management are to ensure that the end product conforms with customer specification and is produced on time and within budget.

- The **project life cycle** can be broken down into the stages of project definition, planning, implementation, completion and review.

- **Estimating** is always hazardous. Relatively small estimating errors can dent profits significantly.

- **Work breakdown structure** is the analysis of work into tasks. This can be used to estimate costs (by defining the resources needed for each task), and to schedule activities by determining which activities depend on which.

- **Project planning tools** include **network analysis**, **Gantt charts** and **resource histograms**.

- **Innovation** can be a major source of competitive advantage but brings a burden of cost and uncertainty. **Intrapreneurship** is entrepreneurship carried on within the organisation at a level below the strategic apex.

- Barriers to innovation can be overcome using top management commitment and training and personal development.

- Innovation performance can be measured by the **rate** of new product launches or by customer satisfaction ratings.

- Research may be **pure**, **applied** or **development**. It may be intended to improve **products** or **processes**.

- R&D should support the organisation's strategy and be closely co-ordinated with marketing. Research may be analysed into **product research** and **process research**. Product research is as much concerned with existing products as with new ones.

Quick Quiz

1   Define 'project'.

2   What are the distinctive problems of project management?

3   What are the objectives of project management?

4   What four different types of estimate can be given?

5   What is work breakdown structure?

6   What is technical cost investigation?

7   What is a Gantt Chart?

8   What is crashing?

9   What is the difference between pure and applied research?

10   What problems does innovation bring?

Answers to quick quiz

1   A project is 'an undertaking that has a beginning and an end and is carried out to meet established goals within cost, schedule and quality objectives' (Haynes, Project Management).

2   Teambuilding; expected problems; unexpected problems; delayed benefit; specialists; stakeholders

3   Quality, budget, timescale

4   Ball park; comparative; feasibility; definitive

5   Analysis of a project into units or tasks to identify what must be done and in what sequence, and to identify the optimum allocation of resources

6   Investigation of costs by the client's technical experts

7   A horizontal bar chart relating tasks to time used for project control

8   Crashing changes the critical path by devolving sufficient extra resources to finish the project in minimum time

9   Pure research has no obvious commercial or practical end in view. Applied research does.

10   Regulatory approval; uncertain demand; R&D costs; lower cost imitators

Now try Question 10 at the end of the Study Text

Part E
Measurement, evaluation and control

11

Control systems

Syllabus content

- Using accounting measures of performance of marketing activities against objectives
- Defining and using customer-related and innovation measures as part of a balanced scorecard

Introduction

Control in a planning system has two aspects. It monitors and corrects current performance. Also, it feeds into the next planning cycle. Control in effect asks 'Where are we now?', the starting point of the planning process. Similarly, the measures used for control do bear some relationship with, and might be identical to, the detailed objectives and critical success factors determined earlier. Control involves a review of what we have achieved, or what we anticipate achieving in the light of our plans.

1 Effective marketing feedback and control systems

FAST FORWARD

Marketing activities depend upon the actions and reactions of **people**: this complicates the problem of feedback and control.

In contrast to, say, mechanistic production processes, **marketing feedback and control systems need to recognise the volatile nature of human beings**. After all, **markets are people** or rather people's wants and needs, modified by affordability and availability. Problems of unsatisfactory feedback and control can occur.

(a)   People change

(b)   Reasons for change are not always apparent or identifiable

(c)   The same product can be bought by the same person for different purposes eg champagne to celebrate a win on the 3.30, or to drown sorrows after a loss on the 4.00.

(d)   Delays occur in the system due to suppliers being remote from consumers.

(e)   Competitor actions can seriously affect the systems.

(f)   Rarely is complete information affordable so that inadequacies occur in feedback.

(g)   Distortions inevitably occur in the data transfer between people. The more often the data is transcribed the more distortion will occur.

We have already seen the need for **marketing information feedback at each stage of the planning process**.

(a)   Only if marketing managers are kept informed of what is happening and what is likely to happen, can they make sensible decisions. For example, **contingency planning depends upon 'what if' scenarios**. Only when managers receive information indicating a particular scenario is taking place can the right contingency plan be invoked. The information in this case acts as an identifier, a selector and a trigger.

(b)   The dimensions of marketing feedback and control systems are in fact wide-ranging and flexible. One of the most important marketing planning philosophies is to avoid a laissez-faire, complacent attitude to good news. We need to remember that **good sales figures represent the past situation**, so we need to worry about the future longer-term survival and growth.

Some items have greater immediacy than others. Failure to act on a serious complaint could lead to the loss of an important customer, adversely affecting future sales and profitability.

Exam tip

A question might ask about financial and other information in a marketing control system and the potential problems that setting up such a system could create. For example, there are additional problems in developing control systems for service organisations, due to the very nature of services (such as intangibility and the importance of service personnel).

BPP
PROFESSIONAL EDUCATION

A four stage model is suggested.
(1)   Set targets
(2)   Measure achievement
(3)   Examine reasons
(4)   Take corrective action

This is similar to the control model we outline below.

2 Basic control concepts

All **feedback control systems** work in the same way. Progress is measured and compared with plan; discrepancies lead to control action. **Single loop feedback** leads to changes in activity; **double loop feedback** is used to modify the plan itself. **Feedforward control** makes a comparison between the plan and a forecast based on actual current achievement; control action is initiated before activity is complete.

A good starting point in thinking about basic control concepts is to take the example of driving a car. In doing this we receive various **feedbacks** eg visual feedback to tell us if we are driving in the right direction, in the correct position on the road, at the right speed etc. Instruments such as the speedometer and our senses – eyes, touch (vibration) provide the basic data. We measure this data against **standards** such as the speed limit, the highway code/laws etc and where necessary take **corrective action** using control devices like the steering wheel and the accelerator.

The marketing planning and implementation process follows similar precepts. We cannot implement a plan in the first place until we know where we are going. In planning where we are going we need to know where we are now. It also helps if we know where we have come from.

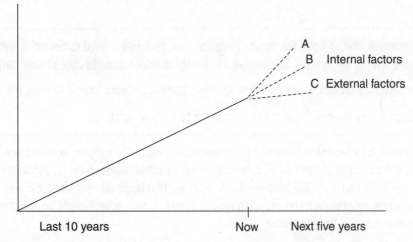

The past determines not only where we are now relative to it but out **future direction** (extrapolation of past trend assuming no change = position B). **Control is, however, only partial in marketing**.

(a)   We can change internal factors (the 7 Ps) positively so as to aim for position A.

(b)   However, external factors (political, economic, sociological, technological and competition) might act positively or negatively, in the latter case dragging us down to position C.

(c)   Nevertheless, the more information we have about the so called uncontrollable external factors, the more we can anticipate, ride or avoid the blows.

Here is a diagram of a generic **control system**.

Control System

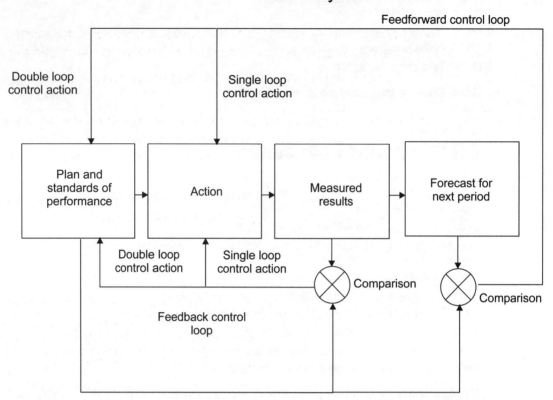

The essence of control is the measurement of results and comparison of them with the original plan. Any deviation from plan indicates that control action is required to make the results conform more closely with plan.

Key concepts

> **Feedback** occurs when the results (outputs) of a system are used to control it, by adjusting the input or behaviour of the system. Businesses use feedback information to control their performance.
>
> **Single loop feedback** results in the system's behaviour being altered to meet the plan.
>
> **Double loop feedback** can result in changes to the plan itself.

Double loop feedback is control information transmitted to a higher level in the system. Whereas single loop feedback is concerned with immediate task control, higher level feedback is concerned with overall control. The term double loop feedback indicates that feedback is used to indicate both divergence between the observed and expected results where control action might be required, and also the need for **adjustments to the plan itself**.

2.1 Feedforward control

(a)   **Control delay**. A timelag may exist between the actual results and the corrective action. However, results can be anticipated.

(b)   **Feedforward control** uses **anticipated** or forecast results, and compares them with the plan. **Corrective action** is thus taken **in advance**, before it is too late to do anything effective. Control is exercised before the results, rather than after the event.

Emmanuel et al describe **four necessary conditions that must be satisfied before any process can be said to be controlled**. These will help us to put control into a wider context still.

(a)   **Objectives** for the process being controlled must exist, for without an aim or purpose control has no meaning.

(b) The **output of** the process must be **measurable** in terms of the dimensions defined by the objectives.

(c) A **predictive model** of the process being controlled is required so that causes for the non-attainment of objectives can be determined and proposed corrective actions evaluated.

(d) There must be a **capability of taking action** so that deviations of attainment from objectives can be reduced.

It is important to understand that this concept of control involves more than just measuring results and taking corrective action. Control in the broad sense embraces **the formulation of objectives** – deciding what are the things that need to be done – as well as monitoring their attainment by way of feedback. Note two important points.

(a) As *Drucker* pointed out, the most crucial aspect of management performance in business is economic success; that is, **financial targets are the vital ones**.

(b) Targets are only useful if performance can be **measured**.

2.1.1 Examples

Feedback	Standards	Control actions
Sales figures	Against budget plus or minus	Stimulate/dampen down demand
Complaints	Number, frequency, seriousness	Corrective action
Competitors	Relative to us	Attack/defence strategies
Market size changes	Market share	Marketing mix manipulation
Costs/profitability	Ratios	Cost cutting exercises
Corporate image	Attribute measures	Internal/external communications
Environmental factors	Variances from norm	Invoke strategic alternatives

Action Programme 1

Sally Keene works for a large department store, as a manager.

(a) At the beginning of each year she is given a yearly plan, subdivided into twelve months. This is based on the previous year's performance and some allowance is made for anticipated economic conditions. Every three months she sends her views as to the next quarter to senior management, who give her a new plan in the light of changing conditions.

(b) She monitors sales revenue per square foot, and sales per employee. Employees who do not meet the necessary sales targets are at first counselled and then if performance does not improve they are dismissed. Sally is not unreasonable. She sets what she believes are realistic targets.

(c) She believes there is a good team spirit in the sales force, however, and that employees, whose commission is partly based on the sales revenue earned by the store as a whole, discourage slackers in their ranks.

What kind of control, control system or control information can you identify in the three cases above?

3 Strategic control

Corporate control systems should be able to influence people towards the achievement of corporate goals. Key factors and managers should be identified and reporting and control systems focused on them. **Critical success factors** should form the basis of control systems.

The **control measures and analytical techniques** that might be relevant for control at a strategic level are as follows.

Type of analysis	Used to control
1 *Financial analysis*	
Ratio analysis	Elements of profitability
Variance analysis	Costs or revenue
Cash budgeting	Cash flow
Capital budgeting and	
Capital expenditure audit	Investment
2 *Market/sales analysis*	
Demand analysis	Competitive standing
Market share or penetration	
Sales targets	Sales effectiveness
Sales budget	Efficiency in use of resources for selling
3 *Physical resource analysis*	
Capacity fill	Plant utilisation
Yield	Materials utilisation
Product inspection	Quality
4 *Human resources analysis*	
Work measurement	Productivity
Output measurement	
Labour turnover	Workforce stability
5 *Analysis of systems*	
Management by objectives	Implementation of strategy
Network analysis	Resource planning and scheduling

3.1 Features of basic strategic control systems

Control must influence the behaviour of individuals and groups towards the implementation of the corporate strategy and towards progressive change.

(a)   **Distinguish between control at different levels** in the management hierarchy (strategic, tactical, operational). Is the control measure intended to have an immediate impact (for example, 'firefighting', at an operational control or budgetary level) or will it take time for the measure to have a tangible effect?

(i)   Define **strategic objectives** (ie the organisation's eventual objectives in terms of competitive strategy).

(ii)   Identify **strategic milestones** on the way to achieving strategic objectives. These could be the specific tasks by which strategic objectives are achieved. These are short-term steps along the way to long-term goals.

(iii)   The **key assumptions** on which the strategy is based must also be monitored. A strategy drawn up from a position of limited competition (eg a protected national market) would have to be changed if the market was opened to foreign companies.

(b)   **Individual managers** should be identified as having the responsibility for certain matters, and authority to take control measures.

(c)   The **key factors for control** should be identified. Managers responsible for taking control action must be informed about what the key factors are, and why they are critical.

(d)   **Control reporting should be timed sensibly**. Depending on the level of control, control reports should vary from occasional to regular and frequent.

(e)   **Apply targets and standards**

- Targets for market share, in absolute and relative terms, compared with competitors
- Targets for relative product quality
- Timetables for strategic action programmes
- Targets for costs relative to the competitors' costs

(f)   Control reports should only contain **relevant information** for the manager receiving the report.

(g)   **Selective reporting**. Selective reporting means identifying **key points for control**.

(i)   The **position of each product** in the product-market matrix or in its life cycle will suggest how much close watching the product needs.

(ii)   A product which performs **inconsistently** might need close watching and control.

(iii)   **Information and control reporting costs money**.

(iv)   The **key item might be qualitative**. For example within the marketing function it might be considered vitally important that there should be a rapid and significant improvement in employee commitment and enthusiasm. Control reporting at the corporate planning level should therefore emphasise these points, and shift back to other matters when appropriate.

3.1.1 Example

Date: March 2006

Source: January 2004 planning document

Mission: Market share

1.   *Long term targets, to be achieved by 2010*

(a)   X% value of market share
(b)   Y% profitability over the decade

Status: March 2006. Market share lower than anticipated, owing to unexpected competition. Profits lower than expected because of loss of scale economies and increased marketing costs.

Outlook. Profit will be improved thanks to cost-cutting measures. Market share target might be missed.

2.   *Critical assumptions*

The home market is growing only slowly, and is becoming mature. There are limited opportunities for segmentation.

Overseas markets are likely to expand by Z% as some are reducing tariffs.

Status March 2006. The home market has matured more quickly than expected. Overseas market growth can compensate for this.

3.   *Critical success factors*

- Exports increased by W%
- Secure distribution arrangements

4.   *Key tasks*

- Launch of budget products for overseas markets
- Setting up of a computerised distribution system to enhance speedy response to demand and to cut warehousing costs
- Get ISO 9000 certification

Note the use of **critical success factors**. We discussed them briefly in the context of resource planning but they are also relevant to control.

Day and Wensley relate these to **advantages** and **outcomes** as follows.

(a)   **Sources of advantage**

- Superior skills
- Superior resources

(b)   **Positional advantages**

- Superior customer value
- Lower relative costs

(c)   **Performance outcomes**

- Customer satisfaction
- Customer loyalty
- Higher market share
- Higher profits

Marketing at Work

Freund relates CSFs with strategies and performance indicators for a life insurance company as follows.

CSF	Strategies	Performance indicators
Able to achieve critical mass volumes via existing brokers/ agents.	Develop closer ties with agents Telemarket to brokers. Adjust agents' compensation.	Number of policies in force. Number of new policies written. Percentage of business with existing brokers.
Able to introduce new products within six months of industry leaders.	Underwrite strategic joint ventures.	Time taken to introduce. Percentage out within six months. Percentage of underwriters having extra certification.
Be able to manage product and product lines, profitably.	Segment investment portfolio. Improve cost accounting. Closely manage loss rate.	Return on portfolio segments. Actual product cost revenue versus budget. Loss ratio relative to competitors.

3.1.2 CSFs that cover both financial and non-financial criteria

Sphere of activity	Critical factors
Marketing	Sales volume Market share Gross margins
Production	Capacity utilisation Quality standards
Logistics	Capacity utilisation Level of service

3.1.3 CSFs that relate to specific elements of the marketing mix

Activity	CSF
New product development	Trial rate Repurchase rate
Sales programmes	Contribution by region, salesperson Controllable margin as percentage of sales Number of new accounts Travel costs
Advertising programmes	Awareness levels Attribute ratings Cost levels
Pricing programmes	Price relative to industry average Price elasticity of demand
Distribution programmes	Number of distributors carrying the product

3.1.4 The trade off between short-term and long-term for control action

Control action must not prejudice **longer-term development** in order to improve results in the short-term.

It is often the case that in order to rectify short-term results, control action will be at the expense of long-term targets. Similarly, controls over longer-term achievements might call for short-term sacrifices.

Examples of the reasons for S/L trade-offs are as follows.

(a) **Short-term losses**. A company has a target of building up its market share for a new product to 30% within four years. It has decided to do this with a low price market penetration strategy. As a short-term target, it wants the product to earn a small profit (£100,000) in the current year. Actual results after three months of the year indicate that the market share has already built up to 18%, but that the product will make a £50,000 loss in the year.

The S/L trade off involves a decision about what to do about short-term profitability (raise prices? cut back on advertising? reduce the sales force?) without sacrificing altogether the long-term market share target.

(b) **Capital expenditure**. K Bhattacharya has written as follows.

'This is one of the most vulnerable areas for detrimental S/L trade-offs. The horizon for returns is most certainly more than a year off, yet costs associated with the implementation of the programme can easily reduce short-term profits. Postponements can almost always release capital and manpower resources needed to generate immediate operating profit.'

(c) **Research and development**. This is another area where short-term profitability is boosted, by cutting back on R & D expenditure at the expense of the longer-term need to continue to develop new products.

(d) **Behaviour**. Very often managers are under pressure to produce good short-term results (for example immediate profitability) in order to get their next promotion.

Marketing at Work

McDonnell Douglas

With $14bn in sales, *McDonnell Douglas* was one of the nation's largest defence companies. It had done a good job of turning around the C-17 transport plane program, which a few years earlier was nearly cancelled by the Air Force over technical flaws and delays. But its commercial aircraft arm, Douglas Aircraft, was a disaster, caught in the tailwinds of Boeing and Airbus. In 1994, McDonnell Douglas's board shocked investors by bringing in an outsider – a brash, controversial former GE executive, Harry Stonecipher – as CEO.

At first Stonecipher insisted that the firm was committed to building passenger airplanes. At one point he said the business was so good that if Douglas wasn't in it already, 'we would be looking for a way to get in'. But years of under-investment had resulted in planes with little imagination, and Douglas would need to spend billions to catch up. **Ultimately, Stonecipher wasn't willing to make that investment, preferring to focus on short-term stock performance**. (BPP emphasis)

During his tenture as CEO, McDonnell Douglas's stock quadrupled (Stonecipher carries a laminated copy of the stock chart in his briefcase), but critics say the failure to invest in R&D would have been disastrous eventually. 'This is a company that would have gone out of business in five years', says Richard Aboulafia, an analyst at Teal Group, an aviation research firm. 'It was headed to oblivion.'

Eventually, McDonnell Douglas merged with Boeing.

Fortune, 9 April 2004

3.1.5 Ensuring that the S/L trade off is properly judged and well balanced

(a)   Managers should **recognise** whether or not S/L trade-offs in control action could be a serious problem.

(b)   **Managers should be aware** that S/L trade-offs take place in practice.

(c)   Controls should exist to prevent or minimise the possibility that short-term controls can be taken which damage long-term targets.

(d)   Senior management must be given **adequate control information** for long-term as well as short-term consequences.

(e)   The planning and review system should **motivate** managers to keep long-term goals in view.

(f)   **Short-term goals should be realistic**. Very often, the pressure on managers to sacrifice long-term interests for short-term results is caused by the imposition of stringent and unrealistic short-term targets on those managers in the first place.

(g)   **Performance measures should reflect both long-term and short-term targets**. There might be, say, quarterly performance reviews on the achievement of strategic goals.

4 The balanced scorecard

FAST FORWARD

> The **balanced scorecard** concept is now widely accepted. The four usual perspectives are: **customer**; **financial**; **internal business**; and **innovation and learning**. Suitable goals and relevant performance measures must be established for each perspective.

The balanced scorecard is a technique designed to ensure that the different functions of the business are integrated together in order that they work to achieve the corporate goals.

Key concept

> The **balanced scorecard** is 'a set of measures that gives top managers a fast but comprehensive view of the business. The balanced scorecard includes financial measures that tell the results of actions already taken. And it complements the financial measures with operational measures on customer satisfaction, internal processes, and the organisation's innovation and improvement activities – operational measures that are the drivers of future financial performance.' (Kaplan and Norton, January–February 1992, *Harvard Business Review.*)

'Traditional financial accounting measures like return on investment and earnings per share can give misleading signals for continuous improvement and innovation'. The balanced scorecard allows managers to look at the business from **four important perspectives**.

- Customer
- Financial
- Internal business
- Innovation and learning

4.1 Customer perspective

'How do customers see us?' The balanced scorecard translates this into specific measures. Here are some examples. You may be able to think of more.

(a)   **Time**. Lead time is the time it takes a firm to meet customer needs, from receiving an order to delivering the product.

(b)   **Quality**. Quality measures not only include defect levels – although these should be minimised by TQM – but accuracy in forecasting.

(c)   **Performance** of the product. (How often does the photocopier break down?)

(d)   **Service**. How long will it take a problem to be rectified? (If the photocopier breaks down, how long will it take the maintenance engineer to arrive?)

To view the firm's performance through customers' eyes, firms hire market researchers to assess how the firm performs. Higher service and quality may cost more at the outset, but savings can be made in the long term.

4.2 Internal business perspective

Findings from the **customers'** perspective must be **turned into the actions the firm must** take to meet these expectations. The **internal business perspective** identifies the **business processes that have the greatest impact on customer satisfaction**, such as quality and employee skills.

(a)   Companies should also attempt to identify and measure their **distinctive competences** and the critical technologies they need to ensure continued leadership. Which processes should they excel at?

(b)   To achieve these goals, **performance measures must relate to employee behaviour**, to tie in the strategic direction with employee action.

(c)   An information system is necessary to enable executives to measure performance. An **executive information system** enables managers to drill down into lower level information.

4.3 Innovation and learning perspective

We briefly discussed the innovation and learning perspective earlier in this Study Text. The question is **'Can we continue to improve and create value?'** Whilst the customer and internal process perspectives identify the **current** parameters for competitive success, the company needs to learn and to innovate to **satisfy future needs**. This might be one of the hardest items to measure.

(a)   How long does it take to develop new products?

(b)   How quickly does the firm climb the experience curve to manufacture new products?

(c)   What percentage of revenue comes from new products?

(d)   How many suggestions are made by staff and are acted upon?

(e)   What are staff attitudes? Some firms believe that employee motivation and successful communication are necessary for organisational learning.

(f)   Depending on circumstances, the company can identify measures for training and long-term investment.

Continuous improvement measures might also be relevant here.

4.4 Financial perspective

From the financial perspective, the question to be asked is: **'How do we appear to shareholders?'** Financial performance indicators indicate 'whether the company's strategies, implementation, and execution are contributing to bottom line management.'

Some analysts consider that financial issues take care of themselves, and that they are only the **result** of the customer, internal process, and innovation and learning issues discussed earlier. This view is rather naive for a number of obvious reasons.

(a)   Money is a resource, and financial measures will ultimately effect a firm's ability to obtain that resource (eg by raising the firm's cost of capital, if shareholders perceive greater risk).

(b)   Well designed financial control systems can actually assist in TQM programmes (eg by identifying variances).

4.5 The vertical vector

Kaplan and Norton's original perspectives may be viewed as hierarchical in nature, with a **vertical vector** running through the measures adopted.

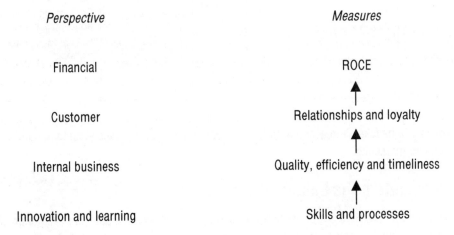

4.6 Understanding the balanced scorecard

Disappointing results might result from a **failure to view all the measures as a whole**. For example, increasing productivity means that fewer employees are needed for a given level of output. Excess capacity can be created by quality improvements. However these improvements have to be exploited (eg by increasing sales). The **financial element** of the balanced scorecard 'reminds executives that improved quality, response time, productivity or new products, benefit the company only when they are translated into improved financial results', or if they enable the firm to obtain a sustainable competitive advantage.

The balanced scorecard can help to measure **performance**. It does not assess **strategy**. As Kaplan and Norton say 'a failure to convert improved operational performance into improved financial performance should send executives back to rethink the company's strategy or its implementation plans.'

4.6.1 Example: a balanced scorecard

Balanced Scorecard

Financial Perspective	
GOALS	**MEASURES**
Survive	Cash flow
Succeed	Monthly sales growth and operating income by division
Prosper	Increase market share and ROCE

Customer Perspective	
GOALS	**MEASURES**
New products	Percentage of sales from new products
Responsive supply	On-time delivery (defined by customer)
Preferred supplier	Share of key accounts' purchases
	Ranking by key accounts
Customer partnership	Number of co-operative engineering efforts

Internal Business Perspective	
GOALS	**MEASURES**
Technology capability	Manufacturing configuration vs competition
Manufacturing excellence	Cycle time
	Unit cost
	Yield
Design productivity	Silicon efficiency
	Engineering efficiency
New product introduction	Actual introduction schedule vs plan

Innovation and Learning Perspective	
GOALS	**MEASURES**
Technology leadership	Time to develop next generation of products
Manufacturing learning	Process time to maturity
Product focus	Percentage of products that equal 80% sales
Time to market	New product introduction vs competition

From a marketing point-of-view, the balanced scorecard enables all the vital perspectives – not just the financial ones – to be taken into account. In fact two of the main perspectives – customer and innovation – relate directly to marketing.

4.7 Implementing the balanced scorecard

The introduction and practical use of the balanced scorecard is likely to be subject to all the problems associated with balancing long-term strategic progress against the management of short-term tactical imperatives. Kaplan and Norton recognise this and recommend an iterative, four-stage approach to the practical problems involved.

(a) **Translating the vision**: the organisation's mission must be expressed in a way that has to be clear operational meaning for each employee.

(b) **Communicating and linking**: the next stage is to link the vision or mission to departmental and individual objectives, including those that transcend traditional short-term financial goals.

(c) **Business planning**: the scorecard is used to prioritise objectives and allocate resources in order to make the best progress towards strategic goals.

(d) **Feedback and learning**: the organisation learns to use feedback on performance to promote progress against all four perspectives.

4.8 Problems with the balanced scoreboard

As with all techniques, problems can arise when it is applied.

Problem	Explanation
Conflicting measures	Some measures in the scorecard such as research funding and cost reduction may naturally conflict. It is often difficult to determine the balance which will achieve the best results.
Selecting measures	Not only do appropriate measures have to be devised but the number of measures used must be agreed. Care must be taken that the impact of the results is not lost in a sea of information. The innovation and learning perspective is, perhaps, the most difficult to measure directly, since much development of human capital will not feed directly into such crude measures as rate of new product launches or even training hours undertaken. It will, rather, improve economy and effectiveness and support the achievement of customer perspective measures.
Expertise	Measurement is only useful if it initiates appropriate action. Non-financial managers may have difficulty with the usual profit measures. With more

Problem	Explanation
	measures to consider this problem will be compounded.
Interpretation	Even a financially-trained manager may have difficulty in putting the figures into an overall perspective.

5 Targets, budgets and ratios

A **budget** is a formal and detailed plan, including targets and the means by which they will be achieved. Problems with budgets include the identification of **limiting factors** and budgetary **slack**. **Variance** reports are a form of feedback, as is the calculation of financial and other **ratios**.

In terms of strategic marketing management, **planned** results often comprise:

(a) Targets for the overall **financial objective**, for each year over the planning period, and other financial strategy objectives such as productivity targets.

(b) Subsidiary **financial targets**

(c) Financial targets in the annual budget (including the sales budget and marketing expenditures budget)

(d) Product-market strategy targets

(e) Targets for each element of the **marketing mix**

5.1 Setting targets

The organisation's objectives provide the basis for setting targets and standards. Each manager's targets will be directed towards achieving the company objectives. Targets or standards:

(a) Tell managers what they are **required to accomplish**, given the authority to make appropriate decisions

(b) Indicate to managers how **well their actual results** measure up against their targets, so that control action can be taken where it is needed

It follows that in setting standards for performance, **it is important to distinguish between controllable or manageable variables and uncontrollable ones**. Any matters which cannot be controlled by an individual manager should be excluded from their standards for performance.

5.2 Budgets as a feedforward control device

Key concept

A **budget** is a plan expressed in money terms. It is also used as the basis for controlling the activities it concerns.

5.2.1 Purposes of a budget

(a) **Co-ordinates** the activities of all the different departments of an organisation; in addition, through participation by employees in preparing a budget, it may be possible to motivate them to raise their targets and standards and to achieve better results.

(b) **Communicates** the policies and targets to every manager in the organisation responsible for carrying out a part of that plan.

(c) **Controls** by having a plan against which actual results can be progressively compared.

(d) **Motivates** by setting challenging but achievable targets.

5.2.2 Preparing budgets

Procedures for preparing the budget are contained in the **budget manual**, which indicates:

- People responsible for preparing budgets
- The order in which they must be prepared
- Deadlines for preparation
- Standard forms

The preparation and administration of budgets is usually the responsibility of a **budget committee**. Every part of the organisation should be represented on the committee.

The preparation of a budget may take weeks or months, and the budget committee may meet several times before the master budget is finally agreed. Functional budgets and cost centre budgets prepared in draft may need to be amended many times over as a consequence of discussions between departments, changes in market conditions, reversals of decisions by management and so on during the course of budget preparation.

5.2.3 The budget period

A budget does not necessarily have to be restricted to a one year planning horizon. The factors which should influence the **budget period** are as follows.

(a)   **Lead times**. A plan decided upon now might need a **considerable time** to be put into operation. Many companies expect growth in market share to take a number of years.

(b)   **In the short-term some resources are fixed**. The fixed nature of these resources, and the length of time which must elapse before they become variable, might therefore determine the planning horizon for budgeting.

(c)   All budgets involve some element of **forecasting and even guesswork**, since future events cannot be quantified with accuracy.

(d)   Since **unforeseen events** cannot be planned for, it would be a waste of time to plan in detail too far ahead.

(e)   Most budgets are prepared over a one-year period to enable managers to plan and control **financial results for the purposes of the annual accounts**.

5.2.4 The principal budget factor

The first task in budgeting is to identify the principal (key, limiting) budget factor. This is the factor which puts constraints on growth. The principal budget factor could be:

(a)   Normally, sales demand, ie a company is restricted from making and selling more of its products because there would be no sales demand for the increased output at a price which would be acceptable/profitable to the company.

(b)   Resources machine capacity, distribution and selling resources, the availability of key raw materials or the availability of cash and so on.

(c)   Once this factor is defined then the rest of the budget can be prepared.

Action Programme 2

What do you think is the crucial difference between the principal budget factors of an organisation producing confectionery and a non-profit orientated organisation such as a hospital?

5.2.5 Budgets and forecasts

(a)   **A forecast is an estimate of what might** happen in the future.

(b)   In contrast, a **budget is a plan of what the organisation would like** to happen, and what it has set as a target, although it should be realistic and so it will be based to some extent on the forecasts prepared.

(c)   However, in formulating a budget, **management will be trying to establish some control over the conditions** that will apply in the future. (For example, in setting a sales budget, management must decide on the prices to be charged and the advertising expenditure budget, even though they might have no control **over other** market factors.)

    (i)   Management might be able to take **control action** to bring forecasts back into line **with the budget**.

    (ii)   Alternatively, management will have to accept that the budget will not be achieved, or it will be exceeded, depending on what the current forecasts include.

Budgets perform a dual role.

(a)   They **incorporate forecasting** and planning information.

(b)   They **incorporate control measures**, in that they plan how resources are to be used to achieve the targets, and they can be flexed for corrective action.

5.2.6 Problems in constructing budgets

(a)   Difficulties in identifying **principal budget factors**

    •   Sales demand may not be known
    •   Resources may not be known

(b)   **Unpredictability** in economic conditions or prices of inputs

(c)   Because of **inflation**, it might be difficult to estimate future price levels for materials, expenses, wages and salaries.

(d)   **Managers might be reluctant to budget accurately**.

    (i)   **Slack**. They may overstate their expected expenditure, so that by having a budget which is larger than necessary, they will be unlikely to overspend the budget allowance. (They will then not be held accountable in control reports for excess spending.)

    (ii)   They may **compete** with other departments for the available resources, by trying to expand their budgeted expenditure. Budget planning might well intensify inter-departmental rivalry and the problems of 'empire building'.

(e)   **Inter departmental rivalries** might ruin the efforts towards co-ordination in a budget.

(f)   Employees might resist budget plans either because the plans are not properly communicated to them, or because they feel that the budget puts them 'under pressure' from senior managers to achieve better results.

Exam tip

> You will have come across budgets and budgeting in your earlier studies or work experience. It is important to recognise that CIM examiners are increasingly requiring that Diploma students demonstrate their appreciation of financial aspects and their implications for both marketing and business. You must be prepared to support plans with budgets both in the context of mini-cases and major case study exercises. These should:
>
> - Indicate your awareness of the process of budgeting and its significance
> - Identify key headings and inclusions.

5.2.7 Sales budget

(a) **A preliminary sales estimate**

- A study of normal business growth
- A forecast of general business conditions
- A knowledge of potential markets for each product
- The practical judgement of sales and management staff
- A realisation of the effect on sales of basic changes in company policy

(b) The **adjustment of the above preliminary sales estimate**

- Seasonal nature of the business
- The viewpoint of optimum selling prices
- Overall production or purchasing capacity
- Viewpoint of securing even manufacturing loads
- Overall selling expenses and net profits
- The financial capacity of the business

(c) The adjusted anticipated sales by value and quantity contained in the sales budget should then be classified by commodities, departments, customers, salesmen, countries, terms of sale, methods of sale, methods of delivery and urgency of delivery (rush or normal).

5.2.8 The expense budgets related to marketing

(a) *Selling expenses budget*

- Salaries and commission
- Materials, literature, samples
- Travelling (car cost, petrol, insurance) and entertaining
- Staff recruitment and selection and training
- Telephones and telegrams, postage
- After-sales service
- Royalties/patents
- Office rent and rates, lighting, heating
- Office equipment
- Credit costs, bad debts

(b) *Advertising budget*

- Trade journal – space
- Prestige media – space
- PR space (costs of releases, entertainment)
- Blocks and artwork
- Advertising agents commission
- Staff salaries, office costs
- Posters

- • Cinema
- • TV
- • Signs

(c) *Sales promotion budget*

- • Exhibitions: space, equipment, staff, transport, hotels, bar
- • Literature: leaflets, catalogues
- • Samples/working models
- • Point of sale display, window or showroom displays
- • Special offers
- • Direct mail shots – enclosure, postage, design costs

(d) *Research and development budget*

- • Market research – design and development and analysis costs
- • Packaging and product research – departmental costs, materials, equipment
- • Pure research – departmental costs materials, equipment
- • Sales analysis and research
- • Economic surveys
- • Product planning
- • Patents

(e) *Distribution budget*

- • Warehouse/deposits – rent, rates, lighting, heating
- • Transport – capital costs
- • Fuel – running costs
- • Warehouse/depot and transport staff wages
- • Packing (as opposed to packaging)

5.3 Variance analysis

It is fine to have a set of budgets and standards, but how do you apply them in practice? The use of budgets as a control device is often achieved through **variance analysis**. Quite complex variance analysis systems are applied to production costs: these need not concern us here, but a brief description of the technique might help, as it is relevant to marketing costs. The essence of a variance is that it directs attention to a specific area of management responsibility.

5.3.1 Example

Assume that, in a month, **budgeted** sales revenue amount to £1m. Actual sales amount to £960,000. The total **sales variance** is thus £40,000 (ie £1m – £960,000). It is adverse as we have sold less than planned. So far so good. But with a little bit more information we can find out a lot more.

Let us assume that, in our original budget, the £1m sales revenue was to result from selling 100,000 units at £10 each. However the cost of a key component rose suddenly, so we had to increase the selling price to £12 a unit. We sold only 80,000 units: total sales revenue amounted to £960,000. There is a total negative sales variance of £40,000 as actual sales are less than we anticipated (£1,000,000). This variance of £40,000 can be analysed into two elements.

(a) **Price variance**. We put up the prices to receive extra revenue from the actual sales

(£12 – £10) × 80,000 = £160,000, a positive or **favourable** price variance

(b) **Volume variance**. We sold fewer, so in volume terms, at the budgeted/standard price of £10 we have a negative or **adverse** volume variance of (100,000 – 80,000) × £10 or £200,000.

(c)		£
	Budgeted sales revenue	1,000,000
	Price variance	160,000
	Volume variance	(200,000)
	Actual sales revenue	£960,000

Clearly, the two aspects of the total sales variance are linked; the analysis explores the background to the failure to achieve the budgeted turnover. Under other circumstances we might find that, for instance, a negative sales variance could be traced entirely to excessive discounting: volume might be satisfactory but only achieved by cutting prices.

Other applications of sales variances include the **sales mix variance**. A firm might sell more of one product in a range and less of another than you anticipated, or there might have been some difference in prices. Variances can also be used in analysing other marketing costs, such as distribution expenditure.

5.4 Tolerance limits for variances at planning level

No corporate plan has the detail or accuracy that a budget has. Consequently, the tolerance limits giving early warning of deviations from the plan should be wider. For example, if tolerance limits in budgetary control are variance ± 5% from standard, then corporate planning tolerance limits might be set at ± 10% or more from targets.

Whatever the tolerance limits are, the reporting of results which go outside (either favourably or adversely) the limits must be prompt. If sales have dropped well below target, the reasons must be established quickly and possible solutions thought about. For example if a company's products unexpectedly gain second highest market share, the questions that should be asked are as follows.

- How did it happen?
- Has profit suffered?
- Can second place be made secure, and if so, how?
- Can the market leader be toppled? (And if so, is this profitable?)

5.5 Ratio analysis

> Marketing mix relevant ratios tend to combine financial and non-financial measures.

A company's financial statements provide sources of useful information about its condition.

The analysis and interpretation of these statements can be carried out by calculating certain ratios and then **using the ratios for comparison**.

(a)   **One year and the next** for a particular business, in order to identify any trends, or significantly better or worse results than before.

(b)   **One business and another**, to establish which business has performed better, and in what ways. You should be very careful, when comparing two different businesses, to ensure that the accounts have been prepared in a similar way.

Below we identify some typical ratios used.

5.6 Profitability and performance ratios

5.6.1 Profit margin

Profit margin is the **ratio of profit before interest and tax over sales turnover**. For example, in 20X0, ARC's profit margin was 17.6% (hence costs as a percentage of sales were 82.4%). **Profit Before Interest**

and Tax (PBIT), is also known as the operating profit. In the accounts of ARC Ltd, the PBIT for 20X1 is £20,640,000 and for 20X0, £9,400,000. The profit margins for the two years are:

20X0	20X1
$\dfrac{9{,}400}{53{,}470} = 17.6\%$	$\dfrac{20{,}640}{98{,}455} = 21\%$

If the ratio of costs to sales goes down, the profit margin will automatically go up. For example, if the cost: sales ratio changes from 80% to 75%, the profit margin will go up from 20% to 25%. What does this mean?

- A **high margin** indicates costs are controlled and/or sales prices are high.
- A low margin can mean high costs or low prices.

Asset turnover is the ratio of sales turnover in a year to the amount of **net assets** which should equate to the amount invested in the business. In the accounts of ARC Ltd, the asset turnover for 20X1 and 20X0 is:

20X0	20X1
$\dfrac{53{,}470}{9{,}000} = 5.9 \text{ times}$	$\dfrac{98{,}455}{16{,}100} = 6.1 \text{ times}$

This means that for every £1 of assets employed in 20X0, the company generated sales turnover of £5.90 per annum. To utilise assets more efficiently, managers should try to create a higher volume of sales and a higher asset turnover ratio.

5.6.2 Return on capital employed (ROCE)

Return on capital employed (ROCE) is the amount of profit as a percentage of capital employed (net assets). If a company makes a profit of £30,000, we do not know how good or bad the result is until we look at the amount of capital which has been invested to achieve the profit. £30,000 might be a good sized profit for a small firm, but this would not be good enough for a 'giant' firm such as Marks & Spencer. For this reason, it is helpful to measure performance by relating profits to capital employed. The ROCE of ARC Ltd for 20X1 and 20X1 is:

20X0	20X1
$\dfrac{9{,}400}{9{,}000} = 104.4\%$	$\dfrac{20{,}640}{16{,}100} = 128\%$

You may already have realised that there is a mathematical connection between return on capital employed, profit margin and asset turnover:

$$\frac{\text{Profit}}{\text{Capital employed}} = \frac{\text{Profit}}{\text{Sales}} \times \frac{\text{Sales}}{\text{Capital employed}}$$

ie ROCE = Profit margin × Asset turnover

This is important. If we accept that ROCE is the single most important measure of business performance, comparing profit with the amount of capital invested, we can go on to say that business performance is dependent on two separate 'subsidiary' factors, each of which contributes to ROCE, **profit margin** and **asset turnover**.

A single ratio is nearly meaningless. What is important is the movement in that ratio over time and the comparison of that ratio with other companies in a similar business.

5.6.3 Operational ratios

Operational ratios relate to the cash cycle of a business.

(a)   A business which cannot pay its debts as they fall due is insolvent. **Liquidity** is a critical and urgent issue, which is why working capital is monitored thoroughly. A company facing crises in liquidity has few options.

(b)   Often external parties, such a banks, will provide extra funds, but in extreme cases **marketing strategies must be devised to raise as much cash as possible**.

Consequently the finance function will monitor **turnover periods**. These ratios, usually expressed in days, measure how long or how many times the business is exchanging cash over a period of time.

Debtors' turnover period, or **debt collection period**: the length of the credit period taken by customers or the time between the sale of an item and the receipt of cash for the sale from the customer.

(a)   This describes the level of debtors compared with the sales turnover. So the ratio for ARC Ltd is:

	2005	2006
$\dfrac{\text{Debtors}}{\text{Sales}}$	$\dfrac{8{,}900}{53{,}470} = 16\%$	$\dfrac{27{,}100}{98{,}455} = 28\%$

(b)   This can be expressed in days. By multiplying our ratio by 365 we recognise that the debtors are on average:

2005	2006
$\dfrac{8{,}900}{53{,}470} \times 365 = 61 \text{ days}$	$\dfrac{26{,}700}{98{,}455} \times 365 = 99 \text{ days}$

We can, of course, do similar turnover calculations for **stock turnover period**. This is the length of time an item stays in stores before use.

$$\frac{\text{Average finished goods stocks (use closing stock)}}{\text{Total cost of goods sold in the period}} \times 365 \text{ days}$$

	2005	2006
Stock turnover period	$\dfrac{5{,}000}{40{,}653} \times 365 = 45 \text{ days}$	$\dfrac{15{,}000}{70{,}728} \times 365 = 77 \text{ days}$

5.6.4 Corporate ratios

Marketing strategies **contribute** towards these, but they are at **too high a level of control** to be useful as control measures over marketing activities in particular.

(a)   **Profitability**. Marketing personnel have little direct control over the cost structure of the company, and so while they do contribute to profitability, they cannot control it.

(b)   **ROCE**, as conventionally measured, is a control measure for the company as a whole.

Marketing relevant ratios are a **mix of financial ratios and non-financial ratios**. For example:

(a)   **Financial ratio only**

(i)   Sales revenue or marketing expenditure can be compared: **over time**, against **budget** or against **competition**.

	2005	2006
Revenue	£10m	£15m

2005/2006 gives an increase of 1.5:1.

(ii)   There may be relationships between different variables. For example

	2005	2006
Revenue	£10m	£15m
Bad debts	0.5m	1.2m
Bad debts/revenue	1:20 or 5%	2:25 or 8%

Comparing these over time suggests that while **income has increased**, the **quality of sales** (in terms of **creditworthiness**) has fallen, as bad debts are 8% of revenue rather than 5%. Perhaps the sales force has been too generous.

(b)   **A mixture of financial ratios and non-financial data**

	2005	2006
Revenue	£10m	£15m
Sales personnel	50	60

Revenue has increased by 50% whereas the sales force has increased by 20%.

	2005	2006
Revenue per sales employee	£0.2m	£0.25m

The sales force is more productive in 2006 than in 2005.

(c)   **Non-financial data only**

This can refer to almost any aspect of a company's operations. We are concerned with marketing.

	2005	2006
Sales orders	250	300
Sales leads	1,000	1,025
Sales personnel	50	60

In 2005, 25% of leads turned into orders, whereas in 2006 this has increased to 29%, so the sales force is more effective. The number of orders by sales person has stayed the same.

The next section identifies some ways you can apply performance measures in the marketing mix.

6 Marketing mix effectiveness

FAST FORWARD

Each element of the marketing mix must be subject to its own measures of performance.

Marketing managers are responsible for monitoring their progress towards the agreed targets and objectives. To do this it is necessary to evaluate the marketing mix effectiveness. This section will consider ways of controlling the effectiveness of four of the mix elements.

- Personal selling
- Advertising and sales promotions
- Pricing
- Channels of distribution

6.1 Personal selling

The effectiveness of personal selling can be measured for:

- The sales force as a whole
- Each group of the sales force (eg each regional sales team)
- Each individual salesperson

If there are telephone sales staff, their performance should be measured separately from the travelling sales staff.

Measures of performance would compare actual results against a target or standard.

- Sales, in total, by customer, and by product
- Contribution, in total, by customer and by product
- Selling expenses (budget versus actual) in relation to sales
- Customer call frequency
- Average sales value per call
- Average contribution per call
- Average cost per call
- Average trade discount
- Number of new customers obtained
- Percentage increase in sales compared with previous period
- Average number of repeat calls per sale
- Average mileage travelled per £1 sales

It is not an easy task to decide what the standards should be. It is important not to assume that the efficient sales person who makes ten calls a day is doing a better job than the colleague who makes fewer calls but wins more orders.

There can be a big difference between (a) net sales (ie sales after returns and discounts) and (b) profits or contribution. The costs of selling and distribution can be a very large proportion of an organisation's total costs, and so the performance of a sales force should be based on productivity and profitability, rather than sales alone.

6.2 The effectiveness of advertising

Performance measures for advertising

(a) **Exposure**. Exposure can be measured in terms of frequency (eg the number of times a TV advertisement is screened) and the number of potential customers reached. One TV advertisement might reach two million people; by repeating the advertisement, the intention would be to reach people who missed the advertisement previously, but also to reinforce the message through repetition to people who have seen it before.

(b) **Awareness**. Awareness of the existence of a product, or awareness of certain particular features of a product. Awareness could be measured by recall tests or recognition tests.

(c) **Sales** (volume and/or revenue). Advertising is often intended to increase sales but the effect of advertising on sales is not easy to measure. Why should this be?

    (i) Advertising is only one part of a marketing mix. Other factors influencing sales might be price changes, whether intermediaries have stocked enough of the products to meet an increase in demand, and competitors' actions.

    (ii) Advertising might succeed in **maintaining** a firm's existing market share, without actually increasing sales.

(d) **Profits**. The difficulties of measuring the effect of an advertising campaign on profits are therefore the same as those described in (c) above. Breakeven analysis might be used to calculate the volume of extra sales required to cover the (fixed) costs of the advertising. In monitoring the effects of a campaign, management might be able to judge whether this minimum increase in sales has or has not, in all probability, been achieved. However, advertising might be necessary to build a brand or for management to invest in it.

(e) **Attitudes**. The aim of a campaign might be expressed in terms of 'x% of customers should show a preference for Product A over rival products'.

(f) **Enquiries**. Advertising might be aimed at generating extra enquiries from potential customers. Where possible, enquiries should be traced to the advertisement. For example, a customer reply coupon in a magazine advertisement should be printed with an identification number or label, identifying the magazine and date of its issue.

It is difficult to measure the **success of an advertising** campaign, although volume of sales may be a short-term guide.

(a) A campaign to launch a new product, however, may have to be judged over a longer period of time (ie to see how well the product establishes itself in the market).

(b) Advertising's main purpose in the communication mix is to create **awareness** and **interest**.

(c) The effectiveness of advertising is therefore usually measured by marketing researchers in terms of **customer attitudes** or **psychological response**. Most of the money is spent by agencies on **pre-testing** the given advertisement or campaign before launching it into national circulation. Relatively less tends to be spent on **post-testing** the effect of given advertisements and campaigns.

Post-testing involves finding out how well people can **recall** an advertisement and the product it advertises, and whether (on the basis of a sample of respondents) attitudes to the product have changed since the advertising campaign.

Marketing at Work

New financial service brands including *Virgin Direct* and *Goldfish* failed to convert high levels of awareness into new business.

'The brands, supported by estimated ad budgets of about £5m and £10m respectively and featuring Richard Branson and Billy Connolly, were ever-present on TV at the end of 1996, with Goldfish securing 30 per cent brand awareness for its credit card and Virgin 13 per cent for its products. But neither converted that awareness into new business, according to exclusive research on new financial service and loyalty schemes conducted by the RSL Strategic Initiatives Monitor.

Its survey showed that less high-profile brands such as *MBNA's* credit card, which had an awareness of only ten per cent, achieved a holding of two per cent – outstripping its higher spending rivals.

Significantly the reasons for changing suggest that credit card holders are looking for immediate benefits rather than the promise of rebates in the future from their cards. Over a third of new cardholders mention low APR (annual percentage rate – broadly, interest rate) and a quarter 'no annual fee' as reasons for taking new cards. In contrast only six per cent were attracted by points or tokens offered, while five per cent claim to have switched because they banked with the card issuer.

6.3 Justifying advertising

It would seem sensible too, to try to consider the effectiveness of advertising in terms of **cost, sales and profit**, but only if the aim of an advertising campaign was directed towards boosting sales. If there is a noticeable increase in sales volume as a result of an advertising campaign, it should be possible to estimate the extent to which advertising might have been responsible for the extra sales and contribution, and the extra net profit per £1 of advertising could be measured.

6.4 The effectiveness of sales promotions

There is often a direct link between below-the-line advertising (sales promotions) and short-term sales volume.

(a) The **consumer sales response** to the following is readily measurable.

- Price reductions as sales promotions (for example introductory offers)
- Coupon 'money-off' offers
- Free sendaway gifts
- On-pack free gift offers
- Combination pack offers

(b) It might also be possible to measure the link between sales and promotions for industrial goods, for example special discounts, orders taken at trade fairs or exhibitions and the response to trade-in allowances.

(c) However, there are other promotions where the effect on sales volume is **indirect** and not readily measurable, for example sponsorship, free samples, catalogues, point-of-sale material and inducements.

(d) Promotions may go hand-in-hand with a direct advertising campaign, especially in the case of consumer products, and so the effectiveness of the advertising and the sales promotions should then be considered together.

A manufacturer can try to control sales promotion costs by:

(a) Setting a **time limit** to the campaign (for example, money off coupons, free gift offers etc must be used before a specified date).

(b) **Restricting the campaign** to certain areas or outlets.

(c) Restricting the campaign to **specific goods** (for example, to only three or four goods in the manufacturer's product range, or only to products which are specially labelled with the offer).

6.5 Pricing

6.5.1 Aspects to pricing

(a) **Discount policy should be directed** towards: encouraging a greater volume of sales, and/or obtaining the financial benefits of earlier payments from customers, which ought to exceed the costs of the discounts allowed.

(b) Sales prices are set with a view to the total **sales volume** they should attract.

    (i) **New product pricing policy** might be to set high **skimming** prices or low **penetration** prices.

        (1) For skimming prices, whether they have been too high, because the market has grown faster than anticipated, leaving the organisation with a low market share because of its high prices.

        (2) For penetration prices, whether the price level has succeeded in helping the market to grow quickly and the organisation to grab its target share of the market.

    (ii) Decisions to raise prices or lower prices will be based on assumptions about the **elasticity of demand**. Did actual increases or decreases in demand exceed or fall short of expectation?

(c)   An aspect of **product-market strategy** and positioning is the mixture of product quality and price. An organisation might opt for a **high price and high quality** strategy, or **a low price and average quality** strategy for example. Actual price performance can be judged:

   (i)   By comparing the organisation's prices with those of competitors, to establish whether prices were comparatively low, average or high, as planned

   (ii)   By judging whether the mix of product quality and price appears to have been effective

Marketing at Work

Some of the most familiar ways to market consumer goods are proving to be costly failures.

Recent research has begun to tell the makers of consumer goods which types of marketing actually work. Marketing is not about to become a science, but it will henceforth be easier to tell one half of the marketing budget from the other.

One surprise concerns price cuts. Packaged-goods firms spend some $70 billion a year on various promotions. Among marketing men, however, price cuts remained as popular as ever. It is an article of faith that they both reward loyal customers and woo new ones. Now even this is in question.

(a)   For a start, consumers say they prefer incentives other than price.

(b)   Price cuts also appear to have little lasting effect on sales volumes. In an unpublished study, a team at Purdue University led by Doug Bowman spent eight years scrutinising how almost 1,600 households in America bought a typical household product such as detergent. The study found that consumers exposed to repeated price cuts learnt to ignore the usual price.

(c)   Neither do price cuts attract new customers. The unexpected explanation for this was that almost all the customers buying the discounted product had tried it before. It seems that brands are built in other ways: price cuts are simply a gift to loyal customers. Little wonder that only a third of all promotions pay for themselves.

Another trick is to dazzle the jaded consumer with variety. At one time, *Procter & Gamble* was selling 35 variations of *Crest* toothpaste and different nappies for girls and boys. The average supermarket in America devotes 20ft of shelving to medicine for coughs and colds. Most of this choice is trumpery.

In fact, more choice does not translate into more sales. Ravi Dhar, of Yale University, examined how students decided what to buy, based on the number of versions of each product-category on offer. As the choice increased, so did the likelihood that students would not buy anything at all. John Gourville at Harvard Business School believes that some types of choice are more troublesome than others. His research suggests that consumers like to be offered choices in a single dimension: different sizes of cereal packet, say. If they are asked to make too many trade-offs, such as whether to buy a computer with a modem or speakers, consumers start to feel anxious or even irritated.

The custom in marketing departments of moving managers off a brand within two years has rewarded those who boost sales, even if their favoured marketing strategy achieves no lasting good. Some firms, such as *Coca-Cola* and *AT&T*, now employ brand equity managers to oversee the long-term health of their brands.

There are also new ways of using detailed information to target promotions. Buzzwords abound – relationship marketing, key account management, and in the world of packaged goods, efficient consumer response (ECR).

6.6 Channels of distribution

Some organisations might use channels of distribution for their goods which are unprofitable to use, and which should either be abandoned in favour of more profitable channels, or made profitable by giving some attention to cutting costs or increasing minimum order sizes.

It might well be the case that an organisation gives close scrutiny to the profitability of its products, and the profitability of its market segments, but does not have a costing system which measures the costs of distributing the products to their markets via different distribution channels.

A numerical example might help to illustrate this point. Let us suppose that Biomarket Ltd sells two consumer products, X and Y, in two markets A and B. In both markets, sales are made through the following outlets.

- Direct sales to supermarkets
- Wholesalers

Sales and costs for the most recent quarter have been analysed by product and market as follows.

	Market A			Market B			Both markets		
	X	Y	Total	X	Y	Total	X	Y	Total
	£'000	£'000	£'000	£'000	£'000	£'000	£'000	£'000	£'000
Sales	900	600	1,500	1,000	2,000	3,000	1,900	2,600	4,500
Variable production costs	450	450	900	500	1,500	2,000	950	1,950	2,900
	450	150	600	500	500	1,000	950	650	1,600
Variable sales Costs	90	60	150	100	100	200	190	160	350
Contribution	360	90	450	400	400	800	760	490	1,250
Share of fixed costs (production, sales, distribution, administration)	170	80	250	290	170	460	460	250	710
Net profit	190	10	200	110	230	340	300	240	540

This analysis shows that both products are profitable, and both markets are profitable. But what about the channels of distribution? A further analysis of market A might show the following.

	Market A		
	Supermarkets	Wholesalers	Total
	£'000	£'000	£'000
Sales	1,125	375	1,500
Variable production costs	675	225	900
	450	150	600
Variable selling costs	105	45	150
Contribution	345	105	
Direct distribution costs	10	80	90
	335	25	360
Share of fixed costs	120	40	160
Net profit/(loss)	215	(15)	200

This analysis shows that although sales through wholesalers make a contribution after deducting direct distribution costs, the profitability of this channel of distribution is disappointing, and some attention ought perhaps to be given to improving it.

7 The auditing process as a control mechanism

A **marketing audit** performs a dual role in checking both where we are and where we have come from. In other words marketing planning is a **cyclical** or **iterative process**.

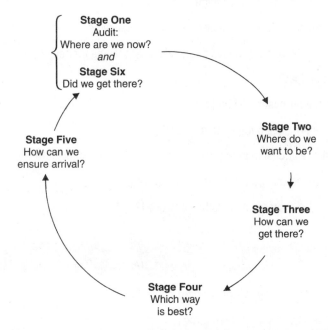

Source: adapted from Wilson, Gilligan, Pearson

Chapter Roundup

- Marketing activities depend upon the actions and reactions of **people**: this complicates the problem of feedback and control.

- All **feedback control systems** work in the same way. Progress is measured and compared with plan; discrepancies lead to control action. **Single loop feedback** leads to changes in activity; **double loop feedback** is used to modify the plan itself. **Feedforward control** makes a comparison between the plan and a forecast based on actual current achievement; control action is initiated before activity is complete.

- Corporate control systems should be able to influence people towards the achievement of corporate goals. Key factors and managers should be identified and reporting and control systems focused on them. **Critical success factors** should form the basis of control systems.

- Control action must not prejudice **longer-term development** in order to improve results in the short-term.

- The **balanced scorecard** concept is now widely accepted. The four usual perspectives are: **customer**; **financial**; **internal business**; and **innovation and learning**. Suitable goals and relevant performance measures must be established for each perspective.

- A **budget** is a formal and detailed plan, including targets and the means by which they will be achieved. Problems with budgets include the identification of **limiting factors** and budgetary **slack**. **Variance** reports are a form of feedback, as is the calculation of financial and other **ratios**.

- Marketing mix relevant ratios tend to combine financial and non-financial measures.

- Each element of the marketing mix must be subject to its own measures of performance.

Quick Quiz

1   What is feedback?

2   What are the sources of advantage?

3   What are the four standard perspectives of a balanced scorecard?

4   What is the role of the balanced scorecard in assessing strategy?

5   What is a budget?

6   What are the purposes of a budget?

7   What is the principal budget factor, usually?

8   What is the relationship between profit margin, ROCE and asset turnover?

9   What are the normal purposes of advertising?

10   How can sales promotion costs be controlled?

Answers to Quick Quiz

1   Information as to progress provide for control purposes

2   Superior skills and superior resources

3   Customer; financial; internal business; innovation and learning

4   It has none; it is for assessing performance

5   A plan expressed in money terms

6   Co-ordinate actions; communicate targets; control progress

7   Sales

8   ROCE = profit margin $\times$ asset turnover

9   To increase awareness and interest

10   By restricting the campaign to specific goals, outlets or time periods

Action Programme Review

1   The plan has to be altered as a result of feedback.

     (a)   This is a **standard**, in other words, a measure of expected performance.

     (b)   Counselling is control action to improve the individual's performance. Dismissal is control action too, if the employee is replaced by someone who performs better, thus raising the performance of the department as a whole.

     (c)   This is feedforward control based on culture.

2   A sweet company's principal budget factor is likely to be demand, as expressed in sales forecasts. A hospital's principal budget factor is almost certainly going to be the funding allocation from the government.

Now try Question 11 at the end of the Study Text

Part F

Mini-cases in the examination

Mini-cases in the examination

Introduction

With the obvious exceptions of the dedicated case study paper, *Strategic Marketing in Practice*, each exam of Professional Post-graduate Diploma level incorporates a 50 mark mini-case study as Part A. Candidates often have difficulty with mini-cases, so this chapter offers detailed guidance on how to tackle them. Question practice can be found in the BPP *Practice & Revision Kit* for this subject – an order form can be found at the end of the Study Text.

1 What is a mini-case?

A mini-case in the examination is a 500–800 word long description of an organisation at a moment in time. You first see it in the examination room and so you have a maximum of 72 minutes to read, understand, analyse and answer the mini-case. The length of the mini-case is likely to be between one and two pages of A4.

The approach is the same for all the subjects and so practice in one area will benefit your other Diploma subjects.

The mini-case carries 50% of the available marks in the examination. Students who fail a Diploma paper are often found to have had difficulties with the mini-case. It is worth noting that a good result on the mini-case can be used to compensate for a weaker performance in part B of the paper.

As mini-cases are fundamental to your exam success, you should be absolutely clear about what mini-cases are, CIM's purpose in using them, what the examiners seek and then, in context, to consider how best they should be tackled.

1.1 The purpose of the mini-case

Diploma examiners require students to demonstrate not only their knowledge of marketing management, but also their ability to use that knowledge in a commercially credible way in the context of a real business scenario.

You cannot pass this part of the paper by regurgitating theory. You must be able to apply the theory to real problems. The mini-case is included to test your competence in analysing information and making clear and reasonable decisions.

1.2 The examiners' requirements

The examiners are the consumers of your examination script. You should remember first and foremost that they need a paper which makes their life easy. That means that the script should be well laid out, with plenty of white space and neat readable writing. All the basic rules of examination technique must be applied, but because communication skills are fundamental to the marketer, the ability to communicate clearly is particularly important.

The examination is your opportunity to market yourself to the examiner, in this case as a marketing professional competent in the skills of analysis and evaluation. As actions speak louder than words, a candidate who has failed to plan the answers or who has run out of the resource time, is unlikely to impress.

Management skills are commonly ignored by candidates who fail to recognise their importance. Management is more about thinking than knowing, more about decision than analysis. It is about achieving action through persuasive communication. It is about meeting deadlines. It is therefore about clear, logical analysis under time pressure, which leads to decisive recommendations presented in simple, clear business English.

The six key factors from the above paragraph are:

- Thinking
- Logical analysis
- Decision
- Action
- Persuasive communication
- Business English

All must be demonstrated to the examiners, especially in the case and mini-case study elements of the Diploma examinations.

If you are entering the Diploma by exemption, take particular note of the examiners' requirements. Certificate holders will have encountered mini-cases before. They should note the change in emphasis from the learning of marketing to its management.

Examiners' reports note the reasons why candidates fail. It makes depressing reading to go back over a series of reports because year after year the examiners make the same points and year after year many candidates ignore them! No examiner can understand why candidates refuse to take notice of their requirements. In everyday life we do what our manager instructs, or we leave the job (one way or another). If candidates would only think of the examiners as senior managers at work, and address them accordingly, the pass rate would shoot up.

1.3 Examiners' comments

Examiners' reports on mini-cases repeatedly stress the same points.

(a) Relate the time allocated to the answer to the marks available.

(b) Answer the question asked. Never use a question as a pretext to answer a different one.

(c) Time planning is crucial to success.

(d) Quality and insight are worth more than quantity and detail.

(e) It is essential to write in role.

(f) Intelligently apply knowledge of theory to a marketing problem.

(g) Do not repeat chunks of the mini-case in the answer.

(h) Do not show any analytical work (for example SWOT) unless specifically requested.

(i) Presentation must be of management quality. Spelling and grammar are important, only a certain laxity will be allowed for the pressures of the exam room.

Direct quotes from examiners' reports reinforce the points made in the previous paragraph.

(a) 'The commonest 'self-destruct' faults

- Bad time management
- Using the question as a pretext to answer a different one
- Poor presentation'

(b) 'Your examiners regard badly constructed and unrealistic case solutions as a particularly serious failing among candidates for the professional diploma of a chartered institute.'

(c) 'The gap between question answering and case solving abilities continues to be very marked.'

(d) 'A wider spread of up-to-date knowledge (greater than Coca-Cola and McDonald's) would give the examiner greater confidence in your competence.'

(e)   'Management of any sort, and particularly marketing management, is about thinking rather than knowing. It is for example about selecting the best strategy rather than simply knowing the range of options available.'

(f)   'Preparation time should be spent in practising techniques as much as in learning content.'

(g)   'Diploma candidates not only need to demonstrate their ability to communicate succinctly as a subsidiary test of marketing awareness but in their own interests of scoring higher marks by getting more valid points across in the limited time available in the exam situation.'

(h)   'It is a shame that such basic mistakes mar what are often otherwise diligent and enthusiastic efforts.'

1.4 The expectations of examiners

Examiners are experienced marketing managers. They know that mini-cases give only limited information and that candidates are working under a tight time constraint. They do not, therefore, require considered, fully rounded answers. There is insufficient data and time. The successful candidate learns to work with what is available, to make reasonable assumptions that help in the decision making process, and to present an answer cogently and concisely.

The examiner can only mark within the criteria that have been established. The requirements are set out very clearly. It is not difficult to satisfy them. The well prepared candidate should not fail the mini-case. Since the information is limited, the time is very constrained, and the examiner is looking for evidence of a managerial approach, any candidate that makes reasonable assumptions about the case, takes clear and sensible decisions, and communicates these succinctly must pass.

Also remember that mini-cases are set for all candidates. Some will know absolutely nothing about the industry, some will work in it and be expert. Candidates take the examinations in centres across the world. Therefore the examiner will not ask technical questions about the industry, nor any tied to a specific culture or economy. Questions have to be more general, more open, less specific. However, you will be expected to have acquired a level of business appreciation and marketing knowledge from your other studies.

1.5 Summary

The requirements are as follows.

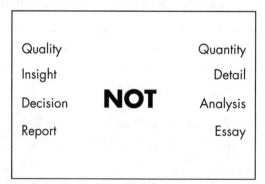

Quality		Quantity
Insight	**NOT**	Detail
Decision		Analysis
Report		Essay

1.6 Management reports in CIM mini-cases

A management report is a specialised form of communication. It is the language used in business. It is not difficult to learn to write in report style, but it does require practice to become fluent. Mini-cases must always be answered in report style.

Management reports are action planning documents and are generally written in the third person. Their role is to make positive recommendations for action. Situational analysis is included only if it is needed to clarify an ambiguity. Examiners complain that many candidates do little more than produce a SWOT analysis as their response to a mini-case. Support material is often included, but as appendices to the body of the report. In CIM mini-case work it is exceptional to include an appendix.

Management reports: the basic rules

- Always head a report with the name of your organisation.
- State to whom it is addressed, from whom it comes, and give the date.
- Head the report (for example 'Marketing research plan for 2004/05').
- Number and sub-number paragraphs. Head them if appropriate.
- Present the contents in a logical order.
- Include diagrams, graphs, tables only if they have positive value.
- Include recommendations for action that are written as intention against time.

If you are forced to use appendices there are two further rules to remember.

- Refer to them within the body of the report (eg 'See Appendix A').
- Indicate when the report concludes (.../ends).

Management reports are written in crisp, no-nonsense business English. There is no room for superlatives, flowery adjectives nor flowing sentences. You are not trying to entertain, simply to present facts as clearly as possible. Think about the style you would adopt if writing a report to senior managers at work.

As we have already said, presentation is of key importance in CIM examinations. The rules are as follows.

- Use a black or a blue pen, never red or green.
- Start your first answer on the facing page of the answer book, never inside the cover.
- Make the first three pages as neat and well laid out as possible, to impress.
- Use plenty of space. Do not crowd your work.
- Number your questions above your answers. Never write in either margin.
- Leave space (four or five lines) between sections of your report.

2 An approach to mini-cases

Mini-cases are easy once you have mastered the basic techniques. The key to success lies in adopting a logical sequence of steps which with practice you will master. You must enter the exam room with the process as second nature, so you can concentrate your attention on the marketing issues which face you.

Students who are at first apprehensive when faced with a mini-case often come to find them much more stimulating and rewarding than traditional examination questions. There is the added security of knowing that there is no single correct answer to a case study.

You will be assessed on your approach, style, creativity and commercial credibility, but you will not be judged against a single 'correct' answer. Treat the mini-case as though it were happening in real life, at work or at a social meeting with a friend. Most of the mini-case is narrative; it tells a story or paints a picture. If a friend says over a drink 'I've got a problem at work' the most usual answer is 'Tell me about it'. The listener will need background information to establish frame reference and to understand the problem. That is what the case narrative is doing. Most of it is background, and it should be read just to grasp the context and flavour of the situation.

It helps to pretend to yourself that the examiner needs your advice. The questions posed indicate the advice which is being sought.

(a)   Just as your friend would not be impressed if you spent half an hour pontificating on how he or she got themselves into this situation, neither will the examiner reward you for analysis of how the situation arose.

(b)   Neither will the examiner be impressed with a long list of 'you could do this ....' 'but on the other hand....' Identify the alternatives, but make a clear recommendation if you want to win friends and influence examiners.

You will be faced with limited information, less than would be available to you in the real world. This is one of the limitations of case study examinations, but everyone is faced with the same constraint. You are able to make assumptions where it is necessary.

A reasonable assumption is logically possible and factually credible. You may need to make and clearly state two or three assumptions in order to tackle a case.

Some students feel uncomfortable that there is no bedrock (an easy, well defined question) on which to build. They feel all at sea and panic.

Preparation is the answer. It is important to practise the technique of handling a mini-case. There are three later in this chapter, and they should be taken individually. For each there are careful instructions and a time guide is given. After you have completed these it will still be necessary for you to develop speed, but the principles needed for success in the examination will have been established. Mini-case scenarios are also included as one of the data sheets in the CIM's *Marketing Success* and these will provide you with regular new material on which to practise.

2.1 An example of a mini-case

This mini-case example is worked through stage by stage to show you the process. This shows you the methodology.

2.2 Direct Lounge Furniture Ltd (DLF)

DLF is owned by two entrepreneurs each of whom built up a separate direct marketing business, one in the East Midlands and one in the West Midlands over a period of some 15 years, before merging three years ago. The main advantages of the merger were joint advertising, wider product ranges, more flexible production and less reliance upon one person. The two owners are good friends and work well together, meeting at least once a week.

Both the two constituent businesses comprise showrooms mainly featuring upholstered three-piece suites finished in Dralon cloth, in a wide variety of styles and colours. This furniture is manufactured in two small factories, each of which has an adjoining showroom.

Sales are achieved by advertising in free newspapers delivered to Midlands households. These advertisements illustrate the furniture on offer, strongly emphasise the lower prices available to the public by buying direct from the manufacturers and of course invite readers to visit the showrooms without obligation.

Upon visiting the showroom the public can look around the products on offer, discuss their individual requirements with a salesperson and be shown round the factory to emphasise the quality of the workmanship, wooden frames etc.

This marketing formula works very well and sales/profits are booming. Customers feel they are involved in the design of their own furniture and that they are getting good value. DLF enjoy high proportions of recommendations and repeat sales.

Buying behaviour patterns are however changing. People are tending to buy individual items rather than the standard three-piece suite (two armchairs plus a 2/3/4 seater settee) and to seek co-ordination with curtains, carpet etc. In partial response to this the East Midlands showroom offers made-to-measure curtains in Dralon to complement or match the upholstery. Another change in the industry is in the foam used for upholstering which was formerly highly flammable and when on fire gave out dense black smoke causing many deaths. Legislation has now been passed enforcing the use of safer foam.

The media exposure of the fire hazard has caused the public to be more careful when choosing furniture and increasing affluence has also resulted in a move up-market by more households.

DLF are well aware that their formula appeals mainly to the more price-conscious households, who have been tolerant of the somewhat less than sophisticated showroom and factory conditions associated with direct marketing of this nature.

2.2.1 Question

You have been called in by DLF as a consultant to advise on expansion options. After conducting a marketing audit and a SWOT analysis you are now evaluating the options for:

- Product development only
- Market development only
- A combination of both product and market development

Submit your report giving the advantages and disadvantages of each of these three options in more detail, stating what control techniques you would recommend in each case.

2.2.2 Analysis

You should immediately identify the following characteristics about the business.

- DLF is a small business.
- They operate in a local market.
- They specialise in the direct marketing of consumer durables.

These characteristics should start to inform your thinking about the case and the nature of the business, for example you can now make the following connections.

(a) *Small business:* may mean limited resources.

(b) *Local market:* local communication media.

(c) *Direct marketing:* control over marketing mix but cost of storage and delivery, credit provision etc.

(d) *Consumer durables:* infrequent purchase, influenced strongly by style, colour, not brand names etc.

The secret of case study questions is to really play the role you have been given. You need to be able to picture this business, its products and showrooms. As soon as you have a mental picture you will be able to fit easily into the role of marketing consultant.

Now read through the case again and identify the key points, strengths, weaknesses etc. You can do this on the examination paper to save time. You need to really think about the narrative and what it is telling you.

Alternatively, or in addition, you can convert the information onto a SWOT chart to help clarify the picture. Remember that you are not presenting this to the examiner, so use a page at the back of your answer book and do not waste too much time on it.

> Remember that weaknesses can always be converted into strengths and that threats can usually be turned to opportunities. Do not waste time worrying about how to categorise an element. It is usually more important that you have identified it.

SWOT of Direct Lounge Furniture Ltd

Strengths	*Weaknesses*
• Owners are friends	Could be a weakness if they fall out; may imply informal systems and procedures
• Established	
• Financially strong; sales and profits high	Resources for expansion limited for a small business

• Good reputation
  –price
  –workmanship
	Perceived as bottom end of market
	
	• Limited geographic market
	• Two unsophisticated showrooms
	• Product oriented
	• Limited product portfolio
	• Little marketing activity

Opportunity	*Threats*
• Higher customer incomes	• Legislation
• Safety awareness pushing demand towards higher value products	• Changing customer needs and attitudes Increased standard of living amongst current customers
• New materials and production techniques which may become available	• Possibility of increased competition

Marketing audit is an assessment of the current marketing activity of DLF. We have uncovered some clues when developing the corporate SWOT.

(a)   The company is product oriented not marketing oriented.

(b)   There is advertising activity but no evidence of a co-ordinated marketing function, therefore no marketing procedures, plans etc.

(c)   We can do a SWOT on the marketing mix.

   (i)   *Product*

      Strength: good workmanship, low prices, range of suites

      Weakness: not a varied product portfolio, one material used, traditional ideas of customer needs

   (ii)   *Promotion*

      Weakness: limited to local advertising, not targeted or controlled. Product oriented by featuring pictures of products

      Strength: good local image and reputation for value for money

   (iii)   *Place*

      Weakness: limited to two showrooms. No information on waiting lists etc

   (iv)   *Price*

      Strength: current pricing policy is a strength while market is price conscious, but the market is changing

Marketing opportunities do exist and some have been identified for us.

(a)   To diversify into new products

   • Curtains
   • Other furniture

(b)   To develop a wider market

(c)   To develop new segments in the current geographic market

(d)   To reposition DLF as a quality product provider

Review the question carefully. We have done the SWOT and the marketing audit. Our response should be based on our analysis of the company. It should not be just a presentation of the analysis.

We are required to evaluate three options and to submit a report indicating the advantages, disadvantages and control techniques in each case.

It is important that you attempt all parts of this question if you want a chance to gain the maximum marks. In this case the question requirements give you an automatic structure to your report.

Before going further you will find it useful to spend 55 minutes preparing your own answer to the question. Compare it with the suggested solution we have provided. Remember that there is no single right answer. Use our solution only as a guide and as an indicator of the process involved.

2.2.3 Solution

Report to:	Managing Directors Direct Lounge Furniture Ltd
From:	A Consultant
Date:	5 April 20XX
Subject:	Evaluation of product/market opportunities for DLF Ltd.

1	**Background**
1.1	Following our initial analysis of DLF's current situation we have found that although the company is in a secure financial position, with no doubt about short-term survival, the medium-term picture is rather bleak.
1.2	The DLF product range is limited to lounge suites, traditionally configured and covered in one fabric, Dralon. This type of lounge furniture is probably in the mature stage and possibly in the decline stage of its life cycle. The DLF position has been weakened by the following macroenvironmental changes.

- Changing customer needs and expectations in home furnishings.
- Higher incomes making demand increasingly price inelastic.
- Safety fears encouraging customers to trade up.

1.3	We would therefore confirm your personal assessment that for DLF to thrive in the medium and long term, positive action must be taken to develop new product/market strategies. It is important that this action is undertaken before declining demand has an adverse impact on profitability and erodes the resources necessary for exploiting a new opportunity.

The options

2	**Product development only**
2.1	Product development could cover any activity from modification of the existing product (lounge suites), to adding new products to the range. We will assume that the option is basically the former.

2.2   *Advantages*

(a)   This would be a market oriented development, allowing products to be designed to meet identified customer needs.

(b)   You are experienced in the business, its production and operational requirements, materials etc.

(c)   You have an established reputation in the business of lounge furniture.

(d)   Product development would allow ranges and lines to be developed to meet the needs of a variety of market segments and would provide a number of opportunities to develop and enhance the business. The workmen have the skills to develop a quality 'made to order' package.

2.3   *Disadvantages*

(a)   You are positioned at the value for money end of the market. Repositioning for a new segment of the market would require a considerable marketing effort and may be easier with a new kind of product, for example dining room furniture.

(b)   Proliferation of product choice would increase the costs of stockholding, requiring a greater variety of raw materials etc.

(c)   Existing showrooms may be unsuitable for attracting a different group of customers.

(d)   Product portfolio is limited. Recession and declining demand for lounge furniture affects the whole business.

2.4   *Controls*

(a)   Enquiry and sales data by product line would be important to assess the profitability of new products offered.

(b)   If the product range was extended to provide all lounge furnishings, for example curtains, cushions, and tables, it would be important to measure the scale of value added sales, by customers purchasing additional items.

(c)   Information on customers would help to identify whether target markets are being attracted. As most products will be delivered, it should be relatively easy to monitor geographic locations and possibly develop a simplified process for classifying residential neighbourhoods.

(d)   There should be controls on production activities such as average stock levels. Order times etc would also be important to monitor efficiency of the operations as a more customer oriented product policy was developed.

3 Market development only

3.1   This would involve looking for new customers for the existing product range. It would imply increasing the geographic spread of the business.

3.2   *Advantages*

(a)   It would require no change to the existing operation at production level.

(b)   It would allow the profitable value for money target customer base to be extended. These are customers who DLF already know well.

(c)   It would require no additional investment in the production resources.

3.3 Disadvantages

(a) It would leave the company product oriented, looking for customers for products, instead of developing products for customers. In the long run this approach will make DLF very vulnerable to competition.

(b) Although this strategy may boost sales in the short run, we know that customer needs and wants are changing and that this low price, traditional product is in decline.

(c) It would require investment in distribution to set up either showrooms or agencies in new areas. These may prove difficult to control.

3.4 Controls

(a) Controls would need to focus on any new distribution channels and salespeople established. Cost of sales and conversions of enquiries would help DLF establish the rate at which the new market became aware of their products.

(b) Given the indicators of general decline in DLF's market, control information would be needed to monitor average customer purchases (two sofas and no chairs), demand for matched curtains, average spend and other purchase patterns. This would provide valuable control information for sales forecasting.

4 Product and market development

4.1
At its extreme, for example moving into high quality kitchen units, product and market developments could be a major diversification, involving not only products but also customers with whom DLF is unfamiliar. However, diversifying into TV cabinets and coffee tables for a made to measure premium market would involve less risk.

4.2 Advantages

(a) It allows DLF to have an effective new start, researching the market to identify product/market opportunities which could be developed.

(b) Assuming that the current cash cow business will be retained at least in the short run, this strategy would diversify the business and so reduce the risk of sudden changes in demand caused by external variables.

(c) A product/market development would allow DLF to completely reposition themselves in the furniture market.

4.3 Disadvantages

(a) The strategy would be risky. The extent of the diversification would indicate how much risk is involved.

(b) It would be expensive, involving investment in both marketing and production.

(c) There is a danger of attempting to develop too many opportunities simultaneously, losing sight of the core business and over-extending resources.

4.4   *Controls*

      (a)   Such a major shift in strategy would require close control. New product sales levels would need to be monitored as would the value of business from new market segments.

      (b)   New distribution channels and promotional activities would probably be needed and these would also require evaluating to assess their effectiveness.

      (c)   Plans and budgets for the separate parts of the business would need establishing, together with administrative systems and procedures. These are unlikely to exist in the current small scale operation.

5   **Conclusions and recommendations**

      (a)   Action is needed to ensure the medium-term survival of DLF.

      (b)   The business has the strengths to extend its product range to meet the needs of new customer segments, in particular high quality, made to order products at premium prices. This extension of the product portfolio should be developed after careful research of the target market.

      (c)   The company should clearly review its mission and should establish financial objectives for the operation. Corporate and marketing plans must be developed as well as a management information system.

A Consultancy will be happy to offer any further assistance to DLF in this activity.

3 Other questions in the examination

Although the questions in Section B are of the more traditional examination style, you must still make certain that you do not answer them in a purely academic manner.

Ensure that you support theory with real world examples and illustrations, use the introductions and conclusions to comment on the value of the concept in question, disadvantages of a technique and so on. You should evaluate every question in terms not only of its content, but also the context in which it is being asked.

Most students will have the knowledge to pass the exam, it is using that information in the 'context' of the question which causes the downfall. A question about the role of planning in the public sector should be answered differently from the same question set in a private sector context.

Make sure you answer the questions set out and watch out for variations in mark allocation made within a question.

These suggested solutions which follow are just that. There is no single correct answer, but use them as a comparison for your own work and an example of the style, approach and the depth needed in the exam.

Remember to practise answers in exam conditions. You will have only 30 minutes per question in the exam room. After allowing planning and review time allow a little over 20 minutes writing time per question. Quality not quantity is required.

Chapter Roundup

- This chapter has explained the nature and purpose of a mini-case. We have used examples from past examination papers to demonstrate how to use our recommended technique and extracts from examiners' reports have illustrated the examiners' requirements and common mistakes made by candidates.

Question and
Answer bank

1 Participation
45 mins

What are the disadvantages of a participative style of leadership? How can these be minimised?

(25 marks)

2 Motivation
45 mins

Outline the principles of motivating staff. Using illustrations from your own observations, which of these principles seem to you to work in practice, and which do not? Give reasons for each of your answers.

(25 marks)

3 Marketing task
45 mins

As markets fragment and life cycles get shorter and less predictable, the nature of the marketing task is changing. Identify the causes of these changes and say how a marketing manager can respond.

(25 marks)

4 Champion of change
45 mins

The recently-appointed Chief Executive Officer (CEO) of the F Steel Company is intent on making the organisation more competitive. He has made it clear that costs are too high and productivity too low. The trade union that represents the steel workers in F Steel Company is well-organised and has promised the workers that it will defend their wage levels and working conditions.

Required

(a) State the forces for change and causes of resistance in the F Steel Company. Classify these according to whether they can be considered as deriving from internal or external sources.

10 marks)

(b) Recommend how the newly-appointed Chief Executive Officer in the F Steel Company might go about managing the process of change.

(15 marks)

(25 marks)

5 Brand stretching
45 mins

As a marketing planner for a financial services company, identify the key elements of a brand strategy and the criteria that should be used in brand stretching decisions.

(25 marks)

6 Integrity
45 mins

The discovery of heavily overstated profits in some of the largest US corporations in 2002 undermined investor confidence in company accounts and called into question the integrity of senior managers, their professional staff and the presumed independence of external auditors.

Required

(a) Describe the *key influences* on the ethical conduct of senior management of business corporations, their professional staff and those involved with auditing their accounts.

(12 marks)

(b) Explain what both businesses and professional bodies can do to influence the ethical behaviour of their organisational members. **(13 marks)**

(25 marks)

7 Expenditure   45 mins

As a marketing manager write a short article for inclusion in a company magazine suggesting how the amount of money spent on marketing communications might be strategically important. Use examples to illustrate your article. **(25 marks)**

8 Hotel company   45 mins

You have applied for a job with a small hotel company that is establishing a formal marketing function for the first time. As part of the interview process, you have been asked to make a short presentation that explains the characteristics of marketing in the service sector. Prepare some notes covering the areas you intend to deal with in your presentation. **(25 marks)**

9 RUS plc   45 mins

RUS plc operates a chain of hotels. Its strategy has been to provide medium-priced accommodation for business people during the week and for families at weekends.

The market has become increasingly competitive and RUS plc has decided to change its strategy. In future, it will provide 'a high-quality service for the discerning guest'.

Required

(a) Explain the relevance of a programme of 'total quality management' for RUS plc in the implementation of its new strategy. **(12 marks)**

(b) Summarise the financial and organisational implications of RUS plc's new strategy. **(13 marks)**

(25 marks)

10 Fleet Water Services Ltd   27 mins

Fleet Water Services Ltd (FWSL) has been formed by centralising a number of regional management units of *Fleet Water*, the holding company. FWSL, which provides a variety of technical services, has been formed so that Fleet Water will benefit from economies of scale. FWSL will sell its services to other companies in the water industry, firms in industries such as brewing and chemicals, and public sector organisations such as hospitals. Water is to be priced according to usage. Water firms need to introduce metering technology; user firms are seeking to manage their use of water more effectively, and FWSL is there to help them.

A major issue to be faced relates to information. FWSL requires a strategy for the use of the information resource. FWSL also needs to install new information systems to get up and running; of these, an accounting system is felt to be most urgent.

Required

FWSL's managers are aware that project management techniques will need to be used in introducing new systems.

(a)   What are the distinguishing characteristics of project management and how can its success be defined?   **(6 marks)**

(b)   Describe the project management techniques which can be used to introduce new information systems to FWSL, and to minimise the risk of the project failing to meet its objectives.   **(9 marks)**

(15 marks)

11 Feedback and control system   45 mins

What factors should be taken into account in the development of a marketing feedback and control system? In what ways might the information possibly be used?   **(25 marks)**

1 Participation

Disadvantages of participative style

There are a number of potential disadvantages of a participative style.

(a)   The degree of participation can vary. A consultative style of leadership allows some participation, and so too does a democratic style. A potential disadvantage of the participative style is that a manager might intend to allow participation to a limited extent, whereas subordinates expect to have an increasingly greater say in decisions that are taken.

(b)   A long time might be required to reach decisions, and the decision reached might be an unsuitable compromise.

(c)   Employees might be motivated to consider the interests of their own group, without having any loyalty for the organisation as a whole. A junior employee in one small section might participate in the decisions of his section, but will have little influence over decisions by his department or division.

(d)   The superior might be able to adopt a participative style, but be unable to reward subordinates for their work. If there is no progress from more effort to more rewards, subordinates might quickly lose interest and motivation.

(e)   Some work does not lend itself to a participative style. Highly programmed, routine work is a case in point. Unless subordinates are allowed to re-structure the jobs in their section so as to remove the monotony from jobs, participation in decision-making will be futile because decisions will be programmed or automatic.

(f)   Not all employees necessarily want to participate in decision-making. Some might be content to accept orders.

(g)   There might be disagreements between subordinates so that some decisions cannot be reached by common agreement. In such cases, the people losing the argument might resent the decision which is taken against them and might try to sabotage subsequent activities in order to prove themselves right.

Minimisation of disadvantages

The disadvantages of a participative style of management might be overcome as follows.

(a)   The extent of participation should be established clearly for everyone to understand. In other words, the leadership style should be consistent.

(b)   Authority should be delegated sufficiently to enable small groups to take decisions about matters which are of some interest to them. One way of doing this in a large organisation might be to split the organisation up into many semi-independent divisions, and to encourage decentralisation within each division.

(c)   Jobs should be re-structured so as to provide challenging work for work groups.

(d)   The participative style should be promoted by senior management and implemented throughout the organisation, provided that the circumstances allow this to be one without adverse consequences.

(e)   Managers should be given powers to reward or punish subordinates, so that subordinates will believe that by making more contributions to group discussions they will eventually receive fair reward.

(f)   Senior managers must pay careful attention to co-ordination of the goals and activities of sub-units within the organisation.

(i)   The goals of the organisation should be made clear to all employees. Decisions by groups should be taken after giving full consideration to the needs of the organisation.

(ii)   A procedure for resolving inter-group differences should be provided. Likert suggested the idea of a linking pin in which the leader of one group is a participating member of a more senior gap, so that there is a continual overlap throughout organisation. The ultimate task of co-ordination would be carried out at board level.

2 Motivation

Background

Motivation is essential if you are to get the 'best' performance from any team. Motivation affects both what individuals do but more importantly their attitude to doing it. In particular front line staff in direct contact with customers have to be motivated to deliver a quality service and 'care' about customers.

Theories of motivation

Because motivation is so important to the effectiveness of a team, it has attracted a lot of attention from management writers. Herzberg identified a range of factors which whilst not acting as positive motivators can and do act as disincentives to work. These are called hygiene factors, and include working conditions, like lighting and heating.

Managers must first ensure that the hygiene factors are in place and can then consider positive motivators, such as job satisfaction. Another theory is Maslow's hierarchy of needs.

Maslow identified a hierarchy which indicates that people have levels through which they progress normally satisfying the most basic needs before moving up through the hierarchy. Although this does not always hold true for many people, the hierarchy does indicate that managers have to think about changing the motivators used, as staff move through the hierarchy, ie at low levels staff may be motivated by money, but at higher levels status and recognition of peers, time off or other rewards like job security may be more effective.

What works?

What actually works as a motivator will depend on the individual and his or her needs at that time. A poor student working in catering can be effectively motivated by financial rewards (tips) to offer high levels of customer care!

In sales teams, motivational schemes are often fairly sophisticated, with awards on the 'best' sales person, incentive gifts, prizes and competitions. This is necessary to get over the particular problems of staff working in isolation, often away from direct support.

In other cases individuals are motivated by the possibility of promotion and status, like those motivated to study for CIM examinations. Participation and involvement in work or a project can also act as a powerful motivator. Teams which are involved and committed to an objective or vision are often highly successful.

It is the job of the manager to find out what motivates staff in any particular environment or situation, and to take action to devise positive schemes to motivate them.

3 Marketing task

Examiner's comments. Better answers focused on a spectrum of issues accelerating the pace of change including demographics, global business and greater competition. Some candidates saw the words, 'product life cycle' and simply talked about the four stages of this model and consequently were awarded very few marks.

Marketers are facing a number of new **strategic challenges** as the environment changes. These include increasing pressure from governments to take a greater account of **green**, **consumer** and **community relations** issues, the growing power of global companies and concentration of power within industries, changing social and cultural trends which bring about fragmentation of markets and innovation based on new technologies and emergent industries which stem from this. The focus of this question will be on the last two of these issues; **market fragmentation** and shorter/less predictable **life cycles**, the cause of these changes and how they affect the practice of marketing.

(a)   **Market fragmentation**

People eat both health food and junk food and have a repertoire of brands depending upon the occasion. A few years ago, accessing daily news was something you generally did by listening to the BBC. Now you can listen to any of the hundreds of celestial, satellite and cable channels, read any one of hundreds of newspapers or magazines, listen to any of the myriad of radio stations or search for a particular topic on the Internet.

(b)   Shorter and less predictable product **life cycles** are a characteristic of high technology products and services. New technology and innovations have escalated over the last 30 years, with new products, concepts, channels and technology being launched at a massive rate. High technology products almost have a built in obsolescence, as technology development never stays still. Predicting the diffusion of innovation rate is very difficult.

Causes of market fragmentation and lack of predictability of life cycles

(a)   **Social change**

The CIM/Henley Centre report, '*Metamorphosis in Marketing*' details how consumer behaviour and attitudes are changing. Traditional consumer life stages are changing. Wells and Guber's traditional family life cycle model which depicts a staged progression from youth to marriage and family to empty nesters is now a much less predictable path. A career for life is no longer the norm, redundancy and self-employment are rising, growing work and affluence of women, so too divorce, caring for elderly parents and middle age inheritances – all of these factors disrupt the pattern and lead to more consumer segments in many markets. The growth in 'minority' lifestyles is creating opportunities for niche brands aimed at consumers with very distinct purchasing habits.

(b)   **Technological innovation** is bringing the ability to create large numbers of product variants without corresponding increases in resources. This is causing markets to become overcrowded. The fragmentation of the media to service ever more specialist and local audiences is denying mass

BPP
PROFESSIONAL EDUCATION

media the ability to assure market dominance for major brand advertisers. This creates **space for niche players** and speeds up the diffusion of **innovation thus shortening life cycles**. The advance in information technology is enabling information about individual customers to be organised in ways that enable highly selective and personal communications. It also fuels **quicker 'me-too' product launches** which potentially shorten product life cycles.

How should the marketing manager respond to these challenges?

Finer segmentation, in response to market fragmentation, looks certain to play an even more crucial role in the marketing strategies in the years ahead. The move from traditional mass marketing to 'micro marketing' is rapidly gaining ground as marketers explore the incremental profit potential of niche markets.

Perhaps the most important response has to come in relation to **long-term marketing strategy**. With less predictable life cycles, marketing managers must redefine the guidelines provided by the traditional PLC. In order for PLC theory to be relevant, some kind of reliable method for **projecting lifespans** of the product is needed. With technology advancing so rapidly, historical data is no longer sufficient to be a useful predictive tool. It has been suggested that the concept of the **Technology Life Cycle** is superior to the PLC concept. A key difference in thinking is that high-tech firms must make a critical decision regarding focus. A company can attempt to follow a technology through its life cycle or specialise in one stage. Whichever is chosen, speed of response becomes vital.

Hooley and Saunders (1993) suggest that in fragmented markets success depends on finding niches where **particular product specifications** are needed, as in the computer software market. As each niche provides little opportunity for growth, a firm needs to find a number of niches with some degree of commonality, to allow economies to be achieved.

In contrast to niche players, brands such as Marks and Spencer and McDonald's over-arch social differences and appeal to **standard needs on an international scale**. As such, marketers are having to stretch their vision to encompass the details and speed of micro-marketing and rapid new product development, global branding, the cost pressures of tertiary brands and the image and service pressures of having a differentiated offering.

4 Champion of change

(a) **Forces for change – internal**

Forceful new CEO
Poor operational performance
High costs
Low productivity

Forces for change – external

Competition from foreign, subsidised steel-makers
High export prices caused by appreciation of the domestic currency
Weak domestic demand for steel
Customer complaints

Forces resisting change – internal

Long-serving managers' complacency
The trade union's attitude

Force resisting change – external

Growing demand in Pacific rim countries

(b)   *Lewin* suggests that after the forces for and against change have been established, effort should be put not only into breaking down those opposing it (which is a natural management response), but also into building up the influence of those supporting it.

This process is the first or 'unfreeze' phase of the *Lewin/Schein* change model. The CEO will have to set up both a programme of education and support for the complacent managers and enter into forceful negotiations with the trade union. The basic aim is to frighten both parties with evidence of looming disaster. This is clear enough from the company's competitive situation. *Ansoff* points out that an early crisis can be triggered in order to improve willingness to change.

The second phase of the *Lewin/Schein* change model requires action to change behaviour, laying down new patterns and reinforcing them. Residual resistance should be confronted with free circulation of information about plans for the future and why they are required. Individuals must be helped to change their attitudes and behaviours. An extensive programme of organisational development is probably required for the F Steel Company. There should be proper application of positive and negative reinforcement in the shape of rewards and sanctions.

The final phase of the model is 'refreeze'. This prevents the staff from slipping back into their old ways and attitudes by a combination of exhortation, reward for good performance and sanctions against the backsliders.

External forces are less susceptible to this treatment than internal ones. In the case of the F Steel Company, representations could be made to government about both the exchange rate and the unfair competition, perhaps through a trade association or other umbrella body. However, it is necessary to recognise that even if action is forthcoming, it is unlikely to be prompt.

5 Brand stretching

Examiner's comments. Not a popular question, and whilst many candidates identified brand strategy, they did not extend this to cover the specific issue of brand stretching.

Introduction

Experts now view **brands** as the **link between** a company's marketing activities and consumers' perceptions of these activities. In the 1990s this brand revolution is particularly relevant to sectors such as financial services. The difficulties consumers have in understanding intangible products and the extent to which the service **becomes** the brand, both present marketing challenges together with the need to exploit brand equity through brand **stretching activities**.

Elements of Brand Strategy

Arnold (1992) in *The Handbook of Brand Management*, outlines a five stage brand management process.

1.   **Market analysis**: Market definition, Market segmentation, Competitor positions, Trends: PEST and Micro factors

2.   **Brand situation analysis**: Brand personality, Individual attributes. Internal analysis = is advertising projecting the right image? Is the packaging too aggressive? Does the product need updating? Fundamental evaluation of the brand's character.

3.   **Targeting future positions**: Future developments. Brand strategy: any brand strategy should incorporate what has been learnt in steps 1 and 2 into a view of how the market will evolve and what strategic response is most appropriate. Target markets, brand positions and brand scope are the elements of brand strategy.

4.   **Testing new offers**: Individual elements of mix and test marketing the total offer.

5. **Planning and evaluating performance**: Level of expenditure. Type of support activity. Measurement against objectives: awareness and availability, attitudes. Information on tracking of performance feeds into step 1 on analysis.

From this we see that brand strategy involves decision on three issues: target market(s), brand positioning and brand stretching.

Brand stretching

Brand stretching refers specifically to the use of an existing, successful brand being used to launch products in an unrelated market. (Note: a brand extension is the use of an established brand name on a new product within the same broad market.)

The starting point for this activity is to identify the current brand's core values. Brands should only be **stretched** in these cases.

(a) The **core values of the brand have relevance** to the new market into which it is to be launched. Marks & Spencer with its retail operations has established a strong brand image for quality, value and integrity. All these values are also important in the financial services market. This has allowed Marks & Spencer to stretch their brand successfully into the financial services sector.

(b) The **new market area will not affect the value of the brand in its core market**. Virgin's brand name has been successfully stretched into a number of markets including financial services. However the brand may now be affected by the problems it is experiencing operating train services in the UK.

There is a school of thought that states that it may be easier for service companies to stretch umbrella brands across markets. Financial services companies using umbrella brands can also run into database marketing programmes across their whole service range, American Express being a good example. In general though, most financial service brands are currently too weak to support much brand stretching activity.

6 Integrity

Pass marks. All professional bodies are concerned about the recent decline in ethical standards in commercial organisations. This decline undermines public confidence in both the profession and the wider world of business.

Part (a)

Influences on ethical conduct can be divided into two groups: positive influences and negative ones.

Positive ethical influences

It is possible to discern an **ethical climate** in a society, that forms part of its culture. Notions of right and wrong tend to be conditioned by history, the behaviour of respected leaders, the tenets of the dominant religion and so on. It is possible to discern subtle differences between societies in this respect, and some that are not so subtle. It has been reported, for example, that there is concern in Western Europe at the less rigorous attitudes to corrupt practices in business that Eastern European countries may bring with them when they join the EU. *The Times* reported that 'former communist states have been tainted by corruption since bribery and the black market became a means of survival in over-regulated, centrally planned economies.'

Organisations tend to have ethical climates too, just as they have their own cultures, and like its culture, an organisation's ethical climate is heavily influenced by its external environment. Thus we may discern an important difference between employers in the USA and those in Europe in relation to ideas of corporate social responsibility. It is inappropriate to overemphasise extremes of behaviour, but we might consider the different attitudes that prevail concerning job security on opposite sides of the Atlantic, for example.

Within an organisation, an ethical influence is the **behaviour of senior managers**, to the extent that the influence of artefacts such as corporate **codes of conduct** and **ethics** hotlines can be completely neutralised by unprincipled behaviour. This was a major problem within *Enron*, which paid extensive lip service to ethical behaviour.

Professional institutions have their own codes of **professional ethics**, such as the ethical demands commonly made on auditors and the specific requirements for objectivity and impartiality made by their own professional bodies. These codes can put members under considerable strain when they demand behaviour that is at variance with what is accepted in an organisation. As one code says, sometimes a professional may have no alternative but to resign.

Negative ethical influences

Personal amorality is likely to exist in any organisation to a greater or lesser extent, quite apart from actively immoral or illegal behaviour. Such amorality, or lack of care about right and wrong must inevitably lead to unethical conduct.

Financial pressures will be a major problem. These may take the form of personal financial problems resulting from, for instance, gambling, drug use or simple over-spending. Such problems drive individuals to a range of unethical behaviour, ranging from inflated expense claims to outright fraud.

Financial pressures leading to fraud also exist at the **corporate level**. External pressure from shareholders or markets to improve profitability can lead to **bribery** to win contracts and all kinds of **creative accounting**, for example. It is also a specific threat to auditors, since efforts may be made to undermine their impartiality and objectivity. The methods employed may range from simple friendliness and the provision of agreeable lunches for the auditors on site, to threats to take more lucrative consulting business elsewhere if the audit is qualified.

Under such circumstances, unprincipled demands for improved performance are likely to filter down through the organisation as each level of the hierarchy comes under pressure from the one above. One professional body's code specifically identifies **pressure from a superior** as a potential cause of ethical conflict.

Part (b)

It is men and arms that make the force and power of the law

Hobbes, Leviathan

Coercion is the fallback position of all systems of behaviour control, including law and ethical codes. If organisations and professions want their people to behave in accordance with a particular set of rules, they must be prepared to **enforce** them. Professional bodies have a set of law-based procedures for doing just that.

Organisations, too, are capable of enforcing their ideas about ethics. An allegation of unethical behaviour at *Boeing* in late 2003 led to the dismissal of the head of finance and subsequently to the resignation of Phil Condit, Chairman and Chief Executive.

If a willingness to enforce them exists, **codes of ethics** can have an effect, both in organisations and in professions. If breaches of such codes are ignored or condoned, they will be treated with contempt and be worse than useless, since they will demonstrate that senior officers are hypocrites as well as unethical in their behaviour.

Ethics management has several tasks.

- To define and give life to an organisation's defining values
- To create an environment that supports ethically sound behaviour
- To instil a sense of shared accountability amongst employees

There are two approaches to the management of ethics, according to *Paine*, the **compliance-based** and the **integrity-based**.

A **compliance-based** approach is primarily designed to ensure that the company **acts within the letter of the law**, and that violations are prevented, detected and punished. Some organisations, faced with the legal consequences of unethical behaviour take legal precautions such as those below.

- Compliance procedures to detect misconduct
- Audits of contracts
- Systems to protect and encourage 'whistleblowers'
- Disciplinary procedures to deal with transgressions

Corporate compliance is limited in that it relates only to the law, but legal compliance is 'not an adequate means for addressing the full range of ethical issues that arise every day'. This is especially the case in the UK, where **voluntary** codes of conduct and self-regulation are perhaps more prevalent than in the US.

The compliance approach also overemphasises the threat of detection and punishment in order to channel appropriate behaviour. Furthermore, mere compliance with the law is no guide to **exemplary** behaviour.

An **integrity-based** approach treats ethics as an issue of organisation culture. It combines a concern for the law with an **emphasis on managerial responsibility** for ethical behaviour. Integrity strategies strive to define companies' **guiding values**, **aspirations** and **patterns of thought and conduct**. When integrated into the day-to-day operations of an organisation, such strategies can help prevent damaging ethical lapses, while tapping into powerful human impulses for moral thought and action. Such approaches assume that people are social beings with values that can be supported and refined. They attempt to integrate ethical values into the organisation (or profession) by providing guidance and consultation and by identifying and resolving problems.

7 Expenditure

Using our Money Wisely on Marketing Communications

by

A Marketing Manager

The amount of money any company spends on marketing communications, and advertising in particular, is absolutely crucial. Are the communications **working**, are they **effective**, are we getting **good value**, could we get it more **cost effectively**? These are all good questions, which that all management teams must ask themselves regularly and be able to respond to when challenged.

What I intend to do here is to provide some information about how we decide how much to spend on marketing communications. Before we look at these specific areas it is useful to consider what marketing communications is and what it is supposed to do. Then it will be possible to look at the **different approaches to budgeting**.

If you think about the key areas where, each and every day, we **communicate with various audiences**, it should come as no surprise that marketing communications is important to our success and can cost a great deal. Broadly, we communicate with the following.

- Customers
- Dealers
- Employees
- Shareholders
- Financial advisers

- Suppliers
- Local communities
- Competitors
- Media
- Many other interested parties

Of course the level of interaction will vary in intensity with each of these audiences depending upon a number of variables. However, marketing communications is about creating and sustaining a **dialogue**

with each of these **stakeholder** audiences. We need to **inform** audiences about new developments within the company, new products and services and about what we as a company believe and value. We need to **persuade** audiences, especially customers and potential customers, we need to **demonstrate how we are different** and of value to each of them, and we need continually to **remind and reassure** our customers not only who we are but also about our products and services.

BA invested over £60m in their corporate rebranding exercise in order to be identified as a global, not British, airline. Kellogg's, Nestle, Cadbury's, Unilever and the many other fmcg manufacturers invest millions each year on advertising in order to maintain and/or grow their **market shares**. Organisations in the business-to-business sector spend much less on advertising but more on personal selling and sales support. The area where the investment is made is not important to this paper. We are, however, interested in the **effective** and efficient use of **limited resources**.

In order to inform, differentiate, persuade and/or remind (DRIP), we need to invest and allocate some of our finances to marketing communications. Choosing the right level of investment is important but it is not a science. We have learnt over the years and we have a good idea about what the right level of investment might be. Some companies allocate a **percentage of sales** as the appropriation, whilst others just take **last years' figure** and add a percentage for inflation. Others allocate what they can afford whilst a few just **guess**. All of these methods have flaws in that they are neither customer focused nor designed to do the right job.

Some other techniques involve **investing the same as our competitors**. Which competitor and how can we be sure that we are achieving real competitive **parity**? The **advertising/sales** (A/S) **ratio** provides an **industry benchmark** in order that we can understand whether we are investing above or below the industry average.

This ratio has proved useful but it does not provide the answer we are looking for as it focuses only on advertising. As we also use sales promotion, direct and interactive marketing, public relations, the sales force plus internal marketing communication activities, there are severe limitations to this approach.

It was reported that Procter & Gamble wanted to reduce their amount of advertising from 25% to 20% and use the 'savings' to fund price-offs in order to compete more **effectively** with their own-label competitors. A counter view from the company was that they wanted to use their advertising and media expenditure much more **efficiently** yet maintain their overall visibility. This was a strong strategic approach and it courted much criticism and debate.

By gauging the percentage of our communication spend against the total spent by all others in the market, we are able to determine what is known as **share of voice**. These figures can be compared to our **share of market** and through analysis we can determine how much we should spend to achieve the market share we set ourselves. Whilst this is intuitively appealing there are some real difficulties in making this work and it does not really apply to our growing market.

PIMS (Profit Impact of Marketing Strategy) is a database system that uses actual data from real organisations across a variety of industries and market sectors. Through analysis of the database it is possible to determine what **return on investment** can be achieved based upon a number of variables. Depending upon whether a company is market leader, number 2 or just another player it is possible to make judgements about, for example, the level of above and below-the-line promotional expenditure, or the right amount of trade communications.

We can use a number of these methods and compare the outcomes. We should determine what it is we want to achieve (**goals**) and how we think our various **push (trade)**, **pull (consumer)** and **profile (corporate)** communication strategies will work. We then determine the **actual costs** of putting it all into action, and then make changes as necessary. This **objective and task approach** is perhaps the soundest technique of them all, but it does require a great deal of **time** and accurate prediction in order to make it work.

Pedigree Petfoods said that after the tins and the cost of the meat, the third most important factor to be measured and evaluated was the **cost of the media** and **level of discounts** used to advertise their pet food products. This further serves to demonstrate that the level of communication spend can be a very significant part of an organisation's activities and needs a **strategic perspective**.

In order to grow and thrive it will be even more important for our company not only to make **good use** of marketing communications, but to also **invest** in communications in order that it maintains dialogue with the right audience, using with the right message at the right time.

8 Hotel company

Presentation Notes on Services Marketing

By: A. Candidate
Audience: Interview Panel
Equipment needed: Slides, Handout

1. *Introduction*

Good morning ladies and gentlemen. Over the next 30 minutes I would like to outline a number of key characteristics of marketing any service and then relate these to the particular task of marketing an hotel. I'll be happy to take questions at the end of the presentation.

2. *Aims of presentation*

(a) To outline the distinctive characteristics of marketing an hotel service

(b) To consider in what ways the marketing mix should be extended when marketing the services of an hotel

3. *The characteristics of services*

Intangibility

A significant characteristic of services is the relative dominance of intangible attributes in the make-up of the service product. A service is a deed, performance or effort not a product which can be seen, touched and taken away. This makes it difficult to evaluate before purchase and means that customers do not own the service.

How can the hotel manage this intangibility?

We need to use tangible cues to service quality and manage 'physical evidence'. For example, our staff should look professional which includes a hotel uniform and attention to personal grooming. The decor in the rooms should be spotless and follow the hotel's overall decorative identity. The food we serve should be of a high standard and offer our guest variety.

Inseparability

Services have simultaneous production and consumption which emphasises the importance of the service provider and therefore the role of our contact personnel. The conference organiser and the waiter, in our customers' eyes, is the hotel.

Consequently, selection, training and rewarding staff for excellent service quality is very important. The consumption of the service often takes place in the presence of other customers, as in the restaurant, therefore enjoyment is not only dependent on the service provider but other guests as well. It is important to identify and reduce the risk of possible sources of conflict. For example our restaurant layout should provide reasonable space between tables and smoking areas.

Heterogeneity

This characteristic can also be referred to as variability, this means that it is very difficult to standardise the service our guests receive. The receptionist may not always be courteous and helpful, the maids may not remember to change all the towels and so on. Due to inseparability a fault such as rudeness cannot be quality checked and corrected between production and consumption.

This again emphasises the need for rigorous selection, training and rewarding of staff. Evaluation systems should be established which give our customers the opportunity to report on their experiences with our staff. In addition we must ensure that our processes are reliable. For example, the way we book in guests, organise their keys and deal with checking-out. No hotel is perfect, however it is important for any service delivery failures to be responded to immediately.

Perishability

Consumption can not be stored for the future, once a hotel room is left empty for the night that potential revenue is lost.

This makes occupancy levels very important and it is necessary to match supply with demand. For example if our hotel is busy in the week but not at weekends, a key marketing task is to provide incentives for weekend use. To cater for peak demand we can employ part-time staff and multi-skill full time staff. We can also use reservation systems in the restaurant and beauty salon to smooth out demand and ensure that if our customers have to wait that comfortable seating in the reception is provided.

3. *The extended marketing mix*

The marketing mix for products is the well known 4Ps of product, price, place and promotion. For service marketing we add three additional Ps to our tool kit: physical evidence, process and people.

Physical evidence is used to manage the essentially intangible nature of the hotel service. As previously stated, smart staff, an impressive lobby and interior design for all areas of the hotel is important to establish an appropriate position and signal this to customers.

Managing processes helps to deal with the inseparability and heterogeneity characteristics. If standards and processes are adhered to a consistent level of service can be delivered. For example receptionists need to be trained to deal with demanding business people and cleaning staff need to prepare rooms to a consistent standard.

Probably the most important element of the services marketing mix is people. Hotel staff occupy a key position in influencing customer perceptions of service quality. Without training and control, employees tend to be variable in their performance which in turn leads to variable service quality and customer satisfaction.

4. *Conclusions*

Key professors in the field of services marketing, such as Bateson, Zeithaml and Bitner, all suggest that there are three key jobs for service marketers; managing differentiation, managing productivity and managing service quality. Should I be successful in my application today, I too would make these three issues my top priority for the hotel.

Does anybody have any questions?

9 RUS PLC

(a) *Relevance of TQM*

TQM is relevant to both the previous and the new strategy. TQM deals with two issues:

(i) design quality (in other words does the service meet customer needs in the most appropriate way?);

(ii)   conformance quality (in other words does the service actually delivered conform to the service promised?).

TQM is more than just a set of techniques. Developed in manufacturing industry, it is an approach to dealing with production, which involves getting things right first time, zero defects etc. It tries to involve the customers needs in the very process of production. This is obviously relevant to service industries, with the proviso that bad service cannot be inspected and scrapped after it is delivered: services are generally consumed as they are produced. As much of the success in a service industry depends on repeat business, getting things right first time (as that is, indeed, the only time) must be a priority.

TQM also involves a detailed analysis of the process of production. An aspect of TQM is the reduction in variation. Restaurant service should be predictable; food quality must be consistently good.

The culture of TQM also must be considered. Employees must be encouraged to come forward with suggestions, and they must be engaged in the process of improving service.

There is no reason why these considerations should not apply to the family and medium-priced business accommodation as well as to the hotels new strategy. However, as guests will be paying more their expectations will be so much higher. The design quality of the service (what these new customers actually want) is paramount, and conformance quality must be faultless. As there are fewer customers, their repeat business will be even more valuable.

(b)   *Financial and organisational implications*

RUS is chasing a different market, targeting high spending customers whose requirements will be different. Investment in buildings and fixtures includes:

(i)   decoration
(ii)   changes to room sizes (eg conversion of pairs of single rooms into suites)
(iii)   more luxurious furnishings
(iv)   perhaps expanded restaurant and kitchen facilities
(v)   swimming pool, gymnasium etc
(vi)   more opulent public spaces.

Other expenditure will include:

(i)   more staff, to provide the service required
(ii)   more training
(iii)   the greater variety of food offered to guests (hence kitchen costs will rise)
(iv)   advertising to reach the target segment.

There will be fewer customers but they will be paying more.

Organisationally, the new staff must be given more training, and existing staff will have to learn to cater differently for the new customers. Furthermore, there is unlikely to be the same deployment of staff. In the past they catered for family and business customers at different times. The new strategy requires the same type and standard of service to be maintained at all times. More effort will need to be spent on management and marketing. Quality circles should be introduced.

10 Fleet Water Services Ltd

Tutor's note. This is not a full 25 mark exam question.

Part (a)

Project management

Project management is directed at an end. It is not directed at maintaining or improving a continuous activity. It thus has a limited objective within a limited time span. All projects involve, according to Dennis Lock, the 'projection of ideas and activities into new endeavours. No project can ever be exactly the same as anything which has gone before.' The steps and tasks leading to completion can never be described accurately in advance. Therefore, according to Lock, 'the job of project management is to foresee as many dangers as possible, and to plan, organise and control activities so that they are avoided.'

There are therefore some special management problems.

(1)   The work is carried out by a team of people usually assembled for one project, who must be able to communicate effectively and immediately with each other.

(2)   There can be many novel *expected* problems, each one of which should be resolved by careful design and planning prior to commencement of work.

(3)   There can be many novel *unexpected* problems, particularly with a project working at the limits of existing and new technologies. There should be mechanisms within the project to enable these problems to be resolved during the time span of the project without detriment to the objective, the cost or the time span.

(4)   There is normally no benefit until the work is finished. The 'lead in' time to this can cause a strain on the eventual recipient who feels deprived until the benefit is achieved (even though in many cases it is a major improvement on existing activities) and who is also faced with increasing expenditure for no immediate benefit.

(5)   Contributions made by specialists are of differing importance at each stage. Assembling a team working towards the one objective is made difficult due to the tendency of specialists to regard their contribution as always being more important than other people's and not understanding the inter-relationship between their various specialities in the context of the project.

(6)   If the project involves several parties with different interests in the outcome, there might be disputes between them.

Part (b)

Project management techniques

Objectives of project management

(1)   *Defining the project.* The project has a task which it must achieve. A technique for making this clear is the specification prepared by or with the client; constantly changing client specifications can increase the cost of the project and lead to its failure. This defines the scope of the project.

(2)   *Quality* (in the sense of conformance to client specifications, and any appropriate safeguards). The result of the project should achieve what it is supposed to do. Some information systems methodologies have a series of steps which specifically relate to ones which have gone before, right back to the specification.

To ensure the right level of quality is achieved, a systems project will require specific documentation to ensure there have been no short cuts taken. Tests should be carried out and fully documented. For greatest benefit, the quality controls over the project should relate to BS EN ISO 9000. This will also give additional assurance to the client.

(3)   *Budget and timescale* can be dealt with together. In order to plan the project effectively, a number of techniques are used. *Work breakdown structure* is an approach which determines the tasks needed to complete the project, which are then broken down into sub-tasks. These can then by mapped on Gantt charts, or even on critical path networks, to find the optimal allocation of

resources to activities. Some activities can be crashed or shortened by throwing more resources at them; of course playing around with the critical path in this way might have the effect of increasing the cost of the project. Other activities might be less urgent, depending on the critical path. Estimating the timescale is quite important; for many commercial contracts there are penalties for late delivery.

Some of the cost aspects relate to the work breakdown structure, in that costs can be ascribed to the resources used by each activity. Generally speaking, estimates are prepared, based on the work breakdown structure. A standard costing system might be relevant here.

A further issue to be considered is that of *risk*. There is the risk that the project will be late or over budget. This can be managed by ensuring that the specification is as accurate as possible. Effective project management should minimise the risk. Insurance might compensate for some of the immediate financial problems.

In other cases, a project may have to be over-specified with fail-safe mechanisms. In other cases risks can be dealt with by means of contingency plans. Some firms have back-up computer systems if an application is judged to be critical.

11 Feedback and control system

Examiner's comments. Too many answers concentrated specifically on the MkIS rather than broader issues of feedback and control, and the use to which this information can be put.

Planning can be defined as 'deciding what to do', whereas control can be defined as 'ensuring that the desired results are achieved'. The feedback and control process can be illustrated by a simple model.

Goal setting		Performance measurement		Performance diagnosis		Corrective action
What do we want to achieve?	•	What is happening?	•	Why is it happening?	•	What should we do about it?

Feedback and control involves the following.

- Goal setting
- Performance measurement
- Performance diagnosis
- Taking corrective action

Goal setting is the role of the planning element of strategic marketing. Ideally, the standards set will have been developed within an understanding of what the organisation is able to deliver. Specifically, the factors which should be taken into account include the following.

(a)   The **type of control information** required – financial and non-financial

(b)   The **methods used to collect** the information – audits, budgets and variance analysis

(c)   **Who** requires the information?

(d)   What **form the information should take** – weekly, monthly annual reports, presentations, continuous computer based data

(e)   The information **systems** required

(f)   The **resource** implications

(g)   The **behavioural implications** of controlling peoples' activities

This final point is less obvious, but very important if the control system is to work effectively. The involvement of a range of managers and personnel in the evaluation process is vital, together with the need for **good communication**, both within the marketing unit and between departments. Effective implementation of the feedback and control system will require **internal marketing** to employees, **motivation** of personnel and effective **co-ordination** of marketing activities.

Feedback and control information can be used in five distinct areas of operation.

- Financial analysis
- Market analysis
- Sales and distribution analysis
- Physical resource analysis
- Human resource analysis

Market, sales and distribution analyses are particularly relevant for marketing planning.

Type of analysis	Used to control
Market/sales analysis to consider size and growth of market and market share Demand analysis Sales targets Sales budget	Competitive standing Sales effectiveness Efficiency in use of resources for selling

Information on these areas can be gathered through **audits, budgeting or variance analysis**. Marketing audits allow for regular monitoring of the successful implementation of marketing plans. For example, a marketing manager might use the information from the mix audit to recognise that communication targets are not being reached. From this point, corrective action would be needed in the form of a campaign review and redevelopment.

Budgeting is the most common form of control. It is financial in nature and very useful when applied to marketing implementation. Budgets tend to be short-term and based on the annual plan for achievement of the year's **profit and sales forecasts**. Monthly deviations from the sales plan tend to require tactical alterations, for example in the form of price increases or decreases to influence demand.

Where budgeting is **longer-term**, this is more appropriate for **monitoring strategic decisions** such as product portfolio management. For example, in the product plan there will be products identified as question marks or potential stars. The position of each product in the matrix will suggest how much close monitoring and control is needed. Information on high-risk or high-potential new products would be used to manage the risk, and to ensure sales forecasts are accurate to avoid back order or production problems.

Variance analysis leads on from budgeting, and involves detailed analysis of the difference between actual and expected results. This sort of control information might possibly be used to consider sales-price variances, sales-quantity variances, profit variances and market share variances.

Many marketing activities are not evaluated or controlled but are assumed to be effective. Marketers tend to enjoy planning and tactical implementation but shy away from feedback on the results of their initiatives. This is short-sighted, as it severely limits learning from experience and can, at worst, result in inefficient and ineffective marketing plans.

Further reading

P Doyle, *Valued Based Marketing*, Wiley, 2000

J Johansson, *Global Marketing*, Irwin McGraw Hill, 2000

P Doyle, *Marketing Management and Strategy*, Pearson, 2002, 3rd ed

C Gilligan & R Wilson, *Strategic Marketing Management*, Butterworth, Heinemann, 2003, 3rd ed

G Hooley, J Saunders and N Piercy, *Marketing Strategy and Competitive Positioning*, Prentice Hall, 1998, 2nd ed

I Doole & R Lowe, *International Marketing Strategy*, Thomson Learning, 2002, 3rd ed

O Walker, B Harper, J Mullins and J Larreche, *Marketing Strategy*, McGraw Hill, 2003

D Aaker, *Strategic Marketing Management*, J Wiley & Sons, 2000, 6th ed

S Mathur, *Creating Value*, Butterworth Heinemann, 2001, 2nd ed

H Davidson, *The Committed Enterprise*, Butterworth Heinemann, 2002

P Ahmed & M Rafiq, *Internal Marketing*, Butterworth Heinemann, 2002

H Mintzberg, J Quinn & S Ghoshal, *The Strategy Process*, Pearson, 1999

K Ohmae, *The Mind of the Strategist*, McGraw Hill, 1982

R Stacey, *Strategic Management and Organisational Dynamics*, FT Prentice Hall, 2000

G Hamel & C Prahalad, *Competing for the Future*, HBS Press, 1994

M Porter, *Competitive Advantage*, The Free Press, 1985

T Peters & R Waterman, *In Search of Excellence*, Profile Business, 2004

T Burns & G Stalker, *The Management of Innovation*, OUP, 1994

P Kotler, *Marketing Management*, Prentice Hall, 2002, 11th ed

H Ansoff, *Corporate Strategy*, Pam Macmillan, 1986

G Johnson & K Scholes, *Exploring Corporate Strategy, Prentice Hall*, 1999, 5th ed

N Piercy, *Marketing Budgeting*, Groom Helm,1986

E Gummesson, *Total Relationship Marketing*, Butterworth, Heinemann, 1999

D Adcock, *Marketing Strategies for Competitive Advantage*, Wiley, 2000

I Nonaka, *The Knowledge Creating Company*, Oxford Press, 1995

P Senge, *The Fifth Discipline*, Currency, 1994

C Emmanuel, D Otley & K Marchant, *Accounting for Management Control*, Chapman and Hall 1990

P Drucker, *The Practice of Management*, Longman, 1993

S Dibb, L Simkin, W Pride, O Ferrel, *Marketing: Concepts and Strategies*, Houghton Mifflin, 2000

N Piercy, *Marketing-led Strategic Change*, Butterworth Heinemann, 2001

C Hofer, D Schendel, *Strategy Formulation*, South Western College Publishing, 1978

H Simon, *Administrative Behaviour*, Simon & Schuster, 1997

W French & C Bell, *Organisational Development*, Prentice Hall, 1995, 6th ed

JP Jeannet, H Henessey, *Global Marketing Strategies*, Houghton Mifflin, 1995, 3rd ed

M Hammer & J Champy, *Reengineering the Corporation*, Harper Business, 1993

J Oakland, *TQM,* Butterworth Heinemann

Key concepts and index

BPP
PROFESSIONAL EDUCATION

REVIEW FORM & FREE PRIZE DRAW

All original review forms from the entire BPP range, completed with genuine comments, will be entered into one of two draws on 31 January 2007 and 30 July 2007. The names on the first four forms picked out on each occasion will be sent a cheque for £50.

Name: _____ **Address**: _____

_____

_____

How have you used this Text?
(Tick one box only)

☐ Self study (book only)

☐ On a course: college_____

☐ With BPP Home Study package

☐ Other _____

Why did you decide to purchase this Text?
(Tick one box only)

☐ Have used companion Kit

☐ Have used BPP Texts in the past

☐ Recommendation by friend/colleague

☐ Recommendation by a lecturer at college

☐ Saw advertising in journals

☐ Saw website

☐ Other _____

During the past six months do you recall seeing/receiving any of the following?
(Tick as many boxes as are relevant)

☐ Our advertisement in *Marketing Success*

☐ Our advertisement in *Marketing Business*

☐ Our brochure with a letter through the post

☐ Our brochure with *Marketing Business*

☐ Saw website

Which (if any) aspects of our advertising do you find useful?
(Tick as many boxes as are relevant)

☐ Prices and publication dates of new editions

☐ Information on product content

☐ Facility to order books off-the-page

☐ None of the above

Have you used the companion Practice & Revision Kit for this subject? ☐ Yes ☐ No

Your ratings, comments and suggestions would be appreciated on the following areas.

	Very useful	Useful	Not useful
Introductory section (How to use this text, study checklist, etc)	☐	☐	☐
Introduction	☐	☐	☐
Syllabus coverage	☐	☐	☐
Action Programmes and Marketing at Work examples	☐	☐	☐
Chapter roundups	☐	☐	☐
Quick quizzes	☐	☐	☐
Illustrative questions	☐	☐	☐
Content of suggested answers	☐	☐	☐
Index	☐	☐	☐
Structure and presentation	☐	☐	☐

	Excellent	Good	Adequate	Poor
Overall opinion of this Text	☐	☐	☐	☐

Do you intend to continue using BPP Study Texts/Kits/Passcards? ☐ Yes ☐ No

Please note any further comments and suggestions/errors on the reverse of this page.

Please return to: Glenn Haldane, BPP Professional Education, FREEPOST, London, W12 8BR

REVIEW FORM & FREE PRIZE DRAW (continued)

Please note any further comments and suggestions/errors below.

FREE PRIZE DRAW RULES

1   Closing date for 31 January 2007 draw is 31 December 2006. Closing date for 31 July 2007 draw is 30 June 2007.

2   Restricted to entries with UK and Eire addresses only. BPP employees, their families and business associates are excluded.

3   No purchase necessary. Entry forms are available upon request from BPP Professional Education. No more than one entry per title, per person. Draw restricted to persons aged 16 and over.

4   Winners will be notified by post and receive their cheques not later than 6 weeks after the relevant draw date. List of winners will be supplied on request.

5   The decision of the promoter in all matters is final and binding. No correspondence will be entered into.